Management Research

Management Research: European Perspectives brings together experts in the field to take stock of European management research and reflect on its distinctiveness. Building on a successful series of papers published in the *European Management Journal*, this book contains international contributions providing a range of scholarly perspectives on the reality of European management research.

The state of management scholarship has recently been a topic of great interest, focusing on such matters as the role of universities versus businesses in shaping research agendas, the so-called 'rigour–relevance' debate, the use of measurements in quality assessment of research outputs, the role of journal rankings, and the merits of the journal review system. Missing, however, is any discussion of what, if anything, constitutes a European approach to management research, how does it differ from other styles used in the rest of the world and why is there a need for such distinctiveness?

It has been noted that European management scholars have a lower success rate for publishing theoretical papers than their North American counterparts, which is surprising given that Europe has been the cradle of many generative intellectual traditions. European scholars may be the heirs to those traditions, but they are sometimes criticized for failing to channel this legacy into authoritative theoretical contributions in elite US-based management journals. This book provides insightful contributions to the debate and offers critical reflections on what European-based scholars have to offer the study of management.

Sabina Siebert is a Professor of Management at the University of Glasgow, UK.

Routledge Studies in International Business and the World Economy

For a full list of titles in this series, visit https://www.routledge.com/Routledge-Studies-in-International-Business-and-the-World-Economy/book-series/SE0358

65 **Management and Organizations in Transitional China**
Yanlong Zhang and Lisa A. Keister

66 **Global Advertising Practice in a Borderless World**
Edited by Robert Crawford, Linda Brennan and Lukas Parker

67 **Social and Solidarity Economy**
The World's Economy with a Social Face
Sara Calvo, Andres Morales, Video Edited by Yanni Zikidis

68 **Managing Culture and Interspace in Cross-border Investments**
Building a Global Company
Edited by Martina Fuchs, Sebastian Henn, Martin Franz, and Ram Mudambi

69 **Venture Capital and Firm Performance**
The Korean Experience in a Global Perspective
Jaeho Lee

70 **Expatriate Managers**
The Paradoxes of Living and Working Abroad
Anna Spiegel, Ursula Mense-Petermann, and Bastian Bredenkötter

71 **The International Business Environment and National Identity**
Tatiana Gladkikh

72 **European Born Globals**
Job Creation in Young International Businesses
Edited by Irene Mandl and Valentina Patrini

73 **Management Research**
European Perspectives
Edited by Sabina Siebert

Management Research
European Perspectives

Edited by Sabina Siebert

LONDON AND NEW YORK

First published 2018 by Routledge

2 Park Square, Milton Park, Abingdon, Oxfordshire OX14 4RN
52 Vanderbilt Avenue, New York, NY 10017

Routledge is an imprint of the Taylor & Francis Group, an informa business

First issued in paperback 2019

Library of Congress Cataloging-in-Publication Data
A catalog record for this book has been requested

ISBN: 978-1-138-72146-3 (hbk)
ISBN: 978-0-367-88758-2 (pbk)

Typeset in Sabon
by Apex CoVantage, LLC

Contents

Tables and Figure

Tables

Figure

Contributors

Göran Ahrne (PhD, University of Uppsala) is a Professor of Sociology at Stockholm University and a member of the Stockholm Centre for Organizational Research (Score). Current research focuses on the particularities of meta-organizations, the differences between organized and non-organized social relations and the organization of markets. His main interest concerns the role of theories of organization for theories of society and the relations between organizational change and social change. He has published a number of articles on these topics in journals such as *Organization* and *Organization Studies*. He has also published a number of books in both Swedish and English. Among his books in English are *Social Organizations, Interaction Inside, Outside and Between Organizations* and *Meta-Organizations* (with Nils Brunsson).

Thomas Boysen Anker is a Senior Lecturer/Associate Professor at the Adam Smith Business School, University of Glasgow, and holds a PhD in applied philosophy from the University of Copenhagen. His main research interests are business ethics, applied epistemology and social marketing, often working in the intersection between marketing, public health and ethics. His work has been published in such journals as *Journal of Business Ethics*, *Marketing Theory* and *European Journal of Marketing*. He recently published a monograph on the controversial topic of truth in marketing, developing a theory that can account for the truthfulness of functional, emotional and behavioural claims. The monograph is entitled *Truth in Marketing: A Theory of Claim-Evidence Relations* and has been published by Routledge. Anker currently serves as Editor-in-Chief for the *European Management Journal*.

David M. Brock is a Professor at the Guilford Glazer Faculty of Business and Management, Ben-Gurion University of the Negev, and an International Research Fellow for Professional Service Firms, Saïd Business School, University of Oxford. He is a graduate of the University of South Africa, the University of Cape Town and North Carolina State University. Prior to moving to Israel in 2002, he lived in Auckland, New Zealand, working at the University of Auckland Business School; and before that he studied and taught at North Carolina State University. He is founding Editor-in-Chief of the *Journal of Professions and Organization* (Oxford University Press), and serves on the editorial board of the *Journal of Management Studies* and the *Journal of International Management*. His research areas include global strategy, the international diversification of professional service firms, capability building in globalizing service firms and institutional changes in the professions.

Nils Brunsson is a Professor of Management and affiliated to Uppsala University and to Score (Stockholm Centre for Organizational Research) at the Stockholm School of Economics and Stockholm University. He has held chairs in management at the Stockholm School of Economics and at Uppsala University and has served as the Niklas Luhmann Gastprofessor at Bielefeld University. He is a co-founder of Score and SCANCOR (the Scandinavian Consortium for Organizational Research). Brunsson has published almost 30 books in the field of organization studies, including *Mechanisms of Hope, The Consequences of Decision-Making, A World of Standards, Reform as Routine* and *Meta-organizations*, as well as numerous articles. He has studied topics such as organizational decision-making, administrative reform and standardization. His current research interests include the organization of markets, partial organization, meta-organizations and the construction of competition. Brunsson is an honorary member of the European Group for Organization Studies (EGOS).

Catherine Cassell is a Professor of Organisational Psychology and Dean of Birmingham Business School at the University of Birmingham, UK. She has a long-standing interest in the use of qualitative methods in management and organizational research. Together with Gillian Symon she has published four books with Sage on the topic, the most recent being *Qualitative Organisational Research: Core Methods and Current Challenges*. She is also the author of *Conducting Research Interviews for Business and Management Students*, published by Sage in 2015, and, together with Ann Cunliffe and Gina Grandy, is Editor of the forthcoming *Sage Handbook of Qualitative Methods in Business and Management Research*. She established and was inaugural Co-Editor (jointly with Gillian Symon) of the journal *Qualitative Research in Organizations and Management: An International Journal*, and has just stood down as Co-Editor after the journal's first ten years. Her enduring interest in research methodology has led to a number of positions. For example, she was the founding chair of the British Academy of Management's Special Interest group in Research Methodology—a group she is still heavily involved with—and a founding member of the steering committee of the European Academy of Management's Special Interest Group in Research Methods and Research Practice.

Robert Chia is a Research Professor of Management at the Adam Smith Business School, University of Glasgow. He received his PhD in Organizational

Analysis from Lancaster University. He is the author/editor of five books, including *Strategy without Design* (Cambridge University Press, with R. Holt), and has published in *Organization Studies*, the *Journal of Management Studies, Human Relations, Organization Science* and the *Academy of Management Journal* amongst many others. Prior to entering academia, he worked for seventeen years in shipbuilding, aircraft engineering, human resource management and manufacturing management.

Miguel Pina e Cunha is a Professor of Organizational Behavior at Nova School of Business and Economics, Lisbon, Portugal. His research has been published in journals such as the Academy of Management Review, Human Relations, Journal of Management Studies and Organization Studies. He participated on the editorial boards of several journals, including the European Management Journal, Management Learning, Organization Studies and Strategic Entrepreneurship Journal. He co-authored The Virtues of Leadership: Contemporary Challenge for Global Managers (Oxford University Press, 2012).

Barbara Czarniawska is the Torsten & Ragnar Söderberg Senior Professor of Management Studies at Gothenburg Research Institute, University of Gothenburg, Sweden. She is a member of the Swedish Royal Academy of Sciences, the Swedish Royal Engineering Academy, the Royal Society of Art and Sciences in Gothenburg and Societas Scientiarum Finnica. Czarniawska takes a feminist and processual perspective on organizing, recently exploring connections between popular culture and practice of management, and the ways overflows are managed in affluent societies. She is interested in techniques of fieldwork and in the application of narratology to organization studies. She writes in Polish, English, Swedish and Italian; her texts have been translated into Arabic, Chinese, French, Danish, German and Russian. Recent books in English: *Coping with Excess: How Organizations, Communities and Individuals Manage Overflow* (edited with Orvar Löfgren, 2013), *Social Science Research from Field to Desk* (2014) and *A Research Agenda for Management and Organization Studies* (edited, 2016).

Max Ganzin is a PhD candidate at the University of Alberta School of Business. He received a BA in philosophy and an MBA from Brigham Young University. His research interests include institutional work, entrepreneurship, myth-creation, storytelling and the use of rhetorical history in organizations.

Pierre Guillet de Monthoux is a Professor of Philosophy and Management at Copenhagen Business School (CBS), where he equally is Director of the CBS Art Initiative. He has initiated the CEMS schools faculty group for integrating Humanities and Arts in business education and is currently engaged in liberal arts-based management research as a Professor affiliated with Uppsala University Campus Gotland and the Center for Art, Business and Culture at the Stockholm School of Economics. In his research he focuses on making aesthetic philosophy and contemporary art bridge business and society and on how to rethink business education as critical curating facilitating art as experience. This made him co-found the Nomadic University at Åbo Academy Finland and conduct executive experimental art-based leadership workshops through ECAM, the European Center for Art and Management in Scandinavia, Germany, Switzerland, France and Belgium.

Tor Hernes is a Professor of Organization Theory at Copenhagen Business School and Adjunct Professor at the University College of Southeast Norway. He works with issues of time and temporality and organizational life, drawing theoretical inspiration from process philosophy. He publishes extensively on organization and time, where he explores an event-based view informed by process philosophy, particularly works by Alfred North Whitehead. He is currently involved in research on how organizational actors combine near and distant pasts and futures in their time construction, where empirical sites include the dairy industry and the brewing industry. His books on process and organization include *A Process Theory of Organization* (Oxford University Press), which was awarded the George R. Terry Book Award in 2015.

Andreas Kaplan is the Rector and Dean of ESCP Europe Business School Berlin. Previously, he served as Dean for Academic Affairs as well as Director of Brand and Communications, both as part of the School's Executive Committee. Before joining ESCP Europe, he started his academic career at the ESSEC Business School and Sciences Po Paris. Kaplan is particularly interested in the future of management education and the general business school landscape. Notably, he has written the article "European Management and European Business Schools", which defines and explores management in Europe. Further publications analyze the digital transformation in higher education through the arrival of MOOCs and SPOCs. Professor Kaplan counts among the Top 50 Business and Management authors in the world according to John Wiley & Sons. Kaplan completed his Habilitation at the Sorbonne and his PhD at the University of Cologne/HEC Paris. He holds a Master of Public Administration (MPA) from the École Nationale d'Administration (ENA; French National School of Public Administration), an MSc from ESCP Europe and a BSc from the University of Munich.

Robert MacIntosh is a Professor of Strategy and Head of School at Heriot-Watt University. His research focuses on strategy development and organizational change using methods that include ethnography, video diaries and action research. Adopting a broadly processual perspective, he has drawn insights from systems theory, complexity theory, learning and culture to explore what people are actually doing when they claim to be working on strategy. He is a fellow of the Institution of Engineering and Technology and of the Academy of Social Sciences. He is an elected member of Council with the British Academy of Management and has created several dissemination channels, including www.thephdblog.com, www.methodsmap.org and www.stridesite.com. He has consulted extensively with public and private sector organizations and sits on the board of the charity Turning Point Scotland. His status as a shareholder in Aberdeen Football Club demonstrates his sense of optimism.

Donald MacLean combines academic work on strategy with ongoing commercial, public and third-sector consultancy engagements and directorships. He received a BSc in Physics from the University of Strathclyde, a PhD in optoelectronics from the University of Cambridge and an MBA from Kingston University. He spent ten years working in the global optoelectronics industry before joining the University of Glasgow in 1993, where he is now a Professorial Research Fellow in the Adam Smith Business School. He has published extensively on strategy, transformation and complexity theory in a range of international journals, including the *Strategic Management Journal, Journal of Management Studies, Organization Studies* and *Human Relations*.

Alison Minkus received a PhD in Organizational Analysis from the University of Alberta School of Business in 2015. She also holds a Bmus from Brandon University and an MBA from the University of Alberta. Her research interests include the nature of power and change, especially in artistic and historical contexts. Her thesis examined the counterbalancing forces of institutional change and persistence in the New York Philharmonic Orchestra from 1842 to 2012. Other research has addressed corporate art collection practices of the Canadian Pacific Railway in the late nineteenth century and the influence of the Medici banking family in seventeenth-century Florence. Her research has appeared in *Management and Organizational History* and recently, with co-author Yuliya Shymko, in *Routledge Research in Creative and Cultural Industries Management*.

Andreas Rasche is a Professor of Business in Society at the Centre for Corporate Social Responsibility at Copenhagen Business School (CBS) and Co-Director of the CBS World-Class Research Environment on "Governing Responsible Business". He holds a PhD (Dr. rer. pol.) from European Business School, Germany and a Habilitation (Dr. habil.) from Helmut Schmidt University, Hamburg. His research focuses on corporate responsibility standards (particularly the UN Global Compact), the political role of corporations in transnational governance and the governance of global supply networks. He regularly contributes to international journals in his field of study and has lectured on corporate social and environmental responsibility at different institutions. He recently edited *Corporate Social Responsibility: Strategy, Communication, Governance* (Cambridge University Press) and published *Building the Responsible Enterprise* (Stanford University Press). He collaborated with the UN Global Compact in the context of different projects. He is Associate

Editor of *Business Ethics Quarterly*. He joined Copenhagen Business School from Warwick Business School in August 2012. More information is available at: www.arasche.com.

Mike Saks is a Research Professor at the University of Suffolk and Visiting Professor at the University of Lincoln, University of London, University of St Mark and St John, UK, and University of Toronto, Canada. He studied for his doctorate at the London School of Economics and is a Fellow of the Institute of Directors, the Institute of Knowledge Exchange, the Research Council for Complementary Medicine and the Royal Society of Arts. He was Provost at University Campus Suffolk (UCS), Senior Pro Vice Chancellor at the University of Lincoln and Dean of Faculty of Health and Community Studies at De Montfort University. He is currently a Board member of Rose Bruford College of Theatre and Performance—having previously been on the Executive Board of Essex University and the University of East Anglia, which owned UCS. He has published 15 books and multiple articles/chapters on health, professions, regulation and research methods—and given many keynote addresses at international conferences. He is a member of the Innovation Council and has been a chair/member of many National Health Service and other healthcare committees, as well as an adviser to governments and professional bodies internationally. His collaborators in funded research range from the Russian Academy of Sciences to the University of Toronto. He was until recently the President/Vice President of the International Sociological Association Research Committee on Professional Groups, and is now on the Board of the International Sociological Association Research Committee on the Sociology of Health and the Editorial/Advisory Boards of several international journals.

David Seidl (PhD, Cambridge University) is a Professor of Management and Organization at the Department of Business Administration at the University of Zurich and is a Research Associate at the Centre for Business Research (CBR) at Cambridge University. He is also a senior editor of *Organization Studies* and editorial member of several other journals, including *Organization*, *Journal of Management Studies, Scandinavian Journal of Management Studies* and *Strategic Organization*. Current research focuses on the dynamics of standardization, the practice of strategy, the communicative constitution of organization and the practical relevance of management studies. He has published widely on these topics in leading international organization and management journals, including *Academy of Management Annals*, *Organization Science*, *Strategic Management Journal* and *Journal of Management Studies*. He has also (co)authored and (co)edited several books, including the *Cambridge Handbook of Strategy as Practice* (Cambridge University Press) and *Niklas Luhmann and Organization Studies* (Copenhagen Business School Press).

Sabina Siebert is a Professor of Management at the Adam Smith Business School, University of Glasgow, UK. With a background in linguistics, literature and cultural studies, she started her career as a tutor in British Culture at the University of Łódź before moving to the Business School at Glasgow Caledonian University and then on to the Adam Smith Business School. She is also a Visiting Professor at the University of Gothenburg, Sweden. Her current research interests include organizational trust and trust repair, sociology of the professions and management in the creative industries. She employs a range of qualitative methodologies including discourse analysis, narrative analysis and organizational ethnography. In 2016 she was awarded the British Academy Mid-Career Fellowship to investigate trust within the biomedical sciences, particularly focusing on the relationship between trust and the phenomenon of 'overflow' in science. She has published in various journals, including *Academy of Management Journal*, *Organization Studies*, *Human Resource Management Journal*, *Sociology*, *Social Science and Medicine* and *Work Employment and Society*. In the years 2013–2017 she was the Co-Editor and then Editor-in-Chief of the *European Management Journal*.

Roy Suddaby is the Winspear Chair of Management at the Peter B. Gustavson School of Business, University of Victoria, Canada, and a Research Professor at Newcastle University Business School. He is an Honorary Professor and Otto Monstead Visiting Professor at Copenhagen Business School and Distinguished Visiting Professor at the University of Technology Sydney. Professor Suddaby is an internationally regarded scholar of organizational theory and institutional change. His work has contributed to our understanding of the critical role of symbolic resources—legitimacy, authenticity, identity and history—in improving an organization's competitive position. His current research examines the changing social and symbolic role of the modern corporation.

Haridimos Tsoukas is the Columbia Ship Management Professor of Strategic Management at the University of Cyprus, Cyprus, and a Distinguished Research Environment Professor of Organization Studies at Warwick Business School, University of Warwick, UK. He obtained his PhD at the Manchester Business School (MBS), University of Manchester, and has worked at MBS, the University of Essex, the University of Strathclyde, and the ALBA Graduate Business School (Greece). He has published widely in several leading academic journals, was the Editor-in-Chief of *Organization Studies* (2003–2008) and has served on the Editorial Board of several journals. He was awarded the honorary degree of Doctor of Science by the University of Warwick in 2014. With Ann Langley he is the Co-Founder and Co-Convener of the annual International Symposium on Process Organization and Co-Editor of the *Perspectives on Process Organization Studies*, published annually by Oxford University Press. He has co-edited several books, including *The Oxford Handbook of Organization Theory* (with Christian Knudsen, Oxford University Press, 2003) and *Philosophy and Organization Theory* (with Robert Chia, Emerald, 2011). He is the author of *Complex Knowledge* (Oxford University Press, 2005) and *If Aristotle Were a CEO* (in Greek, Kastaniotis, 2012, 4th edition).

Tammar B. Zilber is an Associate Professor of Organization Theory at the Jerusalem School of Business, The Hebrew University, Israel. Her research focuses on the dynamics of meaning and action in institutional processes. Focusing on the micro-foundations of institutions, she examines the role of discursive acts (like narrating) in constructing institutional realities; the institutional work involved in creating and maintaining fields, given field multiplicity; the spatial and emotional mediations of institutional dynamics; the interrelations between institutional logics and institutional work; and the translation of institutions over time and across social spheres. Her work is based on qualitative methods, among them narrative research, field-level ethnography and semiotics.

Acknowledgements

Management Research: European Perspectives is a collection of essays previously published in the *European Management Journal*. I would therefore like to thank Vicki Wetherell from Elsevier for granting permission to reprint the revised version of the *EMJ* papers in this book.

This book would not be possible without the willingness of all the authors to contribute and share their ideas. I personally learned a lot from the authors, and thoroughly enjoyed working with them.

I would also like to thank people who were in various ways involved in running the *EMJ* during my editorship: Michael Haenlein, Thomas Anker and Robbie Paton. It was great fun working with them, and I hope that the *EMJ* is a better journal because of the team's hard work.

Finally, my biggest thanks go to Joannah Duncan for being an absolutely excellent managing editor for *EMJ*, and project manager of this book.

Introduction

Is There a Distinctive Approach to Management Research in Europe?

Sabina Siebert

Management Research: European Perspectives is a collection of articles originally published in the 'Reflections' section of the *European Management Journal* (*EMJ*). This section was launched, during my time as Editor-in-Chief and Co-Editor, to open discussions about management research in Europe and provide a forum for provocative, reflective contributions, not necessarily restricted to a standard academic article format. The Reflections section developed and surpassed my expectations, with a great number of fascinating contributions not only from scholars working in Europe but also from those based farther afield who provided different perspectives on European management realities.

The aim of this book is to take stock of European perspectives on management research and answer the following question: Is there a distinctive approach to management research in Europe? To address this question I have gathered together a selection of reflections, which have been revisited, revised and updated by the authors. Most of the original articles evoked strong reactions from the academic community when they were published in *EMJ*—leading to email exchanges with the authors, discussions at conferences and letters to the editor. Some attracted rejoinders and subsequent responses. In preparing this book, I have taken into account these reactions and hope the collection is now richer than the sum of the original *EMJ* articles.

In the world order as it is today (though many believe it is going to change soon), the definition of 'non-European' extends beyond 'North American' (Clegg, Linstead & Sewell, 1999). However, many commentators like simple dichotomies, and the 'European' and 'North American' approaches to the study of management are often juxtaposed, caricatured and crudely simplified. The North American studies are said to rely mostly on 'boxes and arrows', be predominantly normative, favouring variance theory over process theories, and look for simple cause-and-effect relationships. Such studies are also said to renounce past scholarship and treat methodological rigor as the overarching principle underpinning good research, whereas the European studies are seen as overly critical to the point of having nothing left to criticize (e.g. Latour, 2004) and focusing their efforts on finding long dead and forgotten thinkers, preferably Eastern European, whose ideas will allegedly help to re-interpret organizational realities. Koza and Thoenig (1995, p. 2) referred to the dichotomy between North American and European approaches as like 'ships passing in the night' and summed up with these words:

> Why have European and United States scholars failed to produce a unified research program? Prejudice is probably part of the explanation. It is common to hear from some European scholars that, with a few exceptions, US colleagues are arrogant, narrow-minded or stuck in normal science syndromes. For some US scholars, the profile of an average European researcher is of an individual who is not rigorous (which means neither quantitatively oriented nor using a deductive approach), wasting time with general ideas and unable to deliver cumulative knowledge outside very complex monographical studies.
>
> (Koza & Thoenig, 1995, p. 3)

Stereotypes of North American and European approaches to management research proliferate, and they are not helpful. Fortunately, there have also been some serious attempts to define, synthesize and characterize management research in Europe (for examples see Kaplan, 2015; Lee & Cassell, 2011; Westwood, Jack, Khan, & Frenkel, 2014). Furthermore, the state of management scholarship in Europe has been touched upon through discussions on the relationship between universities and businesses and its impact on research agendas (Chia, 2014; Steyaert, Beyes, & Parker, 2016), the so-called rigor–relevance debate (Nicolai & Seidl, 2010; Palmer, Dick, & Freiburger, 2009), the use of measurements in assessing the quality of research outputs (Willmott, 2011), the role of journal rankings (Hussain, 2015) and the merits of the journal review system (Davis, 2014). There have also been debates about the prevalence of certain methodologies in different countries (Batt & Banerjee, 2012; Koza & Thoenig, 1995).

There are numerous facets to the European approach to management research, but three main themes emerged from the contributions in this book, which I have attempted to synthesize in the following text.

The first area of distinctiveness is the *transdisciplinarity* of management research in Europe compared with its North American counterpart. In many non-European institutions there is a predominant belief that the strength of an academic discipline lies in its purity and integration (Donaldson, 1995; Pfeffer, 1993), whereas scholars in Europe often adopt a different perspective, which they legitimize by highlighting that management and organization studies emerged originally from the crossing of three different disciplines: psychology, sociology and economics. Consequently, they see no problem in venturing into other fields of intellectual endeavour, such as art, culture, anthropology, history and philosophy. Out of these 'blurred genres', new genres or new cultures emerge:

> Being a mixture of the two original cultures, the third culture also mixed the genres with great gusto: philosophy blended with cybernetics and literature theory (Gumbrecht, 1992), literature with empirical studies (Latour, 1996), and allegories with ethnographies (Geertz, 1973). It was there, in the vibrant fringe of blurred genres, that the new giants arose, all creolized personages: Michel Foucault (historian, philosopher, sociologist, political scientist); Niklas Luhmann (theorist and practitioner of administration, philosopher, cyberneticist, connoisseur of the Classics); Umberto Eco (semiologist, writer, journalist); and Bruno Latour (philosopher, anthropologist, sociologist).
>
> (Czarniawska, 2007, p. 2)

The second area of distinctiveness for management research is the *intellectual underpinnings of theory building*, which, explicitly or not, have roots in philosophy. The European tradition in management often refers to continental philosophy, which encompasses movements such as phenomenology, German idealism, critical theory, structuralism and poststructuralism. By contrast, North American scholars take for granted the assumptions that are typical of analytical philosophy. Although it has been indicated that many contemporary 'continental philosophers', for example Jacques Derrida and Bruno Latour, became famous through making their work known in the USA, their impact reached North American humanities rather than management schools.

It has been claimed that European management scholars publish fewer theoretical papers on the pages of North American management journals (Suddaby, 2014), which is surprising considering the fact that Europe has been the cradle of many of the generative intellectual traditions. Perhaps this is because European understanding of 'theory' is somewhat different. Moreover, North American journals, such as the *Administrative Science Quarterly*, have witnessed a dramatic rise in the Theory, Methods and Discussion sections compared with the notable shrinking of the Results sections (Strang & Siler, 2017). Strang and Siler (2017) explain this shift as a drive to bring management and organization studies closer to physical sciences. Reflecting on the loss of focus on the real phenomena in management research, the authors evoke the image of the prisoners chained to the wall in Plato's cave:

> Concrete facts no longer bring ideas to life; instead, theory animates dull fact as the realization of lively mechanisms and structured interdependencies. Contemporary organizational scholarship is in this sense Platonist. In Plato's allegory of the cave, prisoners chained to a wall see only the shadowy reflections of objects situated outside their field of vision. Knowing nothing else, the prisoners take the shadows for the reality and protest when brought into the light and shown the objects whose reflections have hitherto formed their world. For contemporary students

> of management, similarly, empirical observations become shadows and abstract concepts real.
>
> (Strang & Siler, 2017, p. 20)

At the same time as Strang and Siler (2017) observed a shift towards an increased emphasis on theory in the North American journals, Corley and Schinoff (2017) noticed a certain lack of clarity as to what theory actually is. In their recent study, Corley and Schinoff noted that even the editors of the flagship North American journals—*Academy of Management Journal* and *Academy of Management Review*—'perceived the notion of theoretical contribution as rife with ambiguity and intricacy' (Corley & Schinoff, 2017, p. 11). By contrast, in European management research, a theory is usually a way of explaining a phenomenon under study, and while the philosophical assumptions behind management research need to be incorporated in the work, they are not always explicitly presented in an extended 'methods' section.

The third area of distinctiveness is the role of *context* in management practices. Management research in Europe appears to be more cognizant of the context within which research is conducted; hence, the claims made by scholars are not taken to be automatically generalizable to the rest of the globe. One could argue, after David Hickson's (1993, p. 249) book on management in Western Europe, that 'nowhere on earth is there greater cultural diversity in a relatively small space than in Europe'. Whether this statement is correct or not, it seems that scholars in Europe are perhaps more aware of this diversity, and, when formulating conclusions for their studies, always take into consideration varying political, economic, social and demographic influences (see, for example, Batt and Banerjee's [2012] comparative analysis of the contemporary field of human resource management). This could be attributable to European scholars being more or less forced (perhaps by the North American reviewers?) to remember that there is a different world beyond their country, whereas the great expanse of North America makes it easier for their scholars to forget this fact. Additionally, North American authors realize that the managerial practices they describe are in all probability going to be imitated worldwide, thus generalizability is given at the outset, so to speak.

By identifying these three areas of distinctiveness, I inadvertently arrived at three dichotomies—specialization versus transdisciplinarity, analytical versus continental philosophy and universalism versus contextual perspective. The reflections collected in this book demonstrate that even these dichotomies may at times be misleading, and, in fact, management scholars all over the world have far more in common than might be assumed. Management research is developing rapidly and the make-up of the business management academic community is changing all the time. Over twenty years ago Koza and Thoenig (1995) called for more cross-fertilization of the two communities. In their view, North American journals should co-opt

European colleagues onto their editorial boards and apply more heterogeneous standards for reviewing. Europeans, on the other hand, should make an effort to publish in English and invite more North American colleagues to teach on their doctoral programs. Twenty years on it is safe to say that these changes have already taken place. The number of European scholars attending North American conferences and publishing in North American journals is increasing, and, similarly, more and more people from outside Europe attend European conferences, such as EGOS. Moreover, in recent years the *Academy of Management Journal* has handed out many best paper prizes to European authors. This suggests that the boundaries between once very different approaches are blurring. It is therefore important that this book is not seen as either a collective 'moan' against the 'North American hegemony' in publishing or yet another 'tale from the margin'. The intention behind this book is to celebrate a rich European tradition.

This richness of the European tradition is also reflected in the book contributors' diverse backgrounds and professional careers—which is also a feature of the globalized academia. For example, there are contributors from Canada and Israel, as well as a Pole working in Sweden; a German, Norwegian and Frenchman all working in Denmark; and a Dane and Singaporean working in Scotland. These contributors publish in North American and European journals, and none of them appear to have a sense of superiority or inferiority towards the 'Other'—whoever the Other might be.

Chapter Outlines

Robert Chia argues that what underpins a European-styled management scholarship is the 'rich legacy of diverse historical, cultural and philosophical traditions and contexts that have irretrievably shaped research outlooks, orientations and predispositions on this side of the Atlantic'. In his view, the North American management journals follow overly positivistic and unitary mainstream approaches, and ignore the inherently conflicting nature of knowledge claims arising from the diversity of philosophical, cultural and ideological traditions within the European context. In Europe, there is also a noticeably greater appreciation of diverse perspectives and epistemological pluralism. Chia therefore advocates 'artistic rigour' over adherence to methodological procedures in the research process, which can help reshape the intellectual landscape of management research. Chia argues that such scholarship can encourage scholarly contributions that are not simply scientifically rigorous, but also imaginatively interesting and often counterintuitive.

Tor Hernes proposes four tenets of managerial research that are focused more explicitly on processual issues of managing and organizing and which may help constitute a new soul of management and organization studies. These four tenets point towards 'a localised, embedded and temporally informed understanding of managerial work'. Emphasizing the role of context, Hernes argues that the particular cultural richness and variety found in Europe make it a fertile ground for building a research tradition in organization studies and management that engages with the fluid and processual nature of managerial work. In his view, to capture the nuances of the research context, researchers need to provide rich descriptions and explanations and move away from the excessive demands of scientific rigour and relevance. In his view, the way forward is process-based perspectives that are connecting and reconnecting heterogeneous actors in a world that is permanently on the move.

The notion that rationality and disenchantment are dominant in contemporary organizational neo-institutionalism in North America is challenged by **Roy Suddaby, Max Ganzin** and **Alison Minkus**. In their chapter they argue that rationality and disenchantment cannot exist in the absence of magic, mystery and enchantment. Furthermore, they identify five compelling themes of disenchantment in the world: the rise of populism, the return of tribalism, the resurgence of religion, the re-enchantment of science and the return to craft. The authors expand the lexicon of institutional theory beyond the over-rationalized notions of legitimacy by discussing constructs such as *authenticity, reflexivity, mimesis* and *incantation*. They also identify examples of 'magical thinking' in management, myths and alchemy within markets and the enchantment of institutions.

In her chapter, **Barbara Czarniawska** draws on the diversity of rich intellectual traditions in Europe to demonstrate how they shaped organization studies. She discusses Niklas Luhmann's and Bruno Latour's intellectual contributions and their commonality in using a transdisciplinary approach. Latour refers to himself as philosopher, sociologist, anthropologist or science and technology scholar, whereas Luhmann can be seen as philosopher, sociologist, political scientist, law scholar or practitioner of administration. Their inspiration came from art, literature, engineering and biology, and they both contributed to our understanding of organizations and organizing. But only the European version of it! Czarniawska argues that there must be something uniquely European about their work that does not resonate in the USA.

For **Pierre Guillet de Monthoux**, management academics are beginning to bridge the divide between North America and Europe as international awareness of the old world intellectual traditions is growing. In his view, European management scholarship is still published 'under the Anglo-Saxon publication radar', but there is increasing appreciation of European scholars' attempts to return to approaches excluded by the narrow analytical thinking dominating new world managerialism. Guillet de Monthoux proposes the term 'turn-taking' (linguistic turn, narrative turn, etc.) as a way of understanding how European management scholarship opens up to societal phenomena as play, critique, artistry and aesthetics to co-create business realities. These 'turns' taken inside the management field engage European scholarship in a fascinating new quest for the reality of business in society.

Donald MacLean and **Robert MacIntosh**'s contribution draws on the concepts of paradox and poetry in strategic management. They argue that strategy research implicitly subscribes to a view of human action that is typically rational or normative and does not take into account the inherent creativity of individual actions. Paradox and poetics are, in the authors' view, a means of revisiting the established problem of implementation failure. They liken the role of the contemporary transformational leader to that of 'the bard', in the tribal clan systems of the Scottish Highlands and Ireland, who endeavoured to translate actions and activities into an art that both entertained the clan and helped sustain social order and coherence. By creative narratives, people in organizations may be able to grapple with the paradoxes of emergent and deliberate strategies.

In their chapter, **Göran Ahrne, Nils Brunsson** and **David Seidl** argue that the field of organization studies has increasingly lost sight of organizations as its central object of research. They put forward two proposals for the future of organization studies that could increase the discipline's significance and relevance for understanding processes outside organizations. Firstly, the authors advocate a return to the classics that emphasize the distinctiveness of organization as a particular type of social order. Secondly, they call for an extension of the notion of organization beyond (formal) organizations, which would allow a transfer of insights, theories and concepts from organization studies research to other fields. Because almost all aspects of the social world involve a degree of organization, organization studies, with insights into organizational orders, should be placed at the heart of the social sciences.

Thomas Boysen Anker states that Europe finds itself in a challenging situation dominated by economic and political uncertainty, which has deep ramifications for businesses and society. By drawing specifically on the Brexit vote for the UK to leave the EU and the ensuing political crisis, Anker raises the fundamental ethical question: 'Should businesses play an active, constructive role in promoting global democracy by reinforcing and inducing democratic values and mindsets?' Although there are no easy answers to this question, Anker argues that businesses in Europe can play a constructive role in establishing political equilibrium by actively designing core internal and external business activities that enable conditions of democracy.

Emphasizing the role of context in management research, **Miguel Pina e Cunha** and **Haridimos Tsoukas** start with the premise that organization scholars have often criticised the discipline as being distant from practical managerial problems. They then tackle another form of distance—from citizens' problems. Specifically, they draw on the financial crisis in Europe to demonstrate the need for massive state reform. Having explored social reforms in Greece and the 'persistently Kafkaesque nature' of reforms in Portugal, they explore the notion of a vicious circle of state reform that impedes real change. The authors agree with Hernes (in this volume) that incessant demands for 'theoretical contribution', rigour and relevance remove management research even farther away from the world of practitioners. They suggest that three topics associated with state reform should be considered in future research in Europe: the conflict between institutional logics at different levels of analysis, the persistent paradoxes and dialectics of change and the process of change.

Andreas Rasche studies the link between firms and politics, specifically focusing on two concepts: corporate political activity and political corporate social responsibility. Rasche argues that most intellectual contributions to each approach come from North America and Europe respectively and that European and North American scholars have undertaken the *paradigmatic framing* of both concepts. He further identifies differences in the approaches to studying corporations as political actors and suggests that these differences can be explained by answering two questions: *Where* does the political engagement of firms take place? and *Why* do firms become politically active? In his analysis, he draws on the characteristics of European/North American management research as well as the political environment on both sides of the Atlantic.

In their contribution, **Mike Saks** and **David M. Brock** reflect on the dynamic nature of the domain of professions and organizations and comment specifically on the key interlinked aspects of professions and organizations in the European context. They draw on the literature from two complementary traditions of understanding professions in organizations: the sociological analysis of professions and organizational theory. Acknowledging the strong North American roots of research into professions, the authors identify the unique contribution made in recent years by European scholars. These insights into new and more established professions are usually underpinned by two theories: neo-Weberian and neo-institutionalist. Saks and Brock go on to use a case study of health professionals to illustrate the insights that these two theoretical perspectives can provide.

In her chapter, **Catherine Cassell** recognizes the strengths that emerge from the diversity in epistemological traditions and methods in European qualitative management research. She draws attention to concerns increasingly expressed by qualitative researchers about the growing pressures of standardization. Cassell concludes by saying that qualitative management researchers should cherish methodological diversity and resist attempts to homogenize the reporting of their work in academic journals. She warns against the production of formulaic pieces of research in North American journals, which can have negative consequences for the methodological diversity of management research.

Andreas Kaplan looks at management research through the lens of business school education in Europe and proposes that 'European management entails cross-cultural, societal management based on an interdisciplinary approach'. In his view, European business schools foster similar values as they are: international in scope and created to deliver value for society at large; as well as interdisciplinary in nature and practically oriented. Kaplan emphasizes the diversity of management approaches in Europe, which is evident in both the types of research published by European scholars (more contextual in nature) and the business schools' education models that promote a deep social, philosophical and ethical understanding.

The contribution by **Tammar B. Zilber** further problematizes the dichotomy between North American and European 'models'. For her, as a management scholar working in Israel, issues of 'us' and 'them' are even more complex. She tells an interesting tale of a journey from the periphery to the centre, and in her chapter the center–periphery interface has many aspects: linguistic, social and even geographical. For Zilber, as a management scholar situated in Israel, the Other against which she defines herself is North American academia (which is symbolically reflected in the US spelling of 'center'); but she also admits that her journey had a number of 'stopovers' in Europe and that her research was inspired by European traditions. Zilber argues that the experience of being on the periphery gives one an advantage—it provides opportunities for scholars to use their peripheral position creatively in the process of knowledge production.

Final Thoughts

The diversity of themes and perspectives in this book, and the positive tone of each chapter, will hopefully contribute to our understanding of management research. Such an understanding and reflective approach to management practice I believe will inform personal and institutional research agendas and management education.

It must be remembered, though, that this book has come together at a time when the world is in turmoil, and strange things are happening politically. Although nobody can foresee the consequences of these changes, such political upheaval is likely to affect organizations and the people working within them, and it is therefore only fair to assume that it will also affect management research. These effects may be not only ideological and philosophical, but also practical in terms of how research is funded or organized. Only the future will reveal the new centre and the new periphery, who will be leading and who will be following and what place both North American and European management research will have in the new world order.

References

Batt, Rosemary & Banerjee, Mallika (2012). The scope and trajectory of strategic HR research: Evidence from American and British journals. *International Journal of Human Resource Management*, 23(9), 1739–1762.

Chia, Robert (2014). From relevance to relevate: How university-based business schools can remain seats of "higher" learning and still contribute effectively to business. *Journal of Management Development*, 33(5), 443–455.

Clegg, Stewart R., Linstead, Stephen. & Sewell, Graham (1999). Only penguins: A polemic on organization theory from the edge of the world. *Organization Studies*, 20(7), 103–117.

Corley, Kevin G. & Schinoff, Beth S. (2017). Who me? An inductive study of novice experts in the context of how editors come to understand theoretical contribution. *Academy of Management Perspectives*, 31(1), 4–27.

Czarniawska, Barbara (2007). On creole researchers, hybrid disciplines and pidgin writing. Conference Proceedings, Linköping: Linköping University Electronic Press.

Davis, Gerald F. (2014). Why do we still have journals? *Administrative Science Quarterly*, 59(2), 193–201.

Donaldson, Lex (1995). *American anti-management theories of organization: A critique of paradigm proliferation*. Cambridge: Cambridge University Press.

Geertz, Clifford (1973). *The interpretation of cultures*. New York: Basic Books.

Gumbrecht, Hans Ulrich (1992). *Making sense in life and literature*. Minneapolis: University of Minnesota Press.

Hickson, David J. (1993). Many more ways than one. In D.J. Hickson (Ed.), *Management in Western Europe: Society, culture and twelve nations* (pp. 249–261). Berlin: Walter de Gruyter.

Hussain, Simon (2015). Journal list fetishism and the "sign of 4" in the ABS guide: A question of trust? *Organization*, 22(1), 119–138.

Kaplan, Andreas (2015). *European business and management*. London: Sage.

Koza, Mitchell, P. & Thoenig, Jean-Claude (1995). Organizational theory at the crossroads: Some reflections on European and United States approaches to organizational research. *Organization Science*, 6(1), 1–8.

Latour, Bruno (1996). *Aramis, or the love of technology*. Cambridge, MA: Harvard University Press.

Latour, Bruno (2004). Why has critique run out of steam? From matters of fact to matters of concern. *Critical Inquiry*, 30(2), 225–248.

Lee, Bill & Cassell, Catherine (2011). *Challenges and controversies in management research*. London: Routledge.

Nicolai, Alexander & Seidl, David (2010). That's relevant! Different forms of practical relevance in management science. *Organization Studies*, 31, 1257–1285.

Palmer, Donald, Dick, Brian & Freiburger, Nathaniel (2009). Rigour and relevance in organization studies. *Journal of Management Inquiry*, 18(4), 265–272.

Pfeffer, Jeffrey (1993). Barriers to the advance of organizational science: Paradigm development as a dependent variable. *Academy of Management Review*, 18(4), 599–620.

Steyaert, Chris, Beyes, Timon & Parker, Martin (2016). *The Routledge companion to reinventing management education*, Oxon: Routledge

Strang, David & Siler, Kyle (2017). From "just the facts" to "more theory and methods, please": The evolution of the research article in *Administrative Science Quarterly*, 1956–2008. *Social Studies of Science*, 1–28, doi:10.1177/0306312717694512.

Suddaby, Roy (2014). Challenges in publishing theory. Unpublished lecture, University of Glasgow, Glasgow.

Westwood, Robert, Jack, Gavin, Khan, Farzad & Frenkel, Michal (2014). *Core-periphery relations and organization studies*. Basingstoke: Palgrave Macmillan.

Willmott, Hugh (2011). Journal list fetishism and the perversion of scholarship: Reactivity and the ABS list. *Organization*, 18(4), 429–442.

1 Reflections on the Distinctiveness of European Management Scholarship

Robert Chia

Introduction

In a much publicized announcement reported in the Guardian on 9 December 2013, the 2013 joint Nobel Prize winner for Physiology and Medicine, Randy Schekman, revealed in his acceptance speech that he would no longer send research papers to the top-tier academic journals, *Nature*, *Cell* and *Science*. He claims that although these 'luxury' journals are supposed to be the epitome of quality, they have, in fact, inadvertently distorted research priorities and constitute a 'tyranny' in the research publication process that must be broken. Schekman maintains that these journals are more preoccupied with aggressively curating their own brands to increase subscriptions than with stimulating important research. Thus, like 'fashion designers who create limited-edition handbags or suits' they artificially restrict the number of papers they accept and then market their journals through the notion of 'impact factor'; a score now widely accepted within the academic world as an accurate measure of a journal's quality. For Schekman, however, this way of measuring and justifying what are supposed to be better journals is as damaging as the bonus culture is to banking. One major consequence is that pressure to publish in these journals has encouraged younger researchers especially to conform to these norms of expectations in publication terms rather than to do more important and often peripheral pieces of work that actually lead to genuine scientific progress.

Reacting to these comments, the 18 January 2014 editorial of the medical journal *Lancet* (Kleinert & Horton, 2014) proceeded to reflexively ask how its own journal publication process within the field of medical science research ought to change in response to this criticism from one of its best. Perhaps, in the same light, Schekman's very public comments ought to give us in management research some food for thought with regard to our own journal publication ranking process and the direction the 'publications game', which seems to preoccupy much of management academia these days, is taking us. This, together with the perennial question surrounding the relevance/irrelevance of management theory to practice that continues to rumble on, should provide sufficient grounds for us to seriously rethink and reconsider the future of management scholarship, particularly within the European management academic context. To be sure these concerns about research contribution and relevance are now beginning to be raised even within the 'top' management journals themselves.

In his Editorial in the February 2014 issue of the *Academy of Management Journal*, the incoming editor Gerard George signaled what appears to be an important 'shift' in emphasis for the journal's publishing priorities. George (2014, pp. 1–6) argues, quite rightly, that the traditional emphasis on 'technical rigor' and 'theoretical contribution' has distracted attention away from the 'soul of relevance' and the 'applied nature of our field'. A major consequence of this persistent insistence on theoretical rigor is that published studies like 'black cats in a coal cellar' become 'increasingly indistinguishable from previous ones' especially when the specific contexts within which these studies have been conducted are surreptitiously removed. George's comments are reminiscent of the late Sumantra Ghoshal's (2005, p. 77) astute observation (following von Hayek, 1974/1989) that the 'pretense of knowledge' which accompanies management theories that adopt a scientifically rigorous approach to analyzing and explaining management phenomena is effectively driving out good management practices. Hayek had previously, in his 1974 Nobel Prize lecture, criticized his own economics discipline for adopting a natural science approach to emulate the kind of theoretical rigor and objectivity displayed and admired in the latter. He maintained that, as a consequence, what looks like impressive social science 'is often the most unscientific' because it is based on a 'false belief that the scientific method consists in the application of a ready-made technique' (von Hayek, 1974/1989, p. 6). Despite this warning on the dangers of adopting a scientistic attitude in management scholarship, management research continues to be defined in terms of the kind of rigor associated with the natural sciences.

Thus, instead of adopting a 'scholarship of common sense' (Ghoshal, 2005, p. 81) that views the researcher, more like Darwin or Freud, as an adventurer ('conquistador') or detective rather than a mathematician or man of science, traditional management research has tended to insist on scientific rigor as the only acceptable basis for theory generation. Instead, of encouraging the pursuit of fresh and bold ideas and the adoption of less conventional research approaches to seek out anomalies that are intriguing and often counterintuitive, and hence potentially useful, there appears to be an increasing standardizing and homogenizing of research preoccupations and findings (Cassell, this volume), as evidenced in much of what ends up being published. George, therefore, proposed that the core of management scholarship ought to be re-conceptualized in terms of a proper balance between rigor and relevance. It is within the terms of this increasing disaffection with the current journal publications processes and emphases and how they are distorting research priorities and preoccupations that I would like to situate this invited chapter contribution.

For management and organization journals firmly based within the British and European philosophical, cultural and social traditions and context, perhaps it is timely to take stock of their own publishing mission and priorities vis-à-vis theory and practice and to show in more refreshingly novel ways how genuine management scholarship (one that is grounded in a 'scholarship of common sense') can actually contribute meaningfully to the real world of practice without necessarily compromising their academic *raison d'être*. In this short reflective piece, therefore, I shall attempt to develop a counterintuitive and possibly contentious argument that emphasizes three interrelated issues that European-based management journals ought to take into consideration in strategically positioning themselves with regard to this rigor/relevance debate in order to genuinely further management scholarship *and* at the same time make a useful contribution to business practice.

First, I want to make the controversial point that the conventionally accepted schism between academic rigor and relevance to the world of practice is an unhelpful and indeed false distinction, one that obscures the oftentimes more nuanced ways in which genuine academic rigor and scholarship can contribute to the world of practice. I shall argue instead that the very best of rigor in scholarship mirrors and is, in principle, indistinguishable from that of the very best kind of thinking evident in business and management practices. In this very important sense, therefore, to be truly rigorous, in terms of a 'scholarship of common sense' is to be genuinely useful and practically relevant. Secondly, I want to suggest that British and European scholarship with its rich intellectual base and sense of history, culture and tradition is best placed to show the way to this exemplary form of academic openness *and* scholastic imagination that management research ought to emulate if it is to achieve the kind of relevance it seeks. Being very imaginatively theoretical can be actually very practical, so much so that Lewin's (1951, p. 169) dictum, 'There is nothing so practical as a good theory', remains as true as ever. Finally, I shall argue that European-based management and organization journals have immense potential in reshaping the intellectual landscape, priorities and parameters of management research by encouraging the kind of *intellectual entrepreneurship* (Chia, 1996) and *adventurism* that was perhaps more evident in a previous scholastic era but now is increasingly missing in mainstream management research outputs. This entails the scholarly practice of playfully and imaginatively transgressing established boundaries of thought (*entre*) with a view to grasping (*prendre*) opportunities for making fresh connections and reconfiguring relationships to produce important novel insights previously unthought or unthinkable. It is about resisting the systematic rationalization that Max Weber (in Gerth & Mills, 1948, p. 51) noted accompanied the inexorable march of modernity and instead reversing this process of 'disenchantment' (Chia, 1998, p. 1) through a return to primitivism and the re-enchantment of the world (Suddaby, this volume). Such a primitivism involves relentlessly striving to attain the kind of innocent, pristine and child-like seeing that provides the basis for true entrepreneurial exploits. Displaying this entrepreneurial propensity in academic scholarship renders redundant the rigor/relevance distinction because it encourages the same kind of concrete appreciation and imaginative generalization required for expanding horizons of comprehension both in academia and in the very best of business ventures.

The Rigor/Relevance Debate: A False Distinction

> The true method of discovery is like the flight of an aeroplane. It starts from the ground of particular observation; it makes a flight in the thin air of imaginative generalization; and it again lands for renewed observation rendered acute by rational interpretation.
>
> (Alfred North Whitehead, *Process and Reality*, 1929, p. 5)

Rigor in management scholarship usually refers to an unwavering commitment to an established set of methodological procedures that emphasize: thoroughness and precision in terms of familiarity with the extant conceptual literature surrounding the field of study; care and comprehensiveness in terms of the gathering of extensive empirical evidence to support one's contention; and logical soundness and justification in terms of the claims being made and the casual relationships imputed. In the typical management journal publication process, one is not in a position to make any kind of credible knowledge claim or to be successful in getting published without having diligently observed these procedural protocols. The current conventional knowledge-creating process, therefore, as such is inherently 'conservative'; it demands an almost ritualized acknowledgement of previous contributors, continuous evidential (mostly quantitative) justification and logical rigor at every step of the development of an argument. One possible consequence of rigidly adhering to such a formulaic notions of 'rigor' is a resultant *rigor mortis*; an intellectual 'stiffness' of the mind that discourages any kind of speculative conjecturing, including especially the initial capacity to gloss over long stretches of incomprehension and to focus on only those aspects that appear immediately appealing or promising. This latter approach is deemed unscientific or not rigorous enough. Yet, it is often this tendency, noticeably widespread among young children, that characterizes the true method of discovery. The art theorist Anton Ehrenzweig (1967, pp. 6–7) describes this ability to take 'flying leaps' over areas of incomprehension as a 'syncretistic approach', in contrast to the more linear logical method adopted in scientific investigations. It is a feature of inquiry much more understood in the arts than the sciences. This 'syncretistic approach' provides us with an alternative understanding of what 'rigor' in an artistic sense might mean.

A 'syncretistic approach' encourages 'a diffused, scattered form of attention that contradicts our normal logical habits of thought' (Ehrenzweig, 1967, p. xii). It elevates 'unconscious scanning' over conscious thought so that one gradually learns to 'handle "open" structures with blurred frontiers which will be drawn with proper precision only in the unknowable future' (p. 42). In this regard, the urge to prematurely achieve form and proper gestalt is actively resisted. Here scholarly rigor entails not so much the rigid following of procedural protocols, but rather of relentlessly striving to attain an '*uncompromising democracy*' of vision; one that refuses to accept pre-existing conceptual distinctions between the various elements that make up a phenomenal experience. This is the very 'essence of artistic rigour' (Ehrenzweig, 1967, p. 29). *Artistic rigor* as such, in contrast to the kind of scientific rigor that journals often demand as a condition for publication, involves the honing and refinement of an empirical sensitivity and the development of a capacity for imaginative generalization that was much tolerated in a previous scholastic era where the mantra of methodological rigor and obsession with so-called 'evidence-based' research had not yet taken a stranglehold over research concerns, priorities and preoccupations. Instead, it was one that was often grounded in everyday (oftentimes singular) empirical observations and then subsequently energized by a fertile and imaginative mind that stretched understanding and comprehension beyond the bounds of logical, linear habits of thought. Like the trajectory of an aeroplane, it often starts from a singular moment of acute observation. It then takes flight in the 'thin air' of 'imagination generalisation' before landing to produce novel and important discoveries and insights hitherto unthought or unthinkable (Whitehead, 1929, p. 5). This is the kind of 'scholarship of common sense' that best describes the inductive and iterative sense-making process undertaken by many influential thinkers in the past as Ghoshal (2005, p. 81) convincingly points out. It is therefore quite unsurprising how many of the established and enduring concepts and theories that continue to provide the foundational basis for management and organizational theorizing have been produced this way rather than through the rigid methodological approaches now widely emphasized in business schools.

Adam Smith's (1759/1976, pp. 184–185) important notions of the 'invisible hand' (sadly often misunderstood) and his arguments for the benefits of the 'division of labor' after observing operations in a pin manufacturing plant in Kirkcaldy (Smith, 1776/1991, p. 10), for instance, were formulated, not so much on the basis of massive amounts of empirical data systematically collected, but rather upon deeper sustained reflection of isolated, singular and often casual observations. What was important in arriving at his monumental insights was not so much the quantity of data collected as 'evidence', but the acute empirical sensitivity he displayed and his capacity for achieving that sense of sympathetic 'fellow-feeling' with those he came into contact with on his visits and in his travels. He possessed that rare quality of pristine seeing which the art critic John Ruskin (1927, Vol. 4, p. 27) called an 'innocence of the eye'; an almost naïve ability to see clearly and then to take flying leaps of 'imaginative generalisation' to arrive at his seminal conceptualizations. Such an artistic 'rigour', well recognized amongst art scholars and practitioners alike, is what makes for the kind of 'radical empiricism' that William James (1912/1996, p. 42) considered to be the true basis of research as opposed to the kind of 'false empiricism' practiced by logical positivists. This revised understanding of 'rigor', not as rigidly following established procedural protocols, but as the relentless striving to attain an 'uncompromising democracy' of vision, is what is missing from management scholarship today. Curiously, as I have intimated, it is this same kind of 'artistic rigor' that underpins the successes of the very best of entrepreneurs and enterprises.

The relentless search for ever-newer products/services that add value to people's lives remains a central purpose and preoccupation of many business enterprises; it underpins a business's success. A cultivated and refined empirical sensitivity to people's needs, a capacity for imaginative generalization and the creative ability to reconfigure assets, resources and expertise to produce novel offerings that add value to people's lives are what really makes a business sustainably successful. Travelling through the busy streets in Bangalore, Ratan Tata, the founder of Tata Corporation, one of India's largest multinationals, found himself caught up in the usual traffic congestion that he had had to endure virtually every day of his working life. On this occasion, however, in an unguarded mind-wandering moment of 'pure seeing', he *noticed* for the first time, a single scooter carrying an entire family with father driving, the elder child standing in front and the wife behind holding a baby. Such a sight is not uncommon in India (Chacko, Noronha, & Agrawal, 2010). But for Ratan Tata, that particular day, in a moment of absorbed 'unconscious scanning' (Ehrenzweig, 1967, p. 42), this flicker of movement that caught his attention sowed the smallest seeds of an idea that was to have important consequences. His intuitively syncretistic approach led him to take a 'flying leap' in his imagination that eventuated in the conception of a 'scooter-car' that would be functional and affordable for the small family he saw on the scooter. Ratan Tata's subsequent doodling preoccupations during management meetings revolved around designing this 'scooter-car', which eventually became a reality when the Tata Nano was launched to much acclaim at the Delhi Auto show in January 2008.

What makes a business genuinely competitive and viable in a truly globalized business environment is its ability to relentlessly value-innovate to meet customers' often unexpressed/unconscious needs through this naïve ability to see with an 'innocence of the eye'. The Japanese industrialist Konusuke Matsushita (1978/1986, pp. 63–65) associates this ability with the possession of what he calls a *sunao* mind—a meek, tractable and untrapped mind. Thus, 'The *sunao* mind gives . . . clarity of vision . . . and the conviction to act in accordance with it'. For this reason, Matsushita (2002, p. 45) insists that it is the cultivation of this *sunao* mind amongst executives that is paramount in his group of companies. We can therefore conclude that the relentless honing of an empirical sensitivity to event-happenings is a prerequisite for achieving excellence in business. This empirical sensitivity, together with the syncretistic capacity to take 'flying leaps' over areas of imprecision and incomprehension in order to arrive at some sense of coherence, is what makes for artistic rigor in the best of scholarship and the best of business practices, thereby rendering the rigor/relevance debate redundant. But this kind of intellectual openness in academic scholarship has been increasingly eroded by an over-eagerness to appear immediately relevant.

The Ancient Tradition of Academic Scholarship in Britain and Europe

> [A] university . . . aims at raising the intellectual tone of society . . . at purifying the national taste . . . at giving enlargement and sobriety to the ideas of the age.
>
> (John Hendry Newman, *The Idea of a University*, 1907/1996, pp. 125–126)

Universities are institutions of 'higher' learning, and the ancient universities in Britain and Europe such as Bologna, Oxford, Cambridge, Paris, Salamanca, St Andrews and Glasgow have been seats of higher learning for no less than five centuries; they existed well before the discovery of America and the setting up of American universities. Many, if not most, of these ancient universities have Christian monastic origins. The University of Glasgow, for instance, was issued its papal bull (charter) by Pope Nicholas V in 1451. Such a rich and overflowing intellectual tradition has inevitably shaped, and continues to shape, academic outlooks, priorities and predispositions in Britain and Europe and hence the nature of management scholarship on this side of the Atlantic. Within this broader and more diverse European philosophical, historical and cultural tradition and context, universities were detached places of solitude, contemplation and scholarship. It is this sense of the need and value of detachment which still underpins the natural impulse of many university academics leading them to be often criticized for their 'ivory tower' thinking. Yet, *contrary to the prevailing view, it is perhaps this very detachment and deliberate indifference to practical concerns that give universities and the real scholars therein their true strength and their potential practical value to business and society*. This is something the ancient universities in Britain and Europe still cherish. It is what gives them their true 'competitive advantage'. Paradoxically, it is their difference in outlooks and diversity of views that enable them to make a real difference to the business world (Chia, 2014) because it challenges the latter to expand its horizons of comprehension and hence the scope and range of decisional possibilities conceivable. A university's fundamental *raison d'être*, therefore, is to make the unthinkable thinkable and hence to open up new vistas of comprehension.

One major consequence is that an individual immersed in this kind of scholarly atmosphere inevitably acquires 'a delicate taste, a candid, equitable . . . mind, a noble and courteous bearing in the conduct of life' (Newman, 1907/1996, p.89). Such a cultivated predisposition or 'habitus' (Bourdieu, 1990) is eminently useful to business enterprises because it engenders the kind of empirical sensitivity and syncretistic capacity that is vital for effective managerial decision making and/or the initiation of entrepreneurial ventures. The role of a university, therefore, is to preserve 'the connection between knowledge and the zest of life' (Whitehead, 1932, p. 139) by encouraging the open, imaginative and passionate consideration of what we believe we know. Thus, a 'fact' learnt is not a mere fact. Instead, it must be 'invested with all its possibilities' and be 'energizing as the poet of our dreams and as the architect of our purposes' (ibid). Facts must lead us to their wider-ranging implications. Yet, there is an increasing danger that this passionate and imaginative approach to research and learning and the real value it can offer to the world of practical affairs is being eroded within university-based business schools because of the debilitating overemphasis on procedural protocols. Paradoxically, the urgency to generate research outputs that appear (superficially) relevant is surreptitiously undermining the university's genuine ability to contribute to the latter. Ironically, the university business school is in danger of rendering itself irrelevant by trying too hard to be relevant and useful!

The philosopher Alan Bloom (1987) in a trenchant critique maintains that many American universities have capitulated to the demands of public opinion and abandoned their scholarly ideals, thereby impoverishing the souls of their students. For him, the kind of shallow scholarship associated with this rush towards 'relevance' paradoxically breeds a kind of 'openness to closedness' (Bloom, 1987, p. 36); it precipitates a numbing 'indifference' that immunizes students and researchers from the more basic desire to seek answers to deeper and more fundamental questions about the human condition. True openness in scholarship for Bloom means resisting the charms that make us comfortable with what we already know; it entails an interminable process of relentlessly questioning the very basis of knowledge itself. Scholarly research, as such, is not simply about systematically generating tangible and cumulative knowledge outputs, but also about the systematic refinement of empirical sensitivity and the instilling of a deep appreciation of the limits and limitations of knowledge generated and hence awareness of our own ignorance.

To *re-search* is, after all, to search again and again interminably for ever-better ways of explicating observed phenomena and our lived experiences. Academic scholarship, as such, must entail relentlessly and interminably 'moving upstream' (Chia, 1996a; Serres, 1982), to critically examine the philosophical presuppositions underpinning knowledge-claims and ready-made explanations. This tendency to move 'upstream' in academic theorizing is something quite instinctive within the European intellectual tradition, and manifests itself quite evidently in British and European management scholarship.

What underpins and influences this broader British and European academic mentality is the rich legacy of diverse historical, cultural and philosophical traditions and contexts that have irretrievably shaped research outlooks, orientations and predispositions on this side of the Atlantic. It has produced a curiously mixed and more healthily guarded outlook on something as fundamental as the capitalist enterprise and its claimed benefits (see for instance the recent much-acclaimed voluminous tome on capitalism by Thomas Piketty, 2014). Several European management scholars have already noted the distinctiveness of the European management approach and have suggested that more emphasis needs to be made to differentiate European management research from that of their North American counterparts (Boone & Bosch, 1997; Demeron & Durand, 2009; van den Bosh & Prooijen, 1992. Unlike the largely more positive and unitary mainstream management research emphases that seem to typically characterize American-based journal publication outputs (with some notable exceptions), there appears to be a more balanced awareness of the inherently conflicting nature of knowledge claims arising from vastly different philosophical, cultural and ideological traditions within the European context. As a consequence, there is a noticeably greater tolerance of diversity of perspectives in the published journal outputs; epistemological pluralism is more widely embraced amongst British and European scholars. Evidence that a different 'soul of relevance' that 'addresses the localized, embedded, fluid and contingent nature' of managerial challenges (Hernes, this volume) exists and persists in European management scholarship.

Whilst, admittedly, there is some evidence of increasing awareness of these philosophical debates and their implications for management scholarship within the United States, it is something deeply embedded within the collective psyche of European management academia. As a result, a certain European 'style' or *modus operandi* is clearly discernible; one that actively shapes research interests, preoccupations and outputs on this side of the Atlantic. Yet, of late, the increasing pressure to publish in 'high impact' American-based journals is now beginning to overshadow such traditional research concerns. To be fair, a number of these American-based journals have, on their part, begun to internationalize their editorial teams and this augurs well for the future of management scholarship, since it is more likely to be sympathetic and appreciative of the diverse range of epistemological, methodological and stylistic approaches reflected in manuscript submissions.

One distinctive sub-field of management research that has been clearly inspired by this quintessentially European academic outlook, for instance, is that of *critical management studies* (Alvesson & Willmott, 1992; Grey & Willmott, 2005; Parker, 2002). This research movement, initially inspired by Labour Process theories and especially the seminal work of Braverman (1974), subsequently drew heavily from the writings of Marx and the Frankfurt school of critical theory and more latterly from post-structuralists including especially the work of Michel Foucault, Jacques Derrida and Gilles Deleuze to critically interrogate the inner workings of the capitalist enterprise and the logic of representation. These philosophical and ideological critiques of capitalism and management theory and practice were relatively unknown in the United States in the early 1980s. Although there has been an increasing take-up and acceptance there in more recent years, it is quite evident that the impetus and inspiration for this movement derives from a propensity for British and European and management scholarship to draw from its own rich and diverse philosophical roots. Critical management studies, sitting side by side with more mainstream management concerns, provides one indication of how genuine 'openness' in academic scholarship can be enhanced through the existence of multiple competing views on the phenomena of management and organization. The real value of having such competing perspectives is not so much to champion an irretrievably hopeless epistemological relativism, but rather to force competing theories and perspectives to 'rub' against each other *and* against brute empirical reality so that an intellectual space or 'clearing' can be created and genuinely fresh insights and understanding rendered possible.

Further, the stimulus for legitimizing such alternative meta-narratives in British and European management scholarship was arguably initiated by Burrell and Morgan's (1979) seminal publication, *Sociological Paradigms and Organizational Analysis*, and this was followed by Morgan's (1986) very influential *Images of Organization*. Together, they were probably the first important theoretical contributions that systematically drew together and comprehensively showed how different ontological, epistemological, ideological and methodological assumptions and concerns can give rise to radically different accounts of managerial and organizational life and their practical consequences. These two key texts, together with Geert Hofstede's (1980) influential contribution on how national cultures affect organizational and management practices, have helped pave the way to greater awareness and acceptance of the plurality and diversity of perspectives on management and organizational theorizing on this side of the Atlantic.

There were other important contributions, of course, including that of the Aston group in the 1960s (primarily Derek Pugh, David Hickson, Bob Hinings and John Child), whose work was seminal in shaping and influencing the direction of organization theory on both sides of the Atlantic. Then there was Michel Crozier's (1964) analysis of the bureaucratic phenomenon (written on a visit to the United States), as well as Stewart Clegg's (1975) comprehensive analysis of power and domination. These, besides many others, helped shape the distinctiveness of European management scholarship. But it is additionally critical to note that up to the mid-1980s most management and organizational behaviour/theory departments in many British universities and in many European ones were located within the Arts and Social Sciences faculties rather than in stand-alone business schools as in the United States. It was therefore more likely that theoretical developments and advancements within the broader social sciences and humanities inevitably affected and informed academic outlooks, predispositions and preoccupations within management and organization studies. This legacy has played a critical role in shaping the uniqueness of British and European management scholarship—one in which greater tolerance of diversity and pluralism of perspectives is evident in journal publication outputs specific to this region.

My contention is that European management scholarship, drawing from this rich and diverse cultural and intellectual tradition, has the potential to achieve a better balance between the overly enthusiastic advocacy of the capitalist enterprise and an overly critical scrutiny of its inherent weaknesses in order to clear the ground for a more constructively critical and genuinely empirically rooted study of the phenomena of management and organization—one grounded on the intriguing tenets of practice, temporality, becoming and heterogeneity (Hernes, this volume). Moreover, it can show that the very best of scholarly rigor, in its more artistic sense, is inherently relevant and valuable to the business of wealth creation, as I have previously argued. This 'soul of relevance' is realizable through what I call *intellectual entrepreneurship*, one characterized by the art of *relevation/revelation.*

The Art of Relevation/Revelation: Intellectual Entrepreneurship in Management Scholarship

> It is not easy for dry academicians to accept that syncretistic primary-process techniques rather than analytic clarity of detail are needed by the creative thinker to (deal with) the vast complexities of his work.
>
> (Ehrenzweig, 1967, p. 46)

To re-search is to imaginatively seek out ever-newer meanings to both exceptional and ordinary everyday experiences, familiar and unfamiliar happenings and taken-for-granted conceptual formulations. It is as much process as it is content-output. It entails re-thinking concepts, renewing observations, reliving experiences and re-enacting memories; it is learning to see, think and imagine anew. More fundamentally, research entails the development of a syncretistic *art* of discerning and revealing hidden relationships and invisible/latent connections; it is about *relevation/revelation.*

Drawing from etymological roots of the term 'relevant' (*reliever* or *relevāre*, in Latin, meaning to lighten, or to raise again) and the medical term *levation*, meaning the act of gradually raising up, 'relevate' implies relaxing pre-existing conceptual constraints so that the unnoticed, overlooked or unattended becomes increasingly viewed as being pertinent and relevant to research considerations. Similarly, the term 'revelate' derives from the Latin root *revelo*, meaning to 'unveil' so that what was previous invisible, hidden from view or 'latent' is shown to be fundamentally and inextricably '*re-lat-ed*' to our concerns and preoccupations. Relevation/revelation helps expand the scope and range of issues considered significant or otherwise to a particular research emphasis; it effectively re-frames a given problematic and in so doing forces a new comprehension of the empirical reality encountered.

To 'relevate/revelate' is therefore to imaginatively provoke, through a variety of scholarly means, a heightened empirical sensitivity to peripheral event-happenings, hidden relationships and latent connections so that the seemingly 'irrelevant' becomes increasingly perceived as pregnant with implications and hence vital to immediate theoretical and practical considerations. Such an open and expansionary outlook describes the kind of intellectual entrepreneurship much needed in management academic scholarship today. Just like the practice of entrepreneurship in business, where what is crucial for success is not so much knowledge and expertise as it is a cultivated attitude, demeanor and predisposition to seek out new possibilities to value-innovate, so also it is in academic scholarship—in one case, empirical sensitivity, scholastic imagination and academic rigor, in the other empirical sensitivity, business imagination and management rigor in business practices. Thus, the perceptual openness and imagination demanded, the veracity of the end sought and the uncompromising attention to fine details all are manifestly evident both in the best of management scholarship and in the most successful of enterprises. Both approaches rely on what the philosopher Alfred North Whitehead (Whitehead, 1932, p. 4) calls the 'art of the utilisation of knowledge'; the capacity to imaginatively reconfigure and create new relationships among knowledge, resources and competencies to formulate a new theory or a new product/service. This is what I mean by 'relevate/revelate'.

Practically, the capacity to relevate/revelate serves to guard against the sometimes obsessive preoccupation within academia to rigidly adhere to procedural protocols that generate the kind of insipid 'theoretical contribution' that makes research outputs indistinguishable in the way that George has rightly pointed out. Similarly, in business, it guards against the organizational tendency to rigidly focus upon and relentlessly pursue an immediate tangible end without giving sufficient regard to the wider and longer-term potential unintended consequences of such actions/decisions. This organizationally myopic condition is precipitated by what the sociologist Robert Merton (1936, p. 901) calls the 'imperious immediacy of interest' and it is this tendency to over-focus on the immediate and the short term that inevitably gives rise to negative unintended consequences that are often the underlying causes of eventual corporate failures (Mackay & Chia, 2013) in the longer term.

Relevating/revelating, therefore, entails cultivating an ever-widening appreciation for the necessarily socially embedded, historically shaped and inextricably contextual nature of managerial scholarship and as a corollary the necessarily contextual and socially embedded nature of any entrepreneurial venture or managerial decision-making process. It heightens awareness of the potency of *latent* connections always already existing in every business and social 're-*lat*-ionship' situation and alerts decision makers to this 'invisible presence' always already motivating 'the movement of being' (Cooper, 2005, p. 1706). The ability to discern the *latent* in any relationship and hence to show how the seemingly 'irrelevant' can be eminently relevant, lies in the best of academic scholarship, in the most successful of entrepreneurial ventures, and in the most astute of political decision making. The cultivation of this 'art' of *relevation/revelation* and hence the capacity for subtle discernment is particularly emphasized in traditional scholarly activities, and it is this aspect of the research process that must be revived and encouraged in the journal publications process. This is the kind of exciting possibility open to European-based management journals. It is one created by an increasing realization that 'scientific rigor' and 'theoretical contribution' are not the be-all and end-all of journal publication outputs. Rather, it is an acknowledgement that for an 'applied' field of study, management scholarship must rely more on a 'scholarship of common sense' which is rigorous in an artistic rather than in a scientific sense. The capacity to be empirically sensitive and to adopt a syncretistic approach to understanding social phenomena is one that can be hugely insightful intellectually, and practically relevant and valuable to the world of practice.

Conclusion

Management scholarship and the journal publication process have been increasingly criticized for being overly elitist and largely irrelevant to the needs of business. There is some justification for such criticisms. Yet, paradoxically, university business schools must resist the urge to be superficially relevant in order to be genuinely useful. This is because the very best of management research scholarship does not entail painfully adhering to procedural protocols. Rather it relies on a 'scholarship of common sense' that actively mirrors the very best of business and management practices in emphasizing the attainment of an 'uncompromising democracy' of vision as the founding basis for both intellectual and business endeavours. Artistic rigor, much more than scientific rigor, is needed. Openness, empirical sensitivity and the capacity for achieving 'flying leaps' of imagination are to be preferred to procedural adherence in both the research process and the imaginative reconfiguring of assets, expertise and resources to create new value-adding products/services.

The rediscovery of this alternative understanding of academic rigor, one based more on the arts than the sciences, derives from a deeper appreciation of the intellectual richness and diversity of perspectives that are clearly more evident in the British and European intellectual traditions. It accounts for a more readily found scholarly openness to the plurality of perspectives that can be proffered on any observed social phenomenon. Such an inclusive pluralism augurs well for the future of management scholarship; it encourages the kind of *intellectual entrepreneurship* and *adventurism* that was perhaps more evident in a previous scholastic era but is now increasingly absent in much of mainstream management research. This is where a European management scholarship has immense potential in actively reshaping the intellectual landscape, priorities and parameters of management research by encouraging this kind of scholarly contribution that is not simply scientifically rigorous, but imaginatively interesting and often counterintuitive; contributions that reveal opportunities for making fresh connections and reconfiguring relationships to produce important novel insights previously unthought or unthinkable. Such a cultivated entrepreneurial propensity in academic scholarship renders redundant the rigor/relevance distinction because it encourages the same kind of imaginative generalization and hence expansion of horizons of comprehension that is quintessential to the very best of business enterprise.

References

Alvesson, Mats & Willmott, Hugh (Eds.) (1992). *Critical management studies*. London: Sage.

Bloom, Allan (1987). *Closing of the American mind*. New York: Simon & Schuster.

Boone, Peter F. & Van Den Bosch, Frans A. J. (1997). Discerning a key characteristic of a European style of management. *International Journal of Management and Organization*, 26(3), 109–127.

Bourdieu, Pierre (1990). *The logic of practice*. Cambridge: Polity Press.

Braverman, Harry (1974). *Labor and monopoly capitalism: The degradation of work in the twentieth century*. New York: Monthly Review Press.

Burrell, Gibson & Morgan, Gareth (1979). *Sociological paradigms and organizational analysis*. Aldershot: Gower.

Chacko, Philip, Noronha, Christabelle & Agrawal, Sujuta (2010). *Small wonder: The making of the Nano*. New Delhi: Westland.

Chia, Robert (1996). Teaching paradigm-shifting in management education: University business schools and the entrepreneurial imagination. *Journal of Management Studies*, 33(4), 409–428.

Chia, Robert (1996a). *Organizational analysis as deconstructive practice*. Berlin: Walter de Gruyter.

Chia, Robert (1998). Introduction. In R. Chia (Ed.), *Organized worlds: Explorations in technology and organization with Robert Cooper* (pp. 1–19). London: Routledge.

Chia, Robert (2014). From relevance to relevate: How university-based business schools can remain seats of "higher" learning and still contribute effectively to business. *Journal of Management Development*, 33(5), 443–455.

Clegg, Stewart (1975). *Power, rule and domination*. London: Routledge & Kegan Paul.

Cooper, Robert (2005). Relationality. *Organization Studies*, 26(11), 1689–1710.

Crozier, Michel (1964). *The bureaucratic phenomenon*. Chicago: University of Chicago Press.

Demeron, Stéphanie & Durand, Thomas (2009). 2020 vision: A dual strategy for European business schools. *EFMD Global Focus*, 3(1), 22–25.

Ehrenzweig, Anton (1967). *The hidden order of art*. Berkeley: University of California Press.

George, Gerard (2014). Rethinking management scholarship. *Academy of Management Journal*, 57(1), 1–6.

Gerth, Hans H. & Mills, Wright C. (1948). *From Max Weber*. London: Routledge.

Ghoshal, Sumantra (2005). Bad management theories are destroying good management practices. *Academy of Management Learning and Education*, 4(1), 75–91.

Grey, Chris & Willmott, Hugh C. (2005). *Critical management studies: A reader*. Oxford: Oxford University Press.

Hofstede, Geert (1980). *Cultures consequences*. Beverly Hills, CA: Sage.

James, William (1912/1996). *Essays in radical empiricism*. Lincoln: University of Nebraska Press.

Kleinert, Sabine & Horton, Richard (2014). How should medical science change? *Lancet*, Vol. 383, 197–198, January, 2014.

Lewin, Kurt (1951). *Field theory in social science; selected theoretical papers*. D. Cartwright (Ed.). New York: Harper & Row.

MacKay, Brad & Chia, Robert (2013). Choice, chance and unintended consequences in strategic change: A process understanding of the rise and fall of Northco automotive. *Academy of Management Journal*, 56(1), 1–23, February, 2013.

Matsushita, Konusuke (1978/1986). *My management philosophy*. National Productivity Board, Singapore (Trans.), Tokyo: PHP Institute.

Matsushita, Konusuke (2002). *The heart of management*. Tokyo, New York, Singapore: PHP Institute.

Merton, Robert (1936). The unanticipated consequences of purposive social action. *American Sociological Review*, 1, 894–904.

Morgan, Gareth (1986). *Images of organization*. Beverly Hills: Sage.

Newman, John Henry (1907/1996). *The idea of a university*. New Haven: Yale University Press.

Parker, Martin (2002). *Against management: Organisation in the age of managerialism*. Oxford: Polity Press.

Piketty, Thomas (2014). *Capital in the twenty-first century*. Boston: Harvard University Press.

Ruskin, John (1927). *The complete works*. London: Nicholson and Weidenfeld.

Schekman, R. (2013). How journals like nature, cell and science are damaging science, December 9, 2013. Guardian, p. 7.

Serres, Michel (1982). *Hermes, literature, science, philosophy*. Baltimore: Johns Hopkins Press.

Smith, Adam (1759/1976). *Theory of moral sentiments*. Oxford: Clarendon Press.

Smith, Adam (1776/1991). *Wealth of nations*. Amherst, New York: Prometheus Books.

van den Bosch, Frans J. A. & van Prooijen, Arno A. (1992). The competitive advantage of European nations: The impact of national culture: A missing element in Porter's analysis? *European Management Journal*, 10(2), 173–177.

von Hayek, Friedrich A. (1974/1989). The pretence of knowledge. *The American Economic Review*, 79(6), 3–7.

Whitehead, Alfred North (1929). *Process and reality*. New York: Macmillan.

Whitehead, Alfred North (1932). *The aims of education*. London: Williams and Norgate.

2 In Search of a Soul of Relevance for European Management Research

Tor Hernes

Misplaced Rigour and Relevance

Robert Chia (in this volume) makes an appeal for academic openness and scholastic imagination in European scholarship, which, he suggests, would enable European research to reshape the intellectual landscape of management research. Chia evokes the ghost of rigour and relevance, which seems to haunt researchers, reviewers and editors alike, as they engage actively in a curious sort of truth-based logic rather than a more pragmatic plausibility-based logic in research. This form of research assessments reverberates through the academic world and leaves its mark on recruitment processes, the daily work of scholars, the knowledge they impart to practitioners and students and the ways in which they project their careers as well as their contributions to the wider research community. Paradoxes abound in this whirlpool of conflicting yet immutable demands. Top journals, while insisting on significant theoretical contribution of papers, also insist on meticulous reviews of previous research, bloated Methods sections and excessive presentations of empirical data, which prevent scholars from properly arguing their theoretical contributions. Paradoxes are also upheld by institutions, which reward publication of papers in top journals where theoretical contribution is demanded, while leaving less time to scholars to engage in research that makes possible those very contributions.

Coupled with incessant demands for 'theoretical contribution', demands of rigour and relevance risk sending the field further away from the world of practitioners. The drive towards misplaced notions of truth imposes incommensurate demands on scholars between the ideology imposed by journals and the fluid world of inquiry with which they engage. Hence George's (2014) claim that attention is distracted away from the 'soul of relevance' and the 'applied nature of our field'. The philosopher Alfred North Whitehead, who maintained a strong concern with the relationship between practice, science and philosophy, described the journey from practice to theory as a journey from the concrete into the abstract. This journey, he pointed out, is necessary for society to evolve. Still, he pointed out, the most critical passage is the journey back from abstractions to living, concrete reality, as abstractions may lead us away from the real complexity of nature (Whitehead, 1938). It is the journey back that sometimes leads to what he famously called 'fallacy of misplaced concreteness' (Whitehead, 1929, p. 2). His point is that theorizing, while describing concrete experience, may lead us to forget the concrete world that theorizing should help us explain and instead become a misplaced version of practice. Still, he suggested: 'There can be no objection to this procedure, however, as long as we know what we are doing' (Whitehead, 1938, p. 10). In other words, researchers should be the masters of the abstractions, and not the other way around.

Incommensurate Ideals, Lying and Shame

A logic of misplaced scientific ideals demands increasing amounts of data to back up even the most trivial claims at times, without being checked by more fundamental questions as to the actual relevance of the data to the dynamic reality on the ground. More data are demanded, as opposed to more precise data, which is why Methods sections of articles in certain journals take on disproportionate dimensions rather than address targeted findings with specific methods. Truth becomes an ideal, and the problem of ideals is that they induce lying as and when they become inconsistent with the reality on the ground (March, 2007). Lying arises when reality and ideals become irreconcilable as March points out. People, however, rarely live up to their ideals, and lying is used as a means to give the impression that ideals are achieved (March, 2007). A problem is that as lying takes hold, the legitimacy of misplaced ideals is maintained, as there is nothing to enable questioning of these ideals. Paradoxically it is the failure to achieve the ideals that actually ends up maintaining those same ideals. As lying increases, the more strongly the ideals are upheld and the more difficult it becomes to question or dismantle them. Instead the process becomes a spiral of increasing demands for ideal behaviour, inducing more lying in turn. Becoming engaged in a process of lying does not mean that people are liars per se. On the contrary, they experience lying as shameful, and it therefore instills them with a sense of guilt. Thus shame emerges among scholars as they grapple with trying to live up to misplaced scientific ideals. The good news is that the shame is caused, not by lack of scientific ability for rigour, but by incommensurate ideals that were misplaced in the first place. Still, the actual process of lying is a social and relational one and becomes institutionally endorsed, as authors, reviewers and editors tend to 'look away' when faced with the fact that the field of management and the ideals of rigour and relevance become incommensurate. Instead there are demands for more data under the pretext that sheer volume will make up for a weak argument. Unfortunately, then, the spiral has no happy ending. Potentially good case studies sometimes end up anaesthetized by perspectives more than by what they reveal of organizational life, which is logical because perspectives have their communities, from which reviewers are recruited, and which cite one another in turn, enabling journals to prosper, publishers to make more money, curricula to be created and beliefs sustained in the relevance of the perspectives taught in the curricula. Again a spiral, separate from the spiral of lying, but entangled with it.

In North America, for example, this spiral is sustained institutionally by the American Academy of Management (AoM), where institutional and editorial responsibilities, celebrated through awards and citations, are entangled with merits in terms of cited papers in top journals in which incommensurate ideals are practiced. As people take up positions, they cannot readily question the merits of publication that got them there in the first place, and it becomes hard to break out of the mold. Such webs of entanglement may become extraordinarily strong. The launching of the journal *Academy of Management Discovery*, dedicated to 'promote the creation and dissemination of new empirical evidence that strengthens our understanding of substantively important yet poorly understood phenomena concerning management and organisations' (http://aom.org/amd/) appears an important initial step out of the spiral. The expression 'creation of new empirical evidence' is worth noting because it suggests a philosophy of science view that departs from the idea of discovery of a reality lying there to be discovered and deciphered to a reality whose richness is engaged with and co-created with those who live it. The aim of the journal resonates in part with the idea of empirical evidence as 'capta' as opposed to 'data', to which I will return at the end of the paper.

The Fallacies of Slicing

When a fluid and partly intangible situation, such as that found in managerial practice, is abstracted (made into a 'thing') in order to make it available for scientific scrutiny inherited from the natural sciences, the concreteness is misplaced (as Whitehead would have it) as and when the thing gets to be taken as the managerial reality, and not a provisional image of it. Again, according to Whitehead, there is nothing wrong with treating as a thing something that is essentially fluid in order to make sense of it, as long as we know what we are doing. There is, in other words, nothing wrong with applying methods, concepts and vocabularies from the natural sciences, as long as we do not treat them as truths. It is when we don't know what we are doing, however, that it becomes a fallacy. The airplane allegory that Chia borrows from Whitehead applies here, as Whitehead's idea was that the imaginative generalization from concrete experience could be seen as a journey in an airplane that would eventually land it back where it came from. If we spend too much time in an airplane we forget what the world on the ground looks like, and the inside world of the airplane slowly begins to replace the earthly reality as we know it. Multiple projections of images from the earth on the cabin screen may delude the passengers into thinking that they are actually looking at an earthly reality and not an image of it.

Incommensurate ideals are intimately related to the misplaced concreteness, found in the slicing of the fluid reality of practitioners into stable categories, which then become congealed as misplaced images of the realities of practitioners. The slicing of reality into categories has served science since Aristotle and is the very basis for the scientific ideals practiced by prominent management journals. It is rooted in organization studies going back at least as far as the 1960s. Slicing enables correspondence between different organizational types and between organizations and their environments to be assessed. It has been the bedrock of organization theory that has given it a standing in the social sciences.

The slicing has, however, come at a high cost, because Whitehead's airplane has not been allowed to land in the richness of organizational life, from which abstractions were initially derived. To be fair, the richness of organizational life has been captured in a broad range of areas of organization theory, where notions such as practice, embeddedness, process, sensemaking, practice, etc. have been applied. A number of interesting studies have also been published, which address the richness of organizational life, in a variety of journals. In spite of their quality, the studies are not sufficient to stem the wave of misplaced natural science criteria, which continue to prevail in a number of prestigious journals.

The last time there was a grand narrative that contrasted with natural science ideals was paradoxically the era of postmodernism, which was manifestly an anti-grand-narrative movement. Still, although it advocated deconstruction, it became a normative force, then inevitably a political force, which is the way things go in academia, as thought worlds turn into thought communities, which may take on tribal dimensions in turn. Unfortunately it became a force without direction, which is logical, given its underlying principle of deconstruction, but nevertheless sad, because it could not match the powerful force of its opponent, the natural science ideals. Thus misplaced scientific ideals prevail because their narrative is directed towards the lofty ideal of natural science, which treats facts as truths, and not as workable possibilities. Hence a flight is boarded that leaves behind the world of practice without its passengers knowing how or where it will return.

No wonder postmodernism could not make it. It could not fight a fair battle with misplaced scientific ideals, which can at any time brand the weapon of rightness, which may again slip into righteousness. Postmodernism could only offer moral appeal. In a paradigm of misplaced scientific ideals, reviewers tend to ask, 'show us that it is true', rather than 'show us why this is interesting', or 'show us why this is novel', or 'show us why this is relevant to practice'. True, we are sometimes asked to demonstrate novelty, but not without the sometimes unjustified proof burden that comes with misplaced scientific ideals. We cannot argue against misplaced scientific ideals, because they can only see the world through their own language and logic. In this sense it is mute to other communicative worlds. The extent to which it will heed other logics can only be seen when those logics are translated into its own language of rigour and relevance.

In Need of a Soul of Relevance

The challenge of organization and management studies lies in finding its 'soul of relevance' and creating patterns of narratives that support that very soul. Interpreted in a moral sense, the word 'soul' has its perils. Still, it is worth retaining, because of its emotional implications. Science, and not least organization and management studies, should not shy away from excitement, delight and, why not, beauty? I see no obvious reason why in science beauty should be reserved for mathematicians' aesthetic pleasure of pursuing elegant lines of reasoning (see also Guillet de Monthoux in this volume). Delight comes with excitement and beauty. Managerial work is emotional, for better or for worse, and theories about it should be no less so. Weick (1995b) is credited with saying that a good theory explains, predicts and delights, and in a field with a soul, prediction and explanation may come with excitement, delight and beauty. A soul is not created by merely talking about it, but is created through the emergence of criteria of relevance that energize a field around some common patterns of narratives from the field of study. It is not the soul per se, but the narratives and their associated criteria of relevance and, yes, rigour, that may further energize the field of European management studies.

In order to provide a viable alternative to a world of misplaced scientific ideals, a different rationality needs to be developed, which becomes accepted as such. In a relatively recent paper in *Academy of Management Review*, Sandberg and Tsoukas (2011) drawing upon Heidegger's phenomenology, argue for a practical rationality to the study of organization and management. They suggest that there are in particular three problems with the scientific rationality which at present detracts from scholars' attention to the real world of organizing: '(1) it underestimates the meaningful totality into which practitioners are immersed, (2) it ignores the situational uniqueness that is characteristic of the tasks practitioners do and (3) it abstracts away from time as experienced by practitioners. By doing so theories developed within the framework of scientific rationality fail to do justice to the logic underlying practice' (p. 341). Sandberg and Tsoukas make a strong plea for a different rationality, one which makes sense for practice. I concur with Sandberg and Tsoukas. The alternative is not to argue against existing misplaced scientific ideals, but to engage with practice and the particular rationality that practice offers. Whereas Chia makes a plea for a logic characterized by openness and scholastic imagination, Sandberg and Tsoukas are more explicit in defining the elements of a new logic. My contribution here is an extension by means of four tenets of managerial research focused more explicitly on processual issues of managing and organizing, which help constitute the type of rationality that Sandberg, Tsoukas and Chia argue in favour of. It is in the process of things that I believe a new soul of management and organization studies may be constructed.

Tenet 1. Practice as Constitutive of Organization

A number of organizational scholars involved with the practice field connect practice to strategy (Gherardi, 2000; Jarzabkowski, 2005; Whittington, 2006) or to routines (Feldman & Pentland, 2003). Drawing inspiration from theorists such as Heidegger (1927), Bourdieu (1977) and Schatzki (2010), they bring attention to what actors actually do in organizations and how actor-worlds are constructed. Still, practice can be broadened from mere focus on activity to the original pragmatist view of practice as a locus of scientific knowledge. Practice should be seen as the ever-constituting force of organizing and organizations. Practice is not something that goes on within organizations, but constitutes those very organizations, and in so doing constitutes how they evolve. Rather than see practice as activity framed by organizations as contexts, practice instantiates those very contexts. Scholars such as Weick and March, who have been prominent in shaping the field of organization and management studies, have consistently worked from pragmatist perspectives, where thinking and understanding have been accompanied and framed by actions. Such thinking is central to pragmatist philosophers, such as Dewey, Mead and Schütz, who were explicit about action being the essential activity of the constitution of meaning and its accompanying structures. Drawing more explicitly on pragmatism will not only help keep focus on actions, but also provide a more focused and consistent philosophy of science perspective to the study of organization and management. What then becomes interesting to study are the ways in which practices uphold—or enable the emergence of—some organizational arrangements rather than others, and what characterizes those practices as well as their linkages. This requires that practices are seen as potentiality for forms of organizing, and not mere representations of those forms.

A view of practice as a constitutive force of organization is a way for actors to keep a sense of the overall organization and how it is moving while staying focused on selected elements. It is also a way for scholars to better understand the intricacies of how organizations are developed and led through many localized acts. For example, Jonathan Ive, chief designer at Apple, describes how Steve jobs would 'read' the company on an almost daily basis by inspecting models of various products in the design lab:

> When Steve comes in, he will sit at one of these tables. If we're working on a new iPhone, he might grab a stool and start playing with different models and feeling them in his hands, remarking on which ones he likes best. Then he will graze by the other tables, just him and me, to see where all the other products are heading. He can get a sense of the sweep of the whole company, the iPhone and iPad, the iMac and

> laptop and everything we're considering. That helps him see where the company is spending its energy and how things connect. And he can ask, "Does doing this make sense, because over here is where we are growing a lot?" or questions like that. He gets to see things in relationship to each other, which is pretty hard in a big company. Looking at the models on these tables, he can see the future for the next three years.
> (Isaacson, 2013, p. 346)

Practices are intimately entangled with the things the organization makes, regardless of whether it makes products or services. Studies of management have largely tended to treat management per se as a profession detached from the actual reality of the organization. For example, forms, styles and structures of organizing have been privileged over the actual processes of organized work, whereas studies, as for example Orr (1998) in his studies of photocopier maintenance at Xerox, show that work processes and artefacts are intrinsically important to the modern workplace. Although the world of work involves an ever-expanding use of abstractions, there will always be an element of doing things. It is a practice-based rationality rather than an organization science rationality that leaders and a different paradigm should articulate. Leaders and managers, as much as anyone else, operate in a situated and localized world of interaction with material and human actors, where decisions follow actions rather than precede actions. Hence a practice logic applies to management as much as to other types of actors, and the practice logic of management is equally driven by instinct, intuition and spontaneity as that of workers and operatives. At the same time managers also have to implement decisions at a larger scale than other practitioners, which calls for understanding of how logics of practice interact with administrative and institutional logics. Therefore, to do justice to realities of organizational life, scholars may do better by more fully appreciating the spatio-temporal tangledness (Hernes, 2008) in which practitioners (including leaders and managers) are embedded, which includes their immediate environment, while at the same time transcending the boundaries of their immediate environment.

Tenet 2. Time as Ontology

Practitioners are acutely aware of operating in time. Not only are they aware of the obvious clock time, but they are also aware of grappling with time as the underlying force of what they are doing. In addition to being seen as linear time, such as represented by clocks and calendars, time may also be seen as ontology; and considered as ontology, it becomes pervasive throughout acts of organizing. Actors are seen as Heidegger would have it, "thrown into time", and it is from the flow time they carve out their temporal existence (Hernes, 2014). Focus on time offers the possibility to understand how, for example, history and the past may weigh in on decisions about future strategies (Schultz & Hernes, 2013; see also Cuna and Tsoukas in this volume). Time also offers the possibility to better understand the notion of the present and it takes part in shaping events, which in turn provides temporal understanding of organizational becoming. It is the temporal dimension that provides organizational actors with an understanding of the becoming of their organization. It is present in the myriads of moments and episodes every day, which connect into temporal patterns which again shape actors' understanding of the organization whose construction they are a part of. These moments and episodes are connected in a variety of ways, including by social media, stories, plans and artefacts, which confer agency upon them (Emirbayer & Mische, 1998). Thus organizational development and change may be understood, not as driven by managerial rationality, but by intensity of moments and episodes of organizing in the flow of time (Hernes, 2014).

Time as ontology has been curiously neglected, not just in organization and management studies, but also in the social sciences. Most studies assume a Newtonian view of time, by which time is seen as a stable scale against which motion and change are measured. This is a curious fact, given that in theoretical physics, time and space have been treated as an interwoven continuum for nearly a century, marked by the empirical validation of Einstein's general theory of relativity in 1919. Time as ontology demands that acts are seen as events, where each event is given agency to (re-)define both its past and its future. A managerial decision, for example, is not seen as a final decision, but as an event that takes place in time and contributes actively to the temporal world making of the organization as it connects past and future in a formation of events (Hernes, 2014). Time, in this view, is seen as a main constitutive force of the reality that actors find themselves in, because decisions are suspended between past and future and help actors acquire a sense of where they come from in the light of where they are heading and vice versa. A company, for example, is defined as the direction in which it is developing from its past to a possible future, articulated in the present. A more consistent focus on how actors operate in the present moment may help explain how the more elusive and stochastic moments and acts affect organizational continuity and change. Organizations are established, developed and changed through very complex sets of actions, ranging from the subconscious to the conscious, from the informal to the formal and from micro moments to larger-scale strategy processes.

Getting a grip on the richness of organizational development requires that researchers do not assume a priori that big events are the actual drivers, but remain open to the possibility that small moments or non-events (MacKay & Chia, 2013) may be decisive, or that certain combinations of events over time are more conducive to certain effects than others. For example, in a recent research project, in which we studied the exercise of dynamic capabilities at Ulstein Group, a Norwegian ship design and construction company, it became evident that much of their overall strategic change over the last decade came about through their ability to act on weak and ambiguous signals in a very short moment of time (Hernes, 2014). In order to better understand how actors seize brief moments of opportunity and act on them, it is necessary to make time and timing the main foci of analysis, coupled with a focus at the level of practice. This becomes all the more important with increased use of social media, which may be analyzed as multiple encounters in time between people and concepts, mediated by technologies.

Tenet 3. Becoming as Essence

Following the death of Steve Jobs in October 2011 Apple continued to grow and in May 2013 was more affluent, dominant and profitable than ever before. Although major indicators were largely positive, certain analysts were reluctant about the future of Apple. Their reluctance was demonstrated by a significant drop of the Apple share value. Such a drop could not be readily explained by looking at the actual figures of Apple's performance, but requires that one looks more closely at the more subtle dynamics of the way Apple was potentially heading in relation to what it had been in the past. Looking at the actual indicators is like what is called a logic of 'being', treating a phenomenon as an isolated epoch during a period of time, disconnected from its past and future. According to a logic of being, Apple's share value should not drop, because the main indicators of that period were positive. The drop in share value, however, may be explained within a logic of becoming as opposed to being. Apple's success has historically been associated with its ability to regularly take the world by surprise and present novel products that would set a standard for competitors, suppliers and customers. Jobs' famously ritualistic 'one more thing' at the end of his appearance at Apple's public product launch meetings signalled a near permanent ability to surprise. Despite the positive indicators, analysts seemed worried that Steve Jobs's legacy did not live on inside Apple, in other words that Apple might not be becoming the Apple that had existed during the past few years.

A 'being' view, such as represented by Lewin's (1951) 'unfreeze—change—refreeze' model, depicts organizational evolution as periods of stability punctuated by sudden change. It is a view that has proved particularly tenacious in the management literature (Schultz & Hernes, 2013; Sonenshein, 2010; Tsoukas & Chia, 2002). However, the periods of stability are entirely fictitious entities, which are in effect averaged-out states of affairs based on an incomplete observation at one (or several) point(s) in time. The assumption of punctuation between stable states is hugely consequential for the understanding of organizations and management. First, it detracts from understanding the actual dynamics of change. As Langley and Tsoukas (2010) point out, knowing that organizational practice B is generally more effective than organizational practice A reveals almost nothing about how to move from A to B. Second, it treats continuity as a non-entity. Continuity takes place in the punctuations, but they are considered void, hence continuity does not enter the picture. Still, any glimpse into organizational life will reveal how it is not just about change, but also about the struggle for continuity, without which change does not make sense. Third, it takes away focus from what is going on in terms of activity that opens for alternative forms of organization. Organizational life exhibits not just actuality, but also potentiality, which means that things can turn out otherwise.

Taking a becoming view as opposed to the step-wise approach described above means to engage with what Weick (1995a) and Feldman (2000) refer to as organizing as an ongoing accomplishment. It demands that one takes the radical step from seeing organizations as accomplished states to being in a continuous process of becoming, in other words studying the actual work of organizational becoming. In relation to the above point about time as ontology, becoming is seen as becoming in time, as it describes the ongoing work involved in projecting past experience into future ambitions or projecting future ambitions onto past experience. It is this very work that is revelatory of the contingent state of the organization through the choices that are faced. In other words, it reveals the organization to its members in the light of its potentiality. While organizing consists of actualizing potentialities, potentialities for acting otherwise accompany acts of organizing those actualities (Hernes & Irgens, 2013). In this view, what analysts saw in the case of post-Jobs Apple was not a problem of being or actuality, but a problem of becoming and potentiality.

Tenet 4. Heterogeneity of Factors

When the word 'work' is used above, it is meant in a broad sense and can in principle be performed by any conceivable actor, whether human, conceptual or material. Traditional organization and management theorizing has tended to draw a distinction between human actors and structure, represented by material artefacts. One result of such a dichotomy has been that structure has become seen as a constraint within which human actors operate. However, organizational life is rife with examples of human actors organized through material artefacts. Artefacts constitute the very means of stabilizing any human intent into a sustainable pattern in a 'world on the move' (Hernes, 2014, p. 1). Any form of stabilization requires the use of materiality, where materiality defines the human actors as much as human actors define the materiality (Latour, 1999). In fact, there is no obvious place, if any, to be drawn between humans and materiality. Bateson (1972, p. 318) illustrates the dilemma of distinction by referring to the blind man and the stick:

> If you ask anybody about the localization and boundaries of the self, these confusions are immediately displayed. Or consider a blind man with a stick. Where does the blind man's self begin? At the tip of the stick? At the handle of the stick? Or at some point halfway up the stick? These questions are nonsense, because the stick is a pathway along

> which differences are transmitted under transformation, so that to draw a delimiting line *across* this pathway is to cut off a part of the systemic circuit which determines the blind man's locomotion.

If one wants to understand the processual world of practitioners, it is better to study how that man–stick relationship articulates organizational arrangements rather than try and draw a distinction between the two, which leaves the analysis with an unnecessary static image of what is going on. The richness of actors should not be limited to humans and material artefacts, but extended to include non-substantial actors, such as talk, narratives and concepts (Czarniawska, 2004). When, for example, a story is told, it is not only a means of representation of a certain situation, but it also performs work in sustaining or changing an organizational arrangement. It is this work that needs to be studied, analyzed and explained. Fortunately, theories and methodologies exist in the social sciences as well as in organization and management studies to support such endeavours. Studies inspired by actor-network theory (ANT) or science and technology studies (STS) have been employed by a number of researchers to understand how heterogeneous sets of actors interact.

It becomes important to explain how heterogeneous sets of actors connect and reconnect. In such a world standards sometimes replace organizations, human judgement is sometimes replaced by audit systems, artefacts sometimes constitute memory, concepts sometimes perform institutional work and brands perform the work of identification. Acknowledging a heterogeneous world implies accepting that while human actors perform work upon concepts and artefacts, they are also performed upon by artefacts and concepts. In other words, they become through acts in encounters with artefacts and concepts. A leader gets to be seen not only through what he/she does, but through the concepts he/she uses, and the technologies through which he/she interacts. The study of management would then exploit the truly relational and contingent world of managing, as managers perform as part of a nested whole of technologies, artefacts, concepts and stories.

Conclusion

The four tenets briefly discussed above point towards a localized, embedded and temporally informed understanding of managerial work. Together they point towards the work of connecting and reconnecting heterogeneous actors in a world that is permanently on the move (Hernes, 2014). The particular cultural richness and variety found in European business and industry makes it a fertile ground for building a research tradition in organization and management that engages with the fluid and processual nature of managerial work. Focus on practice, time, becoming and heterogeneity enables a closer scrutiny of the actual work of managing, and how differences in nuances relate to differences at the organizational level. The translation of nuances requires richness of description and explanation, because no organizational setting or context is assumed to be the same or even similar. In view of the above, scholars would do better to move away from the incommensurate demands of scientific rigour and relevance, and towards what Chia, with reference to Ehrenzweig (1967), calls *artistic rigour*. Chia makes the point that artistic rigour involves the honing and refinement of an empirical sensitivity and the development of a capacity for imaginative generalization. Still, imagination does not work without some form of coherent image of what managerial work is about. European management research now has the possibility to define managerial work, and hence its agenda for studying it, around a thoroughly process based language.

Recognizing that no context is the same, the classic idea of generalization of research findings loses much of its sense. On the other hand, just as considering organizing as an ongoing accomplishment, generalization is also seen as an ongoing process of work and, as Chia suggests, creative work. One of the tenets of Whitehead's philosophy was that stabilizing, the temporary creation of what he called unity, demands creativity, which runs counter to conventional ideas of creativity being all about diversification and multiplicity. Creative work of this kind cannot be content to rely on the search for a reality that lays there ready to be deciphered. Therefore, doing management research is less about analyzing data and more about engaging with what Checkland and Holwell (1998) call 'capta'. Whereas the word 'data' lends to research an image of neutrality in the sense that findings appear independent of the way in which we arrive at them, the notion of capta is conducive to the creative discovery of things that matter in the practical world of managing. 'Capta' remind the writer and the reader that they are subject to selection as well as discovery and that they are active rather than passive factors of research (Hernes, 2008). Whereas data are bits of information collated into patterns of findings, capta provide richer accounts of what is going on and point towards possibilities as they aim to articulate a complex and fluid reality. Artistic rigour also becomes involved in the translation of what is learned from one setting to another. Capta do not travel effortlessly ready to be applied, as they make no sense in the absence of active work of interpretation and re-interpretation. On the contrary, the very work of translation shapes the meaning of them as it is carried out to benefit other actors at other places and other times.

The practice of management is disparate, and while celebrating its diversity, we need to search for those frameworks, models, sets of concepts that lend it some form of unity, which is what demands creativity. Unity is not to be taken as some kind of solid block of rigorously interrelated concepts, but as the soul that the various patterns of narratives point towards. Unity may be expressed in the various combinations of the above tenets, and as they are combined in managerial research they may help provide a sense of a soul. A soul cannot be perceived per se, but may be felt through the patterns of narratives that surround it. The above tenets are suggested elements of narratives that may point towards a soul of European management research. Upholding management research around a sense of soul implies persistent and creative work.

References

Bateson, Gregory (1972). *Steps to an ecology of mind.* Chicago: University of Chicago Press.

Bourdieu, Pierre (1977). *Outline of a theory of practice.* Cambridge: Cambridge University Press.

Checkland, Peter B. & Holwell, Sue (1998). *Information, systems, and information systems.* Chichester: Wiley.

Czarniawska, Barbara (2004). On time, space, and action nets. *Organization*, 11(6), 773–791.

Ehrenzweig, Anton (1967). *The hidden order of art.* Berkeley: University of California Press.

Emirbayer, Mustapha & Mische, Anne (1998). What is agency? *American Journal of Sociology*, 103(4), 962–1023.

Feldman, Martha S. (2000). Organizational routines as a source of continuous change. *Organization Science*, 11(6), 611–629.

Feldman, Martha S. & Pentland, Brian (2003). Reconceptualizing organizational routines as a source of flexibility and change. *Administrative Science Quarterly*, 48, 94–118.

George, Gerard (2014). Rethinking management scholarship. *Academy of Management Journal*, 57(1), 1–6.

Gherardi, Silvia (2000). Practice-based theorizing on learning and knowing in organizations. *Organization*, 7(2), 211–223.

Heidegger, Martin (1927). *Being and time.* Oxford: Blackwell Publishers.

Hernes, Tor (2008). *Understanding organization as process: Theory for a tangled world.* London: Routledge.

Hernes, Tor (2014). *A process theory of organization.* Oxford: Oxford University Press.

Hernes, Tor & Irgens, Eirik (2013). Keeping things mindfully on track: Organizational learning under continuity. *Management Learning*, 44(3), 253–266.

Isaacson, Walter (2013). *Steve Jobs: The exclusive biography.* New York: Simon & Schuster.

Jarzabkowski, Paula (2005). *Strategy as practice: An activity-based approach.* London: Sage.

Langley, Ann & Tsoukas, Haridimos (2010). Introducing "perspectives on process organization studies". In T. Hernes & S. Maitlis (Eds.), *Process, sensemaking and organizing* (pp. 1–26). Oxford: Oxford University Press.

Latour, Bruno (1999). *Pandora's hope: Essays on the reality of science studies.* Cambridge, MA: Harvard University Press.

Lewin, Kurt (1951). *Field theory in social science; selected theoretical papers.* D. Cartwright (Ed.). New York: Harper & Row.

MacKay, Brad & Chia, Robert (2013). Choice, change, and unintended consequences in strategic change: A process understanding of the rise and fall of Northco automotive. *Academy of Management Journal*, 56, 208–230.

March, James G. (2007). Ibsen, ideals, and the subordination of lies. *Organization Studies*, 28, 1277–1285.

Orr, Julian E. (1998). *Talking about machines: An ethnography of a modern job*. New York: ILR Press.

Sandberg, Jörgen & Tsoukas, Haridimos (2011). Grasping the logic of practice: Theorizing through practical rationality. *Academy of Management Review*, 36(2), 338–360.

Schatzki, Theodore R. (2010). *The timespace of human activity: On performance, society, and history as indeterminate teleological events*. Lanham, MD: Lexington Books.

Schultz, Majken & Hernes, Tor (2013). A temporal perspective on organizational identity. *Organization Science*, 24(1), 1–21.

Sonenshein, Scot (2010). We're changing or are we? Untangling the role of progressive, regressive, and stability narratives during strategic change implementation. *Academy of Management Journal*, 53(3), 477–512.

Tsoukas, Haridimos & Chia, Robert (2002). On organizational becoming: Rethinking organizational change. *Organization Science*, 13(5), 567–582.

Weick, Karl E. (1995a). *Sensemaking in organizations*. Thousand Oaks, CA: Sage.

Weick, Karl E. (1995b). Definition of theory. In N. Nicholson (Ed.), *Blackwell dictionary of organizational behavior* (pp. 565–567). Oxford: Blackwell.

Whitehead, Alfred North (1929). *Process and reality*. New York: The Free Press.

Whitehead, Alfred North (1938). *Modes of thought*. New York: The Free Press.

Whittington, Richard (2006). Completing the practice turn in strategy research. *Organization Studies*, 27(5), 613–634.

3 Craft, Magic and the Re-Enchantment of the World

Roy Suddaby, Max Ganzin and Alison Minkus

Introduction

Nearly one hundred years ago, Max Weber identified an emerging 'disenchantment' with the world. He used the term 'disenchantment' to capture a sense of weary nostalgia for what humanity must give up in order to progress. Disenchantment, he argued, was the inevitable outcome of the ongoing expansion of rationality in modernity. Weber saw disenchantment as a natural result of the displacement of tradition, myth and superstition by reason—a displacement that he felt defined the transition to modernity.

Weber's theory of rationalization describes a range of social changes that emerged from the Enlightenment, sweeping away medieval ways of thought (Bell, 2012). Secularism supplanted religion, scientific and expert knowledge replaced myth and magic and, most profoundly, bureaucratic formal social structures like the organization, the guild and the nation-state began to erode traditional collectives like the family, clan, tribe and community (Berman, 1981).

For Weber, disenchantment meant 'the knowledge or belief . . . that there are no mysterious incalculable forces that come into play, but rather that one can, in principle, master all things by calculation' (Weber, 1946, pp. 129–139). Weber's thesis of relentless rationalization was intimately connected to the industrial revolution. He presciently predicted the rationalizing impact of industrialization, where massive factories, organized by trans-national corporations attached to global consumptive markets, achieve ever-greater economies of scale in an emergent world-society.

Weber's thesis of unremitting rationality is a central premise of neo-institutional theory. Isomorphism, the structuration of organizations fields and the global diffusion of modern management practices are extensions of Weber's core idea of the metastasis of formal-rational ways of knowing and being in the world. Neo-institutionalism also shares Weber's sense of disenchantment with its inherent assumption that human agency has been abdicated to institutions. Borrowing from Weber's haunting image of the iron cage, where human will is increasingly suborned to social structures of our own making, neo-institutional theory has been soundly criticized for its persistent unwillingness to attribute change to human agency (Suddaby, 2015).

In this essay we challenge the assumption that inexorable rationalization and disenchantment is the only narrative of modernity. Although the empirical evidence of disenchanting rationality is impressive, there is equally impressive evidence of a countervailing narrative of re-enchantment in the world.

Some of this evidence is not positive. The resurgence of fundamentalist religion, the rejection of sensible science and an increasingly tribal populism all speak to a worrisome rejection of rationality in recent history.

But much is positive. The resilience of the family, the resurgence of craft modes of production and the optimistic persistence of aesthetics, myth and other aspects of human reflexivity all speak to the positive potential of re-enchantment. Yes, there are powerful forces of disenchantment in the world, but there is also a vast but unexamined element of social and organizational life that is simply not amenable to calculation, science or rationality.

We explore this alternative view in this essay, where we draw together the disparate threads of a competing discourse that challenges the prevailing view of rationality as both inexorable and universal. Our core argument is that rationality and disenchantment cannot exist in the absence of enchantment and arationality. We challenge the teleological assumption of progress that is implicit in neo-institutionalism—i.e., that humanity is engaged in a civilizing project of rationality that will, ultimately, erase the influence of myth, magic and mystery in social and organizational life.

We present our argument in three stages. First, we describe the core components of Weber's theory of rationality that form the basis of neo-institutional organization theory. Then we present evidence drawn from both academic research and the popular press that challenge each of these assumptions by offering a competing narrative of ongoing enchantment. Finally, we introduce four competing constructs—authenticity, reflexivity, mimesis and incantation—each a form of a "rational magic" that contradicts and counterbalances neo-institutionalism's assumptions of ever-expanding reason.

Formal Rationality

Max Weber's primary contribution to social theory was to identify the critical role of reason in social history. Broadly stated, Weber argued that the drive toward rationality—the mastery of all things by calculation—informed all areas of human life. The quest for calculability, Weber suggested, underpins all social innovation, perhaps most obviously industrial capitalism, which rests on a range of subsidiary inventions—double entry accounting, the division of ownership and labor, measuring the time-value of money, bureaucratic organizations—each of which enhances the ability to calculate processes of industrial production.

Weber's use of the term *rationality* was never precise and has been the subject of much debate. Most scholars acknowledge four basic types of rationality in Weber's writing; practical, theoretical, substantive and formal (Habermas, 1984; Kalberg, 1980), each of which uses slightly different forms of calculability. Practical rationality implies a form of calculation required to achieve a desired end, based on pragmatic reasoning. Theoretical rationality is perhaps closest to scientific calculability in that it involves abstract reasoning through deduction and the use of increasingly precise symbolic meanings. Substantive rationality involves calculation based on values where a course of action is deemed appropriate based on the degree of congruence of a give cluster of shared beliefs. Formal rationality requires calculations of universal social rules, regulations and the collective expectations of others.

While Weber clearly viewed these categories as ideal types in which any given act might involve varying degrees of each type of rationality (Hirsch, 1997), neo-institutional theorists have clearly emphasized theoretical and formal rationality in articulating their core argument, i.e. that norms of economic rationality are constructed by social institutions (DiMaggio & Powell, 1983; Meyer & Rowan, 1977; Scott, 1995). More emphatically, neo-institutional theorists have wholly adopted Weber's central thesis that modernity is marked by widespread acceptance of rational ways of organizing and knowing and an inevitable expansion in practices of reason.

Most research in neo-institutional theory has been devoted to elaborating this thesis of rampant rationality. Isomorphism, or the notion that organizations become increasingly similar to their institutional environments as the result of increasing structuration of organizational fields (DiMaggio & Powell, 1983), is perhaps the best example. John Meyer and colleagues (Bromley & Meyer, 2015; Meyer, Boli, Thomas, & Ramirez, 1997) extend the concept of structural isomorphism to the global level of analysis, demonstrating how certain formal rationalities (i.e. environmentalism, feminism, corporatization) now operate beyond the nation-state in an emerging and continually expanding world-society.

But we also see Weber's ideas of rationality crystallized in studies of institutional change, which inevitably offer 'progressive' narratives of the displacement of traditional ways by more formally rationalized ones. For example, traditions of professionalism are always replaced by bureaucratic or corporate modes of production (Suddaby & Greenwood, 2005; Thornton, 2004), larger social identities always supplant individual ones (Rao, Monin, & Durand, 2003) and the adoption of new practices always favour 'modernist' rationalities of science and professionalism over "primitive" practices of craft and amateurism (Garud, Jain, & Kumaraswamy, 2002; Zilber, 2002). Ultimately, neo-institutional theory reinforces the Weberian narrative of the inevitability of formal rationality through science and technology, on one hand, and professionally bureaucratic modes of organizing, on the other.

Disenchantment

Weber predicted that the rationalizing arc of modernity would be accompanied by an increasing sense of loss as the old 'nature-centered' world of myth and magic gave way to the new 'human-centered' world of efficiency and control. He understood the emotional consequences of modernity and the increasing loss of meaning that inevitably occurred when craft modes of production gave way to the mechanics of the assembly line, when the courthouse replaced the church and the physician supplanted the midwife.

The emotional impact of the disenchanting effect of modernity is captured in post-Enlightenment culture—in William Blake's (2008) description of the "dark satanic mills" of the Industrial Revolution in his poem *Jerusalem*, in Charles Dickens' ode to the dehumanizing factory towns of England in *Hard Times*, or Edward Hopper's remarkable painting *Nighthawks*, which captures the aching loneliness of urban life. Equally poignant are the academic studies of disenchantment—from Engels' (1993) heart-wrenching descriptions of *The Condition of the Working Class in London*, to Gramsci's (1988) observation that Fordist production regulates both the production of cars and the sexual libido of workers.

Perhaps the most comprehensive summary of the disenchanting effects of rationality is offered by George Ritzer's (1993) powerful concept of McDonaldization, in which he describes the inherent irrationality of rational systems that, in their quest for efficiency and calculability, dehumanize their participants. Collectively, these, and a host of critical management studies, sketch out the emotional cavity created by the expansion of rationality in modern capitalist society.

Re-Enchantment

But is the narrative of the world really one of inexorable rationalization? Does neo-institutionalism's thesis of structuration, isomorphism and commensuration fully capture the phenomenal reality of all social and organizational life? Or as Robert Nisbet (1980) suggests in *The Idea of Progress*, does it actually offer a highly selective account of the future as an illusion of progress inspired by our secular confidence in a rational future?

Consider the possibility that disenchantment is simply an elitist discourse that privileges progress over primitivism, science over myth and secularism over religion. What if enchantment has not, and never will be, fully expunged by mass industrialization, but, rather, has simply been marginalized by a dominant rationalist world-view that sees the world as binary opposites of good (progress to the future) and bad (regress to primitivism)? What if, as Friedrich Nietzsche argued, the magic and mystery in the world has not been entirely erased, but rather, has been merely suppressed by an equally mythological belief in science and progress?

A cursory examination of current events reveals several powerful themes that support the notion that enchantment does exist but has been systematically ignored because it is inconsistent with rationalized discourses of progress. In the balance of this section we elaborate five such emergent themes: populism, tribalism, fundamentalist religion and spirituality, scepticism of science and the return to craft. In each section we both elaborate popular indicia of enchantment and identify its nascent expression in management research.

The Return of Populism

The US election of Donald Trump offers perhaps the best illustration of the resurgence of populism in global politics. President Trump's populist success is reinforced by the emergence of similarly populist leaders in Britain (Nigel Farage), France (Marine Le Pen), Austria (Norbert Hofer) and the Netherlands (Geert Wilders), each riding a surge of support amongst older, predominantly male voters who reflect religious and ethnic majorities. While populist leaders have appeared with some frequency in developing countries, the simultaneous emergence of a number of populist leaders in Western industrial nations that have come to epitomize neo-liberal economic policies is historically unprecedented.

Because populism reflects a broad range of political beliefs it is difficult to define in ideological terms. Politicians as ideologically diverse as Mao, Hitler and Margaret Thatcher have each been described as populist leaders (Norris, 2005). As Ernesto Laclau argues in *On Populist Reason*, populism is best defined in terms of a shared rejection of "an institutionalized other" (Laclau, 2005, p. 117). Populism reflects a libertarian mistrust of traditional social institutions. It is a discourse that emphasizes:

> faith in the 'decent', 'ordinary' or 'little people over the corrupt political and corporate establishment, national interests . . . over cosmopolitan cooperation across borders . . . , protectionist policies regulating the movement of trade, people and finance over global free trade, xenophobia over tolerance of multiculturalism, strong individual leadership over diplomatic bargaining and flexible negotiations, isolationism in foreign and defence policies over international engagement, traditional sex roles for women and men over more fluid gender identities and roles.
>
> (Inglehart & Norris, 2016, p. 17)

Populism rejects rational notions of progress to a world-society in favour of a return to traditional and more local values. Populism 'enchants' by embracing the myths of the past. We see this in the persistent power of the agrarian myth in Western industrial democracies.

The agrarian myth is the nostalgic belief that the most desirable form of living is the pastoral community of village life (Brown, 2003, pp. 27–29). In *The Age of Reform*, Richard Hofstader (1955, pp. 34–55) notes that the agrarian myth valorizes the role of the farmer as a 'special creature, blessed by God' whose voice is 'the voice of democracy and of virtue itself'. The myth is based on a deeply held belief that the city is a deviation from 'natural' living and 'the yeoman farmer' who works to produce food rather than money and whose honest, grounded values form the backbone of democracy (Hesseltine, 1961, pp. 3–32).

The agrarian myth has been used to justify an oversized influence of the agricultural sector in Western industrial economies. Agriculture is often viewed as a sacred industry and is more likely than other industries to get protective trade legislation (Grant, 1993; Lester, 2007). Rural voters are given a disproportionate voice in the US Electoral College, despite the fact that as early as the 1920s the US Census reported more Americans lived in cities than the country (Badger, 2016). The agrarian myth has also proved a powerful impediment to free trade in the food industry. The irrational protection of inefficient agricultural production, in Europe (Marsh, 1989), the US (Grant, 1993) and Japan (Moriguchi, 1990) is attributed to the resilience of a utopian view of farmers, particularly amongst urban elites (Paarlberg, 1988).

Populism, thus, has a stubborn presence in Western democracies and, as evidenced by the agrarian myth, has lain dormant in our collective consciousness but remains influentially embedded in the political structure. Its recent prominence in national politics, in defiance of the predictions of most scientific polling, offers powerful evidence of a growing re-enchantment in the world.

The Return of Populism in Management Research: The Magic of Crowds

The re-emergence of populist logic in management theory can be seen in our changing attitude toward crowds. In early modernity the crowd was not to be trusted. In his famous treatise *The Crowd*, first published in 1895, Gustave Le Bon (1960) characterized crowds in the most derogatory terms. Crowds were impulsive, irritable, unreasonable, lacked judgement and reacted on the basis of exaggerated sentiment. They were, in short, irrational. Le Bon (1960) likely drew from Scottish journalist Charles Mackay's (1995) book *Extraordinary Delusions and the Madness of Crowds*, first published in 1841, which derided the mob-enthused irrationality of the Crusades, duels and prominent economic disasters such as the Railway Mania of the 1840s, the South Sea Bubble and the Dutch tulip craze.

These authors were, of course, reinforcing the rationalist mistrust of populism in the post–Industrial Revolution era by articulating an anti-populist concern about the role of the masses in democracy. Because crowds were irrational, important social institutions were structured to keep the crowd in check. In law, for example, the 'wheels of justice move slowly' by design, so that over time the sober rationality of the legal system can prevail over the emotion of the posse. Similarly, in politics, the reasoned experience of the landed gentry in the House of Lords in England and the Senate in the

United States is designed to offer a check on the populist irrationality of elected politicians.

Consider the view of crowds in public discourse today. In economics we are advised that crowds are no longer viewed as irrational and emotional, but are now thought to be wise. In his best-selling book *The Wisdom of Crowds: Why the Many Are Smarter Than the Few and How Collective Wisdom Shapes Business, Economies, Societies and Nations*, American journalist James Surowiecki (2004) argues that the aggregate information of large groups of individuals offers superior information and advice compared with any single constituent of that group. He relates the oft-told story of Victorian scientist Sir Francis Galton, who observed, with surprise, that when averaged, the guesses of individual crowd members at an agricultural fair could accurately predict the weight of a cow.

Harnessing the aggregate rationality of the crowd is now an established technique called 'Crowdsourcing', in which a specific problem or item of work is outsourced to an undefined (and generally large) network of people in the form of an open call (Howe, 2006). Wikipedia, the online encyclopaedia that aggregates information from an open source author base, is premised on an enchanted challenge to the assumption that arcane knowledge is the exclusive domain of elites (Giles, 2005). Crowdsourcing or 'distributed problem solving' (Brabham, 2008) retains the populist assumption that crowds, once viewed as emotional, irrational and untrustworthy, are now viable sources of reason.

There are serious logical flaws in the argument that crowds are wise. In order for crowds to be wise they must be diverse, independent, decentralized and aggregated. Unfortunately, modern crowds are shaped by social media algorithms, which tend to violate all of those assumptions. As we demonstrate in the next section, modern cyber-crowds are increasingly balkanized into close-knit and often volatile communities that more closely resemble tribes than the sober sources of collective rationality that Galton and Surowiecki describe. The irony, however, is that even as crowds become more tribal, populist discourse has elevated them to founts of rationality, even in the dismal sciences of management and economics. We have re-enchanted the mob.

The Return of Tribalism

The world is becoming increasingly tribal. Tribalism is often mistakenly assumed to refer to kinship communities defined by blood relations. However, as Emile Durkheim (2014) observed in *The Division of Labour in Society*, tribes or clans are more accurately defined as a form of association based on a feeling of organic solidarity or common belief system reinforced by intense and ongoing personal interaction. A more contemporary definition is offered by Paul James (2006, p. 29), who sees tribes as a competing ideology of organization, distinct from the nation-state or globalism, characterized by "self-reproducing communities framed by the social dominance of face-to-face integration and living". A tribe, in this view, can be anything from a group of soccer hooligans to a professional association (Ouchi, 1980).

In his best-selling book *Tribe: On Homecoming and Belonging*, Sebastian Junger recounts Benjamin Franklin's observation that European settlers in the New World were constantly abandoning their 'civilised' settlements to live with the 'Indians', but few 'Indians' voluntarily left their communities to join white communities. He explains this phenomenon as evidence of the communal power of the tribe, and extends that argument to explain why soldiers who return home, even those without direct combat experience, suffer from post-traumatic stress disorder.

The trauma of war, Junger argues, is not the experience of violence but rather the loss of experience of camaraderie and intimacy of the tribe. Modern civilization, he observes, has given abundant material wealth and comfort. But it has also deprived us of the invaluable sense of community that has been fostered over generations of social evolution. War, he argues, satisfies a primal need for belonging (Junger, 2016).

Junger's theory of tribalism, and the anomic sense of loss of community in modern society, is not new. People are more isolated today than ever before (Lee & Bearman, 2017; McPherson, Smith-Lovin, & Brashears, 2006). We see this in American sociologist Robert Putnam's (2000) influential account of the loss of community and political engagement in the United States in America, *Bowling Alone: The Strange Disappearance of Civic America*. We also see it in French sociologist Michel Maffesoli's (1996) *The Time of the Tribes: The Decline of Individualism*, where he predicts that as the institutions of modernism decline, we nostalgically cling to institutions of the past.

Increasingly, the tribe has reasserted itself over more 'civilised' forms of social organization. The 2016 referendum in support of the United Kingdom to exit the European Union can be seen as an illustration of ethnic tribalism triumphing over globalism. But perhaps the most potent evidence of tribalism can be observed on social media, where the construction of tribal groups is facilitated both by our own prejudices and by sophisticated search algorithms that create recursively reinforcing world-views.

Media guru Marshall McLuhan presciently predicted the "tribalizing power of the new electronic media" in its capacity to "return us to the unified fields of the old oral cultures, to tribal cohesion and pre-individualist patterns of thought" (McLuhan, 1997, p. 124). Tribalism, he observed, "is the sense of the deep bond of family, the closed society as the norm of community" (McLuhan, 1997, p. 124). McLuhan's somewhat pastoral notion of tribalism overlooks the bullying reality of modern cyber-tribalism, which, instead of creating McLuhan's utopian global village, has unleashed a more complicated version of the modern tribe. In the same way, management theorists have found the tribe, like the mob, to be a complex and unpredictable subject.

Tribalism in Management: The Magic of the Clan

Tribalism is an increasingly important subject in managerial discourse. This is perhaps most pronounced in marketing, where both practitioners and researchers have become increasingly conscious of the growing import of 'consumer tribes'. Consumer tribes are "a group of people emotionally connected by similar consumption values and usage . . . of products and services to create a community and express identity" (Mitchell & Imrie, 2011, pp. 39–40). In contrast to the passive consumption of traditional consumers, however, the term 'tribe' is invoked to capture the high degree of agency that these consumer groups bring to the marketplace. Consumer tribes "rarely consume brands and products without changing them; they cannot 'consume' a good without it becoming them and them becoming it" (Cova, Kozinets, & Shankar, 2007, pp. 3–4).

In their 2007 book *Consumer Tribes*, Bernard Cova, Robert Kozinets and Avi Shankar show how tribal sub-cultures are changing contemporary commerce. Consumer tribes have rescued failing brands, as in the case of hipster 'cult adoption' of Pabst's Blue Ribbon beer. Pabst was a brand in danger of cancellation that appealed to low-income consumers until the brand was incongruously "appropriated" by high-income West Coast hipsters from San Francisco and Seattle (Cova et al., 2007). Tribal values of irony helped save a failing brand.

Consumer tribes 'hijack' brands by taking control of their marketing away from executives and by violating copyright protection. They 'pirate' the brand by infusing their own unique, and often deliberately ironic meaning to the product in defiance of its intended image. The phenomenon is tribal in that the group appropriates the brand to express their own idiosyncratic values. Often those values undermine the intended meaning of a brand—for example, when fans produce sexually explicit movies using characters from Harry Potter.

A growing managerial discourse celebrates the organizational advantages of tribal knowledge. Mozilla's Firefox, for example, is celebrated as a successful organization in large part due to the communitarian sharing of 'tribal knowledge'. In his 2006 book *Tribal Knowledge*, John Moore (2006) attributes the global success of Starbucks to the uncodified oral knowledge of the organization held by the employees. Moore's positive attribution of 'tribal knowledge' stands in sharp contrast to its prior treatment in the highly rationalized Six Sigma process of total quality management, where unwritten information passed down orally from generation to generation was considered an inefficient and non-rational management practice.

Arguably the most interesting stream of management research on the re-emergence of tribalism lies in efforts to understand how Marshall McLuhan's cyber-tribes of new electronic media can alter our perception of truth. Using computer modeling techniques to simulate online communications, Van Alstyne and Brynjolfsson (2005) demonstrate that social media has a profound balkanizing effect on intellectual and social interaction. Specifically, they show that, while in the past, geography or separation by physical space was the primary source of limits to human interaction, today our own preferences, facilitated by filtering software, help to intensify and crystallize stereotypes and biases.

Cyber-tribalism, thus, is a new type of iron cage, albeit an increasingly smaller one, in which limits to human cognition are subject to ever-narrowing interpretive frames in an ever-expanding universe of information. Gustave Le Bon warned of the hypnotic suggestibility of the crowd. He did not anticipate, however, the even more dangerous autohypnosis of the Internet, in which our own prejudices and lack of epistemic humility can self-construct an ever-constricting "cyber cage" of our own making.

The Return of Religion

Tribalism, as Edward Shils (1975) observed, is built on a foundation of religion. Sacred rituals, he suggested, are central to the power of all social institutions. Like Durkheim, Shils believes that social practices and institutions, however secularized, cannot escape the influence of religious belief. Stated differently, the institutions of religion never fully disappear but, rather, are simply temporarily suppressed by the sediment of alternative myths until new social circumstances allow them to re-emerge.

Shils's argument is borne out in the global resurgence of fundamentalist religion in the late 1970s. A watershed event in this process was the rise of the Grand Ayatollah Ruhola Khomeini to overthrow the nearly 40-year secular rule of Shah Mohammed Reza Pahlavi in Iran. The revolution created the Islamic Republic of Iran and established a contemporary nation in which a religious-political ideology (*velayat-e faquqih*) supplanted a secular one. At the same time, in the United States, Reverend Jerry Falwell, a prominent Southern Baptist and televangelist, founded the Moral Majority, an organization devoted to fighting what he and his followers perceived as the moral and secular decay of America. The Majority represented a significant shift in American politics in that, up to this point, fundamentalist Christians had largely respected the principle of separation of Church and State. The Majority engaged in political action, encouraging followers to oppose secularism and fight legislation that promoted abortion, homosexuality, euthanasia and related progressive norms. The Moral Majority ensured the election of many conservative political candidates, most notably Ronald Reagan as President in 1980 (Kaplan, 1992).

Religious fundamentalism, however notoriously difficult it might be to define, is understood as a powerful reaction against progressive rationality. In his book *Jihad vs. McWorld: How the Planet Is Both Falling Apart and Coming Together*, Benjamin Barber argues that the nation-state is under threat from the rationalizing forces of global capitalism on one side, and fundamentalist religion on the other. In essence, Barber (1995) is suggesting that the dominant social institutions like the nation-state are being pulled apart by competing and powerful forces of disenchantment and re-enchantment.

An important and growing variant of religion in post-industrial nations is a growing interest in New Age spirituality. In a provocative book titled *Value Change in Global Perspective*, Paul R. Abramson and Ronald Inglehart demonstrate how secular societies have moved beyond simply satisfying base material needs, and as a result their members now focus on finding meaning. Examining data from the World Values Survey, Abramson and Inglehart (1995) observe a growing concern for the purpose and meaning in life. They interpret this as a clear sign that spirituality is growing, not receding and should be interpreted as a new form of religion based on 'post material values'.

While there is considerable debate about which specific beliefs best reflect post-material values, they are based on a degree of existential security among the emerging next generation that gives precedence to self-reflective questions of spirituality and meaning over material survival—one of the defining characteristics of religion. Indeed, one might see the tension between the Moral Majority and the conservative right on one hand and the global neoliberals on the other as less a battle between religion and secularism and more a contest between competing religions, both of which offer different scenarios of how to best re-enchant society.

Religion in Management: Post-Material Values at Work

Spirituality is increasingly present at work. Some of it is overtly religious. A study of North American corporations in 2003 revealed that the corporate chaplain is a defined occupational category and roughly 4000 chaplains minister to the spiritual needs of corporate workers (Garcia-Zamor, 2003). Much, however, is based on 'post-material values'. In a book titled *A Spiritual Audit of Corporate America*, Ian Mitroff and Elizabeth Denton (1999) demonstrate that while most US workers distinguish between religion and spirituality in the workplace, the vast majority express an interest in spirituality and meaning in their work. Reflecting on these somewhat surprising findings, Mitroff (2003) concludes that finding meaning in work is part of an individual's larger project to find meaning in life.

Scholars interested in workplace spirituality are quick to note how the subject has traditionally been marginalized by mainstream business academia. Gockel (2004) reports that the Academy of Management has been very slow to respond to the trend toward spirituality, despite mounting evidence that firms with a moral or ethical mission tend to outperform firms without one (Baldrige National Quality Program, 2005; Collins & Porras, 1996; Fry & Matherly, 2006; Orlitzky, Schmidt, & Rynes, 2003;), that spiritual values correlate with leadership effectiveness (Reave, 2005) and that positive organizational values improve employee health, commitment and engagement (Fry, Vitucci, & Cedillo, 2005; Giacalone & Jurkiewicz, 2003; Malone & Fry, 2003).

However, a growing body of research has begun to attend to the more enchanted elements of spirituality and meaning at work. Jane Dutton, Kim Cameron and colleagues at the University of Michigan, for example, have established a vibrant research community that attends to positive organizational scholarship (Cameron & Dutton, 2003). The intent of this research is to focus management scholars' attention on the largely ignored questions of generative dynamics in organizations that lead to human strength, resiliency, healing, restoration and meaningful work (Cameron & Spreitzer, 2011; Pratt & Ashforth, 2003).

The turn to meaning and spirituality in work is an effort to re-enchant the modern corporation. It reflects a long-standing fascination with mysticism in organizations (Bartunek & Moch, 1994; Merton, 1951) and an awareness that successful organizational change often requires the magical language of the shaman rather than the rational logic of the scientist (Biggart, 1977; Frost & Egri, 1994). Our current fascination with corporate social responsibility, some argue, is another example of an attempt to inject spirituality and post-material values into the modern corporation (Bubna-Litic, 2009).

The Re-Enchantment of Science

Science offers what is arguably the ultimate expression of modern rationality. The profound success of science and technology in alleviating hunger and disease or in elevating the material wellbeing of humanity makes it extremely difficult to suggest that modernity has generated a loss of faith in the value of science. But, despite its technical success, there is clear evidence that science is losing legitimacy in distinct segments of Western industrial society.

American sociologist Gordon Gauchat (2012) examined public attitudes toward science in the United States between 1974 and 2010. He found that while there is not an overall decline in the public trust of science, there is a distinct and significant decline in trust for science within the sub-population that identifies as politically conservative. Moreover, educated conservatives uniquely demonstrate the greatest decline in trust, a result that suggests the influence of both religion and populism in challenging the objectivity of science.

The populist mistrust of science includes the field of medicine, as demonstrated by the increasing rejection of immunization in North America and parts of Europe. The US National Institutes of Health reports that in many communities the vaccination rates for children have fallen below the threshold required to maintain 'herd immunity'. As a result, these communities are experiencing outbreaks of diseases that we once believed to be eradicated by modern science.

Author Timothy Caulfield, in a book provocatively titled *Is Gwyneth Paltrow Wrong About Everything?* (Caulfield, 2015), argues that the growing mistrust in science is fuelled by modern celebrity. The anti-immunization movement has been driven by entertainment celebrities, such as Gwyneth Paltrow, Jenny McCarthy, Jim Carrey, Bill Maher and Robert DeNiro, who use their powerful media profiles to promote scientifically unproven claims about the adverse effects of immunization. Their motivation, apart from the obvious efforts to grow their own online followers, seems to also involve a somewhat incomplete articulation of the 'post-material' values of meaning and spirituality which, in part, promotes a growing disenchantment with the lack of independent objectivity of medical science.

While the populist challenges to science are somewhat new, there is a long-standing scepticism toward scientific rationality as a disenchanting element of society that reaches back to the critical theorists of the Frankfurt School. The rapid rise of acupuncture, homeopathy and other alternative medicines does not necessarily suggest a complete rejection of the objectivity of science. Rather it suggests that science has become a consumer item or an expression of fashion and taste, the interpretation and use of which is increasingly understood as a source of individual re-enchantment.

Re-Enchanting the Science of Management Education

The critiques of rationality in science have inspired similar critiques of hyper-rationality in management education. In a famous *Harvard Business Review* article titled "How Business Schools Lost Their Way", noted leadership scholar Warren Bennis argues that research in business schools fails to connect with practicing managers because of its narrow focus on scientific rationality. Science, he observes, "is predicated on the faulty assumption that business is an academic discipline like chemistry or geology. In fact, business is a profession, akin to medicine and the law, and business schools are professional schools—or should be" (Bennis & O'Toole, 2005, p. 98).

In his highly influential book *From Higher Aims to Hired Hands*, Rakesh Khurana (2010) argues that in order to attain legitimacy within the university, business schools adopted the model of scientific management promoted by Frederick W. Taylor. But critics note that scientific management failed both in practice and in its application in business schools because scientific rationality erroneously assumes that business decisions can be made independently of social values.

As a result, observes management guru Henry Mintzberg (2004), business schools have adopted an "excessively analytical, detached style" of education that produces "overconfident and underqualified MBAs" with no real grounding in how to run an actual company. The narrow rationality of business education based on amoral theories of maximizing self-interest and the application of algorithmic reasoning has generated a serious backlash by elite business school academics who argue for a more balanced curriculum that embraces critical thinking, the humanities and ethics (Augier & March,

2002; Ferraro, Pfeffer, & Sutton, 2005; Grey, 2004). In our terms, they each ask for a degree of humanistic re-enchantment of management education.

The Return to Craft

The resurgence of craft modes of production in Europe and North America offers a powerful illustration of the re-enchantment of work and economy. While craft has always been an important but somewhat invisible element of contemporary industrial economies, the global financial crisis of 2008 seems to have accelerated a movement to reframe craft from a form of hobby-work to a viable form of commerce.

There are multiple indicia of the growing economic clout of craft production. Etsy.com, an online platform devoted to retailing handmade goods, observed a 5,000 percent increase in sales between 2008 and 2011 (etsy.com). The total value of sales in 2010 was 314.3 million USD, an increase of 74% over the previous year and a 106% increase over 2008. In 2013 Etsy sales exceeded $1 billion (etsy.com).

The craft beer industry has experienced a similar trajectory of growth since the financial crisis. In 2015, American craft brewers celebrated the sixth consecutive year of double-digit growth in sales with a year over year increase of 13% over annual sales from 2014. The 4,269 craft brewers now make up 12 percent of the total beer consumption market in the US, roughly doubling their market share in just four years. The American Brewers Association acknowledges an aspirational goal of controlling 20 percent of the US beer market by 2020 (Kell, 2016).

The resurgence of craft modes of production has been accompanied by a growing cultural discourse about rediscovering the meaning and value of working with one's hands. In his *New York Times* best-selling book *Shop Class as Soulcraft: An Inquiry into the Value of Work*, Matthew B. Crawford (2009) notes that for nearly a generation Americans have denigrated blue-collar work. Citing Robert Reich's now famous argument that the new American worker must acquire the abstract knowledge required to become a "symbolic analyst" or "knowledge worker", Crawford (2009) observes that skilled labour has become delegitimized, as evidenced by the widespread closure of 'shop' classes—classes devoted to exposing students to work in the trades—in US high schools.

The problem with delegitimizing manual labour, Crawford notes, is that it implies that white-collar workers achieve higher agency, autonomy and financial success than their blue-collar counterparts. The empirical evidence, however, is quite different. The average office worker or computer programmer is as subject to the same deskilling impacts of scientific management as is the typical assembly line worker. Independent tradesmen, Crawford argues, still retain a degree of autonomy over work, a vocational dedication to quality and a sense of purpose and meaning in work that has long since been eliminated in the cubicle-based reality of a typical 'knowledge worker'.

Crawford concludes with the observation that while Western industrial societies have worked hard to create institutions that prevent the concentration of political power, we have failed utterly to prevent the concentration of economic power or to take account of how such concentration damages the conditions under which full human flourishing becomes possible. Crawford echoes many decades of research in management that bemoans the loss of meaning in work and the need to re-enchant the workplace.

Re-Enchanting Institutions

Collectively, the resurgence of religion and spirituality, emerging challenges to scientific rationality and the rise of populism, tribalism and craft modes of production all speak to an oppositional discourse that exposes the questionable assumptions of totalizing progress inherent in post-Enlightenment claims of inexorable rationality. More specifically, these phenomena offer an empirical challenge to the assumptions of neo-institutional theory. Institutionalism has duly explained the inexorable expansion of rationality and disenchantment in the world. But it has been wilfully blind to the contradictory evidence of the stubborn persistence of myth, magic and re-enchantment.

Instead, institutionalism has fallen victim to the disenchanting effects of rationality. Consider how the theoretical richness of the 'old' institutionalism, and its focus on social structures populated by humans, has given way to the thin constructs of neo-institutionalism, where cognition occurs absent individuals (i.e. institutional 'logics') and change occurs absent human agency or reflexivity (i.e. institutional 'entrepreneurship'). In his poignant comments on the virtues of old institutionalism, Arthur Stinchcombe (1997, p. 1) comments on the disenchanted absence of individuals in the constructs of neo-institutionalism:

> But, unlike the institutions of modern institutionalism, *people ran these institutions* by organizing activities on their behalf. Institutions were, in the first instance, *created by purposive people* in legislatures and international unions, and in pamphlets of business ideologists in Northern England. Modern institutionalism, to create a caricature, is Durkheimian in the sense that collective representations manufacture themselves by opaque processes, are implemented by diffusion, are exterior and constraining without exterior people doing the creation or the constraining. [emphasis added]

Institutional theory is in serious need of re-enchantment.

What would a re-enchanted theory of institutions look like? We address this question in the balance of this essay. We sketch out four alternative constructs that offer an 'enchanted re-interpretation' of well-established constructs in neo-institutional theory. First, we examine authenticity as a counterbalance to legitimacy. Second, we introduce the concept of reflexivity in place of the paralyzing notion of embeddedness. Third, we offer the construct of mimesis as an enchanted substitute to isomorphism. Finally, we propose incantation as a counterpoint to diffusion.

Authenticity

Considerable research has demonstrated that, in order to be successful, an organization must be legitimate—i.e. it must comply with prevailing societal norms, values and expectations (Suchman, 1995). This means not only legal compliance, it also means normative compliance with social expectations of how an organization should be structured, governed and managed. For example, corporations ought to have a board of directors, and any corporation without one will find it difficult to gain critical resources.

An equally important, but unarticulated, element of organizational success is authenticity or the ability of an organization to remain true to idealized and unique norms, values and expectations of success. In contrast to legitimacy, which requires an organization to remain true to externally determined social expectations, authenticity requires an organization to remain true to an internalized ideal, identity or historically defined template of what is real, honest, true or essential about an organization, a product or a practice.

The notion of authenticity draws from Plato's notion of ideal forms in which there is assumed to exist an abstracted ideal type from which all empirical observations are to be compared. While notions of what is legitimate for an organization is socially constructed and may vary over time and space (e.g. gambling, once an illegal activity, is now legitimized as 'gaming') as external norms change, notions of authenticity or being true to an endogenously conceived ideal form are resistant to pressures of social construction.

Authenticity offers an important but as yet unarticulated counterpoint to legitimacy. While the construct does not form part of the ongoing conversation in neo-institutionalism, the notion of authenticity was an implicit element in the 'old institutionalism' of Phillip Selznick, who coined the term *institutional character* to capture the internal "ideals and commitments" (Selznick, 1949, p. 181) held by an organization that give it its "distinctive unity and character" (Selznick, 2008, p. 59).

Organizational character, Selznick observes, is the product of an organization's history, an integral element that cannot be easily replicated or removed and which contributes to its distinctiveness. "Not every organization", Selznick (1960, p. 56) observes, "has a set character. When goals are highly specialized and technical, where individuals and groups have only a narrow relation to the organization as a whole, few character-defining commitments may develop. But where some special mission, or a long history, results in more than a purely formal administrative structure, there emerges a quality of uniqueness that suffuses the entire organization".

Selznick's conception of character, thus, is a construct that combines the somewhat ephemeral elements of what we now understand to be organizational culture. However, Selznick (1992, p. 321) noted that character "includes its culture, but something more as well". It also incorporates an element of commitment to a set of ideals or 'critical values' that protected the organization from the somewhat whimsical demands of the external environment by giving the organization a sense of "irreversible commitments" (Selznick, 1957, p. 40) to an internal ideal or sense of organisational self that could best be described as an "institutional imperative" (Selznick, 2008, p. 98).

Ultimately Selznick's conception of character captures the essence of authenticity, which is an enduring ideological commitment to an internalized set of values and sense of identity that helps guide an entity on a range of difficult issues. Selznick's notion of character has been largely ignored by contemporary neo-institutionalists, with the one possible exception of Roger Friedland, whose construct of institutional substance echoes many elements of Selznick's original ideas. Friedland (2009, p. 56) defines institutional substance as an unchanging essence of an institutional field determined by a "regime of values" which defines "the foundation or essence of a thing which cannot be reduced to its accidental properties". Critically, like Selznick's notion of institutional character, institutional substance defies calculability. It is often difficult to articulate, even by those who understand its value. "Like Aristotle's soul as the substance of human, an institutional substance does not exist; it is rather an absent presence necessary to institutional life" (Friedland, 2009, p. 57).

In combination, these three elements—institutional character, essence and substance—contribute to the umbrella construct of authenticity which we define as a powerful and enduring commitment to an internalized set of critical organizational values that are the product of a unique history and critical reflection that gives an organization a coherent identity and purpose. Authenticity is a recognition that organizations are, at their core, human endeavours.

While the term *authenticity* has not yet been articulated in organizational theory, we gain some insights from a variety of themes that appear to help elaborate the term. One such theme is that authenticity involves being true to an organization's history, identity or founding values (Suddaby & Foster, 2017). Prior research has shown that successful organizations often fail by drifting too far from the key factors that originally determined their unique position in the marketplace. Mercedes-Benz, for example, faced near failure when the company drifted too far away from its core competence in high quality engineering (Miller, 1992). Similarly, the Danish toy manufacturer Lego faced bankruptcy after decades of strategic drift away from its foundational values as a source of childhood creativity (Schultz & Hernes, 2013).

In contrast to legitimacy, which is inherently based on a discourse of prevalence, similarity and "normality" (see Baum & Powell, 1995; Hannan &

Carroll, 1995; Suddaby, Bitektine, & Haack, 2017), authenticity is based on a discourse of difference, 'rarity', uniqueness and the logic of identity. Like Baudrillard's (1994) notion of the simulacra, authenticity is not merely the claim of aspiration to be normal, it is rather the claim of aspiring to be real.

Reflexivity

A distinguishing element of authenticity is that it presumes a capacity for human critical reflection. This assumption stands in sharp contrast to canons of neo-institutionalism, which has been sharply criticized for failing to articulate a clear role for individual agency in institutional processes (Suddaby, 2010) and for the marked absence of any explanation of reflective capacity (Mutch, 2007; Suddaby, Viale, & Gendron, 2016).

Instead, neo-institutionalism is premised on the concept of an 'iron cage' in which agents are so embedded in social relations that they fail to recognize their position in the social structure and, as a result, are not capable of understanding how to change it—a theoretical conundrum that has been termed the "paradox of embeddedness" (Greenwood & Suddaby, 2006). Actors, thus, are assigned the assumptive role of Garfinkel's (1967) "cultural dopes", with an extremely limited repertoire of choice and action as a result of a presumed inability to understand the social pressures that surround them.

While neo-institutional theory has devoted considerable attention to resolving the paradox, the proposed solutions focus on gaps in the social-structural edifice that create very limited opportunities for change. Entrepreneurs effect change by occupying structural positions that exist either on the periphery of social structures (Leblebici, Salancik, Copay, & King, 1991), thereby avoiding the totalizing effects of social pressure, or in the center of two or more social fields, thereby acquiring a hyper-muscular capacity to overcome the social pressures of each (Suddaby & Greenwood, 2005). Both explanations rest on the disenchanted assumption that reflexive insight emanates from flaws in the social structure rather than the reflective capacity of the actor.

Reflexivity is a well-established construct in both social (Archer, 2007; Garfinkel, 1967; Horkheimer & Adorno, 1972; Marx, 1992) and organizational theory (Weick, 1995; Chia, 1996; Alvesson, 2003; Antonacopolou & Tsoukas, 2002). Perhaps the most compelling contemporary articulation of reflexivity in social theory is offered by Margaret Archer's work, which focuses explicitly on intra-subjective conversation as a key element of social action. Drawing from American pragmatist Charles Saunders Peirce, Archer (2007) focuses attention on the 'internal conversation' or the ongoing internal deliberations with us as the foundation of human reflexivity.

These internal conversations with different elements of the self (the I, me and myself, as Cooley [1902] would describe them) provides a life-long internal discussion within which the subject forms an internal consensus about a projected life course that best expresses an authentic identity of the self. Reflexivity, according to Archer (2007, p. 4), is "the regular exercise of the mental ability, shared by all normal people, to consider themselves in relation to their social contexts and vice versa".

Reflexivity is also emerging as an explanatory element within neo-institutional theory (Mutch, 2007; Suddaby et al., 2016). Suddaby et al. (2016, p. 229) define reflexivity as "an individuals' general awareness of the constraints and opportunities created by the norms, values, beliefs and expectations of the social structure that surrounds them . . . it is the outcome of an interaction between one's structural position . . . and the general level of social skill, expertise and knowledge that they have".

Reflexivity offers the possibility of re-enchanting institutional theory by articulating a role for the uniquely human capacity for creative insight and self-awareness. Like authenticity, the concept of reflexivity refers to a somewhat ephemeral internal ability that captures Schutz and Luckmann's (1973) notion of "commonsense rationality" as distinct from scientific rationality. In order to justify one's social actions, Schutz argued, they must not only be understood to be rational, they must also be "sensible and reasonable" within the subjective point of view of the actor.

It is important to note that reflexivity and internal conversations are not restricted to the interiority of the individual. Both Peirce (1933–35) and Archer (2007) contemplate the possibility of internal conversations about the life interest and life project of collectives—groups and organizations for example. These conversations are expressed in what Searle (1990) describes as statements of joint commitment that capture collective intentionality that are expressed as "we" statements that often form the basis of institutions, perhaps best illustrated by the opening words of the US Declaration of Independence.

In his work in the sociology of law, Phillip Selznick (1992, 1994, pp. 396–402) identified reflexive rationality as an advanced form of legal interpretation that was superior to formal law because of its ability to create progressive social institutions. Formal law requires the narrow construction of rational interpretation according to the inherent logic of its internal assumptions. So, for example, in a contract dispute a judge must find that a contract exists if the evidence shows a "meeting of minds" between the parties.

Reflexive law, by contrast, avoids slavish attention to procedure and is, instead, attentive to social factors, such as any power differences between the parties, and will restructure contracts based on desired social outcomes. The difference between formal law and reflexive law is like the difference between strict constructionism of the US constitution and judicial activism. It is also like the difference between old and new institutionalism. The former is purposive, agentic and interventionist while the latter is bound by rigid adherence to rules and conventions that cede agency to structures of our own creation.

Reflexivity, thus, offers a re-enchanted view of organizations in which cognizant, self-aware individuals form collective intentions to engage in institutional actions. While these individuals are subject to normative pressures of the institutions they create, these pressures are not cognitively overwhelming. Rather, individuals retain a degree of awareness and sensitivity to their influence. With reflexivity, institutions are enchanting rather than totalizing.

Mimesis

Isomorphism is another disenchanted concept of neo-institutionalism. It is based on the observation that organizations signal conformity to institutional pressures by adopting structures, practices and behaviours that are perceived to be legitimate because they are similar to other organizations in a shared social field. Over time, organizations in a common field will become increasingly similar to each other.

DiMaggio and Powell (1983) identify three distinct types of isomorphism. Coercive isomorphism is a response to social pressures of large central actors in an organizational field, most typically the state. Normative isomorphism is a response to social pressures of arbiters of legitimacy in the field, typically the professions. Mimetic isomorphism is a response to conflicting or ambiguous social pressures in an organizational field in which subject organizations mimic those organizations perceived to be successful or legitimate.

Isomorphism offers a limited and biased view of empirical reality because it marginalizes the role of agency in institutions. It does so by separating beliefs, as subject, from the rationalization of those beliefs into taken-for-granted practices and routines, as object. The concept of isomorphism forces us to attend to the outcome of processes of mimicry—i.e. the expansion of rational forms—with the assumption that the copy is a true but weaker reproduction of an original. Mimesis, by contrast, does not. It is premised on the assumption of an integration of subject and object (original and copy) and focuses attention on the process by which subject and object, or original and copy, become integrated into a new claim of reality (Baudrillard, 1994).

Although both mimesis and isomorphism share an interest in the production of copies, they differ substantially in how the copy is theorized. In the formal rationality of isomorphism the copy is a weak reproduction of the original. The subtext of mimetic isomorphism is that the weak and inefficient copy the 'leader' in the hope of appearing rational. In *Mimesis and Alterity*, however, anthropologist Michael Taussig (1993) observes that mimesis is a form of 'sympathetic magic' in which special power is conferred through the act of copying and through which the copy becomes more powerful than the original.

Walter Benjamin sees mimesis as a form of symbolic interaction that underpins all social institutions. Benjamin (1986, p. 336) granted special attention to mimesis through language as a key means whereby magic occurs as the subject becomes the object:

> In this way language may be seen as the highest level of mimetic behavior and the most complete archive of non-sensuous similarity: a medium into which the earlier powers of mimetic production and comprehension have passed without residue, to the point where they have liquidated those of magic.

We see the power of mimesis in modern business practice where logos, trademarks and brands—mimetic simulacra—are often far more valuable than the products they represent. The trademark, Coombe (1996, p. 206) observes, is the "mass-reproduced stamp of an authorized site of origin that authenticates mass-produced goods bearing the trademark owner's singular distinction, the mark might be seen as channelling the cultural energy of mimesis into the form of the signature".

We see it, too, in human resource practices that position mirroring behaviour as critical to building powerful relationships in the workplace (Bargh & Chartrand, 1999). We also see the power of mimesis in workplace rituals, systematic and programmed copies intended "to show employees the kind of behaviour that is expected of them" (Deal & Kennedy, 2000, p. 14) and which reinforce, recreate and transfer pre-existing status orders to a new statement of social reality (Dacin, Munir, & Tracey, 2010). Mimesis, thus, offers an enchanted view of isomorphism.

Incantation

Diffusion is a central concept in neo-institutionalism. The core argument is that organizational practices and structures are adopted not because of their technical efficiency or operational superiority but because they conform to norms and values in the organizational field. Considerable empirical evidence has been amassed to demonstrate how fads and fashions emerge and diffuse in management, not because of their technical performance but rather because they conform to assumptions about what an organization should do (Abrahamson, 1996).

Critics have been quick to point out some problematic assumptions in diffusion studies. First, it is often assumed that adopting organizations do so passively. Without assessing the motive for adopting, it is difficult to distinguish between adoption for reasons of efficiency versus reasons of mimetic isomorphism (Donaldson, 1995; Haunschild, 2008; Haunschild & Miner, 1997). Second, diffusion studies typically fail to account for changes or translation of structures and practices during the process of adoption (Sahlin & Wedlin, 2008). Scandinavian institutionalism refers to the act of changing a structure or practice during diffusion as a process of "translation" (Czarniawska & Joerges, 1996).

The term translation captures an important but invisible element of diffusion—that the practice of adopting a new structure or process, regardless of the motive, is always mediated by language. Indeed, legitimation, which is the sentiment that underpins diffusion, is also a linguistic construct (Zbaracki, 1998). Language, of course, underpins much human behaviour, but it is the power of language intended to legitimate or persuade that is of particular interest to those who wish to understand how rational actors can be convinced to do things that undermine their technical performance (Suddaby & Greenwood, 2005). In this regard, language is magic.

The power to incant through language has always been a central element of enchantment. Covino (1994) reminds us that the words 'spelling' and 'grammar' have their origins in sorcery and offer a reflection of the capacity of one skilled with words to cast 'spells' by reading from a 'grimoire'. In *The Philosophy of Literary Form*, rhetorician Kenneth Burke (1974, p. 4) reinforces our historical understanding of the magic of words:

> The magical decree is implicit in all language; for the mere act of naming an object or situation decrees that it is to be singled out as such and such rather than as something other. Hence, I think that an attempt to eliminate magic would involve us in the elimination of the vocabulary itself as a way of sizing up reality.

True rhetoric, Burke (1969) argued, is magical because it initiates action. Words have the power to send men to their death in war, abandon their home and families and adopt political structures that will enslave them.

Yet where is the power of incantation in management theory? The hyper-rational world of finance tends to dismiss words as "mere noise" that will be ultimately washed out by the "invisible hand" of an "efficient market" (Fama & French, 1992, 2012). The global financial crisis of 2008 has revealed the notion of an efficient market as yet another myth of rationality (Fox, 2011). However, there is an emerging interest amongst finance scholars to explore the power of rhetoric to magically subvert the rationality of markets. For example, researchers are examining the ways in which the choice of words by central bankers can significantly move the value of currencies (Holmes, 2009) or how the emotions used by finance analysts to describe firms can magically distort the value of a corporate stock (Feldman, Govindaraj, Livnat, & Segal, 2010; Loughran & McDonald, 2011; Tetlock, 2007).

Language and incantation are powerful forms of enchantment and magic that remain largely unexplored in institutional processes. While we have some indication of the legitimating power of words through rhetoric (Suddaby & Greenwood, 2005) and discourse (Maguire & Hardy, 2009) this thread of research remains largely unexplored. Certainly the sterility of diffusion deserves to be re-enchanted by a closer examination of how words and incantation permit the translation and movement of ideas (Czarniawska & Joerges, 1996; Sahlin & Wedlin, 2008).

Re-Enchanting Institutions with Magical Thinking

The intent of this essay has been to draw attention to the hyper-rationality of the modern world—the prominence of science, the spread of secularism and the expansion of rationality—and its deleterious effect on how we study and understand institutions. The hyper-rationality of social science and its focus on quantification and measurement have forced us to focus on the outcomes of institutional processes that produce organizational forms and ideas that conform to modernist notions of progress.

It is important to remember, however, that one of the central concepts of neo-institutionalism is that of rational myths (Meyer & Rowan, 1977), which argues that primitive and often regressive cultural ideas can only be spread in modernity when they are wrapped in the guise of rationality. They are not rational themselves. Quite the opposite; it is the incantation and mimesis of rationality that makes them appear legitimate.

Why then do studies of institutional change always demonstrate the success of modern forms of production (corporate modes of publishing always replace craft modes) or thinking (progressive logics always replace primitive ones) over traditional ones? Where are the accounts of successful efforts to subvert science, slow secularism and challenge capitalism? Where are the studies of enchantment and re-enchantment in the world?

Some are beginning to emerge. Perhaps the best illustration of this is offered by the fascinating account of the enchanted process of training advocates in Scotland—a process called devilling—by Sabina Siebert and colleagues (Siebert, Wilson, & Hamilton, 2016). The trainees (termed devils) must conform to ancient rules and rituals enforced by their mentors (devil-masters). The rules have little relationship to learning the rational, technical elements of law and much to do with the reinforcement of tradition and the ritualistic expression of enchantment through the imposition of seemingly arbitrary commandments (devils may not sit here), which the authors term the "enchantment of space".

While the example of 'devilling' may be an extreme case, the professions are replete with lesser examples of the stubborn persistence of ritualistic thinking. Consider the reluctance of the American medical establishment to give up the irrational 'on call' schedule of physicians in training (Pratt, Rockmann, & Kaufmann, 2006). Or consider the role of primitive routines in reproducing ancient class structures at elite British universities (Dacin et al., 2010) and the power of traditional professionalism to de-legitimate the rationality of multi-disciplinary professional partnerships (Suddaby & Greenwood, 2005). These are all illustrations of the power of re-enchantment.

Stories of enchantment also abound in the hyper-rational world of finance. In his book *The Alchemy of Finance*, billionaire philanthropist George Soros attributes his success in investing to a form of magical thinking. Based on his experience in the markets, he rejects economists' assumption of rationality in the market. Markets, he observes, are made inconsistent by biased perceptions or myths. This he terms the principle of fallibility. He argues that the myths become magnified by human reflexivity, which ultimately makes markets highly mercurial, more like alchemy than science. Rationality and human reflexivity, Soros observes, are incompatible explanations of the market. His success, he argues, is based on his view of markets as reflexive not rational systems best understood by alchemy rather than quantification.

The intent of this essay is to draw attention away from the obvious examples of hyper-rationality in the world and encourage us to attend, as well, to the somewhat marginalized examples of 'arationality'—a term used to capture phenomena which stand outside the domain of what can be understood by reason. Emotions, ethics and much of what makes humanity interesting is inherently arational—a form of 'magical thinking'.

In his acclaimed book *Infinite Jest*, American writer David Foster Wallace confronted the importance of arationality or magical thinking in the absurdity of the hyper-rationality of modern capitalism. Describing how the magical aural intimacy of old telephone conversations has been destroyed by a (fictional) new video technology, Wallace writes:

> The bilateral illusion of unilateral attention was almost infantilely gratifying from an emotional standpoint: you got to believe you were receiving somebody's complete attention without having to return it. Regarded with the objectivity of hindsight, the illusion appears arational, almost literally fantastic: it would be like being able to both lie and to trust other people at the same time.
>
> (Wallace, 1996, p. 144)

Here Wallace describes the inherent and recurrent destruction of intimacy by new technology. Prior generations, of course, would argue that the phone destroyed the magical intimacy of face-to-face conversations. But his critical insight is the observation that new modes of technology are always underpinned by a nostalgic substratum of how we have lost another small aspect of being human and how that can be reclaimed by attending to the a-rational. This is, of course, the core claim of magical realism in fiction—that the hyper-rationality of modernity has largely suppressed our humanity, but it re-appears with the episodic appearance of supernatural or magical events in everyday life.

Magical thinking acknowledges the animism inherent in material objects, such as the speed bump, known in the UK as 'sleeping policemen' with the power to "calm traffic" (Pinch, 2008), or the algorithms used to trade financial derivatives (MacKenzie, 2006) and to curate newsfeeds to social media users (Bashky, Messing, & Adamic, 2015). Social media and its ability to curate ideology and meaning of the self is the essence of animism—i.e. that material objects may, through processes of human signification, acquire agency.

Collectively the constructs of authenticity, reflexivity, mimesis and incantation offer promising alternatives to the increasingly rationalized and disenchanted concepts of legitimacy, institutional embeddedness, isomorphism and diffusion. Their enchantment arises from the degree to which they reflect and reinforce the phenomenological foundations of institutions. Institutions only exist to the degree that we believe they exist. But mere faith in institutions need not deny human reflection, agency or the cathartic power of myth.

We cannot deny the power and influence of the ongoing expansion of rationality. Nor can we deny its associated sense of disenchantment. But, by the same reasoning, we cannot ignore the tenacious persistence of myth, magic and enchantment in human beliefs, social practices and institutions. Our intent is to sketch out the possibility of institutions as Janus-like social structures, looking forward to an increasingly rational future dominated by the exteriority of the social structures we have imposed on ourselves, while, simultaneously, and perhaps somewhat nostalgically, embracing a still unexplored interior world of memory and reflection on the character, essence and authenticity of those social structures. An enchanted view of institutions is simply an acknowledgement that there is more in the dark corners of the universe, and organizations, than either science or rationality will admit.

References

Abrahamson, Eric (1996). Management fashion. *Academy of Management Review*, 21(1), 254–285.

Abramson, Paul R. & Inglehart, Ronald (1995). *Value change in global perspective.* Ann Arbor: University of Michigan Press.

Alvesson, Mats (2003). Beyond neopositivists, romantics, and localists: A reflexive approach to interviews in organizational research. *Academy of Management Review*, 28(1), 13–33.

Antonacopoulou, Elena & Tsoukas, Haridimos (2002). Time and reflexivity in organization studies: An introduction. *Organization Studies*, 23(6), 857–862.

Archer, Margaret S. (2007). *Making our way through the world: Human reflexivity and social mobility*. Cambridge, UK: Cambridge University Press.

Augier, Mie & March, James G. (Eds.) (2002). *The economics of choice, change, and organization: Essays in memory of Richard M. Cyert*. Cheltenham and Northampton, MA: Edward Elgar.

Badger, Emily (2016). As American as apple pie? The rural vote's disproportionate slice of power. *New York Times*, November 21, p. A11.

Baldrige National Quality Program (2005). Accessed February 27, 2017: www.nist.gov/baldrige.

Barber, Benjamin (1995). *Jihad vs. McWorld: How the planet is both falling apart and coming together*. New York, NY: Ballantine Books.

Bargh, John A. & Chartrand, Tanya L. (1999). The unbearable automaticity of being. *American Psychologist*, 54(7), 462–479.

Bartunek, Jean M. & Moch, Michael K. (1994). Third-order organizational change and the Western mystical tradition. *Journal of Organizational Change Management*, 7(1), 24–41.

Bashky, Eytan, Messing, Solomon & Adamic, Lada A. (2015). Exposure to ideologically diverse news and opinion on Facebook. *Science*, 348, 1130–1132.
Baudrillard, Jean (1994). *Simulacra and simulation*. Ann Arbor: University of Michigan Press.
Baum, Joel A. C. & Powell, Walter W.(1995). Cultivating an institutional ecology of organizations: Comment on Hannan, Carroll, Dundon, and Torres. *American Sociological Review*, 60, 529–538.
Benjamin, Walter (1986). *Reflections: Essays, aphorisms, autobiographical writings*. New York, NY: Schocken.
Bell, Karl (2012). *The magical imagination: Magic and modernity in Urban England 1780–1914*. Cambridge, UK: Cambridge University Press.
Bennis, Warren G. & O'Toole, James (2005). How business schools lost their way. *Harvard Business Review*, 83(5), 96–104.
Berman, Morris (1981). *The reenchantment of the world*. Ithaca, NY: Cornell University Press.
Biggart, Nicole Woolsey (1977). The creative-destructive process of organizational change: The case of the post office. *Administrative Science Quarterly*, 22(3), 410–426.
Blake, William (2008). *The complete poetry and prose of William Blake*. Berkeley: University of California Press.
Brabham, Daren C. (2008). Crowdsourcing as a model for problem solving: An introduction and cases. *Convergence*, 14(1), 75–90.
Bromley, Patricia & Meyer, John W.(2015). *Hyper-organization: Global organizational expansion*. Oxford: Oxford University Press.
Brown, Ralph B. (2003). Agrarian myth. In D. Levinson & K. Christensen (Eds.), *Encyclopedia of community: From the village to the virtual world* (Vol. 2, pp. 27–29). Thousand Oaks, CA: Sage.
Bubna-Litic, David (2009). *Spirituality and corporate social responsibility: Interpenetrating worlds*. Surrey, UK: Gower.
Burke, Kenneth (1969). *A grammar of motives*. Berkeley: University of California Press.
Burke, Kenneth (1974). *The philosophy of literary form: Studies in symbolic action*. Berkeley: University of California Press.
Cameron, Kim S. & Dutton, Jane E.(2003). *Positive organizational scholarship: Foundations of a new discipline*. San Francisco: Barrett-Koehler Publishers.
Cameron, Kim S. & Spreitzer, Gretchen M.(Eds.) (2011). *The Oxford handbook of positive organizational scholarship*. Oxford: Oxford University Press.
Caulfield, Timothy (2015). *Is Gwyneth Paltrow wrong about everything?: When celebrity culture and science clash*. New York, NY: Viking.
Chia, Robert (1996). The problem of reflexivity in organizational research: Towards a postmodern science of organization. *Organization*, 3(1), 31–59.
Cooley, Charles H. (1902). *Human nature and the social order*. New York: Scribner's.
Coombe, Rosemary J. (1996). Embodied trademarks: Mimesis and alterity on American commercial frontiers. *Cultural Anthropology*, 11(2), 202–224.
Collins, James C. & Porras, Jerry I. (1996). *Built to last: Successful habits of visionary companies*. New York, NY: William Collins.
Cova, Bernard, Kozinets, Robert V. & Shankar, Avi (2007). Tribes, Inc.: The new world of tribalism. London: Butterworth-Heinemann
Covino, William A. (1994). *Magic, rhetoric, and literacy: An eccentric history of the composing imagination*. Albany: SUNY Press.

Crawford, Matthew B. (2009). *Shop class as soulcraft: An inquiry into the value of work*. London, UK: Penguin.

Czarniawska, Barbara & Bernward, Joerges (1996). Travels of ideas. In B. Czarniawska & G. Sevon (Eds.), *Translating organizational change* (pp. 13–48). Berlin: De Gruyter.

Dacin, Tina M., Munir, Kamal & Tracey, Paul (2010). Formal dining at Cambridge colleges: Linking ritual performance and institutional maintenance. *Academy of Management Journal*, 53(6), 1393–1418.

Deal, Terrence E. & Kennedy, Allan A. (2000). *Corporate cultures: The rites and rituals of corporate life*. Boston, MA: Da Capo Press.

DiMaggio, Paul & Powell, Walter W. (1983). The iron cage revisited: Collective rationality and institutional isomorphism in organizational fields. *American Sociological Review*, 48(2), 147–160.

Donaldson, Lex (1995). *American anti-management theories of organization: A critique of paradigm proliferation*. Cambridge, UK: Cambridge University Press.

Durkheim, Emile (2014). *The division of labor in society*. New York, NY: Free Press.

Engels, Friedrich (1993). *The condition of the working class in England*. Oxford: Oxford University Press.

Fama, Eugene F. & French, Kenneth R. (1992). The cross-section of expected stock returns. *The Journal of Finance*, 47(2), 427–465.

Fama, Eugene F. & French, Kenneth R. (2012). Size, value, and momentum in international stock returns. *Journal of Financial Economics*, 105(3), 457–472.

Feldman, Ronen, Govindaraj, Suresh, Livnat, Joshua & Segal, Benjamin (2010). Management's tone change, post earnings announcement drift and accruals. *Review of Accounting Studies*, 15(4), 915–953.

Ferraro, Fabrizio, Pfeffer, Jeffrey & Sutton, Robert I. (2005). Economics language and assumptions: How theories can become self-fulfilling. *Academy of Management Review*, 30(1), 8–24.

Fox, Justin (2011). *The myth of the rational market: A history of risk, reward, and delusion on Wall Street*. Petersfield, UK: Harriman House Limited.

Frost, Peter J. & Egri, Carolyn P. (1994). The shamanic perspective on organizational change and development. *Journal of Organizational Change Management*, 7(1), 7–23.

Friedland, Roger (2009). Institution, practice, and ontology: Toward a religious sociology. In R. E. Meyer, K. Sahlin & M. J. Ventresca (Eds.), *Institutions and ideology* (pp. 45–83). Bingley, UK: Emerald Group Publishing Limited.

Fry, Louis W. & Matherly, Laura L. (2006). *Spiritual leadership and organizational performance: An exploratory study*. Stephenville, TX: Tarleton State University.

Fry, Louis W., Vitucci, Steve & Cedillo, Marie (2005). Spiritual leadership and army transformation: Theory, measurement, and establishing a baseline. *The Leadership Quarterly*, 16(5), 835–862.

Garcia-Zamor, Jean-Claude (2003). Workplace spirituality and organizational performance. *Public Administration Review*, 63(3), 355–363.

Garfinkel, Harold (1967). *Studies in ethnomethodology*. Upper Saddle River, NJ: Prentice Hall.

Garud, Raghu, Jain, Sanjay & Kumaraswamy, Arun (2002). Institutional entrepreneurship in the sponsorship of common technological standards: The case of Sun Microsystems and Java. *Academy of Management Journal*, 45(1), 196–214.

Gauchat, Gordon (2012). Politicization of science in the public sphere: A study of public trust in the United States, 1974 to 2010. *American Sociological Review*, 77(2), 167–187.

Giacalone, Robert A. & Jurkiewicz, Carole L. (2003). In Robert A. Giacalone & Carole L. Jurkiewicz (Eds.), Toward a science of workplace spirituality. In *Handbook of workplace spirituality and organizational performance* (pp. 3–28) Armonk, NY: M.E. Sharpe.

Giles, Jim (2005). Internet encyclopedias go head to head. *Nature*, 438(15), 900–901.

Gockel, Annemarie (2004). The trend toward spirituality in the workplace: Overview and implications for career counseling. *Journal of Employment Counseling*, 41(4), 156.

Gramsci, Antonio (1988). Americanism and Fordism. In D. Forgacs (Ed.), *A Gramsci reader: Selected writings 1916–1935* (pp. 275–299). London: Lawrence & Wishart.

Grant, Richard (1993). Against the grain: Agricultural trade policies of the US, the European community and Japan at the GATT. *Political Geography*, 12(3), 247–262.

Greenwood, Royston & Suddaby, Roy (2006). Institutional entrepreneurship in mature fields: The big five accounting firms. *Academy of Management Journal*, 49(1), 27–48.

Grey, Christopher (2004). Reinventing business schools: The contribution of critical management education. *Academy of Management Learning and Education*, 3(2), 178–186.

Habermas, Jürgen (1984). *The theory of communicative action* (Vol. 1). Boston, MA: Beacon.

Hannan, Michael T. & Carroll, Glenn R. (1995). Theory building and cheap talk about legitimation: A reply to Baum and Powell. *American Sociological Review*, 60(4), 539–544.

Haunschild, Pamela R. & Miner, Anne S. (1997). Modes of interorganizational imitation: The effects of outcome salience and uncertainty. *Administrative Science Quarterly*, 42(3): 472–500.

Haunschild, Axel (2008). Challenges to the German theatrical employment system: How long-established national institutions respond to globalization forces. In C. Smith, B. McSweeny & R. Fitzgerald (Eds.), *Remaking management: Between Global and Local* (pp. 251–270). Cambridge, UK.

Hesseltine, William Best (1961). Four American traditions. *Journal of Southern History*, 27(1), 3–32.

Hirsch, Paul M. (1997). Review essay: Sociology without social structure: Neoinstitutional theory meets brave new world. *American Journal of Sociology*, 102(6), 1702–1723.

Holmes, Douglas R. (2009). Economy of words. *Cultural Anthropology*, 24(3), 381–419.

Hofstader, Richard (1955). *The age of reform: From Bryan to FDR*. New York: Vintage.

Horkheimer, Max & Adorno, Theodor W. (1972). *Dialectic of enlightenment*. New York, NY: Seabury Press.

Howe, Jeff (2006). The rise of crowdsourcing. *Wired Magazine*, 14(6), 1–4.

Inglehart, Ronald and Norris, Pippa, Trump, Brexit, and the Rise of Populism: Economic Have-Nots and Cultural Backlash (July 29, 2016). HKS Working Paper No. RWP16-026. Available at SSRN: https://ssrn.com/abstract=2818659

James, Paul (2006). *Globalism, nationalism, tribalism: Bringing theory back in*. Thousand Oaks, CA: Pine Forge Press.

Junger, Sebastian (2016). *Tribe: On homecoming and belonging*. New York, NY: HarperCollins Publishers Ltd.

Kalberg, Stephen (1980). Max Weber's types of rationality: Cornerstones for the analysis of rationalization processes in history. *American Journal of Sociology*, 85(5), 1145–1179.

Kaplan, Lawrence (1992). *Fundamentalism in comparative perspective*. Amherst: University of Massachusetts Press.

Kell, John (2016). What you didn't know about the boom in craft beer. Accessed February 27, 2017: http://fortune.com/2016/03/22/craft-beer-sales-rise-2015/.

Khurana, Rakesh (2010). *From higher aims to hired hands: The social transformation of American business schools and the unfulfilled promise of management as a profession*. Princeton, NJ: Princeton University Press.

Laclau, Ernesto (2005). *On populist reason*. New York, NY: Verso.

Leblebici, Huseyin, Salancik, Gerald R., Copay, Anne & King, Tom (1991). Institutional change and the transformation of interorganizational fields: An organizational history of the U.S. radio broadcasting industry. *Administrative Science Quarterly*, 36, 333–363.

Le Bon, Gustave (1960). *The crowd (1895)*. New York, NY: Viking.

Lee, Byungkyu & Bearman, Peter (2017). Important matters in political context. *Sociological Science*, 4, 1–30.

Lester, Julie (2007). The Agrarian Myth as Narrative in Agricultural Policy Making. PhD Thesis. West Lafayette: IN: Purdue University Graduate School.

Loughran, Tim & McDonald, Bill (2011). When is a liability not a liability? Textual analysis, dictionaries, and 10-Ks. *The Journal of Finance*, 66(1), 35–65.

MacKay, Charles (1995). *Extraordinary delusions and the madness of crowds, 1841*. New York: Three Rivers Press.

MacKenzie, Donald (2006). Is economics performative? Option theory and the construction of derivatives markets. *Journal of the History of Economic Thought*, 28(1), 29–55.

Maffesoli, Michel (1996). *The time of tribes: The decline of individualism in mass society*. London: Sage.

Maguire, Steve & Hardy, Cynthia (2009). Discourse and deinstitutionalization: The decline of DDT. *Academy of Management Journal*, 52(1), 148–178.

Malone, Peggy & Fry, Louis W. (2003). *Transforming schools through spiritual leadership: A field experiment*. Seattle, WA: Academy of Management.

Marsh, John S. (1989). The common agricultural policy. In J. Lodge (Ed.), *The European community and the challenge of the future* (pp. 148–166). New York: St Martin's Press.

Marx, Karl (1992). *Capital, volume I: A critique of political economy*. London, UK: Penguin Classics.

McLuhan, Marshall (1997). *Marshall McLuhan essays: Media research, technology, art*. M. A. Moos (Ed.). New York: Routledge.

McPherson, Miller, Smith-Lovin, Lynn & Brashears, Matthew E. (2006). Social isolation in America: Changes in core discussion networks over two decades. *American Sociological Review*, 71(3), 353–375.

Merton, Robert K. (1951). *Social theory and social structure: Toward the codification of theory and research*. New York, NY: The Free Press.

Meyer, John W., Boli, John, Thomas, George M. & Ramirez, Francisco O. (1997). World society and the nation-state. *American Journal of Sociology*, 103(1), 144–181.

Meyer, John W. & Rowan, Brain (1977). Institutionalized organizations: Formal structure as myth and ceremony. *American Journal of Sociology*, 83(2), 340–363.

Miller, Danny (1992). The generic strategy trap. *Journal of Business Strategy*, 13(1), 37–41.

Mintzberg, Henry (2004). *Managers not MBAs: A hard look at the soft practices of managing and management development*. San Francisco, CA: Basset-Koehler.

Mitchell, Cleo & Imrie, Brian C.(2011). Consumer tribes: Membership, consumption and building loyalty. *Asia Pacific Journal of Marketing and Logistics*, 23(1), 39–56.

Mitroff, Ian I. (2003). Do not promote religion under the guise of spirituality. *Organization*, 10(2), 375–382.

Mitroff, Ian I., Mitroff, Ian & Denton, Elizabeth A. (1999). *A spiritual audit of corporate America: A hard look at spirituality, religion, and values in the workplace*. San Francisco, CA: Jossey-Bass.

Moore, John (2006). *Tribal knowledge: Business wisdom brewed from the grounds of Starbucks corporate culture*. Wokingham, UK: Kaplan Publishing.

Moriguchi, Chikashi (1990). Rice and melons—Japanese agriculture in the Showa era. *Daedalus*, 119, 141–140.

Mutch, Alistair (2007). Reflexivity and the institutional entrepreneur: A historical exploration. *Organization Studies*, 28(7), 1123–1140.

Nisbet, Robert A. (1980). *History of the idea of progress*. Piscataway, NJ: Transaction publishers.

Norris, Pippa (2005). *Radical right: Voters and parties in the electoral market*. New York: Cambridge University Press.

Orlitzky, Marc, Schmidt, Frank L. & Rynes, Sara L. (2003). Corporate social and financial performance: A meta-analysis. *Organization Studies*, 24(3), 403–441.

Ouchi, William G. (1980). Markets, bureaucracies, and clans. *Administrative Science Quarterly*, 25(1): 129–141.

Paarlberg, Robert L. (1988). *Fixing farm trade*. New York: Council on Foreign Relations Press.

Pinch, Trevor (2008). Technology and institutions: Living in a material world. *Theory and Society*, 37(5), 461–483.

Pratt, Michael G. & Ashforth, Blake E.(2003). Fostering meaningfulness in working and at work. In K. Cameron, J. E. Dutton & R.E. Quinn (Eds.), *Positive organizational scholarship: Foundations of a new discipline* (pp. 308–327). San Francisco: Berrett Koehler.

Pratt, Michael G., Rockmann, Kevin W. & Kaufmann, Jeffrey B. (2006). Constructing professional identity: The role of work and identity learning cycles in the customization of identity among medical residents. *Academy of Management Journal*, 49(2), 235–262.

Putnam, Robert D. (2000). *Bowling alone: The collapse and revival of the American community*. New York: Simon & Schuster.

Rao, Hayagreeva, Monin, Philippe & Durand, Rodolphe (2003). Institutional change in Toque Ville: Nouvelle cuisine as an identity movement in French gastronomy. *American Journal of Sociology*, 108(4), 795–843.

Reave, Laura (2005). Spiritual values and practices related to leadership effectiveness. *The Leadership Quarterly*, 16(5), 655–687.

Ritzer, George (1993). *The McDonaldization of society*. Los Angeles, CA: Pine Forge.

Sahlin, Kerstin & Wedlin, Linda (2008). Circulating ideas: Imitation, translation and editing. In R. Greenwood, C. Oliver, K. Sahlin & R. Suddaby (Eds.), *The Sage handbook of organizational institutionalism* (pp. 218, 242) London, UK: Sage.

Searle, John (1990). Collective intentions and actions. In P. Cohen, J. Morgan & M.E. Pollack (Eds.), *Intentions in communication* (pp. 401–416). Cambridge, MA: Bradford Books, MIT Press.

Selznick, Philip (1949). *TVA and the grass roots: A study of politics and organization*. Berkeley: University of California Press.

Selznick, Philip (1957). *Leadership in administration: A sociological interpretation*. Berkeley: University of California Press.

Selznick, Philip (1960). *The organizational weapon*. Glencoe, IL: Free Press.

Selznick, Philip (1992). *The moral commonwealth*. Berkeley: University of California Press.

Selznick, Philip (1994). Self-regulation and the theory of institutions. In G. Teubner, L. Farmer & D. Murphy (Eds.), *Environmental law and ecological responsibility: The concept and practice of ecological self-organization* (pp. 396–402). Hoboken, NJ: John Wiley & Sons Inc.

Selznick, Philip (2008). *A humanist science: Values and ideals in social inquiry*. Stanford, CA: Stanford University Press.

Schutz, Alfred & Luckmann, Thomas (1973). *The structures of the life-world*. Evanston, IL: Northwestern University Press.

Schultz, Majken & Hernes, Tor (2013). A temporal perspective on organizational identity. *Organization Science*, 24(1), 1–21.

Scott, Richard W. (1995). *Institutions and organizations*. Thousand Oaks, CA: Sage.

Shils, Edward (1975). *Center and Periphery: Essays in Macrosociology*. Chicago, IL: University of Chicago Press.

Siebert, Sabina, Wilson, Fiona & Hamilton, John (2016). "Devils may sit here": The role of enchantment in institutional maintenance. *Academy of Management Journal*. Published online before print June 7, 2016, doi:10.5465/amj.2014.0487

Stinchcombe, Arthur L. (1997). On the virtues of the old institutionalism. *Annual Review of Sociology*, 23(1), 1–18.

Suchman, Mark C. (1995). Managing legitimacy: Strategic and institutional approaches. *Academy of Management Review*, 20(3), 571–610.

Suddaby, Roy (2010). Challenges for institutional theory. *Journal of Management Inquiry*, 19(1), 14–20.

Suddaby, Roy (2015). Can institutional theory be critical? *Journal of Management Inquiry*, 24(1), 93–95.

Suddaby, Roy, Bitektine, Alex & Haack, Patrick (2017). Legitimacy. *Academy of Management Annals*, 11(1), 451–478.

Suddaby, Roy & Greenwood, Royston (2005). Rhetorical strategies of legitimacy. *Administrative Science Quarterly*, 50(1), 35–67.

Suddaby, Roy & Foster, William M. (2017). History and organizational change. *Journal of Management*, 43(1), 19–38.

Suddaby, Roy, Viale, Thierry & Gendron, Yves (2016). Reflexivity: The role of embedded social position and entrepreneurial social skill in processes of field level change. *Research in Organizational Behavior*, 36, 225–245.

Surowiecki, James (2004). *The wisdom of crowds*. New York, NY: Anchor.

Taussig, Michael T. (1993). *Mimesis and alterity: A particular history of the senses*. Hove, UK: Psychology Press.

Tetlock, Paul C. (2007). Giving content to investor sentiment: The role of media in the stock market. *The Journal of Finance*, 62(3), 1139–1168.

Thornton, Patricia H. (2004). *Markets from culture: Institutional logics and organizational decisions in higher education publishing*. Stanford, CA: Stanford University Press.

Van Alstyne, Marshall & Erik Brynjolfsson (2005). Global village or cyberbalkans. *Modeling and Measuring the Integration of Electronic Communities, Management Science*, 51(6), 851–868.

Wallace, David F. (1996). *Infinite jest*. New York, NY: Little, Brown.

Weber, Max (1946). Science as a vocation. In H. H. Gerth & C. W. Mills (Trans. and Ed.), *From Max Weber* (pp. 129–156). New York: Oxford University Press.

Weick, Karl E. (1995). *Sensemaking in organizations*. Thousand Oaks, CA: Sage.

Zbaracki, Mark J. (1998). The rhetoric and reality of total quality management. *Administrative Science Quarterly*, 43(3), 602–636.

Zilber, Tammar B. (2002). Institutionalization as an interplay between actions, meanings, and actors: The case of a rape crisis center in Israel. *Academy of Management Journal*, 45(1), 234–254.

4 Bruno Latour and Niklas Luhmann as Organization Theorists

Barbara Czarniawska

'What did Luhmann and Latour do to European organization studies?' Were I writing this text 20 years ago, the question would have been 'What did Foucault and Deleuze do to European organization studies?' But it is 2017, and as much as the insights of Deleuze and Foucault have been incorporated into organization studies to the point of being taken for granted, it is Latour—and Actor-Network Theory (ANT) and Luhmann and self-observing autopoietic systems—that are the most original and visible influences today.

In what follows, I am presenting my personal view (see also Czarniawska, 2005, 2014), and will mention some of my personal works influenced by those two authors, but I hope to do justice to at least some part of a still-growing number of organizational scholars who were similarly impressed by the works of those two. I also claim that, although the approaches of two authors were innovative and can be seen as radical, they were in harmony with earlier observations of management and organization scholars.

Latour and Actor-Network Theory

How Macro Actors Are Constructed

For many decades, social scientists dutifully studied the phenomenon of power, usually assuming its existence as a starting point, and then illuminating its effects and consequences. Yet after the end of the power of hereditary monarchies, a legitimate question should be: Who has power, and why is it those people and organizations and not the other? The question was rarely formulated, at least in English, until 1981, when two French authors—Michel Callon and Bruno Latour—published a chapter in an anthology edited by Karin Knorr and Aaron Cicourel.[1] The chapter's title was "Unscrewing the Big Leviathan or How Do Actors Macrostructure Reality and How Sociologists Help Them to Do So". It began by reminding the readers of Hobbes's idea that society emerged from a contract among individuals who form an association and have their wishes expressed by a common spokesperson. In this way, a "Leviathan" is constructed. To outside observers, such a macro actor—a State, a global corporation—appears to be much larger than any of the individuals that form it, and its true character—that of a network—remains hidden and forgotten. And yet Callon and Latour insisted that it is the very construction of such macro actors that needs to be studied, including negotiations, conflicts, even wars—but first of all, the building and maintaining of associations.

As I noted earlier (Czarniawska, 2017a), two sources of inspiration could be detected in Callon and Latour's chapter. One was Michel Serres' (1974/1982) concept of translation (moving anything from one place to another changes not only what is moved, but also the mover—the translator). The other was actant theory (a version of structuralist analysis proposed by Algirdas Julien Greimas). An actant is a being or a thing that accomplishes or undergoes an act; thus actants could be people, but also animals, objects and concepts (Greimas & Courtés, 1982, p. 5).

The use of the Greimasian model is especially visible in Latour's "Technology Is Society Made Durable" (1992), in which he analyzed the history of the Kodak camera and the emergence of a mass market for amateur photographers.[2] The story is built as a story of meetings of "narrative programs" (another Greimasian term) of many actants, with Kodak as a macro actor and a winner.

But stories never end. The once powerful Eastman Kodak is now but a memory, while the Kodak Company, a micro actor, re-emerged from bankruptcy in 2014, and is trying to survive by trying new narrative programs. This turn of events is not strange, as it was not the "nature" of Eastman Kodak that made it into a macro actor in its time. It simply managed to convince many other actants to join their acts with it. Each time an anti-program was launched by competitors, Eastman Kodak managed to attract new allies, thus winning subsequent trials of strength. But digital photography proved to be a competitor too strong to win over, its network too large . . .

Actor-network theory is not a theory, but an approach, a guide to the process of answering the question 'How do things, people and ideas become connected in larger units and remain so?' Indeed, the name is misleading. The more adequate term would be 'an actant-net approach', but in 1981, when Latour and Callon[3] launched ANT, nobody knew who or what actants were, and ANT is a better acronym than "ANA". Its methodological consequences are well summarized by the 'symmetrical anthropology' concept, introduced by Latour in 1993.

Symmetric Anthropology

According to Latour, the idea came to him while playing anthropologist:

> If, I told myself, those who defend the value of science can maintain such a gap between what they say science is, and what I and my many colleagues in the thriving field of science studies, through a very banal

> use of ethnographic and historical methods, can see it is, then it is no wonder that the 'front of modernization' that I had observed first hand in Africa and then in California, had some trouble defining itself positively. There must be something deeply flawed—and also, then, deeply interesting in how the moderns define, defend and project their 'universal values'.
>
> (2010, p. 62)

Traditional anthropology used 'modern' lenses to look at 'premodern' societies; something that Latour found absurd, in comparing his studies of French industrial education in Abidjian and laboratory life in California (Latour & Woolgar, 1979/1986). This conviction deepened during his next study of the failed project of an automated subway called ARAMIS (Latour, 1996). That work is not only an example of how to study according to principles of symmetric anthropology, but also how to write it up.[4]

Aramis, or the Love of Technology is basically a detective story. A Master and a Pupil are given a task to solve the mystery of death of beautiful Aramis, or Agencement en Rames Automatisées de Modules Indépendents dans les Stations. The Master is a sociologist of science and technology, the Pupil an engineer who takes courses in social sciences at École des Mines and Aramis is a piece of transportation machinery, with cars that couple and decouple automatically, following the programming of the passengers. Born in the late 1960s, Aramis promised to be the kind of technology that serves humans and saves the environment, yet in November 1987 it was nothing but a piece of dead machinery in a technology museum. How did it happen? Did the machines fail? Had the engineers used a wrong design? Did the politicians destroy the project? Did competitors conspire to have it dumped?

The reader gets three versions of the narrative, all realist versions, emitted by the Voices of the Field, the New Sociologist of Technology and Aramis himself—all activated in a dialogue with a pupil—an engineer who wishes to learn his technoscience. This work, rich in textual devices, is especially interesting, because it finds an ingenious solution to the well-known problem facing all field researchers: How to avoid smothering the variety of voices in one sleek version and the kind of fragmentation that occurs when all the voices are reported simultaneously.

Not being a philosopher, and therefore with no ambitions to study anthropos as such, I paraphrased Latour's term into a symmetrical ethnology (Czarniawska, 2017b). Management and organization studies are not about human nature, but about certain ways of life, and, more specifically, about certain ways of work. Still, the approach I adopt follows Latour's precepts, which are:

> Use the same terms to explain truths and lies, failures and successes, trials and errors—in other words, render the method judgment free.

Simultaneously study the emergence and conduct of both humans and non-human actants. (This approach requires that greater attention be directed toward things and machines.)
Avoid any a priori declarations concerning the differences between Westerners and non-Westerners, primitive and modern societies, rationality and irrationality, identity (sameness) and alterity (difference).

'Ethnologizing' management and organizing does not mean that these practices need to be mystified or demonized; it is yet another reminder of the fact that "we have never been modern" (Latour, 1993). The fact that contemporary managers engage in rituals must not diminish respect for their work; it must only change the prevalent understanding of modernity, as John Meyer and Brian Rowan already noted in 1977.

Reassembling the Social

Latour's *Reassembling the Social* (2005) is subtitled "An Introduction to Actor-Network Theory", but it is more a summary of rather than an introduction to the approach. He intended it to be used as a textbook, although it is not written as one. Nevertheless, it is used even in management and organization courses, and translations proliferate.

Latour's declared intention was to convince social science students that they need to abandon the taken-for-granted idea that social is a kind of essential property that can be discovered and measured (a stuff of which something is made) and return to the etymology of the word. "Social" is not a material or a property, but a relationship: Something is connected or assembled, in contrast to being isolated or disconnected.

The first part of *Reassembling the Social* contains a presentation of five uncertainties—positions on which ANT differs from or is critical toward traditional sociology. These uncertainties concern the 'nature' of groups, of actions, of objects, of facts and of type of studies conventionally (and incorrectly) called 'empirical'. This part ends with a dialogue with a student who is confused by the difficulty of doing ANT-inspired studies of organizations. The dialogue represents many a doubt voiced by beginning researchers. The fictitious professor of the dialogue may be poking fun at the student (who reciprocates, creating a symmetry), but Latour the author takes the student's difficulties to heart. He admits at the outset of Part II that it is not easy to trace the social, and gives advice on how to study associations. To begin, new maps are needed—or rather maps must be taken literally, as representing a flatland. Thus new scholars of the social will not be moving between local and global or between micro and macro, because there are no such places, only different positions of a zoom. Such scholars will notice that what happens locally rarely occurs in only one place; it is possible to speak of a redistribution of the local or of localizing and globalizing. While doing so, one thing immediately comes into focus: the type of connection. If what seems to be global consists of many connected times and places and what seems to be local is a product of many connected times and places, what kind of connections are those, and what makes them stable? After all, the world of organizations is anything but flat—but how were the hierarchies made, and of what?

The metaphor of the flatland is one way to differentiate the standpoint of the observer from that of an actor (something about which Luhmann will have much to say). An ANT observer is a skeptic who wants to discover how mountains and valleys have been constructed. Such organization study topics as standardization, formalization and classifications of all kinds become obviously relevant in that endeavour.

In the concluding chapter, Latour suggested a political stance of a symmetric anthropologist.

> We first have to learn how to deploy controversies so as to gauge the number of new participants in any future assemblage (. . .); then we have to be able to follow how the actors themselves stabilize those uncertainties by building formats, standards, and metrologies (. . .); and finally, we want to see how the assemblages thus gathered can renew our sense of being in the same collective.
>
> (Latour, 2005, p. 249)

He proposed to replace the traditional political question 'How many are we?' with the question 'Can we live together?' Commonsensical as it may sound, it is a truly revolutionary question, not least in organization theory, in which the distinctions between leaders and followers, men and women, employers and employees, producers and consumers—followed by counting the forces—was a matter of routine for all political factions. The idea of assembling a collective and a subsequent 'progressive composition of one common world' will allow animals, plants and objects to join in, preserving the heterogeneity. After all, "to study is always to do politics in the sense that it collects or composes what the common world is made of" (2005, p. 256). And the social scientist's task is that of representation, in the political sense of the word (Latour, 1988).

Luhmann, the Autopoietic Systems and the Society of the Observers

Organizations as Autopoietic Systems

Chilean biologists Humberto Maturana and Francisco J. Varela introduced the cybernetic notion of autopoiesis (self-reproduction) to immunology (1973). German philosopher and sociologist Niklas Luhmann (1927–1998) observed that social systems (societies, organizations, interactions) are no doubt open in their energy inputs. As communication systems, however, they can be more fruitfully conceived of as autopoietic—self-reproducing and self-referential—just like DNA cells[5] (Luhmann, 1984/1995).

DNA cells, like any other part of an organism, depend on oxygen, water and nutrition for their survival, and in this sense, they are open to the environment.

But their mission is to carry information that will allow for the reproduction of the same organism, no matter what the environment. The possibility of inheriting functional adaptations has long been rejected as fraudulent. It is assumed that evolution happens via random mutation, creating variation, which is, in turn, reduced by selection. Thus, DNA cannot improve upon itself.

Autopoietic systems are not only self-organizing in the sense of structuring their elements and processes, but also self-producing: They construct their elements and processes. They exist in an environment, but the relationships with this environment are of their own making. By saying this, Luhmann spoke in parallel with Karl Weick (1988), whose concept of enactment was close to Luhmann's idea, although in Luhmann's terms the environment is "en-communicated" rather than en-acted.

Luhmann's "cognitive constructionism", as Karin Knorr Cetina (1994) labeled it, is truly helpful in understanding otherwise puzzling developments in formal organizations, which constantly attempt to reform themselves without achieving the desired results (see e.g. Brunsson & Olsen, 1993 for a review of studies of such reforms).

In Luhmann's terminology, people move from acting to observing, from action to communication. The system observes itself; it cannot change, because it observes itself from the same set of categories that constitutes it. But for a while, it stops doing whatever it was doing. One consequence could be reinforcement of its past functioning in the future; another could be a faulty reproduction of previous patterns, which, indeed, can introduce change.

But if so, what do management consultants do, employed by organizations to help them introduce change, and usually plentifully rewarded for doing just that? Luhmann was among the first of social scientists to pay attention to the phenomenon of consulting.

Luhmann questioned any possibility of a successful communication between consultants and their clients, as their acts of communication form two distinct and closed systems (Luhmann, 1989/2005). A communicative event, according to Luhmann, consists of information, utterance and meaning. Whereas the information transmitted and received may be identical, and although all parties may perceive the fact of the utterance, the meaning is produced within the system, where communications can refer only to what belongs to the system itself. Autopoietic systems are, by definition, idiosyncratic, and a successful communication among different systems is impossible. Any communicative event over the system boundaries will become different when processed inside. The systems can shout to each other, as it were, but what reaches them is but a reflection of their own voices. So what, if anything, is the role of management consultants?

According to Luhmann, consultants were supposed to communicate the accessible results of science in such a way that their clients could put them into practice. This would mean either that science is completely understandable (and thus there is no need for consultants) or that consultants speak exactly the same language as their clients (which means that there is no difference between them, and again no need for the consultants).

> That a group of consultants [. . .] cannot communicate itself completely (but is nonetheless capable of communicating internally about this impossibility of external communication) is due to the fact that communication is the operation by means of which the group carries its own autopoiesis, and thus the means by which it regenerates its own unity, as well as the difference between this unity and its environment.
>
> (Luhmann, 1989/2005, p. 355)

From Luhmann's radical viewpoint, clients and consultants live in two worlds, and will never meet. They do try to communicate, however, and with increasing frequency, but not so much with one another as with their own wider system, including those organizations and institutions that shape their world views: institutionalized practices, communities of practices, taken-for-granted norms and values, for instance.

Building on Luhmann's ideas and connecting them to the institutional theory of organizations, Alfred Kieser (2002, p. 216) has noted that this all happens because organizations are able to react "only to the environmental changes as they are recorded and interpreted by the system", and act only according to their own logic—by the means of organizational routines and codes embedding these memories and interpretations—even while trying to change. If this is so, why does consulting exist and prosper? Luhmann has offered an explanation for and justification of the existence of management consultants. In his view, the attempts at communication produced by management consultants serve as an irritant to the client system (Czarniawska & Mazza, 2012). Left to themselves, clients would be enacting their own visions of the world (Weick, 1988) until some serious crisis stopped them. Thus, even if consultants cannot communicate their different vision of the world to their clients, their very attempts to communicate may provoke client reaction in a way that is similar to the external jolts that Greenwood, Suddaby and Hinings (2002) have described as change triggers.

In a similar vein, but with no reference to Luhmann, Clegg, Kornberger and Rhodes (2004) use the word "parasites"—a term borrowed from Michel Serres—to describe the role of consultants in their relationships with clients.[6] In the Clegg et al.'s conceptualization, "parasitic consultants" are able to disturb a system because "they are in between, neither here nor there but in the middle" (2004, p. 39). This suggestion does resonate with Luhmann's concept of consultants as external irritants, who produce changes not by directly relating to clients, but by stimulating (from outside) the client's social system.

Organizing as De-Paradoxifying

One of Luhmann's interests concerned paradoxes and the ways in which people deal with them (Luhmann, 1991). He noted that the usual criticism of paradoxes and the urge to 'solve them' has to do with the fact that they violate logic. Yet logic is but a conventional way of describing the image of the world, which came into being through the Indo-European languages. It is a linear, one-dimensional set of rules, and the fact that people agreed to and adhere to logic (or at least claim doing so) makes it easier to communicate with one another. Or so it is believed. Thus paradoxes are not attributes of social systems, but the result of using the logical analysis as an observation tool (Luhmann, 1986/2005).

According to Luhmann (1995, p. 95), logic is possible only because the world of meaning encompasses all the contradictions: "Otherwise, the minute one first encountered a contradiction, one would fall into a meaning gap and disappear". The very awareness of an alternative would be paralyzing: "Even Buridan's ass, placed, as it were, between two equally tempting bales of hay, will survive, even if it notices that it cannot decide, for that is why it decides nevertheless!" (Luhmann, 1995, p. 360). The donkey is not an observer; if hungry, it will start eating whichever bale, without making a decision. Contradiction—in life and in science—grinds observation to a halt and demands action. Observations can occur only at a distance, establishing distinctions until they become paradoxical.[7] Then it is time to drop the observer's stance, to come closer and start acting.

This is why the prescription for dealing with paradoxes is clear: They must be eliminated. This urge to dissolve paradoxes does not come merely from the unpleasantness of encountering a logical error: No matter how reflective their attitude toward paradoxes, actors necessarily engage in the process of "deparadoxization" (Luhmann, 1991).

In traditional organization studies, as noted by Van de Ven and Scott Poole (1988), a quest for coherent and consistent theory led to the neglect of organizational paradoxes. The paradoxes observed during fieldwork were taken to be cases of "anomalous communication" (Manning, 1992). And yet this anomalous communication lies at the heart of contemporary institutions. In my study of Swedish public sector organizations in the late 1980s (Czarniawska, 1997), I noticed that the existence of paradoxes in everyday organizing seemed not only to paralyze action, but also to stimulate it. My findings were corroborated by Luhmann's suggestion that "because the paradox cripples observation, it can be understood as an inducement, even as a compulsion to solution" (1998, p. 112).

At least three well-known and practiced strategies in organizations exist in order to deparadoxize: temporization, spatialization and relativization. Temporization, according to Hans-Ulrich Gumbrecht, Luhmann's follower and a literature theoretician, amounts to narrativization (1991). The contradictory elements become detached in time and the conflict is resolved in the future. Thurman Arnold had already claimed in 1935 that "[t]his technique is as old as the parables of the New Testament. It is only its dialectical formulation that is modern" (p. 30).

Conflicting issues can be decoupled not merely over time but also in space; thus the strategy of spatialization (March, 1988; Manning, 1992):

The antitheses are simultaneously present, but not in the same place. Separate committees or working groups can deal with contradictory matters simultaneously; once resolved, they may not be contradictory anymore.

Sometimes, however, neither temporization nor spatialization works. The promise of a synthesis in the future was not convincing; the committees meet in the corridor by mistake, and no longer stick to the issues in their domains. Decentralization is perceived by the people subjected to it as centrally ordered—a paradox that is a source of frustration and a cause of apathy for them. The deparadoxization strategy used in this context consists of explaining different perceptions by the different levels of observation, where first-level observers are assumed to be blind to their own positions and roles in the system ("if you were in their place, you would see it differently").

It should be added that even this strategy fits the possibilities of the narrative perfectly. It is a matter of actorial shifting operations (Latour, 1988), whereby the reader or listener can see the world through the eyes of one or another first-level observer but, by virtue of being a second-level observer, can also understand the limitations of that "native" point of view. Luhmann talked in this context not of a narrative but of a rhetorical tradition.

When none of the deparadoxization strategies works, plunging blindly into action may. It requires the creation of a blind spot, a jump into one part of the paradox, into a distinction, therefore losing sight of the site on which the distinction must be made. Acting may produce "a difference that makes difference" (Luhmann, 1991, p. 69). In this way, autopoietic systems resolve their paradoxes themselves, and only an observer perceives it as a problem. "The autopoiesis does not stop when confronted by logical contradictions: It jumps, provided that possibilities of further communication are close enough at hand" (Luhmann, 1986/ 2005, p. 180).

Luhmann was right: Practitioners tend to abhor reflection and escape into action, hoping for its deparadoxizing effects. Indeed, the increased visibility of paradoxes signals an epistemological crisis within a tradition (MacIntyre, 1988), which in an organizational context usually takes the form of a legitimacy crisis or an identity crisis. The direct experience of paradox is threatening to people and institutions; as a topic for reflection—when the experience is indirect—it may lead to renewal. Paradox can thus be seen as an opportunity for the renewal of language and the transformation of institutions.

Luhmann (1998) was not that optimistic: He saw modern society as a society of observers of systems,[8] a society that was forced, therefore, to resign from authority and to espouse ignorance. In present times, his consequent opinion about protests may be of interest:

> Protest movements (. . .) result from the transformation of ignorance into impatience. They replace ignorance through the knowledge that waiting is no longer an acceptable option, because knowing would come too late if at all. They are superior in this reflectivity to all others

> that offer any resistance. But this produces an uncertainty that can slip into irresponsibility. We already have a culture of concern, if not to say a cultivated fear, that is in search of goals. Whether we can get to a culture of unconvinced understanding is still open.
>
> (Luhmann, 1998, p. 103)

In Other Words: Can We Live Together?

What Do Latour and Luhmann Have in Common?

A lot. First of all, transdisciplinarity. Is Latour a philosopher, a sociologist, an anthropologist or a science and technology scholar? He claims different affiliations in different interviews. Was Luhmann a philosopher, a sociologist, a political scientist, a law scholar or a practitioner of administration? Although they both contributed to social sciences, their inspiration came from art and literature, from engineering and biology. Whereas neither of them would consider himself to be an organization scholar (but see Latour, 2012), both appreciated the importance of organizing process and made a strong contribution to refreshing the way it is being studied and written about. They were also keynote speakers at European Group for Organization Studies (EGOS) conferences: Luhmann in 1985, Latour in 1991 and 2012. The two volumes of collected works, *ANT and Organizing* (Czarniawska & Hernes, 2005) and *Niklas Luhmann and Organization Studies* (Seidl & Becker, 2005, 2006), are early and good examples of their influence, which continues (see e.g. Kühl, 2013/2016; Belliger & Krieger, 2016; Mike, 2017).

Next, they were both constructivists, though Luhmann did not use the word (see Czarniawska & Mazza, 2012), and Latour changed the verb "construct" to "assembly", after constructivism had been kidnapped by idealists, who use it in the meaning practically opposite to that intended by, for example, Russian *konstruktivists* (Czarniawska, 2003). The difference lies mainly in the fact that Luhmann was interested in communication, and Latour was interested in things. In Luhmann's opinion (2001, p. 13), philosophers are interested in things, and poets in communication (he was preparing a new project focusing on connections between poetry and social sciences).

They both knew and quoted Gabriel Tarde before 'tardomania' settled in (Latour, 2001; Luhmann, 1998), and were interested in Whitehead's philosophy. And although Latour was skeptical about "autopoietic systems" when treated as "an underlying framework" (2005, p. 156) and "a description of what is the common world" (2005, p. 189), he also called a text an excellent narrative if it prepares us "to take up the political tasks of composition" (Latour, 2001) and quoted Luhmann's works on law systems. Pity that Luhmann could not answer Latour's comments. As I see it, the idea of autopoietic systems does not have to be an underlying framework (and certainly not an ontological axiom), but is a useful way to explain strange phenomena that may be noted while using an ANT approach.

They both wrote in a rather complex way in their mother tongues, though Latour soon started writing in English, while Luhmann is at the mercy of his translators[9] (whose mercy varies, alas).

Finally, if you happen to believe some literature scholars, from Propp (1928/1968) to Booker (2004), who claim that archetypical plots exist, the analogy between those plots and the DNA is only too obvious. Macro actors are built in accordance with the same plot, and organizations reproduce themselves in accordance with the same template.

This text is about European influences on management and organization theory, and there is no doubt that both Latour and Luhmann influenced it—but, again, the European version of it. Our US colleagues somehow did not become interested in those two thinkers, although they should be well known even on the other side of the Atlantic. In 2007, Bruno Latour was ranked by the *Times Higher Education Supplement* as one of the ten most cited authors in the humanities, living or dead, and his first study published in English was conducted in Stanford, California. Niklas Luhmann has been made known to US scholars not least due to the efforts of Hans Ulrich Gumbrecht, a professor at Stanford University. Yet there must be something uniquely European about their work that does not resonate in the USA. They are both better known in Canada and are often quoted together by the same authors (see e.g. Brummans et al., 2014; Cooren, 2015; Cooren, Taylor, & Van Every, 2006). Perhaps, as Moeller (2012) suggested, the US readers of social sciences are used to textbook style, with a pedagogical way of introducing and summarizing the author's arguments. Well, neither of the two wrote in this way, and I for one am grateful.

Notes

1. The same anthology contained a chapter by Niklas Luhmann: "Communication About Law in Interaction Systems" (1981).
2. Several business historians found ANT to be a useful approach in their studies (see e.g. Durepos & Mills, 2012; Ponzoni & Boersma, 2011).
3. Callon's influence on management and organization theory is also obvious, but it is not my goal to tackle it in this text.
4. The influence of this work is especially visible in such organization studies as those of Porsander (2005) and Tryggestad (2005).
5. Maturana protested against the idea that non-biological (social) systems can be autopoietic, but gave up later: "I was not prepared to accept all the consequences of my own theory" Maturana and Poerksen (2004, p. 106).
6. Luhmann was familiar with Serres' notion, however (2000, p. 60).
7. On paradoxical character of decision making, see Pors and Andersen (2015).
8. In Gumbrecht's (2001, p. 52) opinion, Luhmann was less interested in autopoietic systems in his final years, and more in the observer theory. But "self-observation is an essential characteristic of autopoietic systems" (Luhmann, 1990, p. 244).
9. But see Moeller (2012), the chapter "Why He Wrote Such Bad Books". I was not able to read more than an article in German, and know Luhmann's books from the translations, so I am unable to share or oppose this judgment.

References

Arnold, Thurman W. (1935). *The symbols of government*. New Haven: Yale University Press.

Belliger, Andréa & Krieger, David J. (2016). *Organizing networks: An Actor-Network Theory of organizations*. Bielefeld: Transcript-verlag.

Booker, Christopher (2004). *The seven basic plots: Why we tell stories*. New York, NY: Continuum.

Brummans, Boris, H.J.M., Cooren, François, Robichaud, Daniel & Taylor, James R. (2014). Approaches in research on the communicative constitution of organizations. In L.L. Putnam & D. Mumby (Eds.), *SAGE handbook of organizational communication* (3rd ed., pp. 173–194). Thousand Oaks, CA: Sage.

Brunsson, Nils & Olsen, Johan P. (Eds.) (1993). *The reforming organization*. London: Routledge.

Callon, Michel & Latour, Bruno (1981). Unscrewing the big Leviathan or how do actors macrostructure reality and how sociologists help them to do so. In K. Knorr & A. Cicourel (Eds.), *Advances in social theory and methodology: Toward an integration of micro and macro sociologies* (pp. 277–303). London: Routledge & Kegan Paul.

Clegg, Stewart R., Kornberger, Martin & Rhodes, Carl (2004). Noise, parasites and translation: Theory and practice in management consulting. *Management Learning*, 35, 31–44.

Cooren, François (2015). *Organizational discourse*. Cambridge: Polity Press.

Cooren, François, Taylor, James R. & Van Every, Elizabeth J. (2006). *Communication as organizing*. Mahwah, NJ: Lawrence Erlbaum Associates.

Czarniawska, Barbara (1997). *Narrating the organization: Dramas of institutional identity*. Chicago, IL: The University of Chicago Press.

Czarniawska, Barbara (2003). Social constructionism and organization studies. In R. Westwood & S. Clegg (Eds.), *Debating organization: Point-counterpoint in organization studies* (pp. 128–139). Melbourne: Blackwell Publishing.

Czarniawska, Barbara (2005). On Gorgon sisters: Organizational action in the face of paradox. In D. Seidl & K.H. Becker (Eds.), *Niklas Luhmann and organization studies* (pp. 127–142). Lund/Copenhagen: Liber/CBS Press.

Czarniawska, Barbara (2014). Bruno Latour: An accidental organization theorist. In P. Adler, P. du Gay, G. Morgan & M. Reed (Eds.), *The Oxford handbook of sociology, social theory and organization studies* (pp. 87–105). Oxford: Oxford University Press.

Czarniawska, Barbara (2017a). Actor-network theory. In A. Langley & H. Tsoukas (Eds.), *The SAGE handbook of process organization studies* (pp. 160–173). London: Sage.

Czarniawska, Barbara (2017b). Organization studies as symmetric ethnology. *Journal of Organizational Ethnography*, 6(1): 2–10.

Czarniawska, Barbara & Hernes, Tor (Eds.) (2005). *ANT and organizing*. Lund/Copenhagen: Liber/CBS Press.

Czarniawska, Barbara & Mazza, Carmelo (2012). Consultants and clients from constructivist perspectives. In M. Kipping & T. Clark (Eds.), *The Oxford handbook of management consulting* (pp. 427–446). Oxford: Oxford University Press.

Durepos, Gabie & Mills, Albert J. (2012). Actor network theory, ANTi-history, and critical organizational historiography. *Organization*, 19(6), 703–721.

Greenwood, Royston, Suddaby, Roy & Hinings, C. R. (2002). Theorizing change: The role of professional associations in the transformation of institutionalized fields. *Academy of Management Journal*, 45, 58–80.

Greimas, Algirdas Julien & Courtés, Joseph (1982). *Semiotics and language: An analytical dictionary*. Bloomington: Indiana University Press.

Gumbrecht, Hans Ulrich (1991). Inszenierte Zusammenbrüche oder: Tragödie und Paradox. In H.-U. Gumbrecht & K.L. Pfeiffer (Eds.), *Paradoxien, Dissonanzen, Zusammenbrüche. Situationen offener Epistemologie* (pp. 471–494). Frankfurt: Suhrkamp.

Gumbrecht, Hans Ulrich (2001). How is our future contingent? Reading Luhmann against Luhmann. *Theory, Culture & Society*, 18(1), 49–58.

Kieser, Alfred (2002). Managers as marionettes? Using fashion theories to explain the success of consultants. In M. Kipping & L. Engwall (Eds.), *Management consulting: Emergence and dynamics of a knowledge industry* (pp. 167–183). Oxford, UK: Oxford University Press.

Knorr Cetina, Karin (1994). Primitive classification and postmodernity: Towards a sociological notion of fiction. *Theory, Culture and Society*, 11, 1–22.

Kühl, Stefan (2013/2016). *Organizations: A systems approach*. New York: Routledge.

Latour, Bruno (1988). A relativistic account of Einstein's relativity. *Social Studies of Science*, 18, 3–44.

Latour, Bruno (1992). Technology is society made durable. In J. Law (Ed.), *A sociology of monsters: Essays on power, technology and domination* (pp. 103–131). London: Routledge.

Latour, Bruno (1993). *We have never been modern*. Cambridge, MA: Harvard University Press.

Latour, Bruno (1996). *Aramis or the love of technology*. Cambridge, MA: Harvard University Press.

Latour, Bruno (2001). Gabriel Tarde and the end of the social. In P. Joyce (Ed.), *The social in question: New bearings in history and the social sciences* (pp. 117–132). London: Routledge.

Latour, Bruno (2005). *Reassembling the social*. Oxford: Oxford University Press.

Latour, Bruno (2010). Coming out as a philosopher. *Social Studies of Science*, 40(4), 599–608.

Latour, Bruno (2012). "What's the story?" Organizing as a mode of existence. In J.-H. Passoth, B. Peuker & M. Schillmeier (Eds.), *Agency without actors? New approaches to collective action* (pp. 163–177). New York: Routledge.

Latour, Bruno & Woolgar, Steve (1979/1986). *Laboratory life: An anthropologist at work*. Princeton, NJ: Princeton University Press.

Luhmann, Niklas (1981). Communication about law in interaction systems. In K. Knorr & A. Cicourel (Eds.), *Advances in social theory and methodology: Toward an integration of micro and macro sociologies* (pp. 234–256). London: Routledge & Kegan Paul.

Luhmann, Niklas (1984/1995). *Social systems*. Stanford, CA: Stanford University Press.

Luhmann, Niklas (1986/2005). The autopoiesis of social systems. In D. Seidl & K.H. Becker (Eds.), *Niklas Luhmann and organization studies* (pp. 64–82). Lund/Copenhagen: Liber/CBS Press.

Luhmann, Niklas (1989/2005). Communication barriers in management consulting. In D. Seidl & K.H. Becker (Eds.), *Niklas Luhmann and organization studies* (pp. 351–364). Lund/Copenhagen: Liber/CBS Press.

Luhmann, Niklas (1990). *Essays on self-reference*. New York: Columbia University Press.

Luhmann, Niklas (1991). Sthenographie und Euryalistik. In H.-U. Gumbrecht & K.-L. Pfeiffer (Eds.), *Paradoxien, Dissonanzen, Zusammenbrüche. Situationen offener Epistemologie* (pp. 58–82). Frankfurt: Suhrkamp.

Luhmann, Niklas (1998). *Observations on modernity*. Stanford, CA: Stanford University Press.

Luhmann, Niklas (2000). *The reality of the mass media*. Cambridge: Polity Press.

Luhmann, Niklas (2001). Notes on the project "Poetry and social theory". *Theory, Culture & Society*, 18(1), 15–27.

MacIntyre, Alasdair (1988). *Whose justice? Which rationality?* London: Duckworth.

Manning, Peter K. (1992). *Organizational communication*. New York: Aldine de Gruyter.

March, James G. (1988). *Decisions and organizations*. Oxford: Blackwell.

Maturana, Humbert R. & Poerksen, Bernhard (2004). *From being to doing: The origins of the biology of cognition*. Heidelberg: Carl Auer International.

Maturana, Humbert R. & Varela, Francisco J. (1973). *Autopoiesis and cognition: The realization of the living*. Dordrecht: D. Reidel.

Meyer, John & Rowan, Brian (1977). Institutionalized organizations: Formal structure as myth and ceremony. *American Journal of Sociology*, 83, 340–363.

Mike, Michael (2017). *Actor-network theory*. London: Sage.

Moeller, Hans Georg (2012). *The radical Luhmann*. New York: Columbia University Press.

Ponzoni, Elena & Boersma, Kees (2011). Writing history for business. *Management & Organizational History*, 6(2), 123–143.

Pors, Justine G. & Andersen, Nils Å. (2015). Playful organizations: Undecidability as a scarce resource. *Culture and Organization*, 21(4), 338–354.

Porsander, Lena (2005). "My name is lifebuoy": An actor-network emerging from an action net. In B. Czarniawska & T. Hernes (Eds.), *Actor-network theory and organizing* (pp. 14–30). Malmö/Copenhagen: Liber/CBS Press.

Propp, Vladimir (1928/1968). *Morphology of the folktale*. Austin: University of Texas Press.

Seidl, David & Becker, Kai Helge (Eds.) (2005). *Niklas Luhmann and organization studies*. Lund/Copenhagen: Liber/CBS Press.

Seidl, David & Becker, Kai Helge (Eds.) (2006). Special Issue on Niklas Luhmann and organization studies. *Organization*, 13(1).

Serres, Michel (1974/1982). *Hermes: Literature, science, philosophy*. Baltimore, MD: John Hopkins University Press.

Tryggestad, Kjell (2005). Technological strategy as macro-actor: How humanness may be made of steel. In B. Czarniawska & T. Hernes (Eds.), *Actor-network theory and organizing* (pp. 31–49). Malmö/Copenhagen: Liber/CBS Press.

Van de Ven, Andrew H. & Scott Poole, Marshall (1988). Paradoxical requirements for a theory of organizational change. In R.E. Quinn & K. S. Cameron (Eds.), *Paradox and transformation: Toward a theory of change in organization and management* (pp. 19–80). New York: HarperCollins.

Weick, Karl E. (1988). Enacted sensemaking in crisis situations. *Journal of Management Studies*, 25, 305–317.

5 Art, Philosophy and Business

Turns to Speculative Realism in European Management Scholarship

Pierre Guillet de Monthoux

Opening Gambit: The Bankruptcy of Speculative Fiction

Believe it or not, some areas of academia are worse off than business studies. And given that a quarter of college freshmen still pick business programs, that business faculty members remain in demand, and that business journals and publishers continue to ferret out meaningful research, the legitimacy of this statement would seem indisputable. At the same time, however, US-based experts like Mie Augier and Jim March declare that B schools are stuck between "greed as a social virtue and the substitution of lessons of experience for lessons of analysis and research" (2011, p. 322). Ellen O'Connor (2011) echoes these concerns when she advocates a reconnection with great books popular during the early part of the last century, specifically the work of Mary Parker Follett, a leader in classical management theory, and Chester Barnard, groundbreaking pioneer in management theory and organizational studies. The nostalgia for times when American elites had spiritual stature is also identifiable in Harvard Business School professor Rakesh Khurana's *From Higher Aims to Hired Hands* (2009); he concludes that US business schools fall short in turning out managers who achieve "meaning from their work", and even worse, are unable to "creat[e] meaning for others". Moneymaking overshadows the quest for professional value, and curricular absorption in profit-making strategies leaves little room for the ethical development of future managers. Even though admissions data, professional job openings and research opportunities seem healthy, something is amiss in the picture. Recalibrating the benchmarks for business education requires a moral rearmament against the harsh instrumentality that serves outright greed. In most current American writing on business education, for example, management scholars are encouraged to staunch the tide of the value-drowning philosophy that corrupts their curricula; their responsibility is to evangelize the good and offer students the entertaining fictions of dreaming up a better world before stepping into their personal reality of paying off humongous student loans and taking up positions in US corporations pretending to operate in spheres separate from societal politics (Rasche, 2014). Following the narrative turn in research, good samples of poetic vision and excellent storytelling (Czarniawska-Joerges & Guillet de Monthoux, 1994; Dewandre, 2002; Rombach & Solli, 2006; Sköldberg, 2002) do exist in the works of mainly European management scholars, however, and so it may be that the alleged solution to the business school crises could in fact be a cause of future bankruptcies in research and education. Four Euro-based perspectives can help management scholars effect the transition from narrative speculative fictions to a more promising speculative realism constantly empirically preoccupied with searching the soul of relevance for European management research (Hernes, 2014b).

Play and the Real

The US study *Rethinking Undergraduate Business Education: Liberal Learning for the Profession* (Colby, Ehrlich, Sullivan, & Dolle, 2011) departs from standard moralistic complaints. It reports on a recent investigation by the Carnegie Foundation for the Advancement of Higher Education that convincingly recommends a reverse of the half-century streamlining of business education that followed the publication of the first Carnegie Report (Pierson, 1959). While the first report made business academics eager to deliver management as science, the second report leaves behind the simplistic faith-based dualism of either evil-instrumentality-Scylla or do-good-idealism-Charybdis and advocates a third position, a position that has been well received by European management scholars. The report proposes liberal learning, which integrates the humanities, as the third way to better management education.

The Carnegie Report of 2011 immediately kicked off a US–EU debate at the "Copenhagen Roundtable: Integrating the Humanities and Liberal Arts in Business Education", hosted by Copenhagen Business School. Later the conversation snowballed into an intense exchange with US colleagues at an "Aspen Institute Undergraduate Business Education Consortium". Over the next two years, well-attended American Academy of Management Professional Development Workshops at conferences showed continued interest in and response to the issue. The ongoing debate is now materializing in academic publications like the *Journal of Management Education* special issue (Statler & Guillet de Monthoux, 2015), and additional European publications on practicing humanities and social sciences in management education are in the pipeline. Slowly we are trying to make sense of what Jim Walsh, former president of the American Academy of Management, meant when he proclaimed with genuine Yankee enthusiasm, "You Europeans seem much closer to the Carnegie Report than we!"

In the 2011 report Carnegie writers observed how instructors miss the teachable moments provided by what is actually going on around them. Instead of tackling current financial crises head-on, for example, they become more entrenched in the comfort zones of old theory, ignoring the fact that it no longer fits the real terrain of business. It is time to let reflection, practical reasoning and multiple framing accompany analytical thinking in business schools and to get hold of realism from what is offered in a liberal arts education. The Carnegie Report unreservedly challenges a blinding hegemony of logical empiricism in management research, a paradigm that became normal science under the banner of Herbert Simon's "bounded rationality", the successful cocktail of Chicago-school thinking rooted in the rigid analytical philosophy à la Rudolf Carnap. The lack of any competitive perspective may explain why clever criticisms, from James March's biting "Technology of Foolishness" (1971) to Robert Austin's plea for managerial artfulness and trust instead of agency theory (Austin, 1996; Austin & Devin, 2003), seldom go beyond a playful holiday away from the dominating mindset. Concepts like instrumentality and rationality seem immune to criticism and in addition are used as straw men legitimizing the writing of irony (Johansson & Woodilla, 2005). It may be acceptable to play around for a while—to poke fun with prejudice and without the mindfulness to see what really happens—provided you get serious by the end of the day (Manz, 2014)! Playfulness even risks becoming an integral part of the metaphysical reproduction of seriousness by a dominating economic paradigm (Gustafsson, 2011). Playfully tossing liberal arts courses into a weighty business curriculum is a first step, but it is hardly enough. Can we expect a natural integration—perhaps like an osmotic effect—to take place in the heads of clever business students? Will vast numbers of them give teachers of the humanities high scores because they are fun edutainers, jesters in dull management-science courts?

Critique and the Real

Ten years ago Luc Boltanski, a former collaborator with French cultural sociologist Pierre Bourdieu, in cooperation with Eve Chiapello, B-school accounting professor researching artists and managers in cultural enterprises, published a study of *The New Spirit of Capitalism* (2005); the framework of their book is a comparison of French management textbooks from the 1960s and 1990s. They point out that contemporary capitalism depends increasingly on a 'new spirit' motivating work that develops when managers participate in and bring home public political debates. The 'new spirit' differs from the 'old spirit' of capitalism of Max Weber's Protestant ethic, for example, which is a more static view of how capitalist ideology works as quasi-religion. The making of the 'new spirit' depicted by Boltanski and Chiapello is a muddling-through process and not an outcome of neat clashes between practical instrumentality and theoretical idealism. In fact Boltanski actually severed ties with Pierre Bourdieu's more dualistic view of a gap between the cultural and the commercial. Boltanski believed critical influence is not achieved when rooted in the pure universal principles studied in university libraries or liberal arts courses. Reading Boltanski and Chiapello enables us to see the intertwining of humanities and business—what

Carnegie authors simplify as a double helix—as a pretty bleak and bloodless version of how 'new spirit' really emerges. What makes critique perform in French management is a concrete and often violent bricolage stirred up in the melting pots of French politics.

This is a relatively new phenomenon, for management has not always been so intermixed with society in France. Once upon a time it was a subject exclusively for engineering schools and some Hautes Études Commerciales (HECs), semi-public business schools financially dependent on regional chambers of commerce. These schools mimicked elite institutions like the famous Napoleonic engineering school Ecole Polytechnique. They educated not managers but functional cadres (Boltanski, 1982), framing blue- and white-collar company workers in the formal work organization we know from classicists of industrial management such as Henri Fayol. Cadres turned into managers and entrepreneurs between 1960 and 1990, with the May 1968 student revolt being the turning point. In the US an MBA student could abandon society and study monastically in a capitalist cloister of some Ivy League business school. Perhaps that too was a consequence of the French HEC business school moving its campus out of downtown Paris. Nevertheless the French managers that Boltanski and Chiapello depict are pretty street-smart crawlers in the revolutionary backwaters of Lacan, Althusser or Nietzsche. They may well study Michael Porter or his local clones, but French business depends on capitalist sophists performing their Deleuze–Guattarian "lines of flight" and getting their kinky intellectual kicks out of philosophers' protests against their shameless co-option of originally anti-capitalist ideas. It seems the European "new spirit" evolves a world apart from the aseptic campus conversations on the American management model (Djelic, 2001). This form of European management erupts in Parisian street demonstrations and echoes clever catchwords stolen from leftist intellectual salons. Boltanski and Chiapello depict and deplore the dirty business of French capitalism thriving on the chaos created in the 68 movement. They show how capitalists fittest to survive navigate in the company of Marx and Freud; most successful French brands like Club-Med or Agnes B. were shaped by entrepreneurs primarily schooled in Maoist and Trotskyite activism.

The philosophical turn of French capitalism was eased considerably when postmodernism finally unseated the communist party monopoly over French intellectual life, and that philosophy contributed to the blurring of business and society (Dosse, 1998). After the Berlin Wall crumbled, when Ossie-communist playwright Heiner Müller applauded the Wessie management guru Dirk Baecker (1994), intellectual French managers had already welcomed the postmodern thinkers, who, like Bernard Henri Levy and Francois Lyotard, had stopped postulating clear distinctions between culture and commerce. In the US, French theory (Cusset, 2008) was recycled by cultural studies; in Europe alert managers gladly gobbled it up!

The critique perspective has of course long been central to business. Reforms are responses to 'social critique' rooted in indignation about human suffering, injustice and inequality. In Europe, especially in a German Hegelian tradition, 'social critique' co-created modern management already seen in the late nineteenth century. European management doctrines like Betriebswirtschaftlehre (BWL) were the heart of reform management. BWL, still a dominant German academic doctrine on management—traveling mostly under the radar of Anglo-Saxon scholarship—originated as an academic dynastic business founded by Eugen Schmalenbach (1873–1955) in the early twentieth century; it was updated by his successor Erich Gutenberg (1897–1984) and after WWII democratized and pimped with US footnotes by Gutenberg's son-in-law Horst Albach (1931–). Similar examples are the Swiss management doctrine based on system thinking designed by Hans Ulrich (1919–1997) for St Gallen Business School in the 1950s. Historically the German models have roots back to feudal Kameralism, Bismarckian economic reforms co-opting revolutionary Marxian critique; all this was integrated into Nazi managerial corporatism. Few are aware of how much organization theory owes to the Verein für Sozialpolitik, an impressive state think-tank Bismarck founded in 1873. Here experts Max Weber, Werner Sombart and Georg Simmel worked to, in the words of the German economist Schmoller, "lift, educate, and reconcile the lower classes on the basis of the existing order, so that they would fit into the organism in harmony and peace". Later the Frankfurt School helped democratize Marx, and Jürgen Habermas, star student of Horkheimer's and Adorno's Institute for Social Research, actually also inspired German management research. In Scandinavia, stakeholder models of management enabled Social Democrats to secure peaceful cooperation between employers and unions by appropriate management education. No doubt this was inspired by the New Deal ideology that once permeated US business education. In the northern European political context, the demand for stakeholder models to rescue the 'old spirit' of the welfare state still exists. Rock-and-roll revolutionaries of critical management are handy idiots for preserving the old spirit. Today on the left, mantras like 'power is bad' or 'we all are equal' neatly counterbalance neo-liberal slogans about 'the market'. In the long run, critical management primarily fuels on ideals from speculative fictions to the political left and right. Boltanski and Chiapello actually recommend dropping static 'critical theory' and replacing it with a dynamic 'theory of critique'. For management this means leaving the storytelling of critical management for a realist quest for management by critique.

Aesthetics and the Real

This hypothesis of Boltanski and Chiapello was refuted by German sociologist Andreas Reckwitz (2012), for whom the artistic critique today is hyped into an aesthetic reality. The artistic critique was, Reckwitz thinks, an avant-garde mesmerizing of our world by 'creativity' and 'newness'. Therefore a social critique can only reemerge as embedded in a hegemony of aesthetics that thrives on what he calls a "creativity-dispositive". Drawing mostly on European evidence and reflections, Reckwitz argues that we live in a reality of a global aesthetic state (Chytry, 1989, 2009) with management as aesthetic world making (Béjean, 2008; Goodman, 1968, 1978; Guillet de Monthoux, 2004; Hjorth & Steyart, 2009; Kapferer & Bastien, 2009; Riot, Chamaret, & Rigaud, 2013).

The artistic critique of Boltanski and Chiapello voices individuals' objections to modernity in the tradition of bohemian anarchists revolting against bourgeois society in the nineteenth century. To some extent this was supported by old European aesthetics, the special philosophy legitimizing cutting loose from rational, cognitive and moral ties. Aesthetics interacts with ethics but indirectly. Authenticity here rests on freedom from morality and pragmatism. Reckwitz acknowledges the importance of this old aesthetics, the philosophy rendered by European Kantian and Romantic traditions, but acknowledges that the new aesthetics differs. Kant saw aesthetics as his "third" critique; the contemporary aesthetic philosopher Graham Harman (2011, 2012) recently dubbed the new aesthetics a "first philosophy". Artistic critique was seen coming from 'outside', but today's hegemony of aesthetics is strictly an 'inside' phenomenon. The Romantic tradition transformed Kant's aesthetics into transcendental philosophy; it became associated with something beyond and above society. What Reckwitz is treating, however, is a realist aesthetics growing from the inside with an immanent force of its "Eigendynamik" being "Selbstreferenziell" (2012, p. 19). The new aesthetics has an inner intensity unchecked and independent of external causes. The old one was more of a point of view one should balance with ethics and science. In his treatise, Reckwitz describes hegemonic colonization by such a new aesthetic as penetrating diverse fields, including city and regional planning, psychology of creativity, media, as well as management. Management is part and parcel of other practices that also converge, connect and hybridize with art. The hegemony of the new aesthetics makes all our worlds into art worlds to be managed with aesthetic competence and sensitivity. In the sense of Boltanski and Chiapello, we are certainly not all artists, but all is about art. Managers would do well to hang out with designers, artists, curators, architects, actors, dancers, conductors, directors or other performers! In his latest book, coauthored with Arnaud Esquerre, Luc Boltanski (2017) shows that old industrial capitalism has given way to aesthetic ways of making value highly inspired by art worlds; yet another reason for connecting to art!

Not only does the new aesthetics of Reckwitz forcefully drive a Kantian kale between the two other philosophies of science and ethics, it takes over! New aesthetics implies the marginalization of management as a science that has dominated for so long. Management scholars have fought to legitimize their academic status by aping "methodologies" for so long that they will have a hard time switching their (fake) social science identity to an aesthetics one. The aesthetic turn equally relaxes the focus on morals and the idea that only business ethics can keep capitalism in check. Reckwitz acknowledges the problem that the hegemony of aesthetics squeezes both the political and the religious into the margins. Creativity and newness become mainstream—not as the old transcendental 'beautiful and sublime'—but as a cool new aesthetics of the 'interesting', the 'surprising' and the 'original' with a philosophical sensitivity to the immanence of real, not ideal, metaphysical objects. We no more experience 'something' but take bare experiencing itself; we aim for 'feeling that we feel' and 'knowing that we know'. All this—and here we have a significant difference between old and new aesthetics—is conditioned and constructed by what Reckwitz calls "aesthetic apparatuses" enabling "aesthetic episodes" to unfold in economies where we all are performers and audiences (2012, p. 25). Management in the industrial society learns from manufacturing; in the knowledge society, from science—but to the aesthetic economy, art is central. This is much more about reality than fiction, and many European management scholars have seen it coming for quite some time.

Turns to the Real

The Carnegie Reports investigate cases of management education in innovative US business school classrooms; Boltanski and Chiapello compare European management textbooks; and Reckwitz suggests that a hegemony of aesthetics makes those connected to economic activities engage in art, fashion, design, architecture and the affective creation of atmospheres. From outside management scholarship, they all observe how scholars seem engaged in themes like play, critique, artistry and aesthetics. These outside observations reflect 'turns' taken inside the management field and engage European management scholarship in a fascinating new quest for the reality of business in society.

'The aesthetic turn' in management scholarship often manifests itself in conferences and publications. For example the 2012 European Group for Organization Studies (EGOS) conference in Helsinki, Finland, provided a prominent platform for a keynote address as 'an aesthetic turn' by Robin Holt, editor-in-chief of the European journal *Organization Studies*. To those noting how European management—via its connections to the now dominant theme of 'organization' in past decades—drifts toward philosophy, Holt's holding a London School of Economics (LSE) PhD in Wittgensteinian philosophy seems a no-brainer. That a leading European management and organization scholar writes on Heidegger and Nietzsche has, thanks to many years of European management scholarship, become almost self-evident. In fact as the co-author of a highly successful monograph on strategy (Chia & Holt, 2010), Holt once in a jokingly arrogant tone declared his writing strategy to be one of forgetting about previous writings on strategy in management. The aim was to break loose from old clichés and adventurously leapfrog from island to island of previous management research in the hope that one would land in a fresh new reality. A 'turn' knows what it wants to depart from and takes the risk of landing in an unknown reality. Holt's keynote developed into a playful lecture for young researchers, who wanted their submissions to his journal to be successful. Write something beautiful and attractive was the tongue-in-cheek advice of the speaker who for this occasion was elegantly clad by Westwood in a three-piece suit! In conclusion and to prove his point of how management scholarship should be performed, Professor Holt projected a slide with a small sculpture by the 1930s Bauhaus master Maholy-Nagy. Scholarship demands ARTicles, and journal editing is transfigured into aesthetic curating.

Not long afterward, Holt served as a co-editor of the *Oxford Handbook of Process Philosophy and Organization Studies* (Helin, Hernes, Hjorth, & Holt, 2014). Growing out of European research on entrepreneurship, the volume is a collection of essays on how continental philosophy might inspire management and organization. The philosophy proposed is far from analytical philosophy and logics of the kind used by mainstream decision and game theorists, operations researchers or financial economists for programming the computer algorithms of corporations. Analytical philosophy is no longer used by European management scholarship, which considers it a phenomenon of turning a paradigm into a corporate 'paradogma'. The new handbook openly signals a 'turn to continental philosophy' that has long been under preparation by European management scholarship (Albert, Hachtue, & Laufer, 2013; Fogh-Kirkeby, 2000; Gagliardi & Czarniawska, 2006; Göranzon, 1993; Griseri, 2013; Hernes, 2014a) but under the radars of most established research journals and their English-only readers. International awareness of old world intellectual traditions is, however, growing in legitimacy, making European management research actually climb the ladders of academic evaluations, contrary to what is claimed by Tammar B. Zilber (2015). As European scholars attempt to return to the realities excluded by the narrow analytical thinking dominating new world managerialism, no longer is their thinking filtered out and censored by 'straight' Anglo editors; they slowly become appreciated for insightful and intellectually sophisticated publications on management inquiry that qualifies to top management curricula (Alvesson & Sköldberg, 2010; Arbnor & Bjerke, 2009; Guillet de Monthoux & Statler, 2013; Quattrone, 2015; Scharmer, 2009; Steyaert, Beyes, & Parker, 2016; Strati, 1999).

'The linguistic turn' is another poetic Euro-piece performed over the years by European management scholarship as well. It of course resonates as one of many improvisations on the theme of Peter Winch's (1990) classical Wittgensteinian wake-up call for zombies of social science positivism. In the late 1960s Anthony Hopwood, a freshly minted Chicago PhD, rushed back to Europe to turn accounting research toward language. Some may even recall his immense intellectual curiosity that drove him to travel to Scandinavia upon hearing about the first PhD using the work of Michel Foucault in a management dissertation (Daudi, 1986). With political shrewdness he turned his back on positivistic and vocational accounting research and flung open an intellectual business school window, letting in the fresh air of anthropology and post-structuralism of Foucault, Derrida & Co. Hopwood soon curated this Euro-stuff on the scholarly platform of his journal

Accounting, Organization and Society, which in turn probably contributed in part to Oxford University's appointing him dean of the Saïd Business School. Without intellectual attraction and charm, not even a hefty endowment would have done the trick.

The question of whether 'the narrative turn' is a child of 'the linguistic turn' invites a scholarly debate. Certainly its fragrance had the philosophical dash of Austin (1962) further sophisticated by scholarship perfume-maker Barbara Czarniawska, who spiced it with intellectual aromas from Bruno Latour's anthropology-inspired elegant empirical program. Czarniawska attracted both colleagues and PhD students to empirical research of a concrete reality where hard facts became far more fascinating than the logical computer-dreams of management science. Outside the rigid academic bureaucracies of teaching institutions, where deans alienated from scholarly work anxiously count Google Scholar beans and outsource academic judgment to editorial boards, European scholarship exhibited the turns on European platforms such as the EGOS and European Academy of Management (EURAM) conferences. National educational platforms for management PhDs, such as the Finnish KATAJA and the French FNEG, have over the years provided support by making Euro ideas available to young scholars outside the walls of formal education bureaucracies where mediocre administrators nourish pathetic dreams of turning their provincial school into a Harvard or Stanford Business School.

Unorthodox European conferences have long brought together those sick of corporate functionalistic theories of organization. 'The cultural turn', for instance, emerged on a conference platform that also acted as a launching site for 'the symbolic', 'the critical' and 'the art' turns in management. These groups soon formed their own networks and had European conferences and publications of their own. Their gatherings were like improvised campus festivals, worlds apart from the academic labor market of big US management conferences where nervous debt-ridden job candidates presented their papers in sales-pitch mode. The European business school platforms, under the condition of being public, are often arranged to turn away that kind of corporate scholarship, which makes possible a rhizomic growth of subgroups looking for the lights of truth and reality at the end of the academic tunnels of corporate air-conditioned nightmares.

This has seemed refreshing for many a US scholar, especially those who have tenured positions and want to return to intellectual work. Now they seem to team up—for reasons Jim Walsh observes—as European turn-takers encouraging and empowering them as only intellectually excited Yankees can do. James March founded the SCANCOR Center at Stanford to pick the bubbling brains of young European scholars. Linda Smircich of UMASS/Amherst, David Boje of New Mexico State, Alladi Venkatesh of UC/Irvine, Matt Statler of NYU and Jonathan Schroeder of RIT are but a few examples of the many US scholars inverting the trade flux of management. US intellectual demand attracted the European 'critical management turn' and 'the postmodern turn'. Thanks to market-oriented US scholarship, today special issues, handbooks, companions and readers are the merchandise fruits of many European scholarship 'turns'. Friendships over the pond made European scholarship travel beyond the heated debates in pubs, bistros, krogs and kneipes. Once old world 'turns' are received by the new, they gain considerable energy and sometimes even hit the hardheaded European business school bureaucrats when they return as boomerangs from the US.

Turn-taking in European scholarship can only partly be Google-traced as publications. Most European publications are still books. (At the end of this article some of these volumes are listed for inspiration.) In addition, when monographs get boiled down to journal articles, what does not fit easily into US scholarly conversation gets filtered out. That being said, scholarship still relies on people and platforms of the kind I here have exemplified. While most of this process is informal, the turns in Europe have succeeded in inspiring new privately founded (Euro-style endowment—rather than tuition-financed) institutions like the German business schools of Witten-Herdecke, Alanus or Zeppelin. In the 1990s Finn Junge Jenssen, president of the Copenhagen Business School, institutionally sheltered a number of new scholarly turns. He wanted an LSE or Sorbonne for Danish business and implemented his wish by simply putting humanities scholars on the payroll and assigning them a heavy teaching load. Once hired, these faculty members were left on their own to design new courses and programs incorporating whatever turns they fancied. This was how a program for continental philosophy and management—Fløk—was established. Switzerland's University of St Gallen has a special faculty delivering the ingredients of a compulsory study block called 'context studies', which proposes a vast and unorthodox 'liberal arts' selection of humanities and arts courses to business students. Carefully monitored, such institutional inventions may stay on the meandering, adventurous and creative tracks of turns that triggered them. There is, however, a constant 'back-to-basics' temptation to skip scholarship and supplant it with the idealist dreams promising a core of management that from a realist position hardly exists. Maybe that is how UK's Keele University or Utrecht's University of Humanities in the Netherlands slid back to mediocrity with the argument 'we want what we have but not what we get'. This is how visionary daydreaming deans take power and turn business schools into ivory towers of idealism. The turn-taking scholar, on the other hand, knows exactly what he has, but he does not like it at all. He turns away from the speculative fiction that reproduces abstract visions, ideals, models and dreams and feels much more attracted by unknown concrete realities. As Hopwood concludes, "business is so interesting, and most business schools are so boring" (in Miller, 2010).

Speculative Realism for Turn-Taking Management Scholars

Play, critique, artistry and aesthetics are fields where the reality of management is taking place. Turns are ways in which management scholarship embarks on new explorations. Bill Starbuck, long-time ruler of the *Administrative Science Quarterly* and in that function a legendary gatekeeper of methodological 'social science' conformism in management research, now frankly admits that in hindsight articles that added new discoveries to the management field were primarily 'point of view' essays. How such turns occur might be a future task for Boltanski's and Chiapello's new sociology of critique to explain in detail. While we are waiting for the report, however, we can point out one important contribution made by European management scholarship: to recognize turns as more than mere 'points of view' which depend on the playful whimsical visions of individual scholars. In conclusion I will point to speculative realism (Gratton, 2014; Harman, 2010, 2012) as one possibility of acknowledging and engaging in the turn-taking that seems fundamental to the innovative development of European management scholarship.

Turns are not equal to relaxed holidays from reason, but nevertheless they shape management in ways we do not completely understand. They do not add to a body of knowledge by accumulation, however, as we are told science and social science do. Nor does the turn-taking scholar proceed as case writer or business book author documenting and diffusing successful practices by teaching cases as sedimentation of good business behavior. Turn-taking on the contrary seems to shy away from the method focus of accumulation, and scholars are not satisfied in adding to the army of management methodists invading the academic publications and the market for consultancy (Alvesson, 2013; Bouwmeester, 2010; Furusten, 1999). Scholarship is not scholasticism. On the other hand turn-taking does not seem preoccupied with a moralist preaching of the gospel of economic goodness, profitability and success to students, practitioners or politicians. Methods and morals belong to the realm of ideals, while raw reality is the in-between terrain for the turn-taking European scholar attracted to exploring and exploiting the muddles of play, critique, artistry and aesthetics. When asked about the difference between US and Euro film-making, Hungarian director and Oscar winner István Szabó once claimed that North American movies historically had to have happy endings, while films attracting interest in Europe were tragedies, the reason being that American movie makers in the past were European immigrants obsessed with succeeding in Hollywood. It seems turn-taking management scholars in Europe are open to facing management as primarily an interesting tragedy and would thus be less eager to jump into optimistic pragmatic and utilitarian moral and methodological conclusions when interpreting reality.

At the opening meeting of the 2012 Carnegie Consortium, Aspen Institute president Walter Isaacson gave a keynote address about his biography of Apple founder Steve Jobs. In a mode of investigation similar to that of Reckwitz, Isaacson focused on Jobs's strong emphasis on aesthetics but juxtaposed it to his business success in the high-tech world. In 2014, however, when the new president of the Stockholm School of Economics Lars

Strannegård claimed that art and culture are interesting, he did so more in a European key. He does not see art as an instrument of business success. The managerial role of contemporary artists is not like that of the pop artists: to celebrate business. Art is of interest as a foundation for constituting and constructing the context of business. Once Strannegård had made this declaration abandoning narrow means–ends commercialism, his school was able to establish and develop trusting relationships with communities of artists and curators, those who before had feared instrumentalization. Today the Stockholm School of Economics together with the Copenhagen Business School, HEC Paris and the Universities of St Gallen, Bocconi and Aalto have organized an alliance for business school curating supporting extensive research and educational cooperation with important European art institutions. When occasionally students question art and aesthetics on their curricula, the presidents could simply inform them that contemporary art enters the curriculum on the explicit request of the school's patrons and donors; i.e. the same who later look to recruit 'well rounded graduates' instead of calculating 'nerds'.

European management scholars feel close to the artist who discovers reality (Johansson-Sköldberg, Woodilla, & Berthoin Antal, 2016; Raviola & Zackariasson, 2017). They are interested in art that aims at revealing the world much as the Impressionists did when they left the studios of historical painting for landscape documentation in open air. They go back to novels or watch movies—not as fictions and fantasies, but as sensitive ways to render aspects of reality blocked by outmoded styles of representation (Czarniawska-Joerges & Guillet de Monthoux, 1994; Rombach & Solli, 2006). Management scholars do not welcome artists or connect students to art worlds because of their powerful celebrations of bygone virtues of managerial heroism. The scholar senses that management theory and business education ARE dreaming, and therefore art and artists should help us wake up!

This discussion started with the bankruptcy of the idealism preached by do-good business school evangelists. Management textbooks are full of beautiful ideal-types, with masterpieces to be copied and recommendations on what we ought to do and think depending on old templates and mindmaps. The fantasy worlds of organizational images are speculative fictions. Little difference exists between the creative industry of Harry Potter and that of Philip Kotler; both are opiates for managers (Dewandre, 2002). All this has contributed to the actual popularity of new terms in art and philosophy that might help the scholar to understand what scholarship is about in management.

'Speculative realism' is a term advanced by some philosophers (Gratton, 2014; Harman, 2010, 2011) as a non-transcendental metaphysic of objects with many affinities back to well-known European phenomenology and existentialism as well as long forgotten management philosophies such as the praxeological reism of Tadeusz Kotarbinski (1965). Harman defends the Socratic definition of philosophy as 'the love of truth' rather than 'finding truth'. Management that embraces speculative realism must step down from its legitimizing pedestal, the ivory tower of a scientific mindset, for the Socratic philosophical approach to reality is not about science. The reality that interests us here cannot be better grasped, controlled or understood by some scientific method, and that may be why management scholars, implicitly following the Socratic tradition, are today regarded as important contributors to the humanization of social sciences (Dosse, 1998). Reality must, however, also be respected as non-reductionist and concrete. Speculative realists are not focused on better knowing reality as something we think out in the abstract. Upon reflection, the cost for researchers turning to speculative realism is high, for they will have to strip themselves of scientific or social scientific habits they have developed to harness their discipline as a serious science making theory go deeper, or higher, than that we all experience. To Harman this is a necessary price to pay for a scientist in reclaiming a position as a philosopher.

In management it seems to be a credit to pay to remain a turn-taking scholar open to reality and not become a methodist or moralist. It is a price to pay to regain relevance lost by stubbornly pretending to science and social science and to produce mainstream research in rat-race careers. At the same time, however, practitioners increasingly remind us that publication has gone astray and that management research is written but not read. When management scholars turn to philosophy, they might become helpful as practical philosophers by making us skip fiction and get hooked on the thrilling reality we can only, as the Kantian 'thing-as-such', approach and construct in indirect oblique ways. Artists, architects and designers construct objects that may become art in the aesthetic world if scientists and social scientists ignore them and keep their mouths shut. Philosophers, artists and management scholars share a common mission to make objects real by clever bracketing of science and social science. Fluxus art lives the process, concept art experiences the ideas and the situationists shape situations, to name a few of the long list of avant-gardes making real and objective in aesthetic ways management envies and management research cannot explain scientifically (Borch, 2014; Linstead & Höpfl, 2000).

To Harman it seems very plausible that speculative realism is what managers and management scholars are already doing. The European management scholars I tried to exemplify find business fascinating not in theory but in reality. That is why turns seem so attracted by artistic and philosophical ways to break out of the fictions of idealist textbooks and obsolete sedimented best practices. We respect other scholars not as researchers but as metaphysicians who we feel can liberate us from fictions. For instance those who happen to ally with Bruno Latour actually also side with Harman's own (2009) favourite metaphysician, a scholar who has de facto turned his back on scientism or methodologies and instead constantly connects his attempts to approach reality with a European philosophical heritage and art practices. Latour actually considers exhibition-curating as an important scholarly practice. This way of scholarship might be what Europe has to contribute. To paraphrase the words of Devin and Austin (2012 p. 130) when referring to the marketing of design objects, we can then say the management scholar's role will be 'to provide materials for intuition and then help in the contemplation process'.

References

Albert, David, Hachtue, Armand & Laufer, Romain (2013). *New foundations for management research*. Paris: Presses de Mines.

Alvesson, Mats (2013). *The Triumph of emptiness: Consumption, higher education, and work organization*. Oxford: Oxford University Press.

Alvesson, Mats & Sköldberg, Kaj (2010). *Reflexive methodology: New vistas for qualitative research*. London: Sage.

Arbnor, Ingeman & Bjerke, Björn (2009). *Methodology for creating business knowledge*. London: Sage.

Augier, Mie & March, James G. (2011). *The roots, rituals, and rhetorics of change: North American business schools after the Second World War*. Stanford: Stanford Business Books.

Austin, John (1962). *How to do things with words*. Oxford: Clarendon Press.

Austin, Robert D. (1996). *Measuring and managing performance in organizations*. New York: Dorset House.

Austin, Robert D. & Devin, Lee (2003). *Artful making: What managers need to know about how artists work*. Upper Saddle River, NJ: Financial Times Press.

Baecker, Dirk (1994). *Postheroisches management: Ein Vademecum*. Berlin: Merve Verlag.

Béjean, Mathias (2008). *Le management des entreprises á prestations artistiques*. Paris: Ecole Nationale Supérieure des Mines.

Boltanski, Luc (1982). *Les cadres*. Paris: Editions de Minuit.

Boltanski, Luc & Chiapello, Ève (2005). *The new spirit of capitalism*. London: Verso.

Boltanski, Luc & Esquerre, Arnaud (2017). *Enrichissement, critique de la marchandise*. Paris: Gallimard.

Borch, Christian (Ed.) (2014). *Architectural atmospheres: On the experience and politics of architecture*. Basel: Brikhauser Verlag.

Bouwmeester, Onno (2010). *Economic advice and rhetoric: Why do consultants perform better than economic advisors?* Cheltenham: Edward Elgar.

Chia, Robert & Holt, Robin (2010). *Strategy without design: Silent efficacy of indirect action*. Cambridge: Cambridge University Press.

Chytry, Josef (1989). *The aesthetic state*. Berkeley: University of California Press.

Chytry, Josef (2009). *Unis vers cythere: Aesthetic political investigations in polis thought and the artful firm*. New York: Peter Lang.

Colby, Anne, Ehrlich, Thomas, Sullivan, William M. & Dolle, Jonathan R. (2011). *Rethinking undergraduate business education: Liberal learning for the profession*. San Francisco: Jossey Bass.

Cusset, François (2008). *French theory: How Foucault, Derrida, Deleuze & co. transformed intellectual life in the United States*. Minneapolis: University of Minnesota Press.

Czarniawska-Joerges, Barbara & Guillet de Monthoux, Pierre (1994). *Good novels, better management: Reading organizational realities*. Chur: Harwood.

Daudi, Philippe (1986). *Power in the organization: The discourse of power in managerial Praxis*. Oxford: Blackwell.
Devin, Lee & Austin, Robert (2012). *The soul of design: Harnessing the power of the plot to create extraordinary design*. Palo Alto: Stanford University Press.
Dewandre, Nicole (2002). *Critique de la raison administrative: Pour une Europe ironiste*. Paris: Editions du Seuil.
Djelic, Marie-Laure (2001). *Exporting the American model: Postwar transformation of European business*. Oxford: Oxford University Press.
Dosse, François (1998). *Empire of meaning: The humanization of the social sciences*. Minneapolis: University of Minnesota Press.
Fogh-Kirkeby, Ole (2000). *Management philosophy: A radical normative perspective*. Berlin: Springer.
Furusten, Staffan (1999). *Popular management books: How they are made and what they mean to organizations*. London: Routledge.
Gagliardi, Pasquale & Czarniawska, Barbara (Eds.) (2006). *Management education and the humanities*. Cheltenham: Edward Elgar.
Goodman, Nelson (1968). *Languages of art: An approach to a theory of symbols*. Indianapolis: Bobbs-Merrill Company.
Goodman, Nelson (1978). *Ways of worldmaking*. Indianapolis: Hackett Publishing.
Göranzon, Bo (1993). *The practical intellects: Computers and skills*. Berlin: Springer.
Gratton, Peter (2014). *Speculative realism: Problems and prospects*. London: Bloomsbury.
Griseri, Paul (2013). *An introduction to the philosophy of management*. San Francisco: Sage.
Guillet de Monthoux, Pierre (2004). *The art firm, aesthetic management and metaphysical marketing*. Palo Alto: Stanford University Press.
Guillet de Monthoux, Pierre (2014). Terrorist/anarchist/artist: Why bother? *Ephemera*, 14(4), 977–983.
Guillet de Monthoux, Pierre & Statler, Matt (2013). Theory U: Rethinking business as practical European philosophy. In O. Gunnlaugson, C. Baron & M. Cayer (Eds.), *Perspectives on theory U: Insights from the field* (pp. 234–243). Hershey, PA: IGI global.
Gustafsson, Claes (2011). *The production of seriousness: The metaphysics of economic reason*. London: Palgrave Macmillan.
Harman, Graham (2009). *Prince of networks: Bruno Latour and metaphysics*. Melbourne: re-Press.
Harman, Graham (2010). *Towards speculative realism: Essays and lectures*. Ropley: Zero Books.
Harman, Graham (2011). *The quadruple object*. Alresford: Zero Books.
Harman, Graham (2012). Aesthetics as first philosophy: Levinas and the non human. Accessed 15 January 2015: www.nakedpunch.com/articles/147 In Naked Punch.
Helin, Jenny, Hernes, Tor, Hjorth, Daniel & Holt, Robin (2014). *The Oxford handbook of process philosophy and organization studies*. Oxford: Oxford University Press.
Hernes, Tor (2014a). *A process theory of organization*. Oxford: Oxford University Press.
Hernes, Tor (2014b). In search of a soul of relevance for European management research. *European Management Journal*, 32, 852–857.
Hjorth, Daniel & Steyaert, Chris (Eds.) (2009). *The politics and aesthetics of entrepreneurship*. Cheltenham: Edward Elgar.
Johansson, Ulla & Woodilla, Jill (2005). *Irony and organizations: Epistemological claims and supporting field stories*. Copenhagen: Copenhagen Business School Press.

Johansson-Sköldberg, Ulla, Woodilla, Jill & Berthoin Antal, Ariane (Eds.) (2016). *Artistic interventions in organizations: Research, theory and practice*. London: Routledge.
Kapferer, Jean-Noël & Bastien, Vincent (2009). *The luxury strategy: Break the rules of marketing to build luxury brands*. London: Kogan Page.
Khurana, Rakesh (2009). *From higher aims to hired hands: The social transformation of American business schools and the unfulfilled promise of management as a profession*. Princeton: Princeton University Press.
Kotarbinski, Tadeusz (1965). *Praxeology: An introduction to the sciences of efficient action*. New York: Pergamon Press.
Linstead, Stephen & Höpfl, Heather (2000). *The aesthetics of organization*. London: Sage.
Manz, Charles (2014). Let's get serious! Really? *Journal of Management Inquiry*, 33, 339–342.
March, James (1971). The foolishness of technology. *Civiløkonomen*, 18(4), 4–12.
Miller, Peter (2010). Anthony Hopwood obituary. *The Guardian*, Monday, 28 June.
O'Connor, Ellen (2011). *Creating new knowledge in management: Appropriating the field's lost foundations*. Palo Alto: Stanford University Press.
Pierson, Frank C. (1959). *The education of American businessmen: A study of university-college programs in business administration*. New York: McGraw-Hill.
Quattrone, Paulo (2015). Governing social orders, unfolding rationality, and Jesuit accounting practices: A procedural approach to institutional logics. *Administrative Science Quarterly*, 60(3), 411–445.
Rasche, Andreas (2014). The corporation as a political actor: European and North American perspectives. *European Management Journal*, 33, 4–8.
Raviola, Elena & Zackariasson, Peter (Eds.) (2017). *Art and business building a common ground for understanding society*. London: Routledge.
Reckwitz, Andreas (2012). *Die Erfindung der Kreativität: Zum Prozess gesellschaftlicher Ästhetisierung*. Berlin: Suhrkamp Verlag.
Riot, Elen, Chamaret, Cecile & Rigaud, Emmanuelle (2013). Murakami on the bag: Louis Vuitton's decommoditization strategy. *International Journal of Retail and Distribution Management*, 41, 11–12.
Rombach, Björn & Solli, Rolf (2006). *Constructing leadership: Reflections of film heroes as leaders*. Stockholm: Santerus Förlag.
Scharmer, Otto (2009). *Theory U: Leading from the future as it emerges*. San Francisco: Berrett-Koehler Publishers.
Sköldberg, Kaj (2002). *The poetic logic of organization: Styles and changes of styles in the art of organizing*. London: Routledge.
Statler, Mats & Guillet de Monthoux, Pierre (2015). Humanities and arts in management education: The emerging Carnegie paradigm. *Journal of Management Education*, 39(1), 3–15, special issue: Integrating liberal learning, humanities and management education: Putting the Carnegie Report into practice.
Steyaert, Chris, Beyes, Timon & Parker, Martin (Eds.) (2016). *The Routledge companion to reinventing management education*. London: Routledge.
Strati, Antonio (1999). *Organization and aesthetics*. London: Sage.
Winch, Peter (1990). *The idea of a social science and its relation to philosophy*. London: Routledge.
Zilber, Tammar B. (2015). Turning a disadvantage into a resource—working at the periphery. *European Management Journal*, 33, 423–430.

6 The Strategy Cycle

Planning, Paradox and Poetry in the Practice of Strategists

Donald MacLean and Robert MacIntosh

Introduction

Robert Chia (Chapter 1, this book) lays out a thought-provoking call to continue to develop management and organization research in the 'European tradition'. We would suggest an urgency marked by the observation that technology and globalization mean that "organizations are morphing furiously into new forms" (Barley, 2016, p. 2), whilst our organizational research struggles to keep up. Chia contrasts the ideal of rigour with the idea of rigor mortis, urging fellow researchers to push for innovative thinking. In so doing, he alerts us to the potential dangers of a somewhat totalizing orthodoxy that only recognizes, funds and publishes work adhering to the protocols of what is generally considered to be methodologically sound scientific enquiry and which might deliver significant impact (MacIntosh et al., 2017).

In a counter move, he points towards *artistic rigour*; that is an approach to organization scholarship that is informed more by artistic sensitivities and capabilities than by scientific method. A genuine "*democracy of vision*" characterized by a refusal "*to accept pre-existing conceptual distinctions between the various elements that make up a phenomenal experience*" (Chia, 2014, p. 684); one that "*is energized by a fertile and imaginative mind*" and enabled by "*an acute empirical sensitivity*" (op. cit: 685) sometimes focused on "*singular events*", and one that is open to the influence of impressions, intuitions and imagination in bold acts of creativity that often skirt over and beyond otherwise troublesome contradictions, areas of ignorance, uncertainty, etc.

We are delighted to have the opportunity to offer a response to Chia's call by developing his concern that our collective scholarship should more accurately reflect the behavior of businesses, organizations in general and the people comprised by them. Specifically, we focus on what is broadly termed 'strategy or strategic management' (hereafter, simply referred to as strategic management). We are particularly concerned here to reflect on what we have learned from over two decades of working with a multitude of organizations during periods when strategy has been developed.

Our work often takes the form of a particular style of action research (MacLean et al., 2002); yet some of what we say is inevitably informed by our own experiences running businesses and other forms of organization, sitting on various boards and acting as consultants to a wide range of organizations. Mirroring the rigour-relevance tension identified by Chia, our own work is largely concerned with helping individuals in demanding roles to break free from the suffocating effects of outmoded, over-extended managerialism in pursuit of the twin aims of successful collective action and enriched human experience.

What follows is therefore a partial and personal account of strategic management in which we seek to unpack the kinds of strategizing practices we have encountered in organizations. Our aim is to show that strategy is at least as well described in artistic terms as those of rational science. In so doing, we offer some suggestions for those charged with the development and deployment of strategy in their organizations.

We will begin by revisiting the observation that plans do not always come to fruition—before moving to less familiar territory. We introduce the idea of paradox, along with another major significant concept in strategic management—namely that of "emergent strategy"—placing each in relation to planning. Next, we explore what happens during the realization that a particular plan is not coming to fruition, arguing that a form of creative action takes over. This leads us to consider what are essentially poetic faculties before we conclude by focusing attention on something which is surprisingly absent from most mainstream writings on strategic management—namely the situated strategist resplendent in his myriad variety. Our view sets out a rich ecology of strategy styles and approaches which straddle art and science as well as varying between contexts and cultures.

Planning

People often associate the term 'strategic management' with some key terms such as aim, vision, objectives, goals or route map. Having asked many thousands of individuals this question in workshops, classrooms and boardrooms, the most frequent answer received is 'a plan' with subsequent qualifications including that a strategy is a 'high-level' plan; a 'big-picture' plan; it's a plan 'for the whole business'; and perhaps crucially that it's a 'long term' which involves 'the commitment of significant resources' in ways which are 'not easily undone'.

Such descriptions of strategic management should hardly seem surprising, since this was mostly what was (and, in many cases, still is) taught in business schools or conveyed in the canonical texts of the so-called 'content school' of strategic management (Schendel, 1992). From the early work of pioneers such as Chandler (1962), Sloan (1963), Andrews et al. (1965) and Ansoff (1965) through Porter's work on positioning (1985) and onward to more recent offerings such as Barney (1991) on resource-based thinking (see MacIntosh & Maclean, 2015, pp. 14–20 for an overview), the emphasis has been on rationally planned action, usually reserved to the senior levels of the organization—and usually underpinned by ever more sophisticated analyses of the environment, the cultural or ideological fabric of the organization and its resources or capabilities. Typically this gives rise to a limited number of configurations which offer options for attaining some form of competitive advantage over rivals. We would suggest that this is nothing more than a modern expression of Cartesian thinking in which action is structured by prior intellectual effort. It also represents a variation on the familiar rational schema at the heart of most Western education—ends (intent), means (resources and capability) and conditions (environmental trends)—in which analysis and other forms of structured intellectual activity seek to bring these into fruitful, if not optimal, alignment as a blueprint for action. Notably, the traditional mindset in much of the strategic management literature is that action both is done by others and follows the creation of the blueprint or plan.

This view of strategic management remains remarkably pervasive, yet it seems to be losing connection with, or downplaying, another key aspect of strategic management—which we might call 'artfulness'. In short, strategic management in historical terms was primarily concerned with overturning unfavourable odds, with effecting a successful outcome in spite of the balance of probabilities. As laid out in a remarkable review of strategy—from its inception in ancient times through to its contemporary appearance in business—Oxford historian Lawrence Freedman (2013) draws attention to this artfulness which is both rooted in and arises out of a real challenge. To some this may be most familiar in the words of Baldrick,[1] Edmund Blackadder's hapless yet faithful manservant in the BBC TV series *Blackadder*, who routinely offers his master a series of ill-fated cunning plans. Baldrick may seem an unlikely strategist but we would agree with Carter's account of strategic management as a "paradoxical cocktail of far-sightedness, pragmatism, expediency and low cunning" (2013, p. 1047). Strategies (cunning or otherwise) are called for in challenging situations, yet some organizations may face circumstances which are not perceived as particularly challenging. As such, and contrary to current fashions, there is nothing in the concept of strategy that implies that organizations must have one—or, for that matter, unless they are singularly challenged, need they have *only* one.

Strategies 'belong to' challenges, not to organizations per se; and, as Richard Rumelt eloquently argues in his book *Good Strategy, Bad Strategy* (2011), perhaps the most important stage in crafting a strategy is a succinct statement of the challenge, or challenges, faced. Our own contention is that this diagnosis of the organization's evolution and current situation is a form of problem framing (Mitroff & Silvers, 2009).

To craft a strategy statement is, in rational terms at least, remarkably straightforward, since it might simply be thought of as a succinct plan. Having undertaken diagnosis, analysis, articulation of a challenge and consideration of options, the key challenge is in assembling the various elements of strategic management into a coherent whole. In our experience, many strategies are analytically comprehensive but feature sins of both omission and commission. Hence a badly assembled strategy resembles a bicycle with two sets of pedals but no chain and with handlebars where there should be a seat. Fortunately language can help us here. If we respond to the 'humpty-dumpty' challenge of putting things back together again in the right order, by writing our strategy within a comprehensible and meaningful structure, then we can dramatically influence the extent to which it is likely to 'make sense'.

In our practice, well-crafted strategies have a recognizable 'grammar': We encourage strategists to write within structured forms, with one variation being:

> We will [W = intent] double our turnover in [X = timeframe] five years by exploiting our [Y = statement of capability] unique strength in laser packaging to [Z = statement of opportunity] gain a leading position in the emerging optical computer industry.

You can see that this WXYZ format channels the strategist towards the components of the rational ends-means-conditions schema, in our case expressed as intent (double our turnover in five years and gain a leading position), capability (unique strength in laser packaging) and foresight (the emerging optical computer industry). From studying and developing a large number of strategy statements, we have identified 12 such structuring devices that form the grammar of a comprehensive statement of strategy. The following example shows how these 12 choices interlock to form a strategy.

> The challenge we face is that, since our core market is not growing, our continued growth in that sector requires us to take share from our competitors. This growth strategy will be delivered through a combination of market penetration and the acquisition of struggling competitors to achieve economies of scale, allowing us to further exploit our superior ability to manage costs in the production process. We will therefore compete on the basis of cost, offering a consistently high standard of goods at low production costs. We are therefore seeking to become the dominant player within our strategic group by 2015. In so doing we will achieve growth in turnover to at least £25 million and be seen as the preferred provider of competitively priced leather to mid-range suppliers in the automotive industries.

Here we have included the diagnosis, challenge and a coherent configuration of options. The resulting strategy statement is coherent, comprehensive, yet succinct. It can be summarized in a paragraph rather than a weighty document, though of course it could be expanded to such. The 12 structuring devices are set out in Table 6.1.

Table 6.1 The 12 Key Components of a Business Strategy Statement

1. Diagnosis	An assessment of the challenge facing the organization and which the strategy needs to overcome
2. Intent	What the organization is trying to achieve
3. Timeframe	The period covered by the strategy
4. Capability	An active statement of core capability: "it's our ability to"
5. Opportunity	Trends from the operating environment
6. Aim	The outcome of the strategy specified as consolidation, retrenchment or growth
7. Tactic	How the aim will be delivered: market penetration, market development, product development or diversification
8. Method	The mode of execution employed in the strategy: organic growth, acquisition or partnership
9. Competitive stance	The basis on which you will engage in competition: cost, differentiation, premium or Blue Ocean
10. Strategic group	Who you will engage in competition: within current group or in a different strategic group
11. Offering	What the organization does to create value
12. Audience	Who the organization wants to engage

Robert MacIntosh & Donald MacLean, *Strategic Management: Strategists at Work*, 2015, reproduced with permission of Palgrave Macmillan

On one level at least, the development of a strategic plan is therefore a relatively straightforward affair, involving analytical rigour and grammatical discipline. Armed with a logically robust and comprehensive plan, implementation in the context of a well-disciplined organization should, one might think, be relatively straightforward. Yet both our own experiences and the wider strategic management literature suggest that rates of implementation failure run high in the field of strategic management (Pettigrew, 1992). Indeed, Freedman (2013) concludes that plans are rarely executed as originally intended.

Paradox

> The best laid schemes o' mice and men gang aft agley.
>
> (Robert Burns in "To a Mouse" (1785))

Failing to implement strategy might have its causal roots in any number of areas. Perhaps, like Baldrick's cunning plans, the basic idea was ill-fated from the outset. A poor diagnosis, a fuzzy articulation of the particular challenge faced, wayward analysis, flawed assembly of the basic components, a lack of critical evaluation or overly optimistic risk assessment may individually or in concert explain the failure of a given strategy. In a similar vein, failure is often attributed to poor management, a lack of discipline, the catch-all problem of poor communications, the lack of senior management attention or, as Kerr (1975) argues, reward structures which inadvertently incentivize one thing whilst hoping for another.

The academic community has been concerned with the issue of implementation failure for many years, with the most influential contribution being Mintzberg's views on "deliberate strategy" (1994), which he sees as susceptible to both the "fallacy of prediction" and the "fallacy of detachment". Using his own observations of senior managers engaged in strategy work, Mintzberg introduced the term "emergent strategy" as a counter explanation. This occurs through patterning of interactions between individuals and organizations engaged in a myriad of small acts and events influenced as much by localized chance as by any grand plan or overview.

Since Mintzberg's insights were first published, the concept of emergent strategy has grown in legitimacy and is increasingly accepted as an alternative explanation of how strategies actually form. As testament to Mintzberg's influence, we find that an increasing number of business and public sector organizations recognize his description of emergent strategy. Yet there remains something troubling about the concept, something paradoxical at work.

Whilst we would acknowledge that plans rarely see the light of day, the inescapable fact is that both individuals and organizations still expend time and energy developing plans. In the oft-seen and -heard quote from Robert Burns above, our attention is drawn to the phrase "gang aft"—which translated literally from Scots to English means 'go often' or more conventionally, 'often go'. Burns the poet is alluding to the compulsion we feel to plan despite the full knowledge that this rarely produces the desired effect. We have been asking ourselves why this should be the case? In more prosaic and academic terms, if we conceptualize strategic management as an emergent rather than a mechanistic process, what can or should managers and others do instead? Is emergence itself amenable to influence? Our desire to understand these questions led us to complexity theory, which is sometimes described as the new science of emergence.

A full treatment of complexity theory is not our intention here. Coveney and Highfield (1996) offer an overview of the underpinning science and we have produced an overview of complexity thinking as it pertains to organizations (see MacIntosh et al., 2006). A succinct summary would be to say that at the heart of complexity thinking are a series of insights which contrast starkly with much of our thinking in modern times. The traditional scientific view depicts the universe, and many of its constituent parts, as conforming to the principles of Newtonian mechanics, predictably tending towards designed equilibria in accordance with universal laws of cause and effect—progressively deteriorating in the process (under the influence of the second law of thermodynamics). In organizational terms, the legacy of this scientific mindset is the mechanistic metaphor which draws our attention to re*structuring* during periods when supply and demand have temporarily moved out of equilibrium. The intelligent (and therefore logical and rational) manager remains omnipresent to counteract the underlying tendency for things to *dis*organize in accordance with the second law of thermodynamics.

'Complexity thinking' is an umbrella term covering many root disciplines and several subtle but significant distinctions. Nevertheless, there is a tendency in all complexity thinking to focus on a multiplicity of open systems—each exchanging energy with its environment such that the natural state of affairs is for complex systems to reside in non-equilibrium states. These non-equilibrium systems, unlike those governed by the second law of thermodynamics, are apt to generate and transform their own order from within, which is often referred to as a capacity for *self*-organization. They do so under the influence of a set of initial conditions, positive (as opposed to negative) feedback and, depending on the sub-school to which you subscribe (Cilliers, 1998), the operation of particular configurations of interconnection, or sets of order-generating rules or deep structures (MacIntosh & MacLean, 1999). In contrast to the mechanistic metaphor, complexity views organizations as fluid, processual, self-organizing and capable of spontaneous reconfiguration.

If this description seems a little abstract, think of other contexts such as sports, theatre or music where improvisation and emergence seem both commonplace and necessary. Planning, training, rehearsal and various other preparatory activities are seen as necessary preconditions to the opportunity to react 'in the moment' to the specifics of a given situation, whether that be an improvised jazz session, a conversation, a freestyle dance or a sporting encounter. Our major discomforts with the Mintzbergian sense of emergent strategy are that emergence is seen as largely unmanageable, is only recognizable retrospectively and renders the process of developing a plan somewhat redundant. Instead we drew on our own experiences of engagement in emergent processes and embraced one of the central ideas of Nobel Prize winner Ilya Prigogine's exposition of complexity—namely that nature, including our own experience, is inherently paradoxical (Prigogine & Stengers, 1984).

By 'paradoxical' we simply mean characterized by circumstances where two incommensurable truths appear to co-exist (Beech et al., 2004). In the context of our argument here, the distinction between deliberate and emergent strategy is not an academic problem that will one day be solved but, rather, a quintessential feature of the strategy process and/or our descriptions of that process. Indeed, under closer examination, the 'either-or' approach to the debate seems somewhat naïve. Deliberate strategies, or plans, themselves emerge in conversational interaction amongst members of a particular group or community. Likewise, emergent strategies arise out of the deliberate interactions of many politically minded and intentional actors combined with a range of contextual factors such as aesthetics, embodied biographies, chance, attractions, etc. (MacLean & MacIntosh, 2012).

Viewed through a paradox lens, we might ask afresh, what is happening when we engage in the development of plans despite knowing that those plans will be unlikely to come to fruition? In researching many management teams in a range of organizational settings, we found the formation or reinforcement of interconnections—social, emotional and intellectual. These interconnections often enscribe themselves in the organizational setting as deep structures (Drazin & Sandelands, 1992), simple rules (Sull & Eisenhardt, 2012) or rules of thumb (MacIntosh & MacLean, 2015). These basic principles and shared values allow us to work coherently together when confronted with the need to improvise in the face of changing circumstances. As Eisenhower is reputed to have said, "plans are nothing, planning is everything".

Poetry

Paradox is not only a major theme in the academic literature on complexity and emergence—one might argue that it is central to art, and in particular to a different genre of literature, including poetry. In Shakespeare's *Hamlet*, the young prince berates his mother for entering into what he considers to be an unseemly relationship with his recently deceased father's brother:

> I must be cruel only to be kind.
>
> (Act 3, scene 4)

Shakespeare's prose draws our attention because in the same short line, a paradoxical tension is identified. The reader is aroused by the possibilities suggested through this contradiction. This deeper significance is not revealed at first glance; it takes a different, perhaps deeper faculty to glimpse possible interpretations, to grasp alternative meanings, or maybe a mere suggestion of another way of looking at things. This ability to sense that something else is going on, something different from the apparent logic, or plan, and yet nevertheless meaningful and potentially valuable, is what we take Chia (2014) to mean when he refers to an "artistic rigour" imbued with what he calls an "acute empirical sensitivity". In our terms, this ability to discern and articulate—in the midst of complexity and flux—a potential re-ordering of experience, is precisely what certain individuals do when their reality fails to correspond to the planned version. In terms of complexity theory they are part of the same positive feedback processes that they themselves help to create by crafting a form of narrative complexity (Tsoukas & Hatch, 2001) that simply cannot be reduced to generative logic.

Emergence, then, is by no means left to randomness or tidal forces beyond our grasp. Yet participation in the process of emergence is not scientific in the sense of following a rigid protocol. Indeed in some ways it is the antithesis of scientific method and linear, dare we say strategic, thinking. This ability to look beyond logical contradictions, to hold paradox open, to listen to people and circumstances intently and creatively, to talk boldly and with style and to transform our understanding of what is happening, opening up new possibilities and futures, is the very essence of creativity. It is far from undisciplined. It involves and invokes exceptional abilities and faculties honed through devoted practice. But it is not science, it is not even management as most people would recognize it—it is art in the broad sense, or something akin to what John Shotter and Arlene Katz might term "social poetics" (Shotter & Katz, 1996).

This poetic tendency or acute empirical sensitivity chimes with recent developments in neuroscience and cognitive science. Freedman (2013), in his review of narrative strategy, explains so-called system 1 and system 2 thinking.[2] System 2 decisions are described as "conscious, explicit, analytical, deliberative, more intellectual and inherently linear". To convey the essence of system 1 processes, he quotes the philosopher Isaiah Berlin thus (p. 613):

> a capacity for integrating a vast amalgam of constantly changing, multi-coloured, evanescent, perpetually overlapping data, too many, too swift, too intermingled, too caught and pinned down . . . to integrate them in this sense is to see the data as elements in a single pattern, with their implications, to see them as symptoms of past and future possibilities, to see them pragmatically, that is in terms of what you and others can or will do to them, or what they can or will do to others and you.

The suggestion here is also that in the midst of the action, the linear, rational, strategic, planning mind gives way to a very different faculty; that emergence is both created and governed in part by poetic abilities and a web of interacting factors—some of which may have formed or been encountered during the process of planning. Embracing the role that art may have in our organizations may seem a long way from the familiar road to scientific certainty and methodological rigour. Yet this may be precisely why our increasingly scientific attempts to deliver generalizable truths have rendered us peripheral voices in the lives of practicing managers.

Working where we do, our own attention was drawn to the historical role of 'the bard' in the tribal clan systems of the Scottish Highlands and Ireland. Bards operated in a highly uncertain world of tribal conflicts and turbulent environmental conditions. In the words of Brendan Lehane:

> [B]ards kept alive the ancient stories of a race, dramatized new events, and entertained the courts with their long, stylized narratives.
>
> (2005, pp. 28–29)

Becoming a bard involved a training that was "long and hard" (Chadwick, 2002), spanning years, if not decades, and involving highly disciplined schooling. Whilst the chieftains and warriors engaged in conflicts, alliances and contested territories, the bards played a major role in translating such activities into an art which both entertained the clan and helped to sustain social order and coherence by locating individuals in a transformed understanding of what was going on. On occasions, perhaps when things were not going quite according to custom or expectation, they were required to

> step out of the consensus trance reality, observe the psychodynamics of individual or social disease, and then step back in and protest for change.
>
> (McIntosh, 2004, p. 121)

Perhaps this picture of the bard is not so far from the contemporary figure of the transformational leader (Burns, 1978) who inspires others in times of crisis or opportunity and, in the spirit of strategic management outlined in the section on planning, encourages those around him to do more than they originally expected to do (Fu, 2010). Perhaps then we are simply saying that as planned strategy gives way to emergent reality, leadership comes to the fore, and that better leaders are at least as much bard or poet as scientist, engineer or accountant.

People and Strategic Management

In closing our piece, we (re)turn our attention to people. The absence of any mention of full-fledged human beings in the vast majority of the mainstream strategic management literature is a source of both mystery and amusement to our many friends and collaborators in the world of practice. We offer our own explanation for this state of affairs before suggesting what might be done to remedy it.

In our view there are two interrelated causes for the mysterious absence of people in literature relating to strategic management. First, there is an issue of 'levels'—i.e. the distinction between, organizations, individuals and groups. Despite calls for more micro and more practice-oriented studies (see Johnson, Melin, & Whittington, 2003), strategic management is still largely seen as something that 'organizations have' rather than something that 'people do'. Indeed in our view it would be more accurate to say that 'strategy' is linguistic shorthand for an idea that individuals sometimes invoke in one another's presence to explain, justify or otherwise promote a particular course of action. In fairness, there is discernible movement on this front, not least in the form of the so-called Strategy as Practice movement which now appears in the standing groups of most major management research conferences, as well as in the form of the rapidly expanding interest in dynamic capabilities and micro-foundations, (Teece, 2007; Teece, Pisano, & Shuen, 1997).

Our hope is that renewed scholarly interest in people and what they do may also help with what we see as the second and perhaps more stubborn difficulty. This is the, usually unquestioned, subscription to models of human (or, more typically, organizational) action that are predicated on either (a) rationality or (b) cultural/normative behaviour. We have written in more detail about this elsewhere (see MacLean & MacIntosh, 2012). By way of summary, a rational orientation is the familiar optimizing process concerned with ends, means and conditions described in the earlier section on planning. It often goes hand-in-hand with the Newtonian mechanics (described in the section on paradox). In strategic management research, these ideas typically give rise to a view of the organization mechanically acting out a plan—one usually developed by individuals or groups who can behold the organization 'from the outside' as an object. When this rational view is challenged in the literature, an alternative cultural or normative view is typically offered. This involves a view of behavior in the organization—by individuals and groups—as being 'structured' by group norms, values, rules, habits, beliefs, etc. As such, behavior is more concerned with 'fitting in', 'belonging' and 'survival' than optimization, and the underlying organizational metaphor switches from machine or mechanism to tribe, clan or herd within which action (including strategy) is typically post-rationalized.

Our contention is that neither rational nor normative views of action are particularly suited to explaining processes of creativity set out in our earlier discussion of emergence. Whilst many variants and hybrids of the two views arise, it is difficult to escape serious limitations (albeit of their caricatures)—i.e. the 'me-too', post-rationalized, flock-like behavior of the normative school, or the thought-driven, mechanical, problem-solving, unsurprising behavior of the rational school. Indeed in the rational view, easily the dominant one in the strategic management mainstream (and dare we say it the methodological mainstream in strategic management research), the concern for intellectually driven, systematic, predictable, controllable action paints a picture not of people at all, but of the 'organizational body' as some form of decaying mechanism. In causal terms, the surprising lack of attention paid to individual strategists in the strategic management literature is simply a consequence of two underlying views of action, neither of which has a prominent place for the creative human actor. In polemic terms, our unnecessarily mechanical organizations are locked in an unhelpful dynamic with similarly minded educational factories, giving rise over time to an experience of work which might be described as 'dehumanizing'.

Powell (2014) draws attention to a "creeping impersonalism" in the intellectual history of strategic management theory, and suggests that paying more attention to human beings will deliver better research. Whilst we applaud this, we would add that such a move requires the incorporation of a theory of human action that deals first and foremost with human individuals and their interactions in all of their intellectual, physical, emotional and social fullness such that we can deepen our understanding of what people do, creatively, as participants in processes of emergence. It is for this reason that we have adopted a theory that sees creativity as the primary facet of human action—based on the work of social theorist Hans Joas (1996).

Creative action theory synthesizes different pragmatist theories of action and offers a three-dimensional concept of 'creative action' where action is the manifestation of continually evolving intentions emerging from an ongoing dialogue with the situation, bodily expressions of individual human beings and a socially shaped identity which is produced and sustained in interaction with others. Think of a typical meeting. Whilst there may be an agenda, nobody enters (we hope) with a script. Who is present in the room matters. The health, mood, physicality and disposition of those involved count. Participants are not necessarily instrumentalizing their bodies as plans are executed. Sometimes the body takes over—through desire, outrage or gut instinct, and the intellect is witness to unpremeditated expression. Actions may not be rational; nevertheless most actions and gestures are intentional. They may be non-rational (intuitive, imaginative, emotional) but are rarely irrational. No one is in control, but, equally, it would be inaccurate to describe the situation as being out of control. Interaction is central, since some relationships are productive and some are not. Everything that happens, happens through processes of interrelating as people and groups talk, experiment, learn, win and lose arguments, get ignored or are applauded and build a sense of identity and meaningful belonging, or otherwise, together.

Table 6.2 summarizes the key distinctions between rational, normative and creative perspectives on action.

Table 6.2 Three Views of Action

	Rational	*Cultural*	*Creative*
Key concerns	Optimality problem-solving	Belonging, sustainability and survival	Creativity novelty, innovation and transformation
Focal units	The organization	The collective	Situated individuals
Key process	Control	Co-ordination	Negotiation
Process style	Scientific-logical	Cultural-cohesive	Political-interactive
Key concepts	Ends, means and conditions	Norms, rules, routines, structures	Interaction, emergence, identity
Key influences	Economics, natural sciences	Anthropology, cognitive psychology	Politics, social theory
Implications for strategy	The organization is a rational actor seeking to maximize competitive advantage; strategy becomes a cohesive, systematic mechanical process of enacting intellectually derived tasks.	Strategy centres on repeated patterning of resources and activities. The objective becomes stability, sustainability, legitimacy, belonging and survival.	Strategy flows from creative, entrepreneurial and politically oriented actors operating in co-evolving networks. Individuals engage in situated instances of accepted practice and innovative improvization.

What we are drawing attention to here is that in our work with organizations and individuals we draw on all three of the perspectives set out in Table 6.2. The particular blend is influenced by what is at stake, yet we contend that it is difficult to deal with creativity and emergence in strategic management without paying attention to some of the micro-features indicated in the column on creative action. Any longitudinal research engagement we have undertaken eventually gives rise to stories about performance measures and targets, about individuals, situations, episodes, heroes, villains, good times, bad times, personalities, lessons, deals, etc. These are the social and cultural fabric of the organization and allow those involved to reflect on, and talk about, the possible patterns of interconnection, or rules of thumb that seem to be associated, on a recurring basis, with such stories. Just talking about such things, in our experience, and openly acting as expressive, emotional, intuitive and creative individual human beings—as a legitimized aspect of strategic management—is central to sustaining the vitality of organizational life. Figure 6.1 depicts this diagrammatically in what we call the strategy cycle.

This is our explanation of how strategic management actually happens. We do indeed plan, paradoxically knowing that the subsequent reality will be unlikely to conform. We then experiment and improvise, trying to make sense

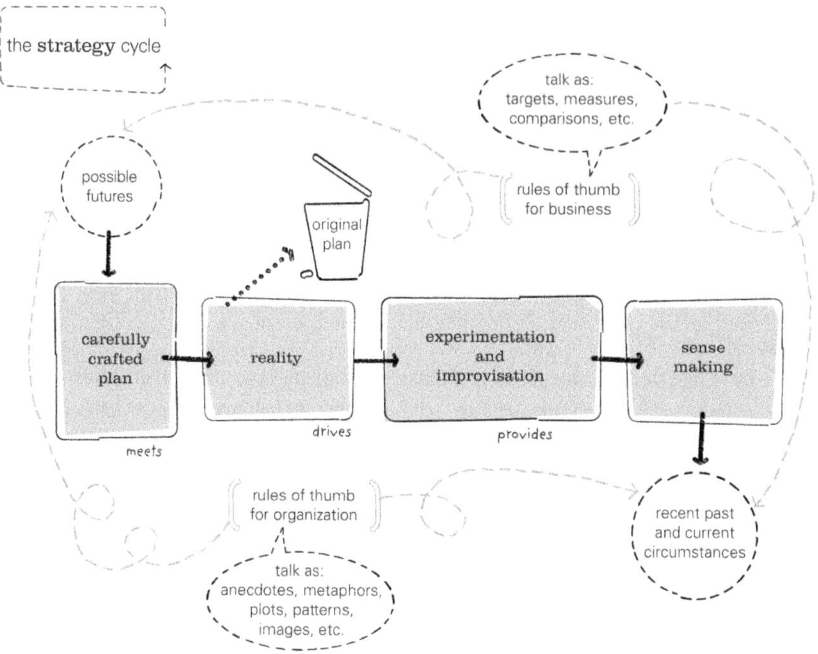

Figure 6.1 The Strategy Cycle

Robert MacIntosh & Donald MacLean, *Strategic Management: Strategists at Work*, 2015, reproduced with permission of Palgrave Macmillan

of an emergent reality, drawing on faculties that are at least as much art as science; 'bardic' in our terms above. The strategist's role is to understand—through conversations, stylized stories and performances—the connections and principles that have created what we experience and simultaneously to glimpse, share and engender participation in new possible futures that may eventually be cast as a new plan.

The Strategy Cycle suggests two points of difference from much of the extant strategic management literature. First, because it argues that strategic management is enacted by situated individuals, there is no universal expression of the cycle, no one-size-fits-all approach to strategy. People and situations vary—indeed, people vary between situations. Our research indicates that individuals navigate this cycle in different ways—skipping bits, 'going backwards', dwelling here or there. For example, in relation to the 'carefully crafted plan' part of the cycle, we have identified three distinct strategy styles[3] which tend to foreground a focus on trends in the environment, internal resources or strategic intent, i.e. strategists tend to be trend driven, resource driven or intent driven, respectively.

However, perhaps a more significant aspect of 'Strategic Styles' is whether the balance of attention to strategic management, and associated talk, focuses on the upper or lower feedback loops in the cycle. Those involved in the strategic management process may choose to focus 'official' conversation on performance, structures, targets or measures. This is by far the most common orientation to strategic management in our own experience, yet a smaller number of individuals or management teams choose to downplay planning and formality altogether, openly espousing a preference for 'making it up as they go along'. Whilst to some this latter orientation might be dismissed as simply lacking the systematic discipline of textbook 'formulate then implement' strategy, in our experience it is more often the result of a deeply held preference for strategy and organization as the ongoing emergence of socially negotiated personal expression and collective creativity. For people in organizations of this type, the idea of mechanically implementing strategy (usually someone else's) is simply alien to their view of how work should be.

In our experience, some organizations balance, over time, their focus on both feedback loops, based in part on personal preference and in part on circumstance. In something of an over-generalization, organizations which are larger, more formal, scientifically orientated or intensive seem to focus on the upper loop. Smaller organizations, more organic or lifestyle- or artistic-oriented ones, seem to prefer the lower. In reality the picture is more nuanced. Indeed in the spirit of this book, the possibility of regional and cultural differences in style could merit further consideration—as we tend to lose sight of the origins of particular styles. This lack of concern for provenance runs the risk of our mimicking 'best practice' at the expense of regional/cultural distinctiveness and creative diversity in the broader ecosystem. By way of example, one of the authors (D.M.) of this chapter has conducted exploratory research in the Scottish Highlands and Islands which would suggest some similarities with the above pattern—larger organizations (relatively few in number) tending towards the orthodox style, focused primarily on the upper feedback loop with talk centred on targets, control, measures, etc, surrounded by myriad smaller, often rural, businesses focused primarily on the lower loop. The potential dangers and costs of such a situation arise not out of a shortfall of homogeneous 'best practice' but out of a failure to recognize, understand and cross-fertilize differences.

These differences in two types of strategic conversation may be analogous to the differences between red and grey squirrels. The former is smaller, more elusive, generally more 'rural', perhaps vulnerable, connected to particular territories, often more remote or 'edge' areas. The latter is larger, more territorially expansive, more aggressive and more commonly found in our business and industrial centres.

Rather than characterizing either as right/wrong, our point is that there are inherent, and potentially valuable, differences in both individual and collective strategy styles. In essence, the two styles discussed above are likely to be extreme ends of a broad spectrum populated by many intermediate varieties. The strategy ecosystem is a rich and diverse one requiring dialogue across its various participants and less by way of shoehorning of people and organizations into preferred 'templates'.

The second point of difference with the strategy cycle is that talk and other forms of interaction are central and that talk itself can vary from informal chat through to highly affective, stylized performance. If we understand 'the organization' and 'strategic management' as concepts invoked in talk and deal with each other as human beings rather than creatures inadvertently caught up in some kind of herd-like response or, worse, as cogs in a machine, then we inevitably find ourselves as full-bodied participants in an emergent and unknowable dynamic—stewarded in part by bardic processes even where those bardic processes are diluted or overlooked.

We must open up to what Chia calls "artistic rigour" (2014). Talk can be art, and such art can be highly influential in social settings—as in the oral tradition of the bards described above. Instead of this, however, John Shotter points towards our tendency, perhaps as a consequence of a relentlessly rational education system, to articulate all the difficulties we experience as 'problems' which ought to have 'solutions' (2011). Further, as Kahneman notes, we each tend, when faced with a difficult question, "to answer an easier one instead, usually without noticing the substitution" (2012, p. 12). Our tendency to concentrate on an abstract 'problem' literally *abstracts* us from the situation itself. We thus become complicit in taking ourselves away from the situation, imagining perhaps that the real difficulty doesn't reside somewhere amidst our interaction with others present.

At this stage in our chapter it seems appropriate to make what is perhaps our major point. These variations in style matter—to us as people who experience much of our lives in organizations. In other words, the strategy cycle in a healthy organization not only can accommodate differences in style but should aim to harness them to the benefit of all concerned. In this sense, our talk really matters to us as people. If we concentrate all of our efforts on the upper loop, all of our talk is somewhat emaciated, focused exclusively on 'function' and usually based on some abstract logic in which people are effectively subordinated to the status of resources. If, on the other hand, we concentrate all of our talk on the lower line, our stories and bardic processes, focused on 'meaning', might create a richer poetic process for us as participants, but the functioning of the collective may suffer. We need both. However, in our experience, partly as a consequence of education, we are considerably more adept (and comfortable) in the domain of problems, abstract logic and function than we are in the domain of one and other as people struggling to express ourselves and create something together. As people, as poets, we have perhaps a lot still to learn from our forebears. Much of our talk in organizations is far from beautiful, far from engaging, far from compelling.

In our view, many of our difficulties in strategic management are 'relational'; they may be 'resolved' through sensitive conversation and 'expressive-responsive' dialogue rather than 'represented' as an abstract technical problem to be solved (Shotter, 2011). The "creeping impersonalism" of strategic management theory referred to by Powell (2014) needs to be addressed by a more mature and confident ability to deal with each other as individual people. We must learn to talk more openly about what we feel, fear, hope, imagine and so forth. And we must acknowledge that being able to do so is an art which we must take seriously if we are to cultivate our abilities. This requires serious study and discipline. As researchers we must therefore pay more attention to these dimensions of lived experience if we are to approach an understanding of emergent change as a creative achievement of human participants. People, poetry and paradox should 'come in' from the edge of strategy.

Notes

1. The BBC comedy series *Blackadder* ran for over four seasons, from 1983 to 1989. Four different generations of the character Baldrick appear, with each season being placed in a specific historical period.
2. The terms 'system 1' and 'system 2' were popularized by Daniel Kahneman but were originally developed by Evans and Stanovich, who themselves point out that the distinction is both "ancient in origin and widespread in philosophical and psychological writing" (2013, p. 223).
3. We have developed a questionnaire which maps individuals against these three strategy styles. It is available at www.stridesite.com.

References

Andrews, Kenneth R., Christensen, C. Roland, Guth, William D & Learned, Edmund P. (1965). *Business policy: Text and cases*. Homewood, IL: Irwin Homewood.

Ansoff, Igor (1965). *Corporate strategy: An analytical approach to business policy for growth and expansion*. New York: McGraw-Hill.

Barley, Stephen R. (2016). 60th anniversary issue: Ruminations on how we became a mystery house and how we might get out. *Administrative Science Quarterly*, 61(1), 1–8.44.

Barney, Jay (1991). Firm resources and sustained competitive advantage. *Journal of Management*, 17(1), 99–120.

Beech, Nic, Burns, Harry, Caestecker, Linda, MacIntosh, Robert & MacLean, Donald (2004). Paradox as an invitation to act in problematic change situations. *Human Relations*, 57, 1311–1332.

Burns, James (1978). *Leadership*. New York: Harper & Row.

Burns, Robert (1785). *To a mouse, on turning her up in her nest with the plough, poems, chiefly in the Scottish dialect*. Kilmarnock: John Wilson Publishers.

Carter, Chris (2013). The age of strategy: Strategy, organizations and society. *Business History*, 55, 1047–1057.

Chadwick, Nora (2002). *The Celts*. London: Folio.

Chandler, Alfred (1962). *Strategy and structure: Chapters in the history of American industrial enterprise*. Cambridge, MA: MIT Press.

Chia, Robert (2014). Reflections on the distinctiveness of European management scholarship. *European Management Journal*, 32, 683–688.

Cilliers, Paul (1998). *Complexity and postmodernism*. London: Routledge.

Coveney, Peter & Highfield, Roger (1996). *Frontiers of complexity*. London: Faber and Faber Ltd.

Drazin, Robert & Sandelands, Lloyd (1992). Autogenesis: A perspective on the process of organizing. *Organization Science*, 3, 230–249.

Evans, Jonathan St. B. T. & Stanovich, Keith (2013). Dual process theories of higher cognition: Advancing the debate. *Perspectives on Psychological Science*, 8(3), 223–241.

Freedman, Lawrence (2013). *Strategy: A history*. New York: Oxford University Press.

Fu, Ping Ping, Tsui, Anne S., Lui, Jun & Li, Lan (2010). Pursuit of whose happiness? Executive Leaders transformational behaviours and personal values. *Administrative Science Quarterly*, 55, 222–254.

Joas, Hans (1996). *The creativity of action*. Cambridge, UK: Polity Press.

Johnson, Gerry, Melin, Lief & Whittington, Richard (2003). Introduction: Micro strategy and strategizing: Towards an activity-based view. *Journal of Management Studies*, 40(3), 3–22.

Kahneman, Daniel (2012). *Thinking, fast and slow*. London: Penguin Books.

Kerr, Steven (1975). On the folly of rewarding A, while hoping for B. *Academy of Management Journal*, 18, 769–783.

Lehane, Brendan (2005). *Early Celtic Christianity*. London: Continuum.

MacIntosh, Robert, Beech, Nic, Bartunek, Jean, Mason, Katy, Cooke, Bill & Denyer, David (2017). Impact and management research: Exploring relationships between temporality, dialogue, reflexivity and praxis. *British Journal of Management*, 28(1), 3–13.

MacIntosh, Robert & MacLean, Donald (1999). Conditioned emergence: A dissipative structures approach to transformation. *Strategic Management Journal*, 20, 297–316.

MacIntosh, Robert & MacLean, Donald (2015). *Strategic management: Strategists at work*. London: Palgrave.

MacIntosh, Robert, MacLean, Donald, Stacey, Ralph & Griffin, Douglas (Eds.) (2006). *Complexity and organization: Readings and conversations*. Abingdon: Routledge.

MacLean, Donald & MacIntosh, Robert (2012). Strategic change as creative action. *International Journal of Strategic Change Management*, 4(1), 80–97.

MacLean, Donald, MacIntosh, Robert & Grant, Sandra (2002). Mode 2 management research. *British Journal of Management*, 13(3), 189–207, December 2002.

McIntosh, Alastair (2004). *Soil and soul*. London: Autumn.

Mintzberg, Henry (1994). *The rise and fall of strategic planning*. Hemel Hempsted: Prentice Hall.

Mitroff, Ian I. & Silvers, Abraham (2009). *Dirty rotten strategies: How we trick ourselves and others into solving the wrong problems precisely*. Stanford: Stanford University Press.

Pettigrew, Andrew M. (1992). The character and significance of strategy process research. *Strategic Management Journal*, 13(s), 5–16.

Porter, Michael E. (1985). *Competitive advantage: Creating and sustaining superior performance*. New York: Free Press.

Powell, Thomas C. (2014). Strategic management and the person. *Strategic Organization*, 12(3), 200–207.

Prigogine, Ilya & Stengers, Isabelle (1984). *Order out of chaos: Man's new dialogue with nature*. New York: Bantam Books.

Rumelt, Richard (2011). *Good strategy, bad strategy: The difference and why it matters*. London: Profile Books.

Schendel, Dan (1992). Introduction to the Winter 1992 special issue on fundamental themes in strategy process research. *Strategic Management Journal*, 13(s), 1–3.

Shotter, John (2011). *Getting it: Withness-thinking and the dialogical . . . in practice*. New York: Hampton Press.

Shotter, John & Katz, Arlene M. (1996). Articulating a practice from within a practice itself: Establishing formative dialogues by use of a social poetics. *Concepts and Transformation*, 1(2/3), 213–237.

Sloan, Alfred (1963). *My life with General Motors*. Garden City, NY: Doubleday.

Sull, Donald N. & Eisenhardt, Kathleen (2012). Simple rules for a complex world. *Harvard Business Review*, 90(9), 68–74.

Teece, David J. (2007). Explicating dynamic capabilities: The nature and microfoundations of (sustainable) enterprise performance. *Strategic Management Journal*, 28(13), 1319–1350.

Teece, David J., Pisano, Gary & Shuen, Amy (1997). Dynamic capabilities and strategic management. *Strategic Management Journal*, 18(7), 509–533.

Tsoukas, Haridimos & Hatch, Mary Jo (2001). Complex thinking, complex practice: The case for a narrative approach to organizational complexity. *Human Relations*, 54(8), 979–1013.

7 Resurrecting Organization by Going Beyond Organizations

Göran Ahrne, Nils Brunsson and David Seidl

Introduction

Organization studies is a large field of research involving thousands of scholars all over the world and taught at universities and at an ever-expanding number of business schools (Augier, March, & Sullivan, 2005). The field has a wide agenda—dealing with almost any type of event in formal organizations and other more general social phenomena such as institutional logics, institutional work, categorization and networks. Organization studies has been open to import concepts and theories from other social sciences and even from natural science, including such disciplines as economics, psychology, science and technology studies and biology. However, organization studies has been less successful in exporting its ideas to other fields of social science; interest in the issues addressed by organization studies is not great outside the field. Many scholars, like Bourdieu, Giddens and Habermas, who presented general societal theories during the late twentieth century, seemed to need no concept or theory of organization and the concept is almost equally weak in economics. The common view among organizational scholars—that organizations matter and that modern society is filled with organizations, such that it can even be characterized as a "society of organizations" (Perrow, 1991) or an "organisational economy" (Simon, 1991)—has had little impact outside the field of organization studies.

In order to make organization a relevant category, one must demonstrate that the social order we find in organizations is not a mere reflection of a more general social order that can be adequately understood by concepts and theories describing society in general. An early example is Max Weber's (1922) theory of bureaucracy, which described organization as a specific phenomenon requiring special concepts and a special theory. A generation later, March and Simon (1958) characterized organizations as a specific type of social order, distinct from other forms of order. Yet, whereas classic organization scholarship was concerned with the particularities of organizations, over the past few decades there has been a drift away from organizations to such other phenomena as institutions and networks.

In this chapter, we develop two proposals for the future of organization studies aimed at increasing its significance and relevance for studies of social processes outside organizations. The first move involves a return to the classics by emphasizing the distinctiveness of organization as a particular type of social order. We argue that this requires a return of decisions to the core of the field. The second move involves the extension of our notion of organization beyond (formal) organizations, thereby allowing insights from organization research to be applied to phenomena studied in other fields and increasing the chance of a transfer of theories and concepts to other disciplines.

The rest of this chapter is structured into five sections. We first elaborate on how the field of organization studies has increasingly lost sight of organization as its central object of research. We then advance our suggestion to return to the classics and put decisions at the core of the field. This is followed by an elaboration of our suggestion to widen the concept of organization to phenomena beyond formal organizations. We then illustrate how organization studies can fruitfully be extended to other domains, such as markets, standards and families. And finally we elaborate on the general implications of the two suggestions and suggest a new research agenda for organization studies.

Organization Studies Losing Sight of the Organization

Although organizations have been studied since the days of Max Weber and even before, the field did not really take off until the 1960s. In their seminal book, *Organizations*, James March and Herbert Simon (1958) summarized organizational research up to that time and laid out issues for further inquiry. They argued that organizations had played "an unobtrusive part in the literature of modern social science" (March & Simon, 1958, p. 2). They attributed that lack of attention to the fact that little was known about organizational research in other social sciences, and it seems that they hoped to remedy that situation with the publication of their book. Their explicit motivation for a special theory of organizations was that organizations influence people's behaviour in a different way than is the case outside of the organizational context. This influence makes a particularly high degree of coordination possible, which "accounts for the ability of organizations to deal in a highly coordinated way with their environments" (March & Simon, 1958, p. 4).

A significant theme of the book was decisions and decision making. March and Simon argued for a perspective from which organization members are seen as decision makers and problem solvers. The book was followed by extensive research into organizational decision making, with March and Simon as forerunners, but with contributions from many others (Brunsson, 2007; Hodgkinson & Starbuck, 2008; March, 1988; Simon, 1960). In particular, the weak relationship between rationality and decision was emphasized. And an important issue became the extent to which and how decisions were implemented (Pressman & Wildavsky, 1973).

Another dominant theme in early organization theory, already present in March and Simon's book, was the relationship between organizations and their so-called environment. Arguably, this perspective came from systems theory in biology, which was fashionable at the time, and in which the distinction between organism and environment was translated to organization and environment (Czarniawska, 2013). In biology, this distinction can be understood as a physical one, whereas for organizations it can only be a metaphor, which can be helpful or misleading.

These themes fit well into an argument for organizations as representing a special social order worthy of its own concepts and theories. The metaphor of organization and environment indicated that there was a fundamental difference between the two. March and Simon (1958, p. 4) contrasted organizations—which they assumed to have individuals as their members—to "the diffuse and variable relations among organizations" and mentioned markets as an example of organizational environments. Although it was noted early that a large part of the environment consisted of other organizations (Perrow, 1991), they were not assumed to be ordered in the same way. March and Simon discussed decisions and communication and compared the high specificity of the transmission of a customer order within organizations with the low specificity of the transmission of rumours in society. Organizational order seemed to be largely a decided order, filled with plans and instructions, an order that differed from the order outside the organization.

In the late 1970s, however, an article by John Meyer and Bryan Rowan (1977) sparked the development of a new approach in North-American (and later also in European) organization scholarship, which came to be known as neo-institutional theory and provided a fundamental criticism of the earlier perspective on organizations (see Suddaby, in this book). According to proponents of this theory, the image of organizations as locally decided orders was exaggerated at best and misleading at worst. Instead, a more traditional sociological perspective was revived. Organizations were treated as local editions of a major societal institution, and much if not most of their behaviour was seen as determined by institutions rather than by local decisions unique to each organization. In essence, organizations were conceptualized not so much as local orders, but as orders representing wider social institutions. Accordingly, the driving force of change in organizations was seen to lie not in the internal conditions and organizational decisions, but in changes in ideas, perceptions and norms in society at large or in a particular organizational sector or field.

With the rise of institutionalism, the concept of the organizational environment became awkward; although it seemed possible to describe other organizations or markets as being outside a focal organization, it was difficult to describe institutions as existing outside organizations. Organizations were rather conceptualized as being submerged in a wider culture. But most important, the institutional argument was radical and reactionary, at least implicitly, in the sense that it questioned the fairly new and fragile idea that the study of organizations required its own concepts and theories. Yet unexpectedly, the institutional perspective became extremely influential in organization research for three decades. It has also been highly fruitful, giving rise to many new insights in organization studies, many of which are now central parts of the standard knowledge in the field. Still, we believe that it is now worth reviving the search for the special characteristics of organizations that can be found in the classical version of organization studies. The fact that organizations are deeply immersed in a wider culture does not preclude the possibility that they are also special systems with special characteristics. First and foremost, we believe that it is time to revive the fundamental idea of the significance of decisions and decision making in organizations.

Back to the Classics—Decisions at the Centre

On the European scene, at least two attempts have been made to put decisions back at the core of the field, as fundamental phenomena for understanding organizations and for distinguishing them from other social phenomena. One attempt was undertaken by Niklas Luhmann, who in the 1960s started to analyze organizations as systems of decision, a project that ended in 2000 with the posthumously published book *Organization and Decision* [*Organisation und Entscheidung*] in 2000 (Seidl & Mormann, 2015; see also Czarniawska, in this book). Inspired by March and Simon (1958), Luhmann argued that organizations differed from other forms of social order in that they were based on decisions, which Luhmann conceptualized as a particular form of communication. Decisions, he argued, differed from 'ordinary' communications in that they informed not only about a particular content (i.e. the selected option), but also about the fact that this content is the result of a selection (Luhmann, 2005). In other words, the decision highlights its own contingency—the fact that there are other options that could have been selected; only by highlighting this fact can the decision be recognized as a 'real' decision rather than a necessity.

Luhmann argued that because of their specific form, decisions are particularly precarious communications: highlighting the existence of other options makes it easy for ensuing communications to question the selected one: Why was it selected over others if they are all 'real' options? At the same time, this form of communication is an extremely powerful order-generating mechanism. Drawing on March and Simon's (1958) concept of "uncertainty absorption", Luhmann argued that decisions reduce the uncertainty for ensuing communications: To the extent that a decision is accepted by ensuing communications, those communications can take the selected option as given and can ignore the uncertainty involved in the original decision making. This allows organizations to handle greater levels of complexity than other forms of social order. It enables firms to mass-produce goods, schools to provide education on a large scale and governments to administer states (Luhmann, 2000; Seidl & Becker, 2006).

Having put decisions at the core of his organization theory, Luhmann traced all organizational structures and processes back to decisions. Drawing again on March and Simon (1958), he argued that organizational structures could be conceptualized as decision premises. These decision premises, which are the result of earlier decisions, define the scope for further decisions. For example, organizations decide on decision programs (e.g. plans) or on channels for decision communications (e.g. particular hierarchical structures). Organizational processes, in turn, are conceptualized as processes of decisions, whereby one decision calls forth ensuing decisions, resulting in a self-reproducing stream of decisions. Together, this leads to a radical view of organizations as "systems of decisions that consist of decisions that produce the decisions of which they consist, through the decisions of which they consist" (Luhmann, 1992, p. 166, our translation).

Ahrne and Brunsson (2011) made a more recent attempt to analyze decisions as fundamental for organization. Their purpose was to find a broader conceptualization of organization than formal organizations—yet precise and not too broad. They defined organization as a "decided social order"—an order that is the result of decisions and that could be contrasted to such emergent orders as institutions and networks. Drawing partly on Luhmann (2000), they conceptualized decisions as *communications* of selections about what people are expected to do, how they are being classified and how they are being treated. Organization is characterized by the fact that all the elements necessary for the continuation or repetition of social interaction are the result of decisions, rather than the result of common institutions, norms or status differences. In line with that notion, they identified five fundamental decisions for organized social interaction. (1) It is necessary for those involved in the interaction to know who else is involved. In organization this is accomplished through decisions on *membership*, defining who is a member and who is not. (2) It is necessary for the participants to gain some shared understanding about what they are doing and how to do it. By organization, this is accomplished through decisions on *rules* for the actions of the members. (3) It is necessary for the participants to be able to observe each other to know how to continue. In organization this is accomplished through decisions on how to *monitor* the members. (4) Participants must be able to get other participants to do what is expected of them. In organization this is accomplished through decisions about positive and negative *sanctions*. (5) Participants must have an understanding about who has the initiative and power. In organization this is accomplished through decisions about *hierarchy* (i.e. through decisions about which decisions are binding). These five types of decisions are seen as the elements of organization. They are constitutive for formal organizations; in other words, a formal organization is expected to have access to all these elements in creating its internal order. But organizational elements can also exist outside the context of formal organizations, as we discuss in the next section.

A Step Beyond the Classics: Organization Outside and Among Organizations

A standard assumption that has remained in the field since classical times is that organization studies is about formal organizations. It is no coincidence that March and Simon's book was entitled *Organizations* with an "s" rather than *Organization*. A more abstract definition of organization introduces the possibility that organization can take place in contexts other than those provided by formal organizations (Ahrne & Brunsson, 2011). This was suggested early on by Karl Weick (1969), who proposed that we speak of 'organizing' rather than 'organizations'. Weick extended the term to include *any* form of social order, however, such that 'organizing' becomes more or less synonymous with '(re)production of social order'. We consider this suggestion problematic in that it undermines the potential for organization studies contributing a distinctive perspective on the social world—a perspective that would also be useful in other disciplines. (After all, all disciplines within the social sciences are involved in explaining the [re]production of social order.) In contrast, the proposed concept of organization as 'decided order' allows for the transfer of the term to other domains outside formal organization, while simultaneously preserving its distinctiveness.

This extension of the concept of organization to phenomena outside formal organizations challenges the relevance of the classical distinction between organization and environment and questions the idea that organization and environment are fundamentally different. This leads instead to the new distinction between organized and non-organized social interactions. Hence, in the terminology of both distinctions, one can describe organization as something that happens both inside and outside formal organizations. Such formulations open up new areas for analysis for organization studies, namely for social phenomena outside organizations. But the reverse is also likely; many things that happen inside formal organizations are *not* examples of organization but of networks or institutions, for instance.

An important step in allowing the concept of organization to transfer to domains outside formal organizations is the acknowledgement that a "decided order" does not necessarily require all the five elements of organization—decisions on membership, hierarchy, rules, monitoring and sanctions—to be present at the same time. This conception of organization opens up the possibility that organization may come in parts, such that only one or a few elements of organization are actually used within or outside a formal organization. Ahrne and Brunsson (2011) have written in this context of "partial organization". Some social orders are based only on membership as a means of organizing, whereas the other elements of organization are missing. This is the case with so-called 'customer clubs' initiated by commercial firms: the Ikea Family Club or the British Airways Executive Club, for instance. In other cases, the social order may be based only on hierarchy, as when participants in a meeting nominate somebody as chair.

There are three reasons why organization may only be 'partial'.

(1) People may see no need to use all organizational elements; an order may already exist, for example, and one merely wants to add one or two organizational elements to shape this order. (2) People may not want to add more organization, because they are not willing to pay the cost in the form of necessary effort or the responsibility that tends to come with organization. (3) People are not able to use all the elements, even if they should like to.

As a consequence of the partialness of organization, there is an increased probability that decisions may be challenged and implementation may not happen. Along these lines, Ostrom (1990) argued that all organizational elements—which she referred to as "design principles"—must be employed in order that common pool resources be handled successfully. She showed that the failure to introduce all elements of organization resulted in outcomes detrimental to the majority of interested parties. In other settings, however, partial organization may be highly successful, as we describe below.

Extending Organization Studies to Other Domains

Acknowledging that organization as a form of social ordering can also occur outside formal organizations creates the possibility of applying genuine concepts of organization studies to phenomena that have traditionally been studied from other disciplinary perspectives. In this section, we illustrate the potential of the proposed extension of the concept of organization by showing how it can be applied to the study of standards, meta-organizations, markets, networks and families.

Standardization

Standardization is one phenomenon to which the extended concept of organization has been applied. Standards can be defined as "rule[s] for common and voluntary use, decided by one or several people or organizations" (Brunsson, Rasche, & Seidl, 2012, p. 616). Standards can be found both within and outside formal organizations and have become such a common feature of modern life that one may even speak of a "world of standards" (Brunsson & Jacobsson, 2000; Timmermans & Epstein, 2010). Although there is an established body of literature in organization studies that has examined how organizations—the International Organization for Standardization (ISO), for example—set standards and how organizations are affected by standards, newer studies have started to examine standardization as a way of organizing society (Brunsson, 2000; Brunsson et al., 2012). From this perspective, standards constitute examples of partial organization, as they possess some elements of organization while lacking others: Standardization is based on decided rules but other elements of organization are often missing.

Studying standardization as partial organization has opened various new avenues of inquiry: Several researchers have begun to examine the degree of partialness of standardization as organization. Although many examples of standardization have only a single element of organization (e.g. the decided rules) other examples are almost complete organizations, as they include membership, monitoring and sanctioning. Relatedly, there are studies comparing the effects of different degrees and forms of partialness of organizing. For example, there are many studies that have compared regulation by standards to regulation by state law (e.g. Mörth, 2004). These studies have shown that, due to the lack of some elements of organization, standardization often results in greater degrees of variation in the application of the rules (e.g. Ahrne & Brunsson, 2011), in a competition between different sets of rules (e.g. Reinecke, Manning, & Von Hagen, 2012) and in unclear accountability for the unintended consequences of compliance with the rules (Seidl, 2007).

In view of the different effects of the partialness of standardization as organization, researchers have explored the reasons for choosing this form of organization over more complete forms. It has been shown that standards are often chosen in cases in which the rule setters have no access to all elements of organization (e.g. monitoring and sanctioning). A good example is the area of transnational regulation (Ahrne & Brunsson, 2006), in which the standard setters lack the authority to monitor and sanction compliance with their rules. In other cases, the partialness of standardization is also purposefully chosen, as it has particular advantages. Partial forms of organizing often are less costly—for example, they allow for greater flexibility in the application of the rules (Mörth, 2004), are considered easier to change (Seidl, 2007) and are less easily challenged by unions and protest movements (Ahrne & Brunsson, 2011).

In spite of the missing organizational elements, standardization can still be powerful, particularly when the missing organizational elements are compensated for by contributions from "third parties" (Brunsson & Jacobsson, 2000). Compliance with the rules is often monitored and sanctioned by organizations other than the standard setter, for example, thereby contributing to the enforcement of the originally voluntary rules (Kerwer, 2005). In other cases, there is also a more diffuse set of such third parties as customers or industry partners, who indirectly monitor and sanction rule following by basing their decision to buy products or to cooperate with particular firms on compliance with those rules. Sometimes the lack of monitoring and sanctioning mechanisms is also compensated through high levels of legitimacy and authority for a rule setter (Tamm Hallström, 2004).

Meta-Organizations

Most standards are directed at organizations rather than individuals, thus illustrating how the diffuse and variable relations among organizations that March and Simon wrote about are, in fact, organized. Another more extreme case of the way organizations organize their relationships is when they establish meta-organizations: formal organizations with similar interests or agendas joining forces to establish a common organization, of which they themselves are the members. In other words, meta-organizations have organizations as their members. In meta-organizations the members make joint decisions but still retain their identity as autonomous organizations. Large industry associations and international governmental organizations are well-known examples of meta-organizations.

Meta-organizations substantially reduce the difference between organization and environment. Meta-organizations are established in order to transform part of the environment of each organization to an organized order of the same kind as its internal order. But meta-organizations also change the members' relationship to organizations that do not become members (Ahrne & Brunsson, 2008). For each member, the common internal environment created by the meta-organization offers a kind of protected area, by circumscribing the influence of other more hostile organizations outside the meta-organization. Instead of being exposed to rules and monitoring, for example, from other organizations, the members create a protected zone in which they make their own rules and monitor each other.

Meta-organizations break with the classic assumption that the members of organizations are individuals. The lasting effect of this assumption is probably one reason why meta-organizations have spurred little interest in organization studies and why they, when they are actually analyzed, have often been treated as if they were organizations with individual membership: Scholars have not taken seriously the meta-organizations' claim that their members are other organizations, but instead have defined the organization as the secretariat (with individual employees as the members) and treated the organizational members as a kind of environment (Barnett & Finnemore, 2004; Marcussen, 2002).

As formal organizations, meta-organizations have, in principle, access to all organizational elements. But they tend to have difficulties in using them. In order to be recognized as independent actors, the members of meta-organizations must defend their autonomy and are typically reluctant to accept too much organization. For example, meta-organizations often prefer to issue standards instead of binding rules. There are also limitations to the amount of monitoring members are willing to accept. Using negative sanctions is even more difficult (Ahrne, Brunsson, & Kerwer, 2016).

The most salient organizational element in meta-organizations is membership. The strength of many meta-organizations comes from their ability to decide the criteria for membership and the conditions for access. Meta-organizations are based on some kind of similarity among the members and for both access and continued membership, similarity is required, thus producing or reinforcing organized isomorphism (Ahrne & Brunsson, 2005).

There is a tension between each member's need for organizing itself and the meta-organization's need for some authority to organize its members in order to be considered relevant. This tension makes for change rather than stability. Some meta-organizations have become stronger organizers over time, while others remain weak or are even weakened. Some meta-organizations, such as the EU, have succeeded for a long time to organize its members to a relatively high degree and in multiple ways (Kerwer, 2013), while other meta-organizations, such as some industry associations, are examples of the opposite (Berkowitz & Dumez, 2015). At the extremes, meta-organizations may disappear, either because the members merge—thus turning the meta-organization into an individual-based organization with fewer problems of organizing—or because the meta-organization may be dissolved by the members leaving it, thus reducing the degree of organization (Ahrne & Brunsson, 2008). An intriguing task for organizational research is to discover the processes and factors that influence the degree of organization in meta-organizations and how this plays out over time.

Organizing Markets

It is common in social science to contrast organizations with markets (Coase, 1937; Williamson, 1975). Admittedly, organizations and markets represent different social forms—according to Marshall (1920), they represent the two fundamental forms of the economy. Yet, they are not irreconcilable opposites; in practice they are often combined. Markets often exist within formal organizations; internal markets in firms constitute one example, exchanges such as stock exchanges constitute another. In fact, even the currently dominating neoclassical concept of the market in economics was originally based on studies of markets within organizations—in particular, Léon Walras' studies of exchanges which he explicitly described as "perfectly organized markets" (Walras, 1954, p. 83). Exchanges have also been seen as the markets that come closest to the ideal of being perfectly competitive (Samuelsson, 1969). Most markets, however, exist outside formal organizations. Yet, they are organized.

Contemporary economics has a tradition of emphasizing processes of mutual adaptation in markets (Lindblom, 1979)—to the extent that markets are sometimes described as 'spontaneous' social orders. Some economists and economic sociologists have added institutions as another kind of ordering mechanism (Aspers, 2011; North, 1990). But organization is a further mechanism. Just like formal organizations, markets are ordered not only by mutual adaptation and institutions, but also by organization (Ahrne, Aspers, & Brunsson, 2015): Many markets are organized through decisions about membership: allowing only certain people or organizations to obtain licences to act as sellers of taxi rides or pharmaceuticals, for example. Products sold in markets must comply with decided rules about product safety or rules regarding product labelling. Sellers and buyers are monitored by certification and accreditation activities or by rating institutes. Positive sanctions in the form of prizes and awards are common in many markets, and negative sanctions such as boycotts are sometimes imposed. There are many parties involved in organizing markets: national government authorities; international government organizations; various civil society organizations interested in saving the world or protecting the interests of disadvantaged groups; intermediaries such as brokers, agents or auction houses; associations of sellers or buyers. Many of these are meta-organizations.

Markets offer a fertile ground for organizational research. Students of organization are well equipped to analyze and explain how and why markets are organized and why the kind and form or organization varies among markets. Value conflicts in markets seem to be one driver of market organization (Alexius & Tamm Hallström, 2014). Similar questions can be asked about markets as have traditionally been asked about formal organizations. What is the role of organization when markets are created? Who can become a market organizer and how do market organizers become influential? How do they achieve authority and legitimacy? What drives reorganization of markets?

Networks

Many social relationships outside organizations are described as networks (Nohria & Eccles, 1992). Similar to markets, networks are often regarded as the opposite of organization. Relationships in networks are assumed to be non-hierarchical and 'informal', and networks are seen as being maintained through mechanisms such as reciprocity, trust and social capital (Borgatti & Foster, 2003, Podolny & Page, 1998). Some researchers even see networks as a more reliable and innovative form of cooperation and coordination than formal organizations are (Kanter & Eccles, 1992).

Instead of treating organizations and networks as opposites, our conceptualization of organization allows networks to be seen as social orders with varying degrees of organization (Ahrne & Brunsson, 2011). For example, over the last decades new forms of networks have emerged, such as hacker collectives (Dobusch & Schoeneborn, 2015), online communities (O'Mahony & Ferraro, 2007) and terrorist networks (Schoeneborn & Scherer, 2012) which are partially organized. A social relationship that emerged as a pure network of individuals without any organization often gradually becomes organized with one or more organizational elements, thereby making the relationships more visible both for those involved and from the outside. Some people may develop a list of network members, so everybody knows who is involved in the network, or they can choose a convenor that has the authority to decide about future meetings and can set the agenda. In order to accomplish common action or make common statements, even more organization may be needed. More generally, studies have shown that organization can contribute to the functioning of networks. Starkey, Barnatt and Tempest (2000), for example, in their study of the UK television industry, found that networks that are focused upon intermittent projects develop "latent organizations" that help sustain the network.

Social movements are often blends of emergent and decided orders (den Hond, de Bakker, & Smith, 2015). If a movement must choose a future strategy, it must decide how to make this decision and who shall be allowed to take part in the decision making (Kuechler & Dalton, 1994, p. 289). It is not uncommon that social movements that start as unorganized networks over time turn into formal social movement organizations (Papakostas, 2012).

If we observe relationships that are described as networks in terms of organizational elements, we will probably find many variations of partial organization. In this way, it is possible to dissolve the unproductive dichotomy between organization and network and instead to investigate different uses of organizational elements. There are many intriguing questions. What consequences result from different combinations of organizational elements? Why are only some elements used and not all? What circumstances result in an increase versus a decrease in the degree of organization?

Families

Extending the concept of organization makes it possible to apply organizational concepts even to such phenomena as families. Families are a very different type of social relationship than social movements or networks of friends, for instance, in that their membership is well defined. The family is generally regarded as a central social institution (Laslett, 1973). Much of family life is ordered by institutionalized patterns of behaviour. But families are also partially organized—and to an increasing extent (Ahrne, 2015). Organization begins with the decision to establish a family. Even though the nuclear family revolves around the idea of love defined by the binary code of being in love (or not) (Luhmann, 1986), the establishment of the primary relationship is typically based on a common decision to get married or to live together.

In traditional families, relationships were generally arranged in accordance with institutional norms, but in order to break with such norms, organization is required. Many traditional institutions related to family life are currently being questioned, and there are many competing ideas concerning how a family should function. Family members must make a number of decisions regarding: how to arrange for their marriage, what they can expect from each other and whether they are going to have children.

Modern families face the dilemma of navigating in a complex institutional environment requiring many choices and decisions (Beck & Beck-Gernsheim, 1995). Their decision-making structure, however, is imperfect. Family members often lack a clear notion of how to make common decisions. And as long as the decision makers are exactly two persons, voting can be used neither as a threat nor as a practice. Modern families are probably more like "adhocracies" than "hierarchies" and, as Mintzberg (1993, p. 277) argued, "people talk a lot in these structures". But even if family members talk a great deal, it is not certain that they agree on what decisions to make or on what these decisions may imply. When decision making fails, it is likely that the relationship will relapse into old institutionalized patterns, such as traditional gender roles. Taken together, modern families can be conceptualized as partially organized with membership and perhaps some rules, but without a clear hierarchy.

Seeing families as partially organized turns them into potential objects for organization research. An interesting topic for organization scholars could be to analyse the difficulties of decision making in families and how these difficulties are resolved. As in meta-organizations, the tension between the interests of the individual member and the family as a whole seems to be currently under debate, with widely differing solutions in modern compared with traditional contexts. Against this backdrop, a systematic comparison with meta-organizations seems to be a promising project for understanding both families and meta-organizations. Another theme for further research is the varying extent to which families use monitoring and sanctions, and the ways in which these elements of organization are applied.

The Expansion and Re-Location of Organization

In a globalizing social world, the typical answer to problems of cultural integration is more organization. Organization is a critical part of a global cultural rationalization and, in the words of Bromley and Meyer (2015, p. 4), the "modern impulse" is to encounter any problematic situation with more organizational structures. Standardization is an overwhelming phenomenon in the modern world that covers not only products, but also organizational processes and management systems; it serves not only the purpose of efficient coordination, but also such political agendas as environmental protection or 'fair trade'. The ISO, just one of many standards organizations, has produced more than 20,500 standards since its foundation in 1947 (www.iso.org). Although meta-organizations are not as common as individual-based organizations, they exist in large numbers, and on the international scene there has been a great expansion during the past 60 years. Now more than 10,000 international meta-organizations play key roles in almost every area of social life. There are meta-organizations for almost anything—ranging from the protection of the producers of various goods and services to the provision of different state functions such as the protection of the environment or indigenous people, or even for increasing the popularity of cremation. Contemporary global markets are arenas not only for exchange, but also for what could be called a form of global democracy, with civil society organizations organizing them in the right way: setting rules for decent products and production processes, establishing systems for monitoring in the form of labels and for arranging boycotts.

Contemporary claims for transparency, accountability and democracy stimulate an increasing organization of existing network orders. Increasing demands for information about who is involved in a particular network triggers the construction of member lists, for example; demands for information about who has the power in a particular network triggers the establishment of a decided hierarchy. Even families have to organize more than they did in the past.

For established formal organizations such as firms or states, however, the extensive organization outside them gives less room and need for internal organization. Although they still present themselves as strong and autonomous actors that organize themselves, more and more of what they do is decided elsewhere. If organizational scholars continue to study exclusively traditional, formal organizations, such as firms, their research risks becoming increasingly less relevant for understanding society at large and societal change.

General Implications and a Research Agenda

In this chapter, we have elaborated upon recent developments in European organization research, which place organization back at the centre of organization scholarship. The suggested reorientation in organization studies is based on two fundamental movements. The first movement is a return to the classics of organization studies and its appreciation of organization as a distinctive type of social order based on decisions (as they are defined in the "Back to the Classics" section above). The second movement takes the concept of organization beyond its classic meaning and transfers it to phenomena beyond the formal organization. This is made possible in two ways: by allowing for different degrees of organization and by relaxing some of the traditional assumptions about the characteristics of organization—the assumption that only individuals, not organizations, are organized, and the assumption that the organizational environment is not organized.

These suggested movements are largely a reaction to the dominance of institutionalism and its variants in organization studies, which have shifted attention away from organization as a central concern for organization scholars. The perspective presented here shares with institutionalism the notion that the difference between organization and environment was exaggerated by classical theory. But although institutionalists argued essentially that organizations are similar to their environments because they share the same institutions, we have argued that environments are similar to organizations because both are organized. Institutional theory implies that there is less organization than the classic theorists assumed, whereas we have argued that there is more. Institutionalists have tended to treat most social phenomena as resulting from institutional processes and have largely subordinated organizations to institutions (Greenwood, Oliver, Suddaby, & Sahlin-Andersson, 2008). In contrast, the perspective presented here highlights the distinctive contributions of organization to the ordering of the world. Rather than subordinating organization to institution, organization and institution are treated as alternative forms of social ordering. This allows a comparison of the effects of the two types of social orderings. In contrast to institutions, for example, organization highlights human responsibility and draws attention to the persons with the possibility and right to make decisions. Organization tends to produce more fragile orders than institutions do, as the decided nature of the order highlights its contingency, and is therefore more likely to be contested. Whereas the concept of institution implies an existing order, decisions are attempts with uncertain consequences. Organization highlights the gap between talk and action, and much organization fails to be realized, but it is just as important for understanding organization to explain why some attempts to organize fail as to explain why other attempts are successful.

Distinguishing between organization and institution as types of social ordering also makes it possible to examine the ways in which the two relate to each other. This presupposes, however, a more precise definition of institution, one that allows it to be clearly differentiated from organization. Apart from the fact that the term 'institution' is not used consistently (Greenwood et al., 2008), there is the issue that many conceptualizations of institution include aspects of organization (Ahrne & Brunsson, 2011). Many scholars (e.g. North, 1990; Scott, 1995) consider rules such as state laws that were explicitly decided upon to be institutions, and some scholars (e.g. Christensen, Lægreid, Roness, & Røvik, 2007) even call the organizations that produce rules 'institutions'. Against this background, it seems more fruitful to restrict the term 'institution' to those social orders that are based on taken-for-granted beliefs and norms and to relegate all forms of decided orders to the term 'organization'. Doing that, we can see that organization and institution are often related in intricate ways. For example, institutions provide order to organizations and thereby reduce the amount of organization necessary (e.g. when there are established norms, fewer decided rules are required). Yet, an increase in the number of different institutions may also lead to an increase in the amount of organization required, as it may become necessary to choose between institutions (Greenwood et al., 2011). We can also observe that organizations and institutions can transform into each other. On the one hand, decided orders can turn into institutions. For example, standards may become taken for granted and the fact that they have been the result of decisions may be forgotten (Brunsson & Jacobsson, 2000). On the other hand, institutions can turn into organization. For example, people often introduce standards when they want to change an institution.

Reconceptualizing organization in the way suggested here opens up a range of new avenues for research in organization studies. Now we turn to highlight potential lines of inquiry that seem particularly promising.

1. Against the background of conceptualizing organization as one mode of social order amongst others, the most obvious line of inquiry that comes to mind is to examine the consequences of adopting organizational elements in creating social order, compared with other modes.

We have already noted, for example, that decided orders are often more fragile than institutional orders are. Decided orders have the advantage, however, in that they can handle higher levels of complexity (Luhmann, 2000) and consequently are often introduced when the level of complexity increases (Knudsen, 2005).

2. Another promising line of inquiry concerns the interaction between different types of social order. As we have noted, we often find a combination of different elements of social orderings. Decided rules are often combined with institutional norms and beliefs, for example, or networks are combined with memberships (Ahrne & Brunsson, 2011).
3. Focusing particularly on partial organization, we could explore the consequences of missing organizational elements. On the one hand, we can examine how partialness plays out in the social order. Partial organization is often more unstable, for example, due to the lack of particular organizational elements (Ahrne & Brunsson, 2011; Dobusch & Schoeneborn, 2015). On the other hand, we could examine whether and to what extent partialness is compensated through other forms of social order (e.g. Seidl, 2007).
4. Related to (3), we could examine the factors that lead to an increase or decrease in the amount of organization. We could try to find general factors that hold across various domains: The degree of organization could be related to the extent to which other forms of order are present, for instance. Apart from that, we can examine this question with regard to particular social domains.
5. More generally, we could try to identify and examine different forms and manifestations of partial organization. We expect to find a range of typical constellations of organizational elements. Some organizational elements tend to be combined with particular other elements, whereas other elements may often be found on their own.
6. Finally, this perspective advances possibilities for historical studies on the development and diffusion of various forms of complete and partial organization. Luhmann (2012/2013), for example, showed that formal organizations as forms of social order emerged relatively late in societal evolution, as they presupposed a functionally differentiated society. Previously, there were only partially organised collectivities in which some of the elements of organization were missing.

Overall, the suggested new perspective on organization puts organization studies at the heart of the social sciences. Given that almost all domains of our social world involve some degree of organization, organization studies, with its expertise in examining organizational orders, is particularly well placed to offer fundamental insights into the workings of our world. Positioned in this way, there is an opportunity for a more fruitful and reciprocal exchange of theories and concepts between organization studies and other disciplines within the social sciences. While organization studies can continue importing theories and concepts to examine non-organizational elements within formal organizations, it may also become a fruitful source of theories and concepts for scholars in other disciplines who realize that organization is part of the social systems and processes they want to understand, although they are not studying formal organizations.

Acknowledgements

We thank Leonhard Dobusch for helpful comments on earlier drafts of this chapter. We also acknowledge that Nils Brunsson's research for this article has been funded by Riksbankens Jubileumsfond, Sweden, grant 36520.

References

Ahrne, Göran (2015). The partial organization of intimate relations. *Le Libellio d'AEGIS*, 3(11), 7–19.

Ahrne, Göran, Aspers, Patrik & Brunsson, Nils (2015). The organization of markets. *Organization Studies*, 36(1), 7–27.

Ahrne, Göran & Brunsson, Nils (2005). Organizations and meta-organizations. *Scandinavian Journal of Management*, 21(4), 429–449.

Ahrne, Göran & Brunsson, Nils (2006). Organizing the world. In M.-L. Djelic & K. Sahlin-Andersson (Eds.), *Transnational governance: Institutional dynamics of regulation* (pp. 74–94). Cambridge: Cambridge University Press.

Ahrne, Göran & Brunsson, Nils (2008). *Meta-organizations*. Cheltenham: Edward Elgar Publishing.

Ahrne, Göran & Brunsson, Nils (2011). Organization outside organizations: The significance of partial organization. *Organization*, 18(1), 83–104.

Ahrne, Göran, Brunsson, Nils & Kerwer, Dieter (2016). The paradox of organizing states: A meta-organization perspective on international organizations. *Journal of International Organizations Studies*, 7(1), 5–24.

Alexius, Susanna & Tamm Hallström, Kristina (Eds.) (2014). *Configuring value conflicts in markets*. Cheltenham: Edward Elgar.

Aspers, Patrik (2011). *Markets*. Cambridge: Polity Press.

Augier, Mie, March, James G. & Sullivan, Bilian Ni (2005). Notes on the evolution of a research community: Organization studies in anglophone North America, 1945–2000. *Organization Science*, 16(1), 85–95.

Barnett, Michael N. & Finnemore, Martha (2004). *Rules for the world: International organizations in global politics*. Ithaca, NY: Cornell University Press.

Beck, Ulrich & Beck-Gernsheim, Elisabeth (1995). *The normal chaos of love*. Cambridge: Polity Press.

Berkowitz, Héloïse & Dumez, Hervé (2015). La dynamique des dispositifs d'action collective entre firmes: Le cas des me'taméta-organisations dans le secteur pétrolie. *L'Année Sociologique*, 65(2), 333–356.

Borgatti, Stephen & Foster, Pacey C. (2003). The network paradigm in organizational research: A review and typology. *Journal of Management*, 29(6), 991–1013.

Bromley, Patricia & Meyer, John W. (2015). *Hyper-organization: Global organizational expansion*. Oxford: Oxford University Press.

Brunsson, Nils (2000). Organizations, markets and standardization. In N. Brunsson & B. Jacobsson (Eds.), *A world of standards* (pp. 22–39). Oxford: Oxford University Press.

Brunsson, Nils (2007). *The consequences of decision-making*. Oxford: Oxford University Press.

Brunsson, Nils & Jacobsson, Bengt (Eds.) (2000). *A world of standards*. Oxford: Oxford University Press.

Brunsson, Nils, Rasche, Andreas & Seidl, David (2012). The dynamics of standardization: Three perspectives on standards in organization studies. *Organization Studies*, 33(5–6), 613–632.

Christensen, Tom P., Lægreid, Per, Roness, Paul G. & Røvik, Kjell Arne (2007). *Organization theory for the public sector*. London: Routledge.

Coase, Ronald H. (1937). The nature of the firm. *Economica*, 4(16), 386–405.

Czarniawska, Barbara (2013). Organizations as obstacles to organizing. In D. Robichaud & F. Cooren (Eds.), *Organizations and organizing: Materiality, agency, and discourse* (pp. 3–22). New York: Routledge.

den Hond, Frank, de Bakker, Frank & Smith, Nikolai (2015). Social movements and organizational analysis. In M. Diani & D. Della Porta (Eds.), *The Oxford handbook of social movements* (pp. 291–306). Oxford: Oxford University Press.

Dobusch, Leonhard & Schoeneborn, Dennis (2015). Fluidity, identity, and organizationality: The communicative constitution of *Anonymous*. *Journal of Management*, 52(8), 1005–1035.

Greenwood, Royston, Oliver, Christine, Suddaby, Roy & Sahlin-Andersson, Kerstin (Eds.) (2008). *The Sage handbook of organizational institutionalism*. London: Sage.

Greenwood, Royston, Raynard, Mia, Kodeih, Farah, Micelotta, Evelyn R. & Lounsbury, Michael (2011). Institutional complexity and organizational responses. *The Academy of Management Annals*, 5(1), 317–371.

Hodgkinson, Gerard & Starbuck, William (Eds.) (2008). *The Oxford handbook of organizational decision making*. Oxford: Oxford University Press.

Kanter, Rosabeth M. & Eccles, Robert G. (1992). Making network research relevant to practice. In N. Nohria & R. G. Eccles (Eds.), *Networks and organizations: Structure, form, and action* (pp. 521–527). Boston: Harvard Business School.

Kerwer, Dieter (2005). Rules that many use: Standards and global regulation. *Governance*, 18(4), 611–632.

Kerwer, Dieter (2013). International organizations as meta-organizations: The case of the European Union. *Journal of International Organizations Studies*, 4(Special Issue), 40–53.

Knudsen, Morten (2005). Displacing the paradox of decision making: The management of contingency in the modernization of a Danish county. In D. Seidl & K. H. Becker (Eds.), *Niklas Luhmann and organization studies* (pp. 107–126). Copenhagen: Copenhagen Business School Press.

Kuechler, Manfred & Dalton, Russell J. (1994). New social movements and the political order: Inducing change for long term stability? In R. J. Dalton & M. Kuechler (Eds.), *Challenging the political order: New social and political movements in Western democracies* (pp. 277–300). Cambridge: Polity Press.

Laslett, Barbara (1973). The family as a public and private institution: A historical perspective. *Journal of Marriage and Family*, 35(3), 480–492.

Lindblom, Charles E. (1979). Still muddling, not yet through. *Public Administration Review*, 39(6), 517–526.

Luhmann, Niklas (1986). *Love as passion: The codification of intimacy*. Cambridge, MA: Harvard University Press.

Luhmann, Niklas (1992). Organisation. In W. Küpper & G. Ortmann (Eds.), *Mikropolitik: Rationalität, Macht und Spiele in Organisationen* (pp. 165–185). Opladen: Westdeutscher Verlag.

Luhmann, Niklas (2000). *Organisation und Entscheidung*. Opladen: Westdeutscher Verlag.

Luhmann, Niklas (2005). The paradox of decision making. In D. Seidl & K. H. Becker (Eds.), *Niklas Luhmann and organization studies* (pp. 85–106). Copenhagen: Copenhagen Business School Press.

Luhmann, Niklas (2012/2013). *Theory of society*. Stanford: Stanford University Press.

March, James G. (1988). *Decisions and organizations*. Oxford: Blackwell.

March, James G. & Simon, Herbert A. (1958). *Organizations*. New York: John Wiley.

Marcussen, Martin (2002). *OECD og idéspillet. Game over?* Copenhagen: Hans Reitzels Forlag.

Marshall, Alfred (1920). *Principles of economics: An introductory volume*. London: Macmillan.

Meyer, John W. & Rowan, Brian (1977). Institutionalized organizations: Formal structure as myth and ceremony. *American Journal of Sociology*, 83(2), 340–363.

Mintzberg, Henry (1993). *Structure in fives: Designing effective organizations*. Englewood Cliffs, NJ: Prentice-Hall.

Mörth, Ulrika (2004). *Soft law in governance and regulation: An interdisciplinary analysis*. Cheltenham: Edward Elgar.

Nohria, Nitin & Eccles, Richard G. (Eds.) (1992). *Networks and organizations: Structure, form and action*. Boston: Harvard Business School Press.

North, Douglass C. (1990). Institutions and their consequences for economic performance. In K. Cook & M. Levi (Eds.), *The limits of rationality* (pp. 383–401). Chicago: University of Chicago Press.

O'Mahony, Siobhán & Ferraro, Fabrizio (2007). The emergence of governance in an open source community. *Academy of Management Journal*, 50(5), 1079–1106.

Ostrom, Elinor (1990). *Governing the commons: The evolution of institutions for collective action*. Cambridge: Cambridge University Press.

Papakostas, Apostolis (2012). *Civilizing the public sphere: Distrust, trust and corruption*. Basingstoke: Palgrave.

Perrow, Charles (1991). A society of organizations. *Theory and Society*, 20(6), 725–762.

Podolny, Joel M. & Page, Karen L. (1998). Network forms of organization. *Annual Review of Sociology*, 24, 57–76.

Pressman, Jeffrey L. & Wildavsky, Aaron (1973). *Implementation*. Berkeley: University of California Press.

Reinecke, Juliane, Manning, Stephan & Von Hagen, Oliver (2012). The emergence of a standard market: Multiplicity of sustainability standards in the global coffee industry. *Organization Studies*, 33(5–6), 791–814.

Samuelsson, Paul A. (1969). *Economics: An introductory analysis* (6th ed.). New York: McGraw Hill.

Schoeneborn, Dennis & Scherer, Andreas G. (2012). Clandestine organizations, al Qaeda, and the paradox of (in)visibility: A response to Stohl and Stohl. *Organization Studies*, 33(7), 963–971.

Scott, William Richard (1995). *Institutions and organizations*. Thousand Oaks, CA: Sage.

Seidl, David (2007). Standard setting and following in corporate governance: An observation—theoretical study of the effectiveness of governance codes. *Organization*, 14(5), 705–727.

Seidl, David & Becker, Kai Helge (2006). Organisations as distinction generating and processing systems: Niklas Luhmann's contribution to organisation studies. *Organization*, 13(1), 9–35.

Seidl, David & Mormann, Hannah (2015). Niklas Luhmann as organization theorist. In P. Adler, P. du Gay, G. Morgan & M. Reed (Eds.), *Oxford handbook of sociology, social theory and organization studies: Contemporary currents* (pp. 125–157). Oxford: Oxford University Press.

Simon, Herbert A. (1960). *The new science of management decision*. New York: Harper & Row.

Simon, Herbert A. (1991). Organisations and markets. *Journal of Economic Perspectives*, 5(2), 25–44.

Starkey, Ken, Barnatt, Christopher & Tempest, Sue (2000). Beyond networks and hierarchies: Latent organizations in the UK television industry. *Organization Science*, 11(3), 299–305.

Tamm Hallström, Kristina (2004). *Organizing international standardization: ISO and the IASC in quest of authority*. Cheltenham: Edward Elgar.

Timmermans, Stefan & Epstein, Steven (2010). A world of standards but not a standard world: Toward a sociology of standards and standardization. *Annual Review of Sociology*, 36, 69–89.

Walras, Leon (1954). *Elements of pure economics, or the theory of social wealth*. London: Allen & Unwin.

Weber, Max (1922). *Economy and society: An outline of interpretive sociology*. New York: Bedminster Press.

Weick, Karl E. (1969). *The social psychology of organizing*. New York: McGraw-Hill.

Williamson, Oliver (1975). *Markets and hierarchies: Analysis and antitrust implications*. New York: Free Press.

8 Corporate Democratic Nation-Building

Reflections on the Constructive Role of Businesses in Fostering Global Democracy

Thomas Boysen Anker

Introduction

Europe is going through a testing time. The UK's decision to leave the European Union, and thereby to unravel some 40 years of ever closer union and integration between the member states, is not just about redefining domestic politics. Brexit has deep international ramifications and puts the entire EU to the test, raising the larger political question about peace and stability in Europe. The ideological backbone of the EU is to end the frequent bloodshed between neighbouring countries across the continent. Since its inception, the EU has played a key role in global politics, historically as a main player in the Cold War and most recently as a highly active global player in the fight against terrorism. A disunited—or disuniting—Europe is a political condition, which too often has fertilized radical ideologies, mobilized alienated and disenfranchised citizens in extreme right- or left-wing movements and, ultimately, led to unrest and war. A new European equilibrium is not a desirable option: It's a *sine qua non* for peace and stability. The aim of this reflection on Europe is to outline the crucial constructive role that businesses can adopt to foster this new state of democratic equilibrium. This reflection develops a speculative argument showing that businesses can have direct impact on a range of enabling conditions for democracy.[1] The argument goes one step further by advancing the controversial view not only that businesses can actively contribute to democratic nation-building, but also corporations have non-trivial structural and pragmatic advantages that potentially make them better democratic nation-builders than traditional political agents. Although normative in nature, this reflection does not aim to convince the reader of any political approaches or ideas; rather, my hope is to present a provocative argument to spark reflection on a crucial topic that has deep ramifications for businesses and society.

Definitions of nation-building differ and often conflate the distinctions between state-building and nation-building (Fukuyama, 2008). The most influential definitions comprise the following key constructs: Nation-building is an interventionist process whereby an external political power interferes militarily in a foreign nation and subsequently implements ambitious systems of economic development while seeking to embed recognized processes of democratic decision-making throughout all political institutions, ultimately aiming at establishing a new political order (Fukuyama, 2008; Mylonas, 2013; Somit & Peterson, 2005). Moreover, nation-building aims to establish a community of shared values, emphasizing the creation of shared belief- and value-sets across diverse cultures and ethnic groups. The end goal is for the newly created and shared value-sets to converge on the foundational values of democracy held by the nation-builders.

For the purposes of this reflection, nation-building is the process of designing and implementing activities that have a substantial impact on a range of enabling conditions consciously configured to improve, sustain or introduce clearly defined elements of democracy. This definition is broader than conventional definitions of nation-building in that it emphasizes a dual context of influence: on the one hand, improving and sustaining democratic values and processes, on the other, designing and introducing elements of democracy. The rationale for operating across this twofold context of influence is as follows: First, there is a need to reinforce and stabilize existing democracies enduring periods of political activity that challenges the democratic foundations (e.g. post-Brexit Europe); second, there is a need to fertilize the global citizen-driven public demand for democratization of non-democratic states (e.g. the Arab Spring). Accordingly, this reflection has a special emphasis on the European context but frequently branches out, putting the discussion into global perspective. These two contexts are intertwined in the overall narrative and they will not be addressed separately.

The controversial idea that businesses can—and perhaps even should—design their commercial operations to be conducive to sustaining or developing democratic systems evolves naturally from the increased focus on their political role. Scherer and Palazzo's (2011) paper "The New Political Role of Business in a Globalized World" provides an excellent overview of this area. Their overarching point is that globalization has created a legal and political void, where businesses are initially operating without being guided by regulatory and legal frameworks, because policies that can realistically be implemented and policed by nation-states are limited to a national or transnational scope. To fill the void, businesses have expanded the traditional scope of corporate social responsibility (CSR) to involve a political dimension, where corporations are actively involved in the development of a range of self-regulatory measures and systems and effectively become political actors (Rasche, 2015; Scherer, Palazzo, & Matten, 2014).[2] Scholars often refer to this new branch of studies as political CSR (e.g. Westermann-Behaylo, Rehbein, & Fort, 2015).

The argument of this essay is structured as follows. It begins with clarification of why the Brexit vote has triggered a crisis of European democracy, and why this is a genuine concern for business, which should motivate an active interest in corporate democratic nation-building. The main section then argues that businesses can employ democratic nation-building by consciously designing operations that actively reinforce or implement a range of key enabling conditions of democracy. The emphasis is not on the actual, specific measures that businesses can use to promote democracy, but rather the focal point is on clarifying the underlying structural conditions that enable businesses to promote democracy. Put differently, this essay is not about the pragmatics of corporate nation-building, but about the ontological conditions that put businesses in the unprecedented position of state-like actors able to actively promote values and processes that are conducive to democracy. Having discussed the potential for businesses to engage in corporate democratic nation-building, the essay closes with a short ethical remark, addressing whether corporate democratic nation-building is the ultimate form of political manipulation. Critics will object to the very concept of corporate democratic nation-building as an oxymoron, because the concept seeks to reinforce or introduce political ideas and structures through the exercise of powers that are not politically, let alone democratically, legitimized. On balance, however, the immense opportunity to spread democracy through business activities appears to be an opportunity that we cannot afford to miss.

Brexit, Democracy and Business

Does the Brexit vote constitute a crisis of European democracy? In one sense the answer is: 'definitely not'. The UK is as democratic as before and one may convincingly submit to the view that the 'leave vote' was in fact a spectacular victory of democracy. The UKIP leader Nigel Farage, for example, underscores the Brexit vote as a victory of the little man over big politics and the undue influence of big business. Although one may disagree wildly with the UKIP leader, it is difficult to deny the relevance of this particular observation. According to this political narrative, the underdogs have utilized their democratic rights to create decisive political change. However, while Brexit may be a cause for local celebrations of democracy, it is a democratic catastrophe from a European point of view. This becomes clear by looking into the underpinning conditions that fuelled the Brexit vote.

UK citizens' resistance to the EU can be interpreted as a matter of perceived loss of power. As individual political agents in a democratic system, voters are—and should be—deeply wary of transferring power, money and autonomy to a centralized bureaucracy governed by principles and procedures which they don't trust and which instils a feeling of disempowerment. As Acemoglu and Robinson (2012) observe, modern welfare state democracy is a subgame perfect equilibrium, that is entirely conditional on citizens' willingness to accept the exercise of political power, which in turn is conditional on voters having political leverage in terms of being able to terminate unwanted politicians through robust election mechanisms. Too many UK voters felt they had lost the sense of being democratically in touch with their EU politicians: No clear route to punishment of unwanted politicians seemed available, creating a feeling of disenfranchisement, resentment and—fundamentally—social injustice. Democratic political equilibria break down when citizens become unwilling to make their 'political investments' into shares whose potential performance is impossible to gauge given their dependency on a super-layered bureaucracy, the hyper-complexity of which undermines the political accessibility relation between politics and the people (Acemoglu & Robinson, 2012). Frankly, for many citizens in the UK, the EU—rightly or wrongly—became an incentive incompatible political investment, because those managing the investment lost the ability to explain in plain language the correlation between personal benefit and political investment. Seen from that perspective, opting out of the EU is a perfectly reasonable strategy. If this analysis is correct, then the Brexit vote has sent the EU into a political crisis, hitting the Union in the core of its political heart: The EU is fundamentally a large-scale democratic nation-building experiment designed to create and sustain peace and stability—and thereby prosperity—in Europe. By the very act of leaving the EU, the UK shakes the political ideology which forms the bedrock of the Union. Through leaving the Union due to feelings of disenfranchisement, the UK implicitly challenges the EU as a political project having lost its democratic legitimacy and direction.

The Link Between Democracy and Economic Growth

Is democracy good for business? A large body of economic and political literature discusses the correlation between democracy and economic growth (see Acemoglu, Naidu, Restrepo, & Robinson, 2014; Przeworski & Limongi, 1993 for an overview of the most important literature). Some, both historically and more recently, find democracy to be a hindrance to economic growth (e.g. Lindblom, 1977; Olson, 1982; Schumpeter, 1943; Wood, 1995). Olson (1982), for example, argues that the power of interest groups in developed democracies impedes growth. A case in point is the large infrastructure projects that may have detrimental impact on the environment and local communities, such as a third runway for Heathrow airport in London. The democracy-motivated need for stakeholder buy-in to obtain political approval slows down the advancement of such projects and may ultimately terminate them. In non-democratic countries like China, a select group of decision makers can issue instant approval and thereby grant businesses immediate and unhindered access to implement large-scale projects such as building new airports or power plants. This line of reasoning has influenced some thinkers to question the universal desirability of democratic ideas. In his groundbreaking paper, Barro (1996, p. 23) finds that:

> [w]ith respect to the determination of growth . . . [there are] favourable effects from maintenance of the rule of law, free markets, small

> government consumption, and high human capital. Once these kinds of variables and the initial level of GDP are held constant, the overall effect of democracy on growth is weakly negative.

Central to this reflection's ambition of global corporate democratic nation-building, Barro (1996, p. 24) comments critically on the desirability of exporting Western democracy:

> The more general conclusion is that the advanced Western countries would contribute more to the welfare of poor nations by exporting their economic systems, notably property rights and free markets, rather than their political systems, which typically developed after reasonable standards of living had been attained. If economic freedom can be established in a poor country, then growth would be encouraged, and the country would tend eventually to become more democratic on its own.

In contrast, there are several studies that find a positive correlation between democracy and economic growth. Persson and Tabellini (2009) make the case for a virtuous cycle where accumulation of physical and democratic capital reinforce each other, increasing overall economic prosperity over time. Papaioannou and Siourounis (2008) demonstrate a small but significant positive impact of democratization on long-term economic growth in countries that replace autocratic rule with democratic political systems. Recently, Acemoglu et al. (2014) conducted possibly the most comprehensive and ambitious investigation yet, demonstrating that democratization can increase GDP per capita by no less than 20% over time.

As a whole, the scientific literature on democracy and economic growth underdetermines the causal relationship between level of democratization and positive economic outputs over time (Feng, 1997). However, having democratic societies as a platform for commercial business is nevertheless a pertinent business interest, because macro-economic instability adversely impacts on business performance and GDP growth (Aisen & Veiga, 2013). Established democracies have a high degree of stability, internally and externally. While some highly entrepreneurial businesses capable of exploiting disruptive business models thrive under high levels of uncertainty, most mature and large businesses need high levels of stability to be successful, as stability is a precondition of long-term strategic planning and economic growth (Aisen & Veiga, 2013). Also, the stability offered by democratic rule curbs corruption, minimizes the risk of monopolization of economic opportunities and significantly reduces social unrest, thus providing advantageous enabling conditions for commercial growth and long-term profit maximization (Acemoglu & Robinson, 2012).

Two different approaches are now open: If the operating assumption is that democracy reinforces economic growth, then there is a direct interest in sustaining existing conditions of democracy and introducing enabling conditions in non-democratic markets. If, by contrast, the operating condition is that democracy is a political system which evolves as an emergent condition relative to pre-existing economic growth, then democracy should not be exported or promoted directly: The emphasis should be on exporting economic rather than political systems.

This reflection converges to a synthesizing midpoint between these two approaches: By putting businesses at the core of democratic nation-building, the enabling conditions of democracy are reinforced through a range of clearly defined business activities. In this middle ground, the aim is neither to create economic growth to fertilize the introduction of democracy nor to introduce democracy to create greater prosperity. On the contrary, the idea is that businesses can do both by designing their commercial activities to activate and reinforce clearly defined enabling conditions of democracy. The question whether we should export political or economic systems to developing countries never poses a dilemma, as the disjunction between the options collapses: When businesses design their core commercial activities to promote democracy, then the distinction between choosing either economic or political systems as a basis for nation-building becomes redundant because the ultimate political aim is embedded in the commercial enterprise.

Corporate Democratic Nation-Building

It is useful to distinguish between internal and external pathways to promote democracy within a business context. Internally, nourishing a sense of community and belongingness within the company and adopting transparent governance and dialogic leadership styles may positively impact on employees, reinforcing or instilling democratic mindsets and pro-democratic dispositional attitudes (Fort & Schipani, 2004; Gastil, 1994; Woods, 2004). Externally, stakeholder involvement in core decision making regarding developments that may affect the local community or impact on the environment allows for the wider public to have a say (Fort & Schipani, 2004). From a marketing point of view, my work (Anker, 2014a) analyzes how some commercial brands used marketing campaigns to actively engage in promoting democracy, in some cases with a view to fuel pro-democratic political unrest. I have also reported findings from a preliminary study (Anker, 2014b) which demonstrated how brands can design commercial brand building to be conducive to the development of democratic values in different target groups. Both internal and external approaches underpin the following discussion.

The aim of this section is twofold—firstly, to stimulate scholars and policymakers to think creatively about how societies can harness the immense economic, political and persuasive power of corporations to promote and reinforce key enabling conditions of democracy; secondly, to justify and substantiate the operating assumption that businesses not only can design commercial activities to promote democracy, but are also, in many respects, in a superior position compared with any traditional polity previously involved in Western-style democratic nation-building.

Democratic Mindsets: Creating and Reinforcing Values of Democracy

The branch of marketing known as political marketing has demonstrated how marketing methods can be utilized to promote political ideologies, individual politicians, political parties and political causes (Ormrod, Henneberg, & O'Shaughnessy, 2013). Businesses have an unprecedented potential to engage mass audiences actively with ideological messages and, thereby, to engage in political marketing with unmatched political reach—the reason being that brands carry a semantic charge that can be released with global impact: The language of the logo is instantly recognizable across national and cultural boundaries (Klein, 2000).

In a certain almost absurd sense, the simplified symbolic sign systems of global brands achieve the mythic quest for a universal language[3] through the employment of logos and other brand building blocks. Sound is an interesting example: Carefully designed sounds such as the ones indicating that your MacBook is booting up or notifying you of a new email on your iPhone are semantic constructs that communicate across linguistic barriers. Marketing scholars have found brand-related phonetic symbolism to carry unique meaning across languages and thereby constitute a brand building block that unlocks sources of universal meaning (Lowrey & Shrum, 2007; Shrum et al., 2012). Keller (2008) demonstrates a keen sense of how brands can create a global platform through conscious configuration of brand building blocks. This means that businesses are in possession of communicative powers that far outperform those of traditional political entities and movements. If, therefore, this semantically super-charged power is released across global markets to advocate political ideas, it seems reasonable to assume that businesses may be capable of changing mindsets at a global scale and framing political ideas with true global reach.

In a pilot study, I provided early evidence that this may indeed be the case (Anker, 2014b). I identified a set of societal values that are crucial to the development of democratic mindsets and demonstrated how businesses can design and deploy brand building blocks that create positive associations in the customer mindset to these key values of democracy. For example, democracy is founded on a set of individual rights (e.g. freedom of speech, religion and assembly) and responsibilities (e.g. respect for differences in opinion, beliefs and politics), and these rights and responsibilities are grounded in societal values such as 'diversity', 'self-expression', 'inclusion' and 'equality' (Kymlicka, 2002). Corporations can promote democratic mindsets by activating and positively aligning this core set of democratic values with key brand values. In my conference paper (Anker, 2014a) "The Revolutionary Brand!", I analyzed how three different brands (Vodafone, Coca Cola and

Pepsi) aligned themselves with the citizen-driven demand for democracy during the Arab Spring. I identified three different types of brand engagement in radical political change: active incitement to engagement in political activities; fertilization of the idea of radical democratic political change; and positioning and inducement of political beliefs. The most striking example is Vodafone's campaign, "Power to You", which was launched during the Arab Spring and explicitly encouraged Egyptians to actively protest against the political establishment and demand democratic change (Vodafone, 2011). The official aim of the campaign was "to remind Egyptians how powerful they are" and, effectively, to encourage political dissent. The central campaign platform was a YouTube video which provided a summary of the entire campaign: The video is a rare piece of social media history where a brand both explicitly encourages consumers to engage in radical political activities and takes credit for having played a causally instrumental role in fuelling the uprising which led to the fall of Hosni Mubarak.[4]

The question, then, is not so much whether businesses have the capacity and ability to activate and shape democratic mindsets through the deployment of politically charged communicative vehicles. Rather, the question is whether global target groups would be receptive to business-sponsored political messages and engage in sustained political relationships with brands or exit the communicative relationship because of inherent mistrust of global branding.

Trust and Global Branding

Reading critiques of global branding (Klein, 2000) and textbooks on business ethics (Crane & Matten, 2007; Fryer, 2015), it may come as a surprise that not all consumers are naturally wary of global brands. However, marketing research demonstrates that consumers display significant levels of trust in brands (BBG, 2015; EE, 2015). Contrasting this against political trust, the question is whether brands are perceived to be more trustworthy than the most powerful politicians: Political trust-ratings hit a record low in Western terms during the recent US presidential election, with 50% of voters finding Hillary Clinton to be dishonest, compared with 58% for Donald Trump (CFPI, 2016). It is, of course, simplistic to compare trust in brands with political trust, as political and commercial entities traditionally exist in very different types of domains. But since global corporates have already established themselves as political agents (Scherer & Palazzo, 2011; Scherer et al., 2014), the comparison between established political agents (i.e. politicians) and emerging political agents (e.g. corporates) is relevant and necessary.

Trust is an ethically charged relational concept, comprising at least two fundamental elements: a normative and a transactional construct (BBG, 2015). First, as Deutsch (1973) explains in his seminal work on conflict resolution, the foundation of trust between two people requires the attribution of positive intent to another person. Thus, if A trusts B, then A is attributing to B a set of intentions that are incompatible with B wanting to harm or otherwise disadvantage A. This is the normative component of trust. The second and transactional component of trust is much more pragmatic and linked to practice: Trust is a sort of promise such that if A trusts B, then A has a strong belief that if B says she will do X, then—all other things equal—B will do X. Trust is thereby conceptually connected to keeping one's promises (Anker, Kappel, & Sandøe, 2012). If the normative relation breaks down, then A is no longer trusting B. However, contingent breakdown of the instrumental relation is permissible: Not delivering on one's promises will only undermine the normative relation of trust if non-delivery becomes the expectation.

Compared with politicians, brands have a non-trivial advantage in trust-building. Both types of agents are building the normative trust relation through sustained delivery of promised courses of actions. Yet, the type of agency expected of the differing agents is not the same. Brands are by default expected to deliver on promises made regarding products and services, whereas politicians are expected to deliver on promises of social justice, fairness, education, safety, infrastructure, health and welfare. This means that it is far more difficult for politicians to deliver on their promises. Brands have a clear advantage in terms of ease of long-term delivery of the pragmatic, transactional dimension of trust necessary to sustain normative trust. This observation holds true for both established democratic markets and non-democratic markets. Markets in developing countries add an additional advantage to businesses' capacity for trust-building. Many global brands invest in developmental projects such as promoting literacy, alleviating homelessness and malnutrition and fighting public health crises such as HIV/AIDS (Margolis & Walsh, 2003; Rosen et al., 2003; Scherer & Palazzo, 2011). In developing markets where businesses to a large extent supplement or simply constitute the main platform for promoting societal and individual health and welfare, citizens will not just trust the relevant corporations in terms of expected delivery on the instrumental, transactional criterion of trust; rather, citizens depending on the state-like agency of corporations to uphold minimal levels of public goods are likely to perceive these quasi-state commercial actors as giving back more than they could reasonably be expected within a capitalistic logic of markets.

But even in 'developed nations' with sophisticated states and, in some cases, with extensive welfare states, corporate trust-building is likely to become increasingly important as a powerful political tool. Brexit is a result of broken political promises where the 'return on political investment' was profoundly unclear to the majority of UK voters. The election of Donald Trump as the 45th president of the US expresses a fundamental breakdown of the political promise—not of Barack Obama—but of a political system where disparity of economy and opportunity continues to grow regardless of whether the president is a Democrat or a Republican. Donald Trump may get most things wrong, but on one account his political reading of events was spot on: During his campaign, Trump frequently termed the prospect of his being elected US president as a "Double-Brexit". Brexit and Trump are expressions of the exact same anti-establishment sentiment, engrained in the populace through generally shared feelings of systemic distrust. Global business, by contrast, has by no means failed as an institution; it may have fallen short in an ethical and environmental sense, but not in terms of promise delivery. Consumers have high levels of trust in businesses, and many global brands are among the most trusted in Europe (BBG, 2015; EE, 2015).

Combining the language-crossing global reach of commercial communications with the generally high levels of consumer trust in global brands, corporations constitute an unprecedented propaganda vehicle. Although a speculative, philosophical and interim conclusion, it is difficult to deny that corporations have the potential for very directly impacting on citizens' perceptions of what democracy is and on the values underpinning and facilitating democratic processes and institutions. Contemporary corporations' amalgamation of global communicative reach and high levels of trust implies that commercial businesses have the power to shape democratic mindsets on a global scale.

Democracy and the Politics of Recognition

Social marketing is the application of marketing methods and thinking to influence attitudes, perceptions, ideas and behaviours to promote individual, societal and environmental welfare (Dann, 2010). In its most fundamental and simplistic form, social marketing is the application of the 4Ps of marketing—product, price, place and promotion—to influence citizens to change behaviours or to change their perception of themselves, others or the environment. It is a fundamental insight of applying the 4P framework that promotion alone rarely can achieve the goal, be it sales, brand loyalty or behaviour change in a broader social context. Communication is usually only effective in changing behaviours in tandem with the employment of a range of other marketing tools and techniques. This is a very important insight, which challenges the preceding reflection on the power of businesses to win hearts and minds and promote global democratic mindsets. Influencing people to adopt democratic ideas or, in a broader and looser sense, to simply associate democracy with something positive, is of very little value in and of itself. Mindsets frame the way we think, but they only shape behaviours over time if they are wired to a set of external processes that attach positive social recognition to behaviours that are coherent with the mindset. Deploying its wide-ranging communicative powers to mobilize people to (re)affirm democratic values, businesses can only ever hope to promote democracy in concrete terms if it can influence people to act accordingly. Interestingly, businesses again are in a remarkably strong position compared with traditional political actors, because they have a high degree of control over the conditions under which individual achievement is recognized as socially desirable and praiseworthy.

To unfold the argument, it is necessary to connect to Axel Honneth's philosophy of recognition. In his main work, *The Struggle for Recognition*, Honneth (1995) describes how three principles of social recognition have evolved during history. All societies are thought to develop through these three stages of social recognition. In the first stage, social recognition is ascribed to family units, and individuals receive recognition through their membership of, and place in, a given family structure. Existential meaning is a holistic concept, which develops relative to the internal dynamics of the family. In the second evolutionary stage, social recognition transforms into a legal concept and individuals receive recognition through possession of individual rights such as property rights and rights to freedom of interference by the state. In the final stage, social recognition is attached to recognition of individual achievement. The evolutionary process thus culminates in the individual subject coming to the fore of societal importance: It is through the disciplined development of individual abilities and skilled exploitation of opportunities in the individual's life-world that the subject manifests its willpower to the advancement of subjective and intersubjective value and, ultimately, receives social recognition. This exercise of individualism presupposes individual legal rights, but the ontological status of recognition is entirely different from the first, family-based stage of recognition. The individual is the unit of recognition. Social recognition is not simply a pat on the back or a momentary feeling of worth and purpose. Recognition for individual achievement is the ultimate source of existential meaning and social identity and, as such, is embodied in the human psyche as the central motivation shaping most significant behavioural patterns.

Businesses operating in capitalistic market economies have a central position in the pragmatic ascription of social recognition. We spend an average of 30% of our lives at work, and our perception of individual identity, happiness and well-being is strongly correlated with our work-related activities (Warr, 2011). The workplace constitutes one of the key frames of social recognition and construction of personal identity. Work is not just a means of making money to sustain one's life, it is an identity-project through which we create and fulfil very significant conditions of existential meaning (Warr, 2011; Whiteford, 2000).

Businesses, thereby, become one of the prime issuers of recognition for individual achievement in contemporary society and, by inference, have considerable influence over the social psychological principle shaping a substantial set of our behaviours.

When businesses become a prime normative agent in the ascription of social recognition, being out of work—or being denied access to sufficiently meaningful types of work (i.e. occupational deprivation, Whiteford, 2000)—essentially constitutes a negation of the possibility for recognition of individual achievement. In that way being out of work, or being deprived of meaningful work that receives social recognition, is a manifestation of the individual as a non-contributor to society.

This observation is important for two reasons. First, by controlling access to and ascription of social recognition, businesses can directly promote democratic values by explicitly recognizing managers and staff for engaging successfully with work-related activities that are correlated with values underpinning democratic institutions—for example, at a managerial level by recognizing the adoption of inclusive and consultative styles of leadership (or "democratic rationalities" [Woods, 2004]) that progress solutions through dialogue rather than directive command (Gastil, 1994); at a staff level through the positive recognition of behaviours and attitudes which are coherent with and buttress the societal values underpinning democracy, i.e. by recognizing agency that builds a collective ethos of inclusion, respect for difference and diversity and encouragement of active participation in decision making.

Second, the power of businesses to control the principle of recognition of individual achievement has potentially a very significant connection to the evolving Western political context. If global businesses working across Europe and the US had given more people access to social recognition by widening access to work, and if they had more directly and consciously introduced leadership programmes designed to foster democracy at work and build up a collective ethos of respect for diversity and social inclusion, then the social undercurrent of political disenfranchisement and anti-establishmentism that fuelled the Brexit vote and put Trump in the Oval Office might never have happened.

Concluding Ethical Remark

Is corporate democratic nation-building a constructive, albeit controversial, route to promote global democracy? Or is it the ultimate betrayal of the spirit of democracy?

The core ethical problem is that corporate promotion of democracy happens by means of fundamentally undemocratic methods. A clear-cut example is the previously discussed Arab Spring campaign by Vodafone (2011), where the company used its superior communicative powers to motivate people to engage in political unrest to bring about democratic change. In this example the corporation is not only a political actor promoting democracy, it is a polity acting in favour of democracy by non-democratic means. Business leaders are not democratically elected and their engagement in political causes is a result of decisions taken in non-democratic contexts. It may be a democratic decision within the company, but that does not change the fundamental fact that those engaging in the decision-making processes are not democratically elected and represent the narrow interest of profit maximization. It is a defining feature of the capitalistic market economy that businesses are at liberty to define business models and leadership frameworks insofar as they are compliant with legal requirements. As such, corporate democratic nation-building will always be a non-democratic endeavour.

This raises the fundamental ethical question: Should businesses play an active, constructive role in promoting global democracy by reinforcing and inducing democratic values and mindsets? In my view, there are no easy answers. Obviously, the philosophy of democracy grants citizens a global right to freedom from manipulation, which counts heavily against the idea of corporations as democratic nation-builders. Counterbalancing this right, however, is the pragmatic observation that most attempts by traditional state actors to engage in democratic nation-building have failed spectacularly (Iraq and Afghanistan are obvious examples; see Fukuyama, 2008; Somit & Peterson, 2005). Thus, developing a controversial and innovative mix of state and corporate political agency, harnessing global corporations' potential for internal and external promotion of key enabling conditions of democracy, may be our best chance for global democracy, peace and prosperity.

Notes

1. There are many types of democracy (e.g. direct, indirect and representative) and many competing definitions. However, the defining elements across these definitions are that democracy is a form of government where politicians are elected by the majority in a public vote (Goodin, 2009). Also, democracy presupposes the rule of law and transparent, robust processes for democratic decision making and elections. This paper addresses some of the enabling conditions underpinning the key defining features of all types of democracy.
2. Self-regulatory mechanisms are obviously associated with a potentially strong bias due to the vested interest: Businesses have a very direct interest in developing only regulatory measures that are in the best interest of core business priorities. As such, even advanced and robust self-regulatory frameworks, which have incorporated the "arms-length" principle, are frequently subject to criticism because they can never reach the same level of political integrity as independent government regulation.
3. The dream of a universal language has influenced European thinking since the birth of Western civilization, given that modern European science and philosophy developed out of philosophical theories heavily influenced by Christianity (Kenny, 2010). According to the Old Testament, mankind had a shared language until it committed the sin of wanting to reach Heaven through the construction of the Babel tower. God issued a global punishment—which in some sense runs as an undercurrent to all international conflict—by "confusing their [the people of the Earth's] language, so that they will not understand one another's speech" (Genesis, 11). The sudden imposition of different languages made it impossible for humans to complete the Babel tower, because the ensuing confusion meant they could no longer join forces and collaborate across national boundaries to obtain a shared goal.
4. Vodafone's political campaign has been removed from YouTube due to the controversies it caused and subsequent developments in Egypt. However, the video is still available from Dailymotion's website (see Vodafone, 2011).

References

Acemoglu, Daren, Naidu, Suresh, Restrepo, Pascual & Robinson, James A. (2014). Democracy does cause growth. National Bureau of Economic Research. Working Paper 20004. Cambridge, MA. Accessed December 2016: www.nber.org/papers/w20004.

Acemoglu, Daren & Robinson, James A. (2012). *Why nations fail: The origins of power, prosperity and poverty*. London: Profile Books.

Aisen, Ari & Veiga, Francisco (2013). How does political instability affect economic growth? *European Journal of Political Economy*, 29, 151–167.

Anker, Thomas B. (2014a). The revolutionary brand! Preliminary thoughts on the potential role of commercial brands in radical political change. 9th Global Brand Conference of the Academy of Marketing's Brand, Corporate Identity and Reputation Special Interest Group (SIG), Hertford, UK.

Anker, Thomas B. (2014b). Power to the people: Essay on branding and global democracy. In R.J. Varey & M. Pirson (Eds.), *Humanistic marketing* (pp. 204–215). London: Palgrave Macmillan.

Anker, Thomas B., Kappel, Klemens, Eadie, Douglas & Sandøe, Peter (2012). Fuzzy promises: Explicative definitions of brand promise delivery. *Marketing Theory*, 12(3), 267–287.

Barro, Robert J. (1996). Democracy and growth. *Journal of Economic Growth*, 1(1), 1–27.

BBG (2015). *Consumer trust in brands*. London: British Brands Group.

CFPI (2016). Poll: 2016 presidential candidates score low on financial honesty and transparency. The Center for Public Integrity. Accessed December 2016: www.publicintegrity.org/2016/09/06/20158/poll-2016-presidential-candidates-score-low-financial-honesty-and-transparency.

Crane, Andrew & Matten, Dirk (2007). *Business ethics: Managing corporate citizenship and sustainability in the age of globalization*. Oxford: Oxford University Press.

Dann, Stephen (2010). Redefining social marketing with contemporary commercial marketing definitions. *Journal of Business Research*, 63(2), 147–153.

Deutsch, Morton (1973). *The resolution of conflict: Constructive and destructive processes*. New Haven and London: Yale University Press.

EE (2015). *The role of consumer trust in the economics of brands*. London: Europe Economics.

Feng, Yi (1997). Democracy, political stability and economic growth. *British Journal of Political Science*, 27(3), 391–418.

Fort, Timothy L. &. Schipani, Cindy A. (2004). *The role of business in fostering peaceful societies*. Cambridge: Cambridge University Press.

Fryer, Mick (2015). *Ethics theory & business practice*. London: Sage.

Fukuyama, Francis (2008). *Nation-building: Beyond Afghanistan and Iraq*. Baltimore: Johns Hopkins University Press.

Gastil, John (1994). A definition and illustration of democratic leadership. *Human Relations*, 47(8), 953–975.

Goodin, Robert E. (2009). *The Oxford handbook of political science*. Oxford and New York: Oxford University Press.

Honneth, Axel (1995). *The struggle for recognition*. Cambridge: Polity Press.

Keller, Kevin L. (2008). *Strategic brand management*. Upper Saddle River, NJ: Pearson Education.

Kenny, Anthony (2010). *A new history of Western philosophy*. Oxford: Oxford University Press.

Klein, Naomi (2000). *No logo*. London: Flamingo.

Kymlicka, Will (2002). *Contemporary political philosophy*. Oxford: Oxford University Press.

Lindblom, Charles E. (1977). *Politics and markets: The world's political economic systems*. New York: Basic Books.

Lowrey, Tina M. & Shrum, L.J. (2007). Phonetic symbolism and brand name preference. *Journal of Consumer Research*, 34(3), 406–414.

Margolis, Joshua D. & Walsh, James P. (2003). Misery loves companies: Rethinking social initiatives by business. *Administrative Science Quarterly*, 48(2), 268–305.

Mylonas, Harris (2013). *The politics of nation-building: Making co-nationals, refugees, and minorities*. New York: Cambridge University Press.

Olson, Mancur (1982). *The rise and decline of nations*. New Haven and London: Yale University Press.

Ormrod, Robert P., Henneberg, Stephan C. M. & O'Shaughnessy, Nicholas J. (2013). *Political marketing: Theory and concepts*. London: Sage.

Papaioannou, Elias & Siourounis, Gregorios (2008). Democratisation and growth. *Economic Journal*, 118(532), 1520–1551.

Persson, Torsten & Tabellini, Guido (2009). Democratic capital: The nexus of political and economic change. *American Economic Journal: Macroeconomics*, 1(2), 88–126.

Przeworski, Adam & Limongi, Fernando (1993). Political regimes and economic growth. *Journal of Economic Perspectives*, 7(3), 51–69.

Rasche, Andreas (2015). The corporation as a political actor: European and North American perspectives. *European Management Journal*, 33(1), 4–8.

Rosen, Sydney, Simon, Jonathon, Vincent, Jeffrey R., MacLeod, William, Fox, Matthew & Thea, Donald M. (2003). AIDS is your business. *Harvard Business Review*, 81(2), 80–87.

Scherer, Andreas G. & Palazzo, Guido (2011). The new political role of business in a globalized world: A review of a new perspective on CSR and its implications for the firm, governance, and democracy. *Journal of Management Studies*, 48(4), 899–931.

Scherer, Andreas G., Palazzo, Guido & Matten, Dirk (2014). The business firm as a political actor: A new theory of the firm for a globalized world. *Business & Society*, 53(2), 143–156.

Schumpeter, Joseph A. (1943). *Capitalism, socialism, and democracy*. London: Allen & Unwin.

Shrum, L.J., Lowrey, Tina M., Luna, David, Lerman, Dawn B. & Liu, Min (2012). Sound symbolism effects across languages: Implications for global brand names. *International Journal of Research in Marketing*, 29(3), 275–279.

Somit, Albert & Peterson, Steven A. (2005). *The failure of democratic nation building: Ideology meets evolution*. New York: Palgrave Macmillan.

Vodafone. (2011). Power to You. Video removed from YouTube, but available from Dailymotion's website. Accessed December 2016: www.dailymotion.com/video/xj3azr_vodafone-egypt-jwt-ad-taking-credit-for-jan25-revolution_news?start=2.

Warr, Peter (2011). *Work, happiness, and unhappiness*. Mahwah, NJ: Psychology Press.

Westermann-Behaylo, Michelle K., Rehbein, Kathleen & Fort, Timothy (2015). Enhancing the concept of corporate diplomacy: Encompassing political corporate social responsibility, international relations, and peace through commerce. *Academy of Management Perspectives*, 29(4), 387–404.

Whiteford, Gail (2000). Occupational deprivation: Global challenge in the new millennium. *British Journal of Occupational Therapy*, 63(5), 200–204.

Wood, Ellen Meiksins (1995). *Democracy against capitalism: Renewing historical materialism*. Cambridge: Cambridge University Press.

Woods, Philip A. (2004). Democratic leadership: Drawing distinctions with distributed leadership. *International Journal of Leadership in Education*, 7(1), 3–26.

9 Studying Vicious Circles to Learn about Reforms

Miguel Pina e Cunha and Haridimos Tsoukas

Introduction

If there is a word that keeps being daily repeated in European media, surely that is 'reform'—a claim aggravated by the Brexit (see Anker, this volume). The crisis in the Eurozone, in particular, has made 'reform' very popular with politicians, although not necessarily with organized interests and maybe the population at large. 'Reform' is one of those ambiguous concepts which can mean all sorts of different things. However, one thing is certain: Whatever else it may mean, 'reform' involves changing the state.

In southern European countries, in particular, a big, inefficient public administration, not rarely captured by organized interests and clientelistic practices, has rendered its reform urgent. If nothing else, as the Organisation for Economic Co-operation and Development points out in its country-specific reports, the ability of southern European countries to compete inside the Eurozone will be significantly enhanced by the extent to which they reform the state.

However, the worlds of organization and management theory and public administration tend to live separate lives, as Pfeffer (2006) pointed out. But they should not, since some of the most intractable, 'wicked' organizational problems occur in the spheres of the state and of the meta-organizations of the EU. Changing an entire institutional ecology such as the state, however, is a daunting task, partly because of its size, partly because of the open-ended character of competitive politics in a liberal democracy and, crucially, because of the self-reference problem involved: The organization and functioning of the state reflects the historicity of a society—the way it has historically understood itself as a political community and the way, therefore, it has gone about organizing and governing itself over time (Papoulias & Tsoukas, 1994; Tsoukas & Papoulias, 1996, 2005; Tsoukas, 2012). To put it succinctly, a country has the state it desires to have. The problem of self-reference gets larger the bigger the scale of reform is. A government, for example, that aims to change the historical modus operandi of its public administration (e.g. relinquishing political patronage and cronyism in favour of meritocratic practices) will be faced with a much larger problem than a government that, more narrowly, aims to reform pensions or the health system (Tsoukas, 2012).

State reform should have attracted significant attention from mainstream organizational and management scholars as an extreme case of change management complexity. However, despite exceptions (see, for example, Brunsson & Olsen, 1993), it has not—although public policy and public administration scholars, who, however, tend to be somewhat disconnected from mainstream organization and management theory, have been studying policy and administrative reform for years (Kalyvas, Pagoulatos, & Tsoukas, 2012; Pressman & Wildavsky, 1984; Stone, 2002; Wilson, 2000; Yanow, 1996). In this chapter we discuss reform as a special case of the challenges associated with transformational change, involving technical, organizational, institutional and trans-institutional features. We will focus, in particular, on the vicious circles that state reform often generates in southern European countries.

With the above in mind, we define a double theoretical goal—first, we use reform to learn about organizational vicious circularity; second, we use vicious circularity to learn about reform. We organize the chapter in three core sections. In the next section we present a quasi-methodological note, grounding the discussion in the authors' independent previous work. Then we define the scope of reform and discuss its difficulties and the reason it often triggers vicious circles. Finally, we discuss the process known as the vicious circle, its causes and its role in State reform.

A Methodological Note

The reflections in this essay result from research efforts conducted independently by the two authors. Tsoukas explored social reforms in Greece (Papoulias & Tsoukas, 1994; Tsoukas & Papoulias, 1996, 2005; Tsoukas, 2012), whereas Cunha was attracted to the persistently Kafkaesque nature of the Portuguese state and the discontinuities that impede deep change from occurring (Cunha, 2014). In short, an excess of change obstructs real change. The reflections in this chapter are a synthesis and an extension of this previous work.

Studying Reform to Learn About Vicious Circles

Reform can be defined as "deliberate efforts on the part of some authorities to effect change in a public policy domain, be it education, health, utilities, civil service, the pension system and so on, and to do so in a way that change becomes institutionalised and, as a result, a new relevant modus operandi comes about" (Tsoukas, 2012, p. 75). The term has an inherently positive value as it refers to some process that is designed and implemented to improve a target system. In this sense, 'reform' is invoked by reformers as a solution to some major problem that is related to the functioning of the state or the provision of a collective good.

As Tsoukas (2012) explained, reform involves three levels of impact. First, reformers promise a new way of dealing with the technical issues that prevent a system from being more effective or equally effective in a more efficient way (a concern that acquires added relevance in times of budgetary pressure). This is the domain of first-order change. Second, reforms imply the adoption of a set of new values, presumably more aligned with some of the core tenets of modernity, such as efficiency, performance management, accountability or transparency. It is because of the practical consequences of these new values that the technical issues involved in first-order change need to be tackled. Revising the value-system supporting state organizations refers to second-order change. But in many cases, the above changes require third-order change, i.e. the change of the rules that constitute the political domain itself, involving changes in the institutionalized meaning systems and the historical dispositions (the habitus) of governance. Third-order change does not involve merely organizational transformation (as in the case of second-order change) but, through it, "it impacts on the broader institutional field in which an organization is embedded" (Tsoukas, 2012, p. 77). The organization helps change its institutional field (be it health, education, etc.) as it is changing itself; it is a means and an end at the same time.

Reform is difficult because it demands a context-dependent consonance of purpose and action, which is extremely hard to achieve. At the systemic level, an organization (e.g., a government) must recognize the need to reform itself, i.e. recognize the need to change the way governments have typically governed in a given context. This may be difficult because, for example, the political system may have crystallized around political parties' clienteles, because politically mandated cadres dominate the civil service or because the people have grown accustomed to the idea that the cause of the system's malfunctioning is 'cultural', as is often heard as a justification for institutional inertia.

Interestingly, even in case the government is unable or unwilling to change itself, it may start reform due to international agreements, pressure from lenders or international organizations or simply as a token of modern governance. Starting a reform, therefore, is not necessarily difficult. As Brunsson and Olsen (1993, p. 6) have observed, "reform is easier to initiate than to decide on, and easier to decide on than to implement". The Portuguese case offers a good illustration: It may be so easy to start a reform as, according to Pereira (2013), six "reforms" have been initiated by Portuguese governments in a single decade. One of us has even participated in this effort and can thus offer anecdotal confirmation of Brunsson and Olsen's hypothesis.

Reform: Structural vs Enactive Perspectives

When a reforming government sees the need to change the state without seeing the need to change itself, it will possibly initiate reform with a structural mindset. Seen as a structural problem, reform contains a number of predictable features. First, it is directed towards things: state organizations.

Typically, state organizations are seen through a narrowly legal perspective. The organization exists as established in the law. The law defines how the organization is designed, who runs it, who works there and how it functions. All these formal features are legally established and officially documented. In this sense they constitute reality. State organizations are established by governments. Such a perspective assumes organizations as legal-administrative entities which exist as arms of the State and function as bureaucracies following its orders *sine ira et studio* [without anger and fondness] (Albrow, 1992). This perspective is underpinned by a hierarchical, i.e. top down, view of organizations: Orders descend from top to bottom. Time is secondary to change, as if history does not matter. From a structural viewpoint, reform is ahistorical, as most research on organizational change has tended to be (Pettigrew, Woodman, & Cameron, 2001). In this sense, governments can start as many reforms as they deem necessary—six in a single decade—because what matters is how reform is inscribed in the legal-rational-bureaucratic apparatus of the State.

But there is an alternative way of understanding reform. Tsoukas (2012) has called it "enactive". An enactive perspective is firstly phenomenologically oriented, taking into account actors' meanings and experiences and how they are re-constituted over time; secondly it is process oriented, exploring how multiple actors interact over time by drawing on various forms of symbolic and political capital; and thirdly it is action oriented, inviting actors to attend to their habitual ways of acting (Tsoukas, 2012, p. 71). Seen, therefore, through an enactive perspective, reform is viewed as directed towards actors embedded in sociomaterial practices rather than towards ahistorical beings supposedly pursuing some utility function. An enactive perspective acknowledges that the organization exists insofar as people make it happen. Thus, the law defines a design frame, but designs need to be actively adapted to function. No organization exists in a vacuum of historical space and time. Because laws are, by definition, generalizations established without consideration for circumstance, organizing means constant improvising to maintain the organization's operative capability (Cunha, Miner, & Antonacopolou, 2017). An enactive perspective assumes that organizations are social, material and historical processes: Their existence as state bureaucracies does not preclude *ira et studio*. Orders descend from the top but are rendered operational by their users. Time is important because people and organizations have memories, develop implicit theories and accumulate experiences.

From an enactive perspective, reform is therefore a historically situated accomplishment; every time a government starts a new reform it elicits the memories of past reforms. When a government starts a new reform—say, a sixth in a decade—it revives the experiences of the previous five. Managing organizational forgetting (de Holan & Phillips, 2004) may be as necessary as facilitating new learning. However, forgetting is not particularly well managed by reformers because the initiator of the sixth reform is not necessarily the same one who managed the previous five reforms. The memory asymmetry of 'top' and 'base', therefore, results in the accumulation, at the 'base', of piles of memories of reforms failed, which eventually help accumulate negative emotions (e.g. cynicism), low change readiness and change resistance (e.g. Armenakis & Harris, 1993). From an enactive perspective, the legal-rational-bureaucratic apparatus of the State is only a small part of reform, perhaps the easier part. Changing the law is easy, changing the State is not.

How Reform Produces Vicious Circles

When reformers (1) see reform as a primarily structural endeavour, (2) assume that it should be managed from the top-down, (3) impose the reform through an "authoritarian administrative culture" (Tsoukas, 2012, p. 74) and (4) consider that they need to change the system without necessarily having to change themselves, they are aligning a constellation of organizational factors that will potentially give rise to the emergence of circles, in this case vicious circles, deviation-amplifying loops that turn a bad situation worse (Tsoukas & Cunha, forthcoming). These vicious circles will subsequently impede reform, which means that reformers undermine their own reform attempts. Next we discuss why.

First, when reform is seen as a primarily structural endeavour, it is devoid of sensitivity to culture, context and process. The assumption underpinning it is simple and linear: Reformers change structures and the rest will follow. The problem is that changing structures does not necessarily lead to deep change. In this approach people may be confronted with calls for change that they do not necessarily understand. Sensemaking efforts are potentially futile because of the generalist nature of the call. If, in addition, changes were preceded by other changes that were also unintelligible, people may start using rules in a mindless way (Langer, 1989). Sticking mindlessly to rules relieves people of anxiety. This is one reason why so many state organizations, over time, acquire Kafkaesque traits (Warner, 2007). In a Kafkaesque organization people do not understand the rules and yet they actively participate in their enforcement, thus reproducing and perpetuating them (Clegg, Cunha, Munro, Rego & Sousa, 2016).

Secondly, when a process is imposed from the top it often creates feelings of powerlessness throughout the hierarchy. Over time, people learn that there is nothing they can do. In this sense, reforms are paradoxically supposed to be executed by people who think themselves powerless. The question then is: How can change be produced by people who think that they do not have the power to effect change? Imagining a revolution without revolutionaries can offer an approximation to this practical problem.

Thirdly, when the reform is imposed via an authoritarian administrative culture, the above perception of powerlessness is reinforced and the existing circuits of power are further strengthened—even if reform requires a new power circuitry (Deroy & Clegg, 2015). This system becomes inoculated against change and the idea of reform loses its motivational appeal, potentially becoming just another phase in a rhetorical game without substance.

Finally, when reformers consider that they need to change the system without necessarily having to change themselves, they will be stabilizing the system they claim they want to destabilize. In this sense, each new reform may actually render the system less re-formable as every new attempt will only make the vicious circle stronger. Studying organizational vicious circles may constitute a highly informative way of learning about reform. In the next section we switch the conceptual lens and look at the vicious circle as a way of learning about reform.

Studying the Vicious Circle to Learn About Reform

In the previous section we sought to explore why the process of reform produces vicious circles. In this section we ask: How do vicious circles undermine reform attempts, closing the vicious circle and finally neutralizing the reform itself?

To answer this, we should remember that reform is often imposed via an "authoritarian administrative culture" (Tsoukas, 2012, p. 74). When this is the case, reform is enacted as a process external to organizations, an imposition from above. It is neither understood nor desired by those upon which it is imposed. From a change management perspective, this raises several issues: "[I]n organizational transformation, as well as 'hard' (i.e. technical-cum-managerial) issues, 'soft' questions of communication, trust, and credibility become important" (Tsoukas, 2012, p. 77). The handling of these core ingredients of reform, however, confronts people with interpretive traps that can be translated into vicious circles. Next the three soft questions of communication, trust and credibility are discussed.

Limited Understanding of Communicative Practice

Change, especially transformational change, requires significant communication (Kotter, 1996). If change is understood as a process of immanently generated becoming (Tsoukas & Chia, 2002), it must be appropriated and understood by those who must implement it. A change that is not understood cannot be truly implemented, as the local adaptations that would render the new logic operative will not take place, being impervious to sensemaking and local adaptation. In this sense a change that is communicated without an identified purpose will potentially be perceived as an organizational road to nowhere: The same things will be done in a different way. Communication, especially communication of purpose, is critical, as it renders change meaningful.

The result of the lack of clear purpose, as Vaill (1981) suggested, is predictable: When a purpose is not clear or is not attractive enough to be internalized, the implementation modus operandi will be perfunctory. When work in an organization is routine (as it often is in bureaucracies), coercive (as is also common in state bureaucracies; see Adler & Borys, 1996) and imposed without a clear sense of purpose (Vaill, 1981), people will feel trapped in a cycle of endless, mindless repetition. They may perceive the organization as a vicious circle, i.e. a set of "deviation-amplifying loops, i.e. action loops with counterproductive results" (Masuch, 1985, p. 16). They change without a sense of progress.

Low Trust

Traditional features of the political scene in Greece and Portugal include polarized political systems, the politicization of state-controlled organizations, political patronage and cronyism. The way civil service employees think about reform, thus, tends to be devoid of trust. Since generalized trust is low (Rego, Sarrico, & Moreira, 2006), prior reform attempts failed to deliver and the political arena is often regarded as a marketplace for favour exchange, the people who are supposed to make the change happen are also the first to doubt that it will actually occur. The persistence of authoritarian traits in the administrative culture reinforces the element of distrust, leading to a vicious circle: Because the authority of the state does not produce the intended results (e.g., in terms of budgetary control), the state reinforces its authoritarian grip, deepening the existing power circuitry and, in parallel, the mistrust between 'top' and 'base', i.e. government and citizenry.

Lack of Reform Credibility

From a structural perspective, reform is inscribed on a blank page. Every reform starts anew. From an enactive perspective, however, reform is an ongoing process—hardly anything starts for the first time. At any point in time, a reform is embedded in previous cycles of reform (Tsoukas, 2012, p. 69). In this sense, a new reform is the continuation of some previous reform by other means (Weick & Quinn, 1999). In contexts where previous reforms delivered results, reform readiness may be hypothesized to increase, whereas in contexts where reforms failed to deliver, reform readiness may be hypothesized to decrease and organizational cynicism to increase. This combination of low reform readiness and high cynicism leads to a "tragic circle of self-fulfilling prophecy" (Merton, 1948, in Masuch, 1985, p. 17). When reform becomes a sort of an institutional mantra without material consequences, its positive appeal vanishes and the costs associated with an excess of change rise with every new reform attempt (Abrahamson, 2004). The circle then becomes a normal, even if suboptimal, state of organizational affairs (Masuch, 1985, p. 18). In the case of public bureaucracies, the vicious circle may lead to a situation in which "while growing, public bureaucracies may absorb more and more resources until taxpayers finally run out of money"

(Masuch, 1985, p. 19). At the end, people will pursue a path of action that will lead them increasingly further away from the desired end state.

Every failed reform enters the realm of institutional memory, thus helping provide the matrix within which subsequent reforms will unfold. Rather than reform following the lineal Lewinian scheme (unfreezing-changing-refreezing; Lewin, 1947), its trajectory is far more convoluted and open-ended. The failure of one reform thus leaves a mark in an organization's memory of "reform": As change is never frozen, past reforms symbolically and narratively penetrate into present reforms. Expectations towards future reforms and reformers are already pre-formed in ongoing organizational processes, such as organizational memory (Walsh & Ungson, 1991) and implicit theories of leadership (Detert & Edmondson, 2011).

Reforms, Vicious Circles and European Organization Theory

Management researchers have called for the need to study relevant management problems. It is a laudable objective. As Hernes (2014, p. 852) pointed out, "incessant demands for 'theoretical contribution', demands of rigour and relevance risk sending the field further away from the world of practitioners" and, we add, from the world of citizens. State reform constitutes one of the most formidable problems in the European Union, with EU, national and organizational-institutional logics intervening. Three topics associated with state reform may inform future research in a distinctly European context (Rasche, this volume), in which advanced liberal democracies have developed, over time, generous welfare states and, for a variety of reasons, are now being pushed to reconfigure them. Three topics can be considered as deserving special attention: the conflict between institutional logics at different levels of analysis, the persistent paradoxes and dialectics of change and the process of change.

Conflict of Institutional Logics

Reform of the state in southern European EU member states proved to be an extraordinarily complex process. The state, at the national level (say in Athens or Lisbon), is an intricate network of organizations and their respective stakeholders. The logics of stakeholders are often conflicting, as, for example, happens with municipalities seeking to maintain a decentralized approach, whereas the state, in order to increase budgetary discipline, tends to move in the opposite direction. Above the national institutional landscape, lays the EU institutional field. Brussels is a production center of supra-national institutional pressures that have to be integrated into national legislation. The result of this institutional multi-layering is an inevitable collision of institutional logics. Scholars have recently analyzed the difficulties of articulating institutional logics at the level of the firm (Pache & Santos, 2010). These difficulties are amplified in the multi-tiered political context involving the

EU and its member states, with the former pushing reforms which the latter need to translate (Czarniawska & Joerges, 1996) to their own political and institutional circumstances.

Paradox and Dialectics

The study of state reform offers a privileged setting to study a number of topics that are central in process organizational research. Recent process theorizing has uncovered the paradoxes and dialectics of organizing (Clegg, Cunha, & Cunha, 2002; Eisenhardt, 2000; Langley, Smallman, Tsoukas, & Van de Ven, 2013). State reform constitutes an almost inevitable paradoxical ground for the study of major change interventions (Eisenhardt et al., 2016). The diversity of institutional logics and sectional interests that pervade the EU meta-organizations (Ahrne, Brunsson, & Seidl, 2016) inevitably generates tension. The EU puts institutional layers on top of other institutional layers. The sectional interests of one field are not necessarily aligned with those of other fields. The closer one looks at an organization, the more the contradictions between fields become apparent. Seo and Creed (2002) have argued that contradictions can be a source of positive institutional change. But they can also lead to paralysis and vicious circularity (Clegg & Cunha, forthcoming; Lewis & Smith 2014). Persistent paradoxes and the paradoxification process, i.e. the construction of perceived inconsistencies into a workable narrative (Bergstrom, Styhre, & Thilander, 2014), have in the case of state reform a privileged window of analysis.

Dynamic Unfolding of Change

As Hernes (this volume) has observed, practitioners are acutely aware of the fact that they operate in time. But temporal awareness partly depends on the roles one occupies. For every new reformer, reform is urgent and operates within a strict temporal window, whereas for the subjects of the reform, the duration of the process is longer, with each episode emerging from and being added to previous waves of reforms. As a result, reform offers a setting to explore the friction between temporal perspectives and unique personal experiences around the temporality of reform. An interesting case is the clash between Greece's governments and the country's lenders over the question of reform. Greece's lenders mostly demand reforms that will be financially effective as soon as possible, whereas a sustainable reduction of debt, in the long run, demands fundamental institutional reform, which, however, takes time to be enacted and yield results. In other words, the temporality of the financial markets and lenders diverges from the temporality of institutional reform. More generally, reforming state organizations provides a rich setting to explore the pace of institutional change: How much reform is palatable in a given period of time? How far can transformation go? How do people react to repeated claims of change urgency? Given the importance of rhythm and pace in organizational change (e.g. Klarner & Raisch, 2013), reforming the state can provide a promising context for the empirical study of large-scale change and the layering of first-, second- and third-order change.

Finally, given political calendars and the highly politicized nature of state apparatuses in southern Europe, reforms are often rendered incomplete every time there is a change in cabinet. In this sense, reversal of change (Mantere, Schildt, & Sillince, 2012) is a fascinating topic to explore, especially since in a polarized political system and a politicized bureaucracy, continuity is often not imbued with positive political value. The combination of politicization, unpredictability and reformism constitutes a rich setting for studying change as process rather than episode. The recent reversals in policy domains by the left-wing government in Greece are a good case in point. Reforms enacted by the previous governments in, for example, human resource management practices in the civil service, or in higher education and health, are being explicitly reversed. The intense politicization of public life that is noticeable in southern European countries sets limits to reform continuity, since there is often a limited common (i.e. across-party) understanding with regard to how particular policy domains ought to be structured and functioning. Reform reversal helps explain the common sentiment in southern European countries that reform is a rather Sisyphean task.

Conclusion

The crisis that has severely hit southern Europe in the recent years has revealed that, from a management research perspective, scholars are perhaps underestimating or even ignoring some of the major issues that impact the lives of millions of people, thus risking refraining from studying what matters to those outside the academy (Chia, this volume; Eisenhardt et al., 2016). By and large, state reform has not been studied as extensively as it deserves by management scholars, who tend to be more interested in corporate change. In addition, there is considerable scope for the further study of vicious circles beyond those already studied by organizational researchers (e.g. Garud & Kumaraswamy 2005; Masuch, 1985). Yet vicious circles and 'wicked problems' emphatically confront those who attempt state reform (Camillus, 2008; Tsoukas, 2012).

Understanding the 'wickedness' of these challenges and how they can possibly be 'tamed' (Camillus, 2008, p. 99) constitutes a problem that is not only relevant but also urgent. Reform across Europe is producing a number of unintended consequences, including the collision of national interests in a hitherto trans-national community of nations, causing economic distress and social exclusion, youth unemployment, the rise of nationalism and populism and other major problems. Aging populations, global competition, Eurozone fiscal discipline, budgetary pressures, rising welfare-state costs and so on suggest that state reform is not a passing fad but a chronic issue. The more we seek to study it, the more relevant we will become, increasing scholarly understanding and generating actionable knowledge.

References

Abrahamson, Eric (2004). *Change without pain*. Boston, MA: Harvard Business School Press.

Adler, Paul S. & Borys, Bryan (1996). Two types of bureaucracy: Enabling and coercive. *Administrative Science Quarterly*, 41, 61–89.

Ahrne, Goran, Brunsson, Nils & Seidl, David (2016). Resurrecting organization by going beyond organizations. *European Management Journal*, 34, 93–101.

Albrow, Martin (1992). Sine ira et studio—or do organizations have feelings? *Organization Studies*, 13, 313–329.

Armenakis, Achiles A. & Harris, Stanley G. (1993). Creating readiness for organizational change. *Human Relations*, 46(6), 681–703.

Bergstrom, Ola, Styhre, Alexander & Thilander, Per (2014). Paradoxifying organizational change: Cynicism and resistance in the Swedish Armed Forces. *Journal of Change Management*, 14(3), 384–404.

Brunsson, Nils & Olsen, Johan P. (1993). *The reforming organization*. London: Routledge.

Camillus, John C. (2008). Strategy as a wicked problem. *Harvard Business Review*, 86(5), 99–106.

Clegg, Stewart R., Cunha, João Vieira da & Cunha, Miguel Pina (2002). Management paradoxes: A relational view. *Human Relations*, 55(5), 483–503.

Clegg, Stewart R. & Cunha, Miguel Pina e (forthcoming). Organizational dialectics. In M.W. Lewis, W.K. Smith, P. Jarzabkowski & A. Langley (Eds.), *The Oxford handbook of organizational paradox: Approaches to plurality, tensions, and contradictions*. New York: Oxford University Press.

Clegg, Stewart R., Cunha, Miguel Pina e, Munro, Iain., Rego, Arménio & Sousa, Marta Ooom de (2016). Kafkaesque power and bureaucracy. *Journal of Political Power*, 9(2), 157–181.

Cunha, Miguel Pina e (2014). Uma burocracia insuficientemente burocratizada? Uma estranha explicação sobre a administração da administração pública. In T. Cardoso, P.P. Barros, M. Pinheiro & P.S. Esteves (Eds.), *Para uma reforma abrangente da organização e gestão do sector público* (pp. 43–75). Lisboa: Banco de Portugal.

Cunha, Miguel Pina e, Miner Anne S. & Antonacopolou, Elena (2017). Improvisation processes in organizations. In A. Langley & H. Tsoukas (Eds.), *The Sage handbook of process organization studies* (pp. 559–573). Los Angeles: Sage.

Czarniawska, Barbara & Joerges, Bernward (1996). Travels of ideas. In B. Czarniawska & G. Sevón (Eds.), *Translating organizational change* (pp. 13–47). Berlin: De Gruyter.

de Holan, Pablo Martin & Phillips, Nelson (2004). Organizational forgetting as strategy. *Strategic Organization*, 2(4), 423–433.

Deroy, Xavier & Clegg, Stewart (2015). Back in the USSR: Introducing recursive contingency into institutional theory. *Organization Studies*, 36(1), 73–93.

Detert, James R. & Edmondson, Amy (2011). Implicit voice theories: Taken-for-granted rules of self-censorship at work. *Academy of Management Review*, 54(3), 461–488.

Eisenhardt, Kathleen M. (2000). Paradox, spirals, ambivalence: The new language of change and pluralism. *Academy of Management Review*, 25, 703–705.

Eisenhardt, Kathleen M., Graebner, Melissa E. & Sonenshein, Scott (2016). Grand challenges and inductive methods: Rigor without rigor mortis. *Academy of Management Journal*, 59(4), 1113–1123.

Garud, Raghu & Kumaraswamy, Aran (2005). Vicious and virtuous circles in the management of knowledge: The case of Infosys Technologies. *MIS Quarterly*, 20(1), 9–33.

Hernes, Tor (2014). In search of a soul of relevance for European management research. *European Management Journal*, 32(6), 852–857.

Kalyvas, Stathis, Pagoulatos, George & Tsoukas, Haridimos (Eds.) (2012). *From stagnation to forced adjustment: Reforms in Greece, 1974–2010*. New York: Columbia University Press.

Klarner, Patricia & Raisch, Sebastian (2013). Move to the beat: Rhythms of change and firm performance. *Academy of Management Journal*, 56(1), 160–184.

Kotter, John P. (1996). *Leading change*. Boston, MA: Harvard Business School Press.

Langer, Ellen (1989). *Mindfulness*. Reading, MA: Addison-Wesley.

Langley, Ann, Smallman, Clive, Tsoukas, Haridimos & Van de Ven, Andrew H. (2013). Process studies of change in organizations and management: Unveiling temporality, activity and flow. *Academy of Management Journal*, 56(1), 1–13.

Lewin, Kurt (1947). Frontiers of group dynamics, I: Concept, method and reality in social science. *Human Relations*, 1, 5–40.

Lewis, Marianne W. & Smith, Wendy K. (2014). Paradox as a metatheoretical perspective: Sharpening the focus and widening the scope. *Journal of Applied Behavioral Science*, 50(2), 127–149.

Mantere, Saku, Schildt, Henri A. & Sillince, John A. (2012). Reversal of strategic change. *Academy of Management Journal*, 55(1), 172–196.

Masuch, Michael (1985). Vicious circles in organizations. *Administrative Science Quarterly*, 30(1), 14–33.

Merton, Robert K. (1948). The self-fulfilling prophecy. *The Antioch Review*, 8, 193–210.

Pache, Anne-Claire & Santos, Filipe (2010). When worlds collide: The internal dynamics of organizational responses to conflicting institutional demands. *Academy of Management Review*, 35(3), 455–476.

Papoulias, Demetrios & Tsoukas, Harimidos (1994). Managing reforms on a large scale: What role for OR/MS? *Journal of the Operational Research Society*, 45, 977–986.

Pereira, Paulo Trigo (2013). O que é preciso fazer para termos melhor Estado? Paper presented in the 4th "Jornadas Empresariais da AEP", Porto, October 10.

Pettigrew, Andrew M., Woodman, Richard W. & Cameron, Kim S. (2001). Studying change and development: Challenges for future research. *Academy of Management Journal*, 44(4), 697–713.

Pfeffer, Jeffrey (2006). Like ships passing in the night: The separate literatures of organization theory and public management. *International Public Management Journal*, 9(4), 457–465.

Pressman, Jeffrey L. & Wildavsky, Aaron (1984). *Implementation* (3rd ed.). Berkeley: University of California Press.

Rego, Arménio, Sarrico, Cláudia S. & Moreira, José M. (2006). Trust in Portuguese public authorities. *Public Integrity*, 8, 77–92.

Seo, Meyong-Gu & Creed, W. E. Douglas (2002). Institutional contradictions, praxis, and institutional change: A dialectical perspective. *Academy of Management Review*, 27(2), 222–247.

Stone, Deborah (2002). *Policy paradox* (Revised ed.). New York: Norton.

Tsoukas, Harimidos (2012). Enacting reforms: Towards an enactive theory. In S. Kalyvas, G. Pagoulatos & H. Tsoukas (Eds.), *From stagnation to forced adjustment: Reforms in Greece, 1971–2010* (pp. 67–89). London: Hurst & Company.

Tsoukas, Haridimos & Chia, Robert (2002). On organizational becoming: Rethinking organizational change. *Organization Science*, 13, 567–582.

Tsoukas, Harimidos & Cunha, Miguel Pina (forthcoming). On organizational circularity: Vicious and virtuous circles in organizing. In M.W. Lewis, W.K. Smith, P. Jarzabkowski & A. Langley (Eds.), *The Oxford handbook of organizational paradox: Approaches to plurality, tensions, and contradictions*. New York: Oxford University Press.

Tsoukas, Harimidos & Papoulias, Demetrios B. (1996). Understanding social reforms: A conceptual analysis. *Journal of the Operational Research Society*, 47, 653–863.

Tsoukas, Harimidos & Papoulias, Demetrios B. (2005). Managing third-order change: The case of the public power corporation in Greece. *Long Range Planning*, 38, 79–95.

Vaill, Peter B. (1981). The purpose of high-performing systems. *Organizational Dynamics*, 11(2), 23–39.

Walsh, James P. & Ungson, Gerardo R. (1991). Organizational memory. *Academy of Management Review*, 16(1), 57–91.

Warner, Malcolm (2007). Kafka, Weber and organization theory. *Human Relations*, 60(7), 1019–1038.

Weick, Karl E. & Quinn, Robert E. (1999). Organizational change and development. *Annual Review of Psychology*, 50, 361–386.

Wilson, James Q. (2000). *Bureaucracy*. New York: Basic Books.

Yanow, Dvora (1996). *How does a policy mean?* Washington, DC: Georgetown University Press.

10 The Corporation as a Political Actor

European and North American Perspectives

Andreas Rasche

Introduction

Firms' non-market strategies have been discussed from various theoretical perspectives. In particular, the relationship between corporations and politics has attracted much scholarly attention. Two schools of thought seem particularly noteworthy. On the one hand, the corporate political activity (CPA) literature has emphasized that firms interact with governments in a variety of ways, for instance, by trying to influence policy outcomes. On the other hand, recent discussions in the field of corporate social responsibility (CSR) have highlighted that CSR should be understood politically, because firms increasingly provide public goods (e.g., education) and engage in business regulation, thus assuming state-like obligations. While North American scholars were at the forefront of developing the CPA approach (Baron, 2003; Getz, 1997; Hillman, Keim, & Schuler, 2004), European scholars have predominantly shaped the discussion around political CSR (Scherer, Rasche, Palazzo, & Spicer, 2016; Scherer & Palazzo, 2007, 2011; Whelan, 2012).

Of course, it would be an oversimplification to claim that only European scholars have contributed to the political CSR literature and that only North American scholars have added to the CPA debate, especially when considering that scholarly discourses increasingly transcend regional boundaries (Wagner & Leydesdorff, 2005), to say nothing of the contours of both fields not being clearly identified. What I am arguing is that European and North American scholars have undertaken the *paradigmatic framing* of both perspectives and that the majority of intellectual contributions to each approach come from Europe and North America, respectively. Hence, a comparative perspective is helpful to set both approaches apart on a conceptual level.

Although political CSR and CPA share a common interest in studying the link between firms and politics, surprisingly little reflection has gone into exploring the relationship between both concepts (for a recent exception, see den Hond, Rehbein, de Bakker, & van Lankveld, 2014). While the political CSR literature frames CPA as a "purely instrumental view of corporate politics" (Scherer & Palazzo, 2011, p. 900), it has not looked into the details of CPA scholarship. Exploring commonalities and differences between the two approaches is thus a worthwhile endeavour that allows us to better understand the ways in which scholarship in CSR and CPA can(not) interact with each other.

The objective of this chapter is twofold. First, I aim to show how both approaches to the study of corporations as political actors differ. I suggest that some of the key differences can be explained when contrasting the answers given by both approaches to two questions: (a) *Where*, i.e. in what settings, do the political engagement of firms take place? and (b) *Why* do firms become politically active? I argue that the differences can be explained, at least in part, by the characteristics of European/North American management scholarship as well as by the political environment in both regions. Second, I would like to make the controversial point that both perspectives share a number of commonalities and complement each other. I use these insights as a springboard to outline a brief agenda for future research on the interaction effects between CPA and political CSR.

Political Corporate Social Responsibility

There is not much consensus on what CSR entails as a theoretical concept (McWilliams, Siegel, & Wright, 2006). I use CSR as an umbrella concept that defines the responsibilities of firms towards their stakeholders and the natural environment and that demonstrates how such responsibilities are operationalized (Waddock, 2008). Much of the literature on CSR is based on an economic view, emphasizing that social and environmental responsibilities should only be accepted if there is a strategic reason to do so (e.g., advancing the competitive position of a firm; McWilliams & Siegel, 2001). According to Scherer and Palazzo (2011, p. 904), such a perspective assumes that there is a clear separation between business and government. Businesses should maximize profits, while governmental actors should assume responsibility for those issues that corporations cannot address due to their fiduciary responsibilities to shareholders (see also Friedman, 1970).

The political CSR approach acknowledges the limits of such an economic view under conditions of globalization. Governments can only protect citizens from corporate misconduct if they are able to regulate business behavior in their sphere of influence. Firms, however, increasingly manage global supply and value chains and are thus exposed to heterogeneous legal environments and social demands. This challenges the traditional division of labor between business and government (Scherer & Palazzo, 2011), as gaps in global governance restrict the ability of states to regulate adequately corporate behavior through judicial systems. Scherer and Palazzo (2008) emphasize in particular the role of regulatory gaps. Such gaps occur because the flexibility of (multinational) corporations to move production to countries with weak legal systems cannot be matched by nation-states (whose power remains territorially bound) or international organizations (which lack enforcement capacity). International law, which could serve as a way to close some of these governance gaps, is usually not directly applicable to corporate actors and hence depends on nation-states' willingness and capacity to implement relevant rules.

Gaps in global governance are not restricted to the regulatory dimension. Many global problems cannot be addressed because a number of other governance gaps exist (Weiss & Thakur, 2010, pp. 7–23). First, there are gaps in our knowledge about the nature, magnitude and solutions to a number of global problems (e.g., climate change; Bäckstrand & Lövbrand, 2006). *Knowledge gaps* are problematic, as sufficient consensual knowledge about an issue is a precondition for developing relevant policies. Firms, together with civil society organizations and state actors, can create discursive spaces where relevant knowledge can be collected, analyzed, debated and disseminated (Rasche, 2012). Second, global governance is also hindered by lack of agreement on who can legitimately set global norms (i.e. normative gaps). Defining such norms is important, as they often 'harden' into more binding regulations. Although the United Nations is perceived as a legitimate entity, it cannot simply introduce norms, as norms are dependent on being recognized as accepted standards. Finally, the imbalance between the scale of global problems and the resources and political authority attached to organizations intended to address them causes *institutional gaps*. Institutions like the UN often lack adequate resources and the authority to enforce existing norms and policies, for instance, when considering human rights. Firms increasingly provide resources to international organizations, for instance, through UN–business partnerships (Rasche & Kell, 2010), and thus indirectly assume a political role.

Political CSR emphasizes that firms become political actors due to the existence of such global governance gaps. Scherer and Palazzo (2011) summarize this perspective on the political role of corporations by arguing that "political CSR suggests an extended model of governance with business firms contributing to global regulation and providing public goods" (p. 901). Political CSR sharpens our attention to the fact that many firms have assumed state-like functions (e.g., in the prevention and treatment of HIV/AIDS; Valente & Crane, 2010) and the fact that state and non-state actors are working together in the attempt to find solutions to governance challenges. Recently, Scherer et al. (2016) have introduced an enlarged perspective on political CSR, which highlights the more general role of corporations as political actors, regardless of whether they act as global or local players.

This enlarged view on political CSR acknowledges that firms act as political actors if they engage in public deliberations about public goods and/or if they provide these goods (or restrict public bads) "in cases where public authorities are unable or unwilling to fulfill this role" (Scherer et al., 2016, p. 276). This definition centers on the public good concept. While such goods are usually understood as being non-rival in consumption and possessing non-excludable benefits, the political CSR approach uses an expanded public goods conception (Kaul & Mendoza, 2003). Some goods are not public per se but can be made public by deliberation and collective decisions. For instance, while healthcare and education can be classified as rival goods, there can be policy-induced shifts that make these goods available to all citizens. Political CSR becomes particularly relevant when corporations contribute to such policy-induced shifts (e.g., when making non-rival goods like human rights more non-exclusive).

Corporate Political Activity

The CPA literature looks at the interdependence of business and government from a different, yet also interrelated, perspective. Theories in the CPA domain rest on the assumption that governments are not following laissez-faire economic policies due to the provision of subsidies, price controls, entry barriers and other interventions (Shaffer, 1995, p. 498). Such interventions increase environmental uncertainty. Consequently, firms have an incentive to develop 'domain management' strategies—i.e., to use governmental interventions in a way that support their own strategic objectives (Baysinger, 1984, p. 249). Getz (1997) defines CPA as "any deliberate firm action intended to influence government policy or process" (pp. 32–33). Other scholars highlight the ability (or inability) of firms to strategically adapt to government policies as an important topic in the CPA debate (Shaffer, 1995).

The CPA literature views business–government relations from a managerial point of view. It looks at how firms attempt to control their external environment by protecting and advancing their political interests—for instance, by lobbying policymakers, forming coalitions and making contributions to political campaigns. Getz (1997, p. 55) suggests that firms engage in CPA because either they want to protect themselves from perceived environmental threats (be they real or anticipated), or they want to leverage opportunities in their relationship with government. Hillman and Hitt (1999) further distinguish between a transactional and a relational approach towards political action. The transactional approach is reactive in the sense that firms await the development of public policies in a specific issue area, developing short-term tactics to influence these policies. The relational approach focuses less on single issues, but stresses that some firms build long-term relations with relevant parties across issue areas, so that relevant contacts and resources are already in place when policies emerge.

Much research attention has been placed on the external and internal factors that influence the extent to which a firm engages in CPA. Lux, Crook and Woehr (2011) identify three types of antecedents. First, CPA of firms depends, to some degree, on their institutional environment. For instance, the level of government regulation is usually seen to positively influence business's political activity (Kim, 2008), while the extent to which a firm depends on public contracts (i.e., government sales) also positively relates to CPA (Boies, 1989). Second, market and industry-level factors can also influence CPA. For example, research has found that higher industry concentration (and, hence, more consensus regarding policy issues) stimulates higher levels of CPA, as there are more policy demanders with related interests (Yoffie, 1987). Finally, firm-level antecedents are also used to explain CPA. Prior research shows that larger firms are more likely to engage in political action, e.g., because they possess more resources as well as act as contractual partners for governments (Lux et al., 2011).

Differences Between Political CSR and CPA

I explore differences between CPA and political CSR in light of two questions: (a) *Where*, i.e. in what settings, do the political engagement of firms take place? and (b) *Why* do firms become politically active? I suggest that differences between both approaches can be explained, at least in part, by the characteristics of European/North American management scholarship as well as by the political environment in both regions.

Context of Political Engagement: Where, i.e., in What Settings, Do the Political Engagement of Firms Take Place?

CPA theorizes political engagement by looking exclusively into the relationship of businesses with governments. As Getz (1997, p. 33) argues, "CPA focuses only on behavior undertaken in the governmental arena". The CPA literature assumes that firms implement political activities in those settings where policy issues of interest to them can be addressed (e.g., by national governments or supranational organizations). Political CSR adopts a broader view and assumes that the political engagement of firms is embedded into the wider relationship between businesses, governments and civil society (Scherer & Palazzo, 2007, 2011). This changing relationship is reflected, for example, in the proliferation of multi-stakeholder initiatives (MSIs) such as the UN Global Compact and the Forest Stewardship Council (Rasche & Kell, 2010). By engaging in such initiatives, firms set voluntary standards for business behavior in areas such as human rights and environmental sustainability.

Behind this difference lies a much deeper shift in the steering mechanism underlying political engagement—a shift from a focus on government (CPA) to governance (political CSR). The literature on political CSR has not yet developed a robust understanding of the concept of governance and its relationship with government. In its most general sense, governance refers to the "processes and institutions, both formal and informal, that guide and restrain the collective activities of a group" (Keohane & Nye, 2000, p. 12). Government is one way of exercising governance, but not all governance arrangements necessarily relate to governmental action. According to Rhodes (2012), "*Governance* signifies a change in the meaning of *government*, referring to new processes of governing; or changed conditions of ordered rule; or new methods by which society is governed" (p. 33, my emphasis). While CPA highlights governance through government, political CSR stresses the importance of governance shifts and hence emphasizes a broader perspective on the relationship between firms, governments and civil society actors.

Such governance shifts happen in two directions. First, firms' political engagement is tied increasingly to addressing global governance challenges (upward shift in governance). While the CPA literature has predominantly looked at business–government relations at the national level (mostly with regard to the US political system), political CSR stresses the importance of addressing gaps in (global) governance. Second, political CSR looks at the political engagement of firms in settings that reach beyond centralized state control and include more collaborative forms of governance (horizontal shift in governance). This moves the attention away from political hierarchies and state-based forms of governance to partnerships and networks. It is, however, not a shift away from government per se, as governmental actors still contribute in a variety of ways to collaborative governance arrangements (Gond, Kang, & Moon, 2011).

The way in which both discourses frame the political engagement of firms can be attributed, in part, to the political environment in the EU and the USA. Political CSR's understanding of firms' engagement in politics rests on a multi-stakeholder perspective. Firms *together* with governments and civil society actors are expected to address social and environmental problems. Such a multi-stakeholder view has been part and parcel of the EU strategy on CSR. For instance, the creation of the European Multi-Stakeholder Forum on CSR (CSR EMS Forum) was based on the conviction that "the involvement of all affected stakeholders is key to ensure acceptance and credibility of CSR and better compliance with its principles" (de Schutter, 2008, p. 211). Although the CSR EMS Forum did not succeed in creating a balanced representation of stakeholders, mostly because business started to dominate the Forum, it is still fair to say that European-style CSR was, from its origins, concerned with the broader socio-economic context in which corporations are embedded. Hence, it is not surprising that European scholars started to theorize firms' political actions as being embedded in multi-actor governance.

CPA's focus on governmental actors is influenced by a strong tradition of political donations and campaign contributions in the USA—for instance, through political action committees (PACs), which pool individual contributions to electoral campaigns. As PACs must file regular reports disclosing their receipts, studies have access to a rich source of data frequently used when researching business–government relations (see the overview by Hillman et al., 2004). The US legal environment further enables and supports the prominent role of PACs. In 2010, the Supreme Court of the United States ruled that the government could not prohibit or restrict individual contributions to political campaigns by corporations and other actors (see *Citizen United v Federal Election Commission*, 558 US 310). This gives corporations a pivotal role in shaping US politics, a fact that is mirrored in the CPA literature.

Rationale of Political Engagement: Why Do Firms Become Politically Active?

Scholars working in the CPA field emphasize that firms engage in political activity to improve firm performance (Hillman et al., 2004, p. 839). Firms become politically active for instrumental reasons and out of self-interest. They develop and implement political strategies if the benefits of the engagement outweigh the costs (even if the benefits are collective goods). Self-interest can take many forms (Getz, 1997, p. 55). Firms may benefit from curtailing existing or anticipated legitimacy threats in their policy environment, or they may take advantage of opportunities that exist in their relationship with governmental actors. The CPA literature assumes that firms will try to estimate a policy's net impact on its competitive performance (Schuler & Rehbein, 1997). Lux et al.'s (2011) meta-analysis shows that firms with higher levels of successful CPA exhibit better financial performance.

Political CSR rejects such instrumental reasoning, instead emphasizing that changes in firms' operating environment and regulatory context (e.g., the rise of governance gaps) require them to address social and environmental issues, *regardless* of whether such activities create any financial benefit. It sees the main reason for the political engagement of firms in the decreased possibility to divide labor among governments, businesses and civil society. One important aspect in this context is the shifting nature of organizational legitimacy. Corporations do not legitimize themselves any longer through strategic influence of stakeholder perceptions (e.g., as assumed by CPA's emphasis on public image advertising), as such manipulation increasingly fails due to increased levels of transparency. Instead, firms reach public acceptance by engaging in communication processes with a wide range of constituents (moral legitimacy)—for instance, by participating in multi-stakeholder initiatives and public-private partnerships.

It would be overgeneralizing to argue that the distinction between instrumental reasoning (CPA) and governance-related reasoning (political CSR) could be fully attributed to the different intellectual traditions in Europe and North America. It would be equally misleading, however, to completely ignore the influence of such traditions. Historically, North American business schools have promoted the 'scientization' of management education (Kaplan, 2014), emphasizing the importance of discipline-based scholarship, quantitative methods and positivistic thinking. Collin, Johansson, Svensson and Ulvenblad (1996), for instance, find that US-based journals publish significantly more quantitative studies that are embedded in an objectivist paradigm. CPA's emphasis on instrumental reasoning and its search for causal performance implications rest on this science-based understanding of management.

Political CSR rests much more on inter-disciplinary scholarship, critical thinking and epistemological pluralism. Of course, studies in the political CSR discourse can equally adopt a positivistic lens. Understanding firms' political role in the context of the interactions between different societal sectors, however, requires a much broader research strategy, i.e. a strategy that leaves room for conceptual and speculative work, as well as research based on individual case studies. Such an approach seems to be in line with European management scholarship, which is often described as having a greater openness to a range of epistemological and methodological approaches (Chia, 2014; Dameron & Durand, 2009). This diversity is a legacy of the different cultural, historical as well as philosophical traditions that have influenced management scholarship in Europe. For instance, European scholars have clearly shaped the emergence of Critical Management Studies (CMS) and thus opened management studies towards different ideological critiques.

While a certain European research style can be identified on a more general level, it should also be noted that some of these traditional boundaries are blurring. On the one hand, European scholars increasingly aim at positioning their publications in highly ranked North American journals, resulting in a certain import of paradigmatic orientations into European business schools (Kieser, 2004). On the other hand, some North American journals have also started to become more flexible in terms of research methodologies deemed acceptable. Despite these changes, the different intellectual traditions attached to CPA and political CSR are an important consideration when trying to understand why both approaches come to different conclusions when trying to explain how and why firms become politically active.

Commonalities and Complementarities

Although CPA and political CSR differ in a number of ways, they also share some commonalities. These commonalities become apparent once some of the theoretical assumptions of the political CSR discourse are contrasted with real-life corporate behavior. Two commonalities seem particularly important. First, while the political CSR literature rejects instrumental motivations for the participation of firms in responsible business, suggesting that firms need to live up to their responsibilities *independently* of economic considerations (Scherer & Palazzo, 2011, pp. 905–906), many businesses contribute to global business regulation precisely because such engagement provides them with economic advantages. For instance, research on MSIs shows that the business case is one of the key motivations for firms to participate in such governance arrangements (see, e.g., Janney, Dess, & Forlani, 2009). Firms' motivations to engage in political CSR may be as instrumental as their motivations to engage in CPA. The difference is that the CPA literature focuses directly on this instrumental reasoning, as it is concerned with the link between political action and firm performance, while the political CSR discourse rejects such reasoning (at least on a theoretical level), but can hardly neglect that it is a dominant driver of corporate behavior in practice. In the end, why a particular firm engages in responsible business activities remains an empirical question that is hard to answer in principle. Future research may benefit from questioning political CSR's idealized theoretical assumption that firms become engaged in governance processes because they want to provide basic rights to others (without considering consequences for their own competitive position). This debate points towards the importance of better understanding the relationship between instrumental approaches to responsible business and more intrinsically motivated approaches (see also Schuler, Rasche, Etzion, & Newton, 2017).

CPA and political CSR also share a common interest in the strategic deterrence of stronger government regulation. In the CPA literature, this concern is quite obvious: Firms use their different political activities to respond to an anticipation of a strategic threat (e.g., a bill that is about to pass; Getz, 1997). The main aim is to strengthen the competitive position of a business by influencing government regulation favourably. At first glance, political CSR seems to reject such reasoning, suggesting that firms become engaged in global governance processes because, under conditions of globalization, national governments cannot sufficiently regulate. Such a perspective, however, neglects the fact that global business regulation operates on a continuum between hard and soft law (Abbott et al., 2000), and many firms join voluntary global governance initiatives precisely because they fear that, without voluntary commitment, the regulatory spectrum will move towards harder forms of law. For instance, the International Chamber of Commerce, a business association, supported the creation of the UN Global Compact (an initiative without strong enforcement mechanisms), but opposed the UN Draft Norms on the Responsibilities of Transnational Corporations and Other Business Enterprises with regard to Human Rights (an initiative with tighter enforcement mechanisms; see also Rasche, 2009). Political engagement through CSR can be as much about strategic anticipatory behavior as political engagement through CPA. The democratic deficit that is emerging through such strategic behavior deserves more research attention.

CPA and political CSR can also complement each other. Recent scholarly work shows that CPA has largely neglected its own governance dynamics. How regulated should CPA be? Dahan, Hadani and Schuler (2013) argue that CPA is in definite need of self-regulation, as it constitutes a managerial activity that faces high degrees of complexity and lacks direct observability. This offers managers significant opportunities for discretion (and, hence, abuse), as external or internal controls are hard to implement. The private governance of CPA is important, because without stronger regulation, firms' political activities can lead to ethical challenges (e.g., post-CEO political appointments) as well as result in unsustainable overinvestments (e.g., to keep up with competitors; Dahan et al., 2013). Political CSR can be seen as a framework to discuss how to better govern CPA through self-regulation. There are at least two possible ways in which both debates can complement each other. First, it is possible to call for changes in internal corporate governance structures. Scherer, Baumann-Pauly and Schneider (2013, pp. 495–496), for instance, suggest applying political CSR's underlying principle of deliberation to corporate governance mechanisms, showing the need for broader involvement of stakeholders in corporate oversight and relevant decision processes. Second, it is also possible to govern firms' CPA activities by joining MSIs, which political CSR sees as one way of engaging in governance processes. AccountAbility & UN Global Compact (2005), for instance, have jointly launched a framework that helps firms to assess the responsibility of their own lobbying practices.

Political CSR and CPA can also complement each other indirectly, particularly when a corporation's CSR activities help to make political allies. For instance, firms' involvement in community work (e.g., via corporate volunteering) can facilitate the creation of positive relationships with politicians. These relationships can then act as a platform for information provision or coalition building. Not much is known about the effects of CSR activities on firms' relationships with politicians. It would be important to research to what extent CSR activities can enhance a firm's reputation among legislators and whether an increase in reputation impacts regulatory behavior (e.g., the levels of regulatory autonomy that corporations enjoy). Research in this direction would also need to clarify in what ways such an indirect approach to influence legislators can substitute the effects of direct lobbying strategies.

Some firms also use CPA as a strategy to fulfill their responsibilities towards society. For instance, lobbying activities can help firms to secure the provision of basic rights throughout their supply and value chain. Consider the following example (see Peterson & Pfitzer, 2009, p. 48). Levi Strauss & Co. sources materials from Guatemala. In 2001, the US government threatened to take away the country's duty-free export status, as it felt that local labor laws were not adequately enforced. Levi's lobbied the Guatemalan government to strengthen labor laws as well as organized lobbying activities by its local suppliers. In response, Guatemala tightened some of its labor laws. While Levi's political involvement was mainly based on self-interest, it shows that CPA, if executed in the right context, can also contribute to protecting people's rights.

Concluding Remarks and Future Research

Although European and North American scholars have developed conceptions of the political role of corporations that focus on different empirical phenomena and make different theoretical assumptions, there is still much room for future interactions between both discourses. First, research can take the fact that firms' engagement in both CPA and political CSR challenges corporations' legitimacy as a point of departure for scholarly work that bridges both discourses. The political involvement of firms lacks the democratic legitimacy assigned to elected governments. CPA and political CSR scholars can jointly explore how to address this legitimacy deficit—for example, by looking into how to 'democratise' internal decision-making processes to balance the voices of different stakeholders when deciding upon political activities (Scherer et al., 2013). This would better integrate insights from corporate governance studies, with regard to both the US and the European legal environments. Relevant questions include, but are not limited to: How do boards integrate diverse stakeholder perspectives when reviewing a firm's political activities? What information should firms provide to shareholders about their political engagement? Do different corporate governance systems influence the level and scope of firms' engagement in politics?

A different, yet related, task is to study the ways in which CPA and political CSR are aligned, nonaligned or misaligned within corporations (see also den Hond et al., 2014). Research in this direction should reach beyond the normative claim that CPA and political CSR *should* be aligned, e.g., firms should not publicly claim to protect certain rights while at the same time lobbying against stricter regulation in favour of these rights. Instead, it is necessary to address questions like these: Under what conditions do firms align/non-align/misalign CPA and political CSR? What types of resource complementarities can be developed when aligning political CSR and CPA? In what ways does misalignment damage a corporation (e.g., in terms of increased operational costs or lack of legitimacy)? Addressing these issues shows that increasing the interactions between both discourses, and consequently between North American and European scholarship, is important and timely.

Acknowledgement

I thank Frank de Bakker for helpful comments on an earlier draft of the original paper.

References

Abbott, Kenneth W., Keohane, Robert O., Moravcsik, Andrew, Slaughter, Anne-Marie & Snidal, Duncan (2000). The concept of legalization. *International Organization*, 54(3), 401–419.

AccountAbility & UN Global Compact. (2005). *Towards responsible lobbying: Leadership and public policy*. New York: UN Global Compact Office.

Bäckstrand, Karin & Lövbrand, Eva (2006). Planting trees to mitigate climate change: Contested discourses of ecological modernization, green governmentality and civic environmentalism. *Global Environmental Politics*, 6, 50–75.

Baron, David P. (2003). Private politics. *Journal of Economics & Management Strategy*, 12(1), 31–66.

Baysinger, Barry D. (1984). Domain maintenance as an objective of business political activity: An expanded typology. *Academy of Management Review*, 9(2), 248–258.

Boies, John L. (1989). Money, business and the state: Material interests, *Fortune* 500 corporations, and the size of political action committees. *American Sociological Review*, 54, 821–833.

Chia, Robert (2014). Reflections on the distinctiveness of European management scholarship. *European Management Journal.* 32(5), 683–688.

Collin, Sven-Olof, Johansson, Ulf, Svensson, Katrina & Ulvenblad, Per-Ola (1996). Market segmentation in scientific publications: Research patterns in American vs European management journals. *British Journal of Management*, 7(2), 141–154.

Dahan, Nicolas M., Hadani, Michael & Schuler, Douglas A. (2013). The governance challenges of corporate political activity. *Business & Society*, 52(3), 365–387.

Dameron, Stéphanie & Durand, Thomas (2009). 2020 vision: A dual strategy for European business schools. *EFMD Global Focus*, 3(1), 22–25.

den Hond, Frank, Rehbein, Kathleen A., de Bakker, Frank G. A. & Kooijmans-van Lankveld, Hilde (2014). Playing on two chessboards: Reputation effects between corporate social responsibility (CSR) and corporate political activity (CPA). *Journal of Management Studies*, 51(5), 790–813.

de Schutter, Olivier (2008). Corporate social responsibility European style. *European Law Journal*, 14(2), 203–236.

Friedman, Milton (1970). The social responsibility of business is to increase its profit. *The New York Times Magazine*, 13 September. Reprint in T. Donaldson and P.H. Werhane (Eds.), *Ethical issues in business: A philosophical approach* (pp. 217–223). Englewood Cliffs, NJ: Prentice Hall.

Getz, Kathleen A. (1997). Research in corporate political action: Integration and assessment. *Business & Society*, 36(1), 32–72.

Gond, Jean-Pascal, Kang, Nahee & Moon, Jeremy (2011). The government of self-regulation: On the comparative dynamics of corporate social responsibility. *Economy & Society*, 40(4), 640–671.

Hillman, Amy J. & Hitt, Michael A. (1999). Corporate political strategy formulation: A model of approach, participation, and strategy decisions. *Academy of Management Review*, 24(4), 825–842.

Hillman, Amy J., Keim, Gerald D. & Schuler, Douglas (2004). Corporate political activity: A review and research agenda. *Journal of Management*, 30(6), 837–857.

Janney, Jay J., Dess, Greg & Forlani, Victor (2009). Glass houses? Market reactions to firms joining the UN Global Compact. *Journal of Business Ethics*, 90, 407–423.

Kaplan, Andreas (2014). European management and European business schools: Insights from the history of business schools. *European Management Journal*, 32(4), 529–534.

Kaul, Inge & Mendoza, Ronald U. (2003). Advancing the concept of public goods. In I. Kaul, P. Conceicao, K. Le Goulven & R. U. Mendoza (Eds.), *Providing global public goods: Managing globalization* (pp. 78–111). New York and Oxford: Oxford University Press.

Keohane, Robert O. & Nye, Joseph S. (2000). Introduction. In J. S. Nye & J. D. Donahue (Eds.), *Governance in a globalizing world* (pp. 1–44). Washington, DC: Brookings Institution Press.

Kieser, Alfred (2004). The Americanization of academic management education in Germany. *Journal of Management Inquiry*, 13(2), 90–97.

Kim, Jin-Hyuk (2008). Corporate lobbying revisited. *Business and Politics*, 10, 1–23.

Lux, Sean, Crook, T. Russell & Woehr, David J. (2011). Mixing business with politics: A meta-analysis of the antecedents and outcomes of corporate political activity. *Journal of Management*, 37(1), 223–247.

McWilliams, Abigail & Siegel, Donald S. (2001). Corporate social responsibility: A theory of the firm perspective. *Academy of Management Review*, 26, 117–127.

McWilliams, Abigail, Siegel, Donald S. & Wright, Patrick M. (2006). Corporate social responsibility: Strategic implications. *Journal of Management Studies*, 43, 1–18.

Peterson, Kyle & Pfitzer, Marc (2009). Lobbying for good. *Stanford Social Innovation Review*, 7(1), 44–49.

Rasche, Andreas (2009). "A necessary supplement": What the United Nations Global Compact is and is not. *Business & Society*, 48(4), 511–537.

Rasche, Andreas (2012). Global policies and local practice: Loose and tight couplings in multi-stakeholder initiatives. *Business Ethics Quarterly*, 22(4), 679–708.

Rasche, Andreas & Kell, Georg (2010). *The UN Global Compact: Achievements, trends and challenges*. Cambridge and New York: Cambridge University Press.

Rhodes, Rod A. W. (2012). Waves of governance. In D. Levi-Faur (Ed.), *The Oxford handbook of governance* (pp. 33–48). Oxford and New York: Oxford University Press.

Scherer, Andreas G., Baumann-Pauly, Dorothée & Schneider, Anslem (2013). Democratizing corporate governance: Compensating for the democratic deficit of corporate political activity and corporate citizenship. *Business & Society*, 52(3), 473–514.

Scherer, Andreas G. & Palazzo, Guido (2007). Toward a political conception of corporate responsibility: Business and society seen from a Habermasian perspective. *Academy of Management Review*, 32(4), 1096–1120.

Scherer, Andreas G. & Palazzo, Guido (2008). Globalization and corporate social responsibility. In A. Crane, A. McWilliams, D. Matten, J. Moon & D. S. Siegel (Eds.), *The Oxford handbook of corporate social responsibility* (pp. 413–431). Oxford: Oxford University Press.

Scherer, Andreas G. & Palazzo, Guido (2011). The new political role of business in a globalized world: A review of a new perspective on CSR and its implications for the firm, governance, and democracy. *Journal of Management Studies*, 48(4), 899–931.

Scherer, Andreas G., Rasche, Andreas, Palazzo, Guido & Spicer, André (2016). Managing for political corporate social responsibility: New challenges and directions for PCSR 2.0. *Journal of Management Studies*, 53(3), 273–298.

Schuler, Douglas, Rasche, Andreas, Etzion, Dror & Newton, Lisa (2017). Corporate sustainability management and environmental ethics. *Business Ethics Quarterly*, 27(2), 213–237.

Schuler, Douglas & Rehbein, Kathleen (1997). The filtering role of the firm in corporate political involvement. *Business & Society*, 36, 116–139.

Shaffer, Brian (1995). Firm-level responses to government regulation: Theoretical and research approaches. *Journal of Management*, 21(3), 495–514.

Valente, Mike & Crane, Andrew (2010). Public responsibility and private enterprise in developing countries. *California Management Review*, 52(3), 52–78.

Waddock, Sandra (2008). Corporate responsibility/corporate citizenship: The development of a construct. In A. G. Scherer & G. Palazzo (Eds.), *Handbook of research on global corporate citizenship* (pp. 50–73). Cheltenham, UK: Edward Elgar.

Wagner, Caroline S. & Leydesdorff, Loet (2005). Network structure, self-organization, and the growth of international collaboration in science. *Research Policy*, 34(10), 1608–1618.

Weiss, Thomas G. & Thakur, Ramesh (2010). *Global governance and the UN: An unfinished journey*. Bloomington and Indianapolis: Indiana University Press.

Whelan, Glen (2012). The political perspective of corporate social responsibility: A critical research agenda. *Business Ethics Quarterly*, 22(4), 709–737.

Yoffie, David B. (1987). Corporate strategies for political action: A rational model. In A. A. Marcus, A. M. Kaufman & D. R. Beam (Eds.), *Business strategy and public policy* (pp. 43–60). New York: Quorum.

11 Professions and Organizations

A European Perspective

Mike Saks and David M. Brock

Introduction

The contemporary research area of professions and organizations can be considered as a branch both of the sociology of professions (Saks, 2016) and of the organizational theory that studies the managerial aspects of professional work (Brock, Leblebici, & Muzio, 2014). In the literature these two aspects have all too rarely been brought together, but this chapter attempts to do so in a blended manner in overviewing key aspects of professions working in organizations. It focuses particularly on the European context from which some of the most exciting work is now emerging. We outline the growth of the European contribution in these two traditions from what were originally heavily North American roots. The chapter then goes on to discuss the notion of professions and their organizational setting and how they may most helpfully be analyzed, building on these traditions. Finally, the chapter considers European research published in English-speaking sources on specific professions in their organizational context—illustrating this in more depth through a case study of work on the health professions, before drawing to a conclusion.

From the standpoint of sociological theories of professions, the field of professions and organizations was heavily based on work from the United States, with a range of contributors spanning from Talcott Parsons at Harvard University to Eliot Freidson at New York University. This work was paralleled by an increasing range of literature on professions and their organizational context from Britain, the early span of which was overviewed by Millerson (1964). This initial research was taken forward in new directions in Britain by such contributors as Terry Johnson at the University of Leicester and Michael Burrage at the London School of Economics. At this stage, there was little work on professions and organization in the sociological tradition emerging from continental Europe, but this was to expand greatly, especially around the start of the twenty-first century. At this time, as Adams (2015) points out, there was a burgeoning amount of published research on this subject in journals, books and book chapters—with a particular Western European and Canadian interest in state–profession relations and professional regulation. As Adams has also helpfully shown in her review of the sociological literature, the focus in the United States has shifted to a large degree from regulatory issues to the organizational challenges faced by professional groups—no doubt because of the increasingly strong corporatist environment that has prevailed there.

In the case of the parallel strand of more managerially oriented organizational theory, the literature has centered on an interest in such areas as professional service firms, public sector professional service organizations and multinational and transnational private corporations, together with the organizational implications for the expert knowledge workers that we term professionals. Here the field also has strong North American origins, with most of the early concepts, theories and empirical findings published by scholars based in Canada and the United States. For example, here important advances developed around writers like Richard Scott at Stanford University, Henry Mintzberg at McGill University and Royston Greenwood and Bob Hinings at Alberta University. The initial dominance of the field by North America is indicated in the seminal review chapter by Powell, Brock and Hinings (1999), where scarcely a reference is cited from European-based scholars. However, fast-forwarding to the more recent overview of this area by Empson, Muzio, Broschak and Hinings (2015), about one-third of the references are by scholars currently based in Europe—even though much of the foundational material harks back to North American work from the latter half of the twentieth century.

Further evidence of this more recent trend in both the sociological and organizational literature towards a more Euro-centered focus on professions and organization is that some two-thirds of the 20 competitively peer-reviewed articles published by the new *Journal of Professions and Organization* in 2014 and 2015 have first authors based in Europe. And while these trends may or may not be significant, it is claimed in this chapter that the contribution of European scholars to the field of professional organization is not only substantial, but also distinctive (Chia, 2014). Here Adams (2015) has indicated that the European concentration on regulation and policy represents the most marked difference from the United States literature on professions and organization—although Canadian scholars, as well as those in Australia, have also prioritized this area. However, in all these countries there are many overlapping fields of study of professions—ranging from considerations of gender and ethnicity to discussions on organizational autonomy and interprofessional working. Nonetheless, there seems to be somewhat less commonality with Eastern European societies like Russia where the study of professions is only slowly establishing itself following their disestablishment after the Bolshevik Revolution and their current gradual, and by no means inevitable, re-emergence under President Putin (Saks, 2015b).

Theories of Professions and Organizations

But what exactly is a profession in this regard? Classically there have been great disputes over this term, with the early Anglo-American sociological literature based on defining such groups in terms of such unique characteristics as expertise and altruism that differentiated them from other occupations and enabled them to play a positive role in the wider society (see, for example, Greenwood, 1957; Goode, 1960). This interpretation, however, was seriously questioned following the more skeptical, countercultural years of the mid-1960s/1970s because of, amongst other things, the lack of agreement on the key aspects of professions; unthinkingly taking professional ideologies on trust; and failing to understand professions in the context of a conflictual social structure based on social class divisions—where professions themselves typically follow their own self-interests in increasing their income, status and power (Saks, 2012). As a result of such critiques of the more sugar-coated taxonomic interpretations of professions and the vulnerability of a number of the theoretical alternatives to these to the charge of being too abstract and self-fulfilling, the neo-Weberian approach to professions has emerged as the mainstream theoretical orthodoxy in analyzing professional groups in organizational and other contexts.

The neo-Weberian perspective on professions is based on the concept of exclusionary social closure drawn from the work of the late nineteenth/early twentieth century social theorist Max Weber. Professions in this respect are seen as being primarily centered on the establishment of state underwritten occupational monopolies in the market in neo-liberal economies, linked to the realization of professional projects based on favourable socio-political conditions and astute occupational strategies. In this process, professions are held to be able to regulate market conditions in their own favour by restricting opportunities to a limited group of eligibles—characteristically leading to an increase in their income, status and power (Parkin, 1979). This is well illustrated by the cases of medicine and law in Britain and the United States, which are seen as key exemplars of occupational groups that have won monopolies in the market supported by the state (Berlant, 1975; Burrage, 2006). Although they vary in form from *de facto* to *de jure* monopolies and were established through the federal government and state-by-state licensure respectively, they share core similarities. They can also be seen as at the head of a hierarchy of professions in terms of power and dominance in the market, not just within national boundaries but also across international jurisdictions—including in Britain in relation to the European Union, with its mutual recognition of qualifications (Olgiati, 2003).

This theoretical perspective on profession has many advantages when considering professionals in organizational structures in the Anglo-American context—not least being the definitional clarification it provides, based on the legally circumscribed boundaries of professions. However, neo-Weberian analyses of profession have themselves at times come under attack for being applied with insufficient empirical rigour; being overly critical of professional groups; and failing to place professions and professionalization in the context of the wider occupational division of labour (Saks, 2010). Nonetheless, these criticisms do not so much relate to a design fault, as the occasionally inappropriate operationalization of the neo-Weberian perspective.

More pertinent here is the claim by Sciulli (2005) that, whilst the concept of exclusionary social closure may fit Britain and the United States, it has little wider relevance in Europe. It is of course true that this neo-Weberian model of professions has not historically been as prevalent in continental Europe (Collins, 1990), in part because professionals are often embedded in government bureaucracies (Evetts, 2000). However, there is a continuum of arrangements, and many European societies have forms of exclusionary closure in relation to at least some occupational groups—including in countries such as Germany (see, for instance, Kuhlmann & Saks, 2008; Rogowski, 1995). Together with a more holistic theoretical approach recognizing the importance of understanding failed and ongoing as well as successful attempts at professionalization, this brings any European analysis clearly within a neo-Weberian purview.

Nonetheless, as Adams (2015) observes, one of the most frequent current themes of the international sociological literature on professions relates to challenges facing professions. In Europe, this reflects changes in the socio-political environment in which professions work, with the stronger emergence of neo-liberalism—variously linked to the rise of the New Public Management, entrepreneurialism, marketization and integrated work organizations (Svensson & Evetts, 2010). These trends have led to discussions about deprofessionalization and the declining autonomy of professions—especially in the context of the United States, where there have been the most powerful trends towards corporatization (Saks, 2015b). Such developments have also been theorized through the employment by Evetts (2013) of the concept of organizational professionalism, as opposed to occupational professionalism based on the concept of social closure. This notion is intended to reflect the growing bureaucratization, centralization and rationalization of the work environments of professions—centered more on the Weberian notion of legal–rational authority. However, the importance of such societal changes should not be overstated in Europe, as research suggests that their impact on professional independence has frequently been effectively buffered by factors like professional values, interests and strategy (see for example, Faulconbridge & Muzio, 2008; Jonnergård & Erlingsdo'ttir, 2012).

It is not surprising, though, that a particularly significant and distinctive European literature on hybridization has developed—whereby the classic tensions identified by American contributors like Freidson (2001) between professions and their employing organizations are seen as being more or less successfully managed by the intermediary professionals concerned (Noordegraaf, 2015). Here, as Waring (2014) notes, the growth of professional–managerial hybrids and the blurring of boundaries between professions and organizations can be viewed as creating collective professional interests in more bureaucratic and marketized work places. This sense of professional capture neatly leads on to the neo-institutionalist approach which complements neo-Weberianism and has proved increasingly popular in examining the relationship between professions and their growing large-scale public and commercial organizational locations in Europe and beyond (Adams, 2015). In this respect, the essence of neo-institutional theories of professions, which emerged more from a managerial business school environment, is that professions are one institution amongst others struggling for survival in an ecological domain (Suddaby & Muzio, 2015)—even if, as has been seen, they have often managed well enough in preserving their own group interests in income, status and power.

Interestingly, the perspective of the neo-institutionalists also has earlier links to taxonomy insofar as some of its proponents have sought to delineate the core characteristics of professional service firms operating in areas such as accountancy and law in terms of features like knowledge intensity or low capital requirements (von Nordenflycht, 2010). However, just as with taxonomic approaches to professional groups themselves, there has been disagreement about the central features of a professional service firm (Brock, 2006). There has also been a great emphasis in the current European literature on analyzing these bodies from a neo-Weberian perspective—in terms of their elite position in the wider socio-political order (Reed, 2012). In this analysis, Seabrooke (2014) has spotlighted that there are often transnational, as well as national, dimensions from a linked ecologies perspective. In drawing on the pivotal work in the United States of Abbott (2005), there are potential theoretical pitfalls in examining the interplay between professions, professional service firms, multinational corporations and the state from an ecological perspective. However, these may be to a large degree bypassed if it is recognized that the term 'ecology' is simply a metaphor and not a literal Darwinian template for understanding interactions on the wider political stage (Perreault, Bridge, & McCarthy, 2015).

The Study of Specific Professions and Their Organizational Contexts

So what conclusions have studies drawing on the neo-Weberian approach and neo-institutionalism reached about the professions and organization field in Europe? This chapter selectively illustrates some of the research projects within these perspectives with reference to specific professions in European settings. In terms of the nature of the professional groups considered, though, it should be noted that while in global terms the variety of professions has increased substantially—not least as a result of technological change and de-regulation (Powell et al., 1999)—the range actually studied by researchers does not seem to have kept pace. Many European studies, for instance, have been on medicine and the health professions—which will be considered as a case study in the next section. There has also been a strong parallel focus on mainstream areas like accountancy and law, which have increasingly become the terrain of the professional service firm. Muzio, Brock and Suddaby (2013) describe how this restrictive tendency persists in research into professional organizations in general—despite the fact that, as

Malhotra and Morris (2009) and von Nordenflycht (2010) observe, there is growing heterogeneity among professional services in terms of the nature of knowledge used, jurisdictional control and the nature of client relations. As they point out, moreover, these issues affect such aspects of organizational structure as internal processes, range of specialization, geographic spread of offices, fee structure and the degree of centralization. Yet researchers generally have been reluctant to explore fields of research beyond high-profile traditional professions.

However, a wider variety of professions and professionalizing groups are now beginning to be studied by European research programmes. An important relatively early contribution came from Alvesson (1995), whose work on a Swedish information technology consulting firm highlighted the distinctive flat structure and informal culture in this area. Insight from another Scandinavian researcher into different kinds of engineering firm was provided by Løwendahl (2005), who outlined their customized services, expert employees and strong sense of professional ethics. Such studies have provided the basis for an impressive further body of research into engineering firms, many with Norwegian bases in the offshore oil and gas and shipping industries, as exemplified by Breunig, Kvålshaugen and Hydle (2014) and Kvålshaugen, Hydle and Brehmer (2015). Although not all aspects of engineering itself are marked by exclusionary social closure in a European context (Evetts, 1998), this work underlines the developing breadth of the analysis of professions in organizations in Europe. Unlike in the United States, where the widening range of professional groups was acknowledged and identified at an early stage (Bell, 1976; Freidson, 1986), but not pervasively researched, less mainstream professional groups are now starting to be examined in some detail from a neo-Weberian viewpoint in the European literature on professions and organizations.

In this vein, research into human resource management in professional service firms has distinct European roots and has thrived in Britain and elsewhere. Swart and Kinnie (2003), for instance, examined the ways in which the policies and processes of human resources can contribute to the sharing of knowledge of vital importance to the organization, while Swart, Kinnie, Rossenberg and Yalabik (2014) have analyzed the impact of employee commitment on knowledge sharing in a professional service firm. The contribution by Dutch researchers Doorewaard and Meihuizen (2000), moreover, succeeded in relating vibrant debates about the resourcing of the firm to the professional service context. In so doing, they picked up on the strategic types of Løwendahl (2005), which link control of the resource base by the organization, team or individual with a strategic focus on client relations, problem solving or adaptations to produce nine strategic modes. They then simplified these into two generic strategic orientations for professional service firms—namely, an expertise and efficiency orientation—and showed how certain human resources practices support these strategies. Carvalho and Cabral-Cardoso (2008) from Portugal meanwhile outlined the way human resources were able to achieve both functional and numerical flexibility in a combined and interdependent manner in management consulting firms. The study by Stringfellow and Thompson (2014) of the dynamics of status among Scottish accountants reveals how volatile the core sociological construct of status can be in these contexts.

This human resources professional theme in fact joins up with the neo-Weberian study of a number of other professions in European organizational settings, as well as the wider international context. This is highlighted by Swart and Kinnie (2010), who studied the relationship between human resources and the development of knowledge assets and organizational learning in 16 professional service firms in the Anglo-American context, including law firms, management consultancies, software houses and advertising agencies. Studies of such areas have frequently been linked to the neo-institutionalist approach, as exemplified by research by Adamson, Manson and Zakaria (2015) on the new professional group of executive remuneration consultants in the United Kingdom. This work helpfully enhanced academic understanding of their professionalizing project by placing it within a macro institutional framework. Reciprocally, from a neo-institutionalist perspective, Danish research by Harrington (2015) has considered the position of wealth management professionals across Europe and elsewhere. Following interviews, she has demonstrated how local practices and ideas could develop into transnational institutions—thereby reasserting the theoretical importance of interactions between professionals, their clients, peers and organizational contexts on the specific field of international finance. This underlines the ongoing power of even newly evolving professions on a global stage.

In enhancing our understanding of more established professions in a wider organizational and changing socio-political context, debates over empowerment and disempowerment in a neo-Weberian framework have again been central in the contemporary European literature, whether for lawyers in Britain in the face of increased marketization (Sommerlad, Young, Vaughan, & Harris, 2015) or university lecturers in Finland in response to declining state support (Aarrevaara, 2015). Hybridization has also emerged as a major neo-Weberian theme—not least in relation to longer-standing professions such as accountancy, which is crucially involved in making both visible and calculable the hybrids with which it deals, as well as hybridizing itself through dealings with a range of disciplines inside and outside organizational frameworks (Miller, Kurunmaki, & O'Leary, 2008). Aspects of the regulated domain of accountancy—such as actuaries (Collins, Dewing, & Russell, 2009)—have also been studied in this process. In this respect, Bévort and Suddaby (2016) have examined how accountants interpret competing logics of professionalism as they move from practice into managerial roles and as their organizations shift from professional partnerships to more corporate organizational structures. In analyzing the way in which individual professionals make sense of their new roles and integrate the competing demands of professional and managerial logics, they argue that they construct their own identity scripts based less on inter-subjective interactions than individual cognition and interpretive subjectivity.

This clearly poses some challenges to the professional solidarity that has for long been identified by neo-Weberians as so significant in gaining and maintaining exclusionary social closure (see, for instance, Johnson, 1972). To be sure, such independence from wider organizational constraint has not been possible for some occupational groups in a European context—not least in Soviet Russia where professional groups were for long seen as class enemies in the socialist state (Moskovskaya et al., 2013). From a historical viewpoint, though, Macdonald (1995) has indicated how important solidarity was for architects in winning exclusionary closure in parts of Western Europe, coupled with outlining acceptable political objectives for professionalization for state officials. As the European literature has also emphasized, so has been the European Union professional education policy itself in sustaining architecture as an established profession in the market in an age of supranational regulation (Le Bianic & Svensson, 2008). Crucially too, contemporary studies of professions in Europe have normally placed a heavy emphasis on the study of minority groups in considering professions in their organizational context. This is exemplified by the study by Bolton and Muzio (2008) of professional projects in law, teaching and management in Britain, where growing opportunities for women were offset by continuing evidence of gendered exclusion, segmentation and stratification.

Case Study: The Health Professions

This leads on, finally, to the consideration of the distinctive features of the neo-Weberian and neo-institutionalist European literature on the health professions as a relatively cohesive case study. The main reason for choosing this case is that—as in North America—the medical profession is one of the most widely referenced areas of published work on the professions in Europe. Usually it is discussed in the context of the health professions, the literature for which is also sampled here to give an overview of some of the key issues in this particular field. The reason for the revered position of medicine in published work is that it is seen as a leading profession both in Europe and more globally (Collyer, 2012). This is also reflected in its parallel dominance within the health field, where Turner (1995) has classically categorized allied health professions like nursing as subordinated professions and groups such as dentists and physiotherapists as limited professionals operating in legally defined territories related to parts of the body or therapeutic method, with complementary and alternative medicine practitioners as excluded practitioners. Although there has arguably been some fudging of the boundaries since his categorization was written, it neatly sets out the position of medicine not only as a 'top dog' profession, but as being at the apex of the health professional pecking order.

In this regard, there has been much work focused in Europe on the development of the medical profession from a neo-Weberian perspective from the early contribution of Parry and Parry (1976) through to more recent work by Saks (2015b) that includes coverage of Britain and Russia based on its interplay with the state and the market. This research has been geographically extended by Allsop and Jones (2008) and Burau and Vrangbæk (2008), who chart international variations in medical governance, placing the legal regulation of the profession in a wider organizational context in societies ranging from France and the Netherlands to Denmark, Germany, Italy and Norway. This has been paralleled by general work on the regulatory development of other health professional groups in Europe (Johnson, Larkin, & Saks, 1995; Allsop & Saks, 2002; Carvalho & Santiago, 2015), along with particular studies of such professions—as illustrated in Britain by nurses and midwives (Borsay & Hunter, 2012) and complementary and alternative medical practitioners, some of whom have now gained exclusionary closure through a process of professionalization (Saks, 2015a). One of the key themes in this and other literature, as for professions more generally, has been the broader impact of the New Public Management to which the analysis now turns.

The New Public Management, introduced in neo-liberal societies to enhance the efficiency of public services (Dent, Chandler, & Barry, 2004), has posed a particular and increasing challenge to the wide range of health professions, which are mainly based in the public sector in Europe (Burau, Blank, & Pavolini, 2015). This has again led European writers to introduce the theme of hybridization—not least in the context of the medical profession which has fought hard to retain its power and privileges in the face of increasing managerial controls and the regulatory desires of the state (Saks, 2014). These interactions do not, of course, necessarily lead to complementarity and the ready formation of hybrids because contradictions may emerge (Fischer & Ferlie, 2013), but they do underline the dilemmas of hybridization for doctors (Spyridonidis, Hendy, & Barlow, 2015). In this sense, as Kurunmaki (2004) highlighted in her study of medical expertise in Finland, the knowledge of professions may itself be hybridized. She argued that this occurred with the willing adoption of management accounting techniques by medical practitioners in the wake of the New Public Management reforms, in a manner that was resisted in the United Kingdom.

Professional resistance to managerial agendas in organizational settings has also been reported in relation to other health professions by Carvalho (2014) as regards nursing in public hospitals in Portugal. Here it was found that nurses developed hybrid professionalism by incorporating and reshaping conventional professional norms and values and the dominant discourses of the organizations in which they were employed. This research is supported by a Dutch study of neighbourhood nurses by Postma, Oldenhof and Putters (2015), who argued that these professionals increasingly engaged in organizational issues and absorbed them into their activities through articulation work in order to simultaneously provide and organize care through the integration of public services. Such studies, however, have not lessened long-standing claims from some quarters that medicine and other health professions are being deprofessionalized (Elston, 1991). However, in Britain at least the state shelter of the National Health Service seems to have served to protect the medical profession in a manner that has not occurred in the face of greater corporatization in the United States (Saks, 2015b). In fact, the profession may have become more restratified than deprofessionalized from a neo-Weberian perspective following the rise in standing of general practitioners relative to hospital consultants, with the growing emphasis on primary care (Calnan & Gabe, 2009)—despite shifts towards more state-inspired external professional regulation to increase public protection (Chamberlain, 2012).

This brings into focus the neo-institutional approach, by emphasizing the complexity in which organizations are located in contemporary European neo-liberal societies. In their Swedish study of the micro management of a national report on quality in healthcare, Blomgren and Waks (2015) observed four conflicting institutional logics. These were a democratic logic, a managerial logic, a market logic and a professional logic. This underlines the institutional complexity with which hybrid professionals in organizations have to contend in the health field in order to define problems and to provide solutions aligning with multiple prevailing logics. This complexity is amplified further by the work of Seabrooke and Tsingou (2015), who applied a linked ecologies approach to the way in which professional teams of medical experts, demographers and economists forged issue distinctions in Europe and beyond in relation to low fertility. Such professional transnational interactions are reminiscent of the extensive neo-Weberian research that has also taken place on factors that inhibit and promote interprofessional and inter-organizational collaboration between health and social care professionals for the benefit of the user in more localized European contexts (see, for instance, Pollard, Thomas, & Miers, 2009). Moreover, as with fertility issues, Witz (1992) and Kuhlmann and Annandale (2012) demonstrate that gender has been a crucial vector of interest in studying both single and inter-professional developments in organizations involved in European healthcare.

Conclusion

This chapter has overviewed an extensive literature both from European contributors and on a number of key interlinked aspects of professions and organizations in a European context. In so doing, it has distinctively drawn on both neo-Weberian and neo-institutionalist theories—thereby covering a range of blended work, from the sociology of professions to the more managerialist organizations perspective. These theories have been illustrated with reference to the escalating amount of European research undertaken on professional groups based in the private enterprise and public sectors. European researchers have also contributed a refreshing focus on newly developing professions while deepening insights into the more established professions—centrally including those in healthcare. Two enduring thoughts emerge. The first is that this field encompasses a number of complex intersecting levels, but with rich reward for those committed to enhancing academic knowledge in this area and applying research to real managerial situations in Europe. The second is that the reader cannot fail to be struck by the dynamic nature of the domain of professions and organizations in an ever-changing world, with the fast-moving European context increasingly at its epicenter. In this light, we trust that the ever-growing literature base and route map of the terrain to which attention has been drawn in this jointly crafted chapter will prove useful to readers of this edited collection on *Management Research: European Perspectives*.

References

Aarrevaara, Timo (2015). The Finnish academic profession in health-related sciences and social services. In T. Carvalho & R. Santiago (Eds.), *Professionalism, managerialism and reform in higher education and the health services* (pp. 30–63). Basingstoke: Palgrave Macmillan.

Abbott, Andrew (2005). Linked ecologies: States and universities as environments for professions. *Sociological Theory*, 23(3), 245–274.

Adams, Tracey (2015). Sociology of professions: International divergencies and research directions. *Work, Employment and Society*, 29(1), 154–165.

Adamson, Maria, Manson, Stuart & Zakaria, Idlan (2015). Executive remuneration consultancy in the UK: Exploring a professional project through the lens of institutional work. *Journal of Professions and Organization*, 2(1), 19–37.

Allsop, Judith & Jones, Kathryn (2008). Protecting patients: International trends in medical governance. In E. Kuhlmann & M. Saks (Eds.), *Rethinking professional governance: International directions in healthcare* (pp. 15–28). Bristol: Policy Press.

Allsop, Judith & Saks, Mike (Eds.) (2002). *Regulating the health professions*. London: Sage.

Alvesson, Mats (1995). *Management of knowledge intensive companies*. Berlin: de Gruyter.

Bell, Daniel (1976). *The coming of post-industrial society*. New York: Basic Books.

Berlant, Jeffrey L. (1975). *Profession and monopoly: A study of medicine in the United States and Great Britain*. Berkeley: University of California Press.

Bévort, Frans & Suddaby, Roy (2016). Scripting professional identities: How individuals make sense of contradictory logics. *Journal of Professions and Organization*, 3(1), 17–38. http://jpo.oxfordjournals.org/content/3/1/17.

Blomgren, Maria & Waks, Caroline (2015). Coping with contradictions: Hybrid professionals managing institutional complexity. *Journal of Professions and Organization*, 2(1), 78–102.

Bolton, Sharon & Muzio, Daniel (2008). The paradoxical processes of feminization in the professions: The case of established, aspiring and semi-professions. *Work, Employment and Society*, 22(2), 281–299.

Borsay, Anne & Hunter, Billi (Eds.) (2012). *Nursing and midwifery in Britain since 1700*. Basingstoke: Macmillan.

Breunig, Karl J., Kvålshaugen, Ragnhild & Hydle, Katia Maria (2014). Knowing your boundaries: Integration opportunities in international professional service firms. *Journal of World Business*, 49, 502–511.

Brock, David M. (2006). The changing professional organization: A review of competing archetypes. *International Journal of Management*, 8(3), 157–174.

Brock, David M., Leblebici, Hüsayin & Muzio, Daniel (2014). Understanding professionals and their workplaces: The mission of the journal of professions and organization. *Journal of Professions and Organization*, 1(1), 1–15.

Burau, Viola, Blank, Robert H. & Pavolini, Emmanuele (2015). Typologies of healthcare systems and policies. In E. Kuhlmann, R. H. Blank, I. L. Bourgeault & C. Wendt (Eds.), *The Palgrave international handbook of healthcare policy and governance* (pp. 101–115). Basingstoke: Palgrave Macmillan.

Burau, Viola & Vrangbæk, Karsten (2008). Global markets and national pathways of medical re-regulation. In E. Kuhlmann & M. Saks (Eds.), *Rethinking professional governance: International directions in healthcare* (pp. 29–44). Bristol: Policy Press.

Burrage, Michael (2006). *Revolution and the making of the contemporary legal profession: England, France and the United States*. New York: Oxford University Press.

Calnan, Michael & Gabe, Jonathan (2009). The restratification of primary care in England? A sociological analysis. In J. Gabe & M. Calnan (Eds.), *The new sociology of the health service* (pp. 56–78). Abingdon: Routledge.

Carvalho, Teresa (2014). Changing connections between professionalism and managerialism: A case study of nursing in Portugal. *Journal of Professions and Organization*, 1(2), 176–190.

Carvalho, Teresa & Cabral-Cardoso, Carlos (2008). Flexibility through HRM in management consulting firms. *Personnel Review*, 37(3), 332–349.

Carvalho, Teresa & Santiago, Rui (Eds.) (2015). *Professionalism, managerialism and reform in higher education and the health services*. Basingstoke: Palgrave Macmillan.

Chamberlain, John Martyn (2012). *The sociology of medical regulation*. London: Springer.

Chia, Robert (2014). Reflections on the distinctiveness of European management scholarship. *European Management Journal*, 32(5), 683–688.

Collins, David, Dewing, Ian & Russell, Peter (2009). The actuary as a fallen hero: On the reform of a profession. *Work, Employment and Society*, 23(2), 249–266.

Collins, Randall (1990). Market closure and the conflict theory of the professions. In M. Burrage & R. Torstendahl (Eds.), *Professions in theory and history: Rethinking the study of the professions* (pp. 24–43). London: Sage.

Collyer, Fran (2012). *Mapping the sociology of health and medicine: America, Britain and Australia compared*. Basingstoke: Palgrave Macmillan.

Dent, Mike, Chandler, John & Barry, Jim (Eds.) (2004). *Questioning the new public management*. Aldershot: Ashgate.

Doorewaard, Hans & Meihuizen, Hanne E. (2000). Strategic performance options in professional service organisations. *Human Resource Management Journal*, 10(2), 39–57.

Elston, Mary Ann (1991). The politics of professional power: Medicine in a changing health service. In J. Gabe, M. Calnan & M. Bury (Eds.), *The sociology of the health service* (pp. 58–88). London: Routledge.

Empson, Laura, Muzio, Daniel, Broschak, Joseph & Hinings, Bob (2015). Researching professional service firms: An introduction and overview. In L. Empson, D.

Muzio, J. Broschak & R. C. Hinings (Eds.), *The Oxford handbook of professional service firms* (pp. 1–22). Oxford: Oxford University Press.

Evetts, Julia (1998). Professional identity, diversity and segmentation: The case of engineering. In V. Olgiati, L. Orzack & M. Saks (Eds.), *Professions, identity and order in comparative perspective* (pp. 57–70). Onati: Onati International Institute for the Sociology of Law.

Evetts, Julia (2000). Professions in European and UK markets: The European professional federation. *International Journal of Sociology and Social Policy*, 18, 395–415.

Evetts, Julia (2013). Professionalism: Value and ideology. *Current Sociology*, 61(5/6), 778–796.

Faulconbridge, James & Muzio, Daniel (2008). Organizational professionalism in globalizing law firms. *Work, Employment and Society*, 22(1), 7–25.

Fischer, Michael Daniel & Ferlie, Ewan (2013). Resisting hybridization between modes of clinical risk management: Contradiction, contest, and the production of intractable conflict. *Accounting, Organization and Society*, 38(1), 30–49.

Freidson, Eliot (1986). *Professional powers: A study of the institutionalization of formal knowledge*. Chicago, IL: University of Chicago Press.

Freidson, Eliot (2001). *Professionalism: The third logic*. Cambridge: Polity Press.

Goode, William J. (1960). Encroachment, charlatanism and the emerging profession: Psychology, sociology and medicine. *American Sociological Review*, 25, 902–914.

Greenwood, Ernest (1957). The attributes of a profession. *Social Work*, 2(3), 45–55.

Harrington, Brooke (2015). Going global: Professionals and the micro-foundations of institutional change. *Journal of Professions and Organization*, 2(2), 103–121.

Johnson, Terence (1972). *Professions and power*. London: Macmillan.

Johnson, Terry, Larkin, Gerry & Saks, Mike (Eds.) (1995). *Health professions and the state in Europe*. London: Routledge.

Jonnergård, Karin & Erlingsdo'ttir, Gudbjörg (2012). Variations in professions: Adoption of quality reforms: The cases of doctors and auditors in Sweden. *Current Sociology*, 60(5), 672–689.

Kuhlmann, Ellen & Annandale, Ellen (2012). Bringing gender to the heart of health policy, practice and research. In E. Kuhlmann & E. Annandale (Eds.), *The Palgrave handbook of gender and healthcare* (2nd ed., pp. 1–18). Basingstoke: Palgrave Macmillan.

Kuhlmann, Ellen & Saks, Mike (Eds.) (2008). *Rethinking professional governance: International directions in healthcare*. Bristol: Policy Press.

Kurunmaki, Lisa (2004). A hybrid profession: The acquisition of management accounting knowledge by medical professionals. *Accounting, Organizations and Society*, 29, 327–347.

Kvålshaugen, Ragnhild, Hydle, Katja M. & Brehmer, Per-Olof (2015). Innovative capabilities in international professional service firms: Enabling trade-offs between past, present, and future service provision. *Journal of Professions and Organization*, 2(2), 148–167.

Le Bianic, Thomas & Svensson, Lennart G. (2008). European regulation of professional education: A study of documents focusing on architects and psychologists in the EU. *European Societies*, 10(4), 567–595.

Løwendahl, Bente R. (2005). *Strategic management of professional service firms* (3rd ed.). Copenhagen: Copenhagen Business School Press.

Macdonald, Keith (1995). *The sociology of the professions*. London: Sage.

Malhotra, Namrata & Morris, Tim (2009). Heterogeneity in professional service firms. *Journal of Management Studies*, 46(6), 895–922.

Miller, Peter, Kurunmaki, Lisa & O'Leary, Ted (2008). Accounting, hybrids and the management of risk. *Accounting, Organizations and Society*, 33(7–8), 942–967.

Millerson, Geoffrey (1964). *The qualifying associations*. London: Routledge & Kegan Paul.

Moskovskaya, Alexandra, Oberemko, Oleg, Silaeva, Victoria, Popova, Irina, Nazarova, Inna, Peshkova, Olga, & Chernysheva, Marina. (2013). *Development of professional associations in Russia: Research into institutional framework, self-regulation activity, and barriers to professionalization*. Working Paper BRP 26/SOC/2013. Moscow: Higher School of Economics.

Muzio, Daniel, Brock, David & Suddaby, Roy (2013). Professions and institutional change: Towards an institutionalist sociology of the professions. *Journal of Management Studies*, 50(5), 699–721.

Noordegraaf, Mirko (2015). Hybrid professionalism and beyond: (New) forms of public professionalism in changing organizational and societal contexts. *Journal of Professions and Organization*, 2(2), 187–206.

Olgiati, Vittorio (2003). Geo-political constructionism: The challenge of Europe to the comparative sociology of the professions. In L. Svensson & J. Evetts (Eds.), *Conceptual and comparative studies of Continental and Anglo-American professions* (pp. 55–77). Göteborg: Göteborg University.

Parkin, Frank (1979). *Marxism and class theory: A bourgeois critique*. London: Tavistock.

Parry, Noel & Parry, José (1976). *The rise of the medical profession*. London: Croom Helm.

Perreault, Tom, Bridge, Gavin & McCarthy, James (Eds.) (2015). *The Routledge handbook of political ecology*. Abingdon: Routledge.

Pollard, Katherine, Thomas, Judith & Miers, Margaret (2009). *Understanding interprofessional working in health and social care: Theory and practice*. Basingstoke: Palgrave Macmillan.

Postma, Jeroen, Oldenhof, Lieke & Putters, Kim (2015). Organized professionalism in health-care: Articulation work by neighbourhood nurses. *Journal of Professions and Organization*, 2(1), 61–77.

Powell, Michael J., Brock, David M. & Hinings, C. Robert (1999). The changing professional organization. In D. M. Brock, M. J. Powell & C. R. Hinings (Eds.), *Restructuring the professional organization: Accounting, health care and law* (pp. 1–19). London: Routledge.

Reed, Michael I. (2012). Masters of the Universe: Power and elites in organization studies. *Organization Studies*, 33(2), 203–221.

Rogowski, Ralf (1995). German corporate lawyers: Social closure in autopoietic perspective. In Y. Dezalay & D. Sugarman (Eds.), *Professional competition and professional power: Lawyers, accountants and the social construction of markets* (pp. 114–135). London: Routledge.

Saks, Mike (2010). Analyzing the professions: The case for a neo-Weberian approach. *Comparative Sociology*, 9(6), 887–915.

Saks, Mike (2012). Defining a profession: The role of knowledge and expertise. *Professions and Professionalism*, 2, 1–10.

Saks, Mike (2014). The regulation of the English health professions: Zoos, circuses or safari parks? *Journal of Professions and Organization*, 1(1), 84–98.

Saks, Mike (2015a). Power and professionalisation in CAM: A sociological approach. In N. K. Gale & J. V. McHale (Eds.), *Routledge handbook of complementary and alternative medicine: Perspectives from social science and law* (pp. 30–40). Abingdon: Routledge.

Saks, Mike (2015b). *The professions, state and the market: Medicine in Britain, the United States and Russia*. Abingdon: Routledge.

Saks, Mike (2016). A review of theories of professions, organizations and society: The case for neo-Weberianism, neo-institutionalism and eclecticism. *Journal of Professions and Organization*, 3(2), 170–187. http://jpo.oxfordjournals.org/content/3/2/170.

Sciulli, David (2005). Continental sociology of professions today: Conceptual contributions. *Current Sociology*, 53(6), 915–942.

Seabrooke, Leonard (2014). Epistemic arbitrage: Transnational professional knowledge in action. *Journal of Professions and Organization*, 1(1), 49–64.

Seabrooke, Leonard & Tsingou, Eleni (2015). Professional emergence on transnational issues: Linked ecologies on demographic change. *Journal of Professions and Organization*, 2(1), 1–18.

Sommerlad, Hilary, Young, Richard, Vaughan, Steven & Harris-Short, Sonia (Eds.) (2015). *The futures of legal education and the legal profession*. Oxford: Hart.

Spyridonidis, Dimitrios, Hendy, Jane & Barlow, James (2015). Understanding hybrid roles: The role of identity processes amongst physicians. *Public Administration*, 93, 395–411.

Stringfellow, Lindsay & Thompson, Alex (2014). Crab antics? Contesting and perpetuating status hierarchies in professional service firms. *Journal of Professions and Organization*, 1(2), 118–136.

Suddaby, Roy & Muzio, Daniel (2015). Theoretical perspectives of the professions. In L. Empson, D. Muzio, J. Broschak & B. Hinings (Eds.), *The Oxford handbook of professional service firms* (pp. 25–47). Oxford: Oxford University Press.

Svensson, Lennart & Evetts, Julia (2010). Introduction. In L. Svensson & J. Evetts (Eds.), *Sociology of professions: Continental and Anglo-Saxon traditions* (pp. 9–30). Göteborg: Daidalos.

Swart, Juani & Kinnie, Nicholas (2003). Sharing knowledge in knowledge-intensive firms. *Human Resource Management Journal*, 13(2), 60–75.

Swart, Juani & Kinnie, Nicholas (2010). Organisational learning, knowledge assets and HR practices in professional service firms. *Human Resource Management Journal*, 20(1), 64–79.

Swart, Juani, Kinnie, Nicholas, van Rossenberg, Yvonne & Yalabik, Zeynep Y. (2014). Why should I share my knowledge? A multiple foci of commitment perspective. *Human Resource Management Journal*, 24(3), 269–289.

Turner, Bryan S. (1995). *Medical power and social knowledge* (2nd ed.). London: Sage.

von Nordenflycht, Andrew (2010). What is a professional service firm? Toward a theory and taxonomy of knowledge-intensive firms. *Academy of Management Review*, 35(1), 155–174.

Waring, Justin (2014). Restratification, hybridity and professional elites: Questions of power, identity and relational contingency at the points of professional–organisational intersection. *Sociology Compass*, 8, 688–704.

Witz, Anne (1992). *Professions and patriarchy*. London: Routledge.

12 European Qualitative Research

A Celebration of Diversity and a Cautionary Tale

Catherine Cassell

Introduction

The contribution of qualitative research methods to our understanding of organization and management is now accepted (Buchanan & Bryman, 2007), and lately a number of authors have reflected upon the progress that qualitative management research has made into the mainstream (e.g. Bluhm, Harman, Lee, & Mitchell, 2011; Symon, Cassell, & Johnson, 2016). What is meant by qualitative research is a somewhat 'contested terrain' (Johnson, Buehring, Symon, & Cassell, 2007, p. 37); indeed as Locke (2003, p. 19) highlights, the domain of qualitative research is plural if not potentially confusing to the newcomer. An all-encompassing definition is provided by Alvesson and Deetz (2000, p. 1), who suggest: "Qualitative research has become associated with many different theoretical perspectives, but it is typically oriented to the inductive study of socially constructed reality, focusing on meanings, ideas and practices, taking the native's point of view seriously".

It is important to recognize that whereas there are many commonalities in quantitative methods, there is considerable variety in qualitative management research. Notably the use of qualitative research in North America, Europe and the rest of the world has developed at different rates and been informed by different traditions (Lee & Humphrey, 2006). For example, Üsdiken (2014) notes that there is less qualitative research published in US journals than their European alternatives. Bengtsson, Elg and Lind (1997) suggest that the transatlantic gap is also about methodological approaches in that European research is more frequently idiographic and processual, whereas in contrast US research is dominated by nomothetic approaches, with their emphasis upon quantitative analysis across large samples to test hypotheses. Other chapters in this collection explore these differences in more detail (e.g. see Chia, this volume).

There are also different traditions of qualitative management research within Europe itself—for example, Knoblauch et al. (2005, p. 2), when discussing the variety of qualitative research in Europe, highlight how scientific enterprises such as qualitative research are imprinted by cultures—and not only by 'epistemic cultures', but also by their surrounding institutions, traditions and political as well as economic contexts. They suggest that in the European context this has become particularly visible in countries which have passed through a communist era, such as Poland and Slovenia, where the impact of the specific national traditions of thinking on qualitative methods can be seen.

In this chapter I aim to do two things. The first is to highlight the diversity in European qualitative management research as a way of celebrating its ongoing development within Europe. In recognizing the strengths that emerge from this diversity in epistemological traditions and methods, the second aim is to draw attention to the concerns increasingly expressed by qualitative researchers about growing pressures of standardization (Mingers & Willmott, 2013; Symon et al., 2016). I conclude by arguing that qualitative researchers should take every opportunity to encourage methodological diversity whilst resisting attempts at homogenizing the experience and reporting of qualitative management research.

The Diversity of European Qualitative Management Research

Whereas there is considerable consistency in the philosophical roots that underpin quantitative approaches, qualitative methods are informed by a wide range of different epistemological and ontological traditions (Duberley, Johnson, & Cassell, 2012). European thinkers have been central to the development of these paradigms—for example, the role of European critical theorists, including Marx, Gramsci, Bordieu and Habermas, in underpinning the development of traditions (Hassard & Rowlinson, 2011) which still dominate the field of critical management studies. Whole movements in qualitative research such as postmodernism and post-structuralism have been underpinned by the work of European philosophers such as Foucault, Derrida and Lacan. This diversity in epistemological traditions originating in Europe perhaps partially accounts for the friendliness of European journals to such diverse approaches compared with their US counterparts (Bluhm et al., 2011). The European openness to qualitative research also extends to the publication of a variety of different methods (Bluhm et al., 2011). Such openness reflects the diversity of traditions (as treated in the next section of this volume).

There is also considerable diversity in developments in qualitative research in different parts of Europe. To take some examples, Angermüller (2006) suggests that in France, although qualitative approaches are used, there is little preference for the term 'qualitative' because it implies that a certain kind of methodology is being privileged over another. This is different from Germany, where there has long been a clear split between what are seen as hard and soft sciences, with a resulting impact on the development of qualitative research (Angermüller, 2006). A somewhat different scenario has occurred in Ukraine, where Baranchenko and Yukhanaev (2013) highlight a number of problems with publishing qualitative research, including unfamiliarity with methods; lack of understanding about different philosophies; and history and traditions which focus upon numbers and formulae. The authors suggest that one of the underlying problems with the use of qualitative research is that structural changes in the Ukrainian system of higher education have meant that pressure is put on academics to publish in only approved national journals and to go through a rigorous approval procedure with the Ministry of Education. This is similar to the pressures that emerge from journal quality rankings that have been noted elsewhere in Europe (Mingers & Willmott, 2013). As they highlight:

> Given the tradition of positivism and quantitative research methodology together with unwillingness to acknowledge other methodological approaches in the field of business and management research, young academics are faced with an unsurmountable difficulty with using alternative philosophical paradigms and research designs.
>
> (Baranchenko & Yukhanaev, 2013, p. 27)

This is a somewhat different situation than the Italian experience, for example, where qualitative research has had a long tradition (Bruni & Gobo, 2005).

There has also been an emphasis on different types of methods in different European contexts. For example, in the UK classic organizational ethnographies were produced during the 1960s and 1970s (e.g. Benyon, 1973; Lupton, 1963), whereas in Italy ethnography has had an enduringly long tradition (Bruni & Gobo, 2005). Angermüller (2006) highlights how the French have particularly made a major contribution to the development of post-structuralism and discourse analysis through the work of writers like Foucault and Lacan. This diversity is important because as Buchanan and Bryman (2007) highlight, the more recent methodological innovation within the field of management and organizational research more generally has been located around qualitative and interpretive methods. There are a variety that could be mentioned here, but particularly pertinent examples are more recent applications of story and narrative analysis to organizational research (e.g. Beech, 2008; Gabriel & Griffiths, 2004; Ylijoki, 2005; Humphreys & Brown, 2002); developments in discourse and rhetorical analysis (e.g. Symon, 2008; Jørgensen, Jordan, & Mitterhofer, 2012; Shepherd & Challenger, 2013) and the use of visual methods in organizational research (e.g. Davison, McLean, & Warren, 2012).

Hence the European tradition of qualitative research can be characterized as being informed by a range of different philosophical underpinnings, a variety of methods, a history of methodological innovation and different sets of epistemic and methodological traditions across the continent. Why is this diversity important? My argument is that methodological pluralism offers a wider range of opportunities for investigating different types of research questions, hence presenting more opportunities for insights into different managerial phenomena. Therefore, any methodological restrictions would only serve to limit our potential for understanding the complexities of management more generally.

A Cautionary Tale of Standardization

Having highlighted the rich diversity of qualitative European research, at this point I wish to highlight a source of concern for qualitative management researchers that relates to a variety of increasing pressures for the standardization of qualitative research. There is evidence of a move in this direction. For example, in seeking to address the difficulties in publishing qualitative research that have been identified by some qualitative management researchers, a number of editors of esteemed journals have produced guidelines regarding what makes a quality piece of qualitative research. These guidelines usually start from what are perceived as common problems in the submissions of qualitative researchers. For example, Gephart (2004) identifies these as papers being ‘one-off’ rather than embedded in ongoing research programmes; lack of adequate literature reviews; failure to state explicit goals or research questions; lack of conceptual definition; under-specification of methodology; and failing to re-visit research questions or goals in the Discussion and Conclusions sections. Similarly Pratt (2009, p. 857) identifies some “dangerous paths” to follow that will “limit an author’s ability to publish her or his qualitative research”. He provides a series of alternative paths to compensate for the lack of a “boilerplate” or a “standardised language” for writing up qualitative research. Although these recommendations are there to help qualitative writers, one could argue that such guidelines lead to the production of formulaic pieces of research which can have negative consequences given the diversity of methodological approaches highlighted earlier, a point recognized within the most recent of these editorials from the *Academy of Management Journal* (AMJ) (see Bansal and Corley, 2011).

Furthermore, potential pressures for standardization are apparent in the recommendations for progress that emerge from those such as Bluhm et al. (2011). Within that paper the progress that qualitative management research has made during the last 10 years is equated with citation counts. Given that papers in the American Academy journals are more highly cited than others and that these papers are judged to have a greater methodological transparency than their European counterparts, the authors conclude that

> [g]iven the progress that can be made in qualitative management research through higher standards of transparency of methods and analysis, we recommend that European journals follow the lead of US journals in the adoption of higher standards of methodological description of qualitative research.
>
> (Bluhm et al., 2011, p. 1884)

They conclude, somewhat controversially, that the impact of qualitative management research will be improved by the enhanced standardization of best practices, as seen in US journals. Such prescriptive types of editorials and articles are critiqued extensively by Symon et al. (2016), who argue that they serve to produce "(inappropriate) homogeneous evaluation criteria" with the consequence of "marginalising alternative perspectives and disciplining individual qualitative researchers into particular normative practices" (Symon et al., 2016, p. 1).

There is a significant tension here that is difficult to resolve. On the one hand editors are seeking to enhance the publication opportunities for qualitative researchers through providing sets of guidelines, whereas on the other there are qualitative researchers seeking to use diverse and innovative methods who are keen to shy away from any potential attempts at methodological standardization. The contextual background here is also complicated in that in many of the different journal-ranking lists that impact upon where authors choose to publish, those journals ranked the highest are North American ones such as the US Academy journals. Indeed Cornellissen, Gajewska-de Mattos, Piekari and Welch (2012, p. 210) in their review of matched pairs of qualitative articles published in UK and US journals suggest that authors in seeking to publish in North American journals engage in a balancing act "seeking to gain legitimacy through a particular way of writing up their qualitative data while at the same time trying to stay true to their own philosophical approach and the original integrity of their research project". This has also contributed to the aforementioned North American/European divide in qualitative management research.

The dominance of non-qualitative approaches within North American journals leads to particular problems for European-based qualitative researchers. The pressure to publish in US-based journals is one that many business school academics internationally face, and the performative nature of management and organizational research (Bell, 2011) places particular institutional pressures on qualitative researchers that have been considered elsewhere (Symon, Buehring, Johnson, & Cassell, 2008; Willmott, 2011; Mingers & Willmott, 2013). It would seem then that a potential threat to the diversity of qualitative management research is the establishment of a particular form of a 'gold standard' of qualitative research equated to that published in US journals. However, as Bluhm et al. (2011) do highlight, there is a need for US journals to be more open to a more diverse range of qualitative approaches.

A further concern is the increasing popularity within management research of evidence-based management (e.g. Rousseau, 2006). Qualitative and critical management researchers have highlighted that this can potentially be seen as a threat to methodological pluralism in that what constitutes evidence is a hotly contested topic (Learmonth, 2011). Furthermore, the key methodology used in evidence-based inquiry—the systematic review—tends to select and define as 'good' evidence research based upon traditional positivist informed methodologies such as randomized control trials (Cassell, 2011). This critical view is not shared, however, amongst all qualitative researchers; indeed, as Alasuutari (2010) points out, other qualitative researchers have responded to this debate by trying to develop criteria to support qualitative evidence—for example, in qualitative health research (Dixon-Woods et al., 2006). It seems that what is important here is seeking alternative definitions of evidence that are informed by qualitative research. As Pascale (2016, p. 222) suggests:

> Qualitative scholarship in the 21st century needs a concept of evidence that will enable us to account for the systematic construction of both presence and absence in physical, textual and historical spaces. We need a concept of evidence that will enable us to examine contexts as flows of information, relationships, people, ideas and resources.

Hence we need a definition of evidence that is appropriate for qualitative research.

In summary, the key issue here is to ensure that any disciplinary trends do not have an impact upon the acceptance of methodological diversity. Examples range from standardizing the content of doctoral programmes to concerns about the governance processes surrounding ethical research (e.g. Bell, 2011; Cassell & Symon, 2012).

Conclusions

I have drawn attention here to the rich diversity of European qualitative management research and to potential concerns regarding increasing standardization in the domain. I have argued that methodological diversity and pluralism is something to be cherished, offering a variety of insights into a range of different research questions. In concluding, the onus is not just upon qualitative researchers to resist attempts to homogenize qualitative management research and encourage the use of qualitative methods, but also upon epistemological gatekeepers (Symon & Cassell, 1999) such as editors and reviewers to facilitate methodological pluralism. In line with the diversity and plurality celebrated in this collection, we need an international methodological landscape that reflects and celebrates the diverse traditions that comprise qualitative management research.

References

Alasuutari, Pertti (2010). The rise and relevance of qualitative research. *International Journal of Social Research Methodology*, 13(2), 139–155.

Alvesson, Mats & Deetz, Stanley (2000). *Doing critical management research*. London: Sage.

Angermüller, Johannes (2006). "Qualitative" methods of social research in France: Reconstructing the actor, deconstructing the subject. Art. 19. *Forum: Qualitative*

Social Research, 6(3). Accessed 11 May 2016: www.qualitative-research.net/fqs-texte/3-05/05-3-34-e.htm.

Bansal, Pratima & Corley, Kevin (2011). The coming of age of qualitative research: Embracing the diversity of qualitative methods. *Academy of Management Journal*, 54(2), 233–237.

Baranchenko, Yevhen & Yukhanaev, Andrey (2013). Barriers to using qualitative methods in business and management research in the Ukraine. In Proceedings of the 12th European Conference on Research Methodology for Business and Management Studies, University of Minho, Guimaraes, Portugal, 4–5 July 2013.

Beech, Nic (2008). On the nature of dialogic identity work. *Organization*, 15, 51–74.

Bell, Emma (2011). Managerialism and management research: Would Melville Dalton get a job today? In C. M. Cassell & B. Lee (Eds.), *Challenges and controversies in management research* (pp. 122–137). London: Routledge.

Bengtsson, Lars, Elg, Ulf & Lind, Jan-Inge (1997). Bridging the transatlantic publishing gap: How North American reviewers evaluate European idiographic research. *Scandinavian Journal of Management*, 13(4), 473–492.

Benyon, Huw (1973). *Working for Ford*. Harmondsworth: Penguin.

Bluhm, Dustin J., Harman, Wendy, Lee, Thomas W. & Mitchell, Terrence R. (2011). Qualitative research in management: A decade of progress. *Journal of Management Studies*, 48, 1866–1891.

Bruni, Attila & Gobo, Giampietro (2005). Qualitative research in Italy. Art. 41. *Forum: Qualitative Social Research*, 6(3). Accessed 11 May 2016: www.qualitative-research.net/fqs-texte/3-05/05-3-34-e.htm.

Buchanan, David A. & Bryman, Alan (2007). Contextualising methods choice in organizational research. *Organizational Research Methods*, 10, 483–501.

Cassell, Catherine M. (2011). Evidence-based I-O psychology: What do we lose on the way? *Industrial and Organizational Psychology: Perspectives on Science and Practice*, 4(1), 23–26.

Cassell, Catherine M. & Symon, Gillian (2012). The context of qualitative organizational research. In G. Symon & C. M. Cassell (Eds.), *Qualitative organizational research: Core methods and current challenges* (pp. 1–11). London: Sage.

Cornellissen, Joep, Gajewska-de Mattos, Hanna, Piekari, Rebecca & Welch, Catherine (2012). Writing up as a legitimacy-seeking process. In G. Symon & C. M. Cassell (Eds.), *Qualitative organizational research: Core methods and key challenges* (pp. 185–203). London: Sage.

Davison, Jane, McLean, Christine & Warren, Samantha (2012). Exploring the visual in organizations and management. *Qualitative Research in Organizations and Management: An International Journal*, 7(1), 5–15.

Dixon-Woods, Mary, Bonas, Sheila, Booth, Andrew, Jones, David R., Miller, Tina, Sutton, Alex J., Shaw, Rachel L., Smith, Jonathan A. & Young, Bridget (2006). How can systematic reviews incorporate qualitative research? A critical perspective. *Qualitative Research*, 6(1), 27–44.

Duberley, Joanne, Johnson, Phil & Cassell, Catherine C. (2012). Philosophies underpinning qualitative research. In G. Symon & C. M. Cassell (Eds.), *Qualitative organizational research: Core methods and key challenges* (pp. 15–34). London: Sage.

Gabriel, Yiannis & Griffiths, Dorothy S. (2004). Storytelling in organizational research. In C. M. Cassell & G. Symon (Eds.), *Qualitative methods in organizational research* (pp. 114–126). London: Sage.

Gephart, Robert P. (2004). Qualitative research and the Academy of management journal. *Academy of Management Journal*, 47(4), 454–462.

Hassard, John & Rowlinson, Michael (2011). The potential of radical Research: Marxism, labour process theory and critical management studies. In C. M. Cassell & B. Lee (Eds.), *Challenges and controversies in management research* (pp. 225–242). London: Routledge.

Humphreys, Michael & Brown, Andrew D. (2002). Narratives of organizational identity and identification: A case study of hegemony and resistance. *Organization Studies*, 23(3), 421–447.

Johnson, Phil, Buehring, Anna, Symon, Gillian & Cassell, Catherine M. (2007). Defining qualitative management research. *Qualitative Research in Organizations and Management: An International Journal*, 3(1), 23–43.

Jørgensen, Lene, Jordan, Sylvia & Mitterhofer, Hermann (2012). Sensemaking and discourse analyses in inter-organizational research: A review and suggested advances. *Scandinavian Journal of Management*, 28, 107–120.

Knoblauch, Hubert, Flick, Uwe & Maeder, Christoph (2005). Qualitative research in Europe: The variety of social research. Art 34. *Forum: Qualitative Social Research*, 6(3). Accessed 11 May 2016: www.qualitative-research.net/fqs-texte/3-05/05-3-34-e.htm.

Learmonth, Mark (2011). The relationship between evidence and theory in management research. In C. M. Cassell & B. Lee (Eds.), *Challenges and controversies in management research* (pp. 212–224). London: Routledge.

Lee, Bill & Humphrey, Christophe (2006). More than a numbers game: Qualitative research in accounting. *Management Decision*, 44(2), 180–197.

Locke, Karen (2003). *Grounded theory in management research*. Thousand Oaks, CA: Sage.

Lupton, Thomas (1963). *On the shop floor: Two studies of workshop organization and output*. Oxford: Pergamon Press.

Mingers, John & Willmott, Hugh (2013). Taylorizing business school research: On the "one best way" performative effects of journal ranking lists. *Human Relations*, 66, 1051–1073.

Pascale, Celine-Marie (2016). Discourses of the North Atlantic: Epistemology and hegemony. *Qualitative Inquiry*, 22(4), 219–227.

Pratt, Michael G. (2009). From the editors: For the lack of a boilerplate: Tips on writing up (and reviewing) qualitative research. *Academy of Management Journal*, 52(5), 856–862.

Rousseau, Denise M. (2006). Is there such a thing as evidence-based management? *Academy of Management Review*, 31(2), 256–269.

Shepherd, Craig & Challenger, Rose (2013). Revisiting paradigm(s) in management research: A rhetorical analysis of the paradigm wars. *International Journal of Management Reviews*, 15(2), 225–244.

Symon, Gillian (2008). Developing the political perspective on technological change through rhetorical analysis. *Management Communication Quarterly*, 22(1), 74–98.

Symon, Gillian, Buehring, Anna, Johnson, Phil & Cassell, Catherine M. (2008). Positioning qualitative research in the academic labour process. *Organization Studies*, 29(10), 1315–1336.

Symon, Gillian & Cassell, Catherine M. (1999). Barriers to innovation in research practice. In M. Pina e Cunha & C. A. Marques (Eds.), *Readings in organization Science: Organizational change in a changing context* (pp. 387–398). Lisbon: ISPA.

Symon, Gillian, Cassell, Catherine M. & Johnson, Phil (2016). Evaluative practices in qualitative management research: A critical review. *International Journal of Management Reviews*, Version of Record online, doi:10.1111/ijmr.12120.

Üsdiken, Behlül (2014). Centres and peripheries: Research styles and publication patterns in "top" U.S. journals and their European alternatives, 1960–2010. *Journal of Management Studies*, 51, 764–789.

Willmott, Hugh (2011). Journal list fetishism and the perversion of scholarship: Reactivity and the ABS list. *Organization*, 18(4), 429–442.

Ylijoki, Oili-Helena (2005). Academic nostalgia: A narrative approach to academic work. *Human Relations*, 58(5), 555–576.

13 European Management and European Business Schools

Insights from the History of Business Schools

Andreas Kaplan

Nowhere do cultures differ so much as inside Europe.

(Fons Trompenaars, 1993)

Does European Management Exist?

With globalization entering business education, one might think that all business schools are alike. Many would even argue that business schools are primarily a US phenomenon, exported to the rest of the world. But is this indeed the case? Or do European business schools differ, in fact, from their counterparts in the US? This raises a more general question: Is there even such a thing as "European management"? And if so, what unique knowledge should European business schools impart to future European managers? This article is an attempt to answer these questions (cf. Kaplan, 2014, 2015, 2018).

Europe is made up of approximately 50 countries, in which more than 60 different languages are spoken. While the rise of the European Union has led to European integration in the economic, legal and political spheres, cultural homogenization is not one of the EU's aims. Despite a trend towards globalization, Europe fosters the idea of diversity of cultures and languages; for example, the EU Commission enacts a multilingualism policy encouraging language acquisition, promoting a multilingual economy and giving all EU citizens access to information in their own languages.

The European emphasis on multiculturalism has informed its approach to higher business education—which, some might be surprised to discover, was not imported from the US but rather originated in nineteenth-century France. As will be elaborated in what follows, Europe's multicultural approach, together with other qualities, has historically distinguished European business schools from their predominant US counterparts. Although these differences have blurred in recent years, owing to post–World War II Americanization and a general globalization of management education, Europe's business schools have recently begun to emancipate themselves from American influence.

In the following sections, this article will look at the historical evolution of business schools, in which management education is incorporated and institutionalized, in an attempt to identify the common threads linking European business schools and to pinpoint the distinctions between these schools and comparable institutions in the US. On the basis of this examination, a definition of European management will be derived. Finally, this paper will discuss which knowledge and skills European business schools should impart to their students in order to form successful European managers within a globalized world.

History of Business Schools

The history of business schools in Europe can be broadly divided into two periods: The first, spanning the years 1819–1944, is referred to as the Founding Period. In this period, two types of schools were established: the "Southern" model, led by France and Belgium, and the "Northern" model, led by Germany. The second period, the Assimilation Period, started after World War II and continues to this day. The year 1945 marks the beginning of an Americanization of European business schools, and the year 1997 reflects the beginning of Europe's (re)emancipation. Clearly, the latter processes were influenced by the general phenomenon of globalization as well as by the emergence of new approaches to the study of management (e.g. the increasing emphasis on scientific research).

Founding Period of Business Schools: 1819–1944

The Southern (French/Belgian) Model

In 1819, trader Vital Roux and economist Jean-Baptiste Say co-founded the world's first business school: École Supérieure de Commerce de Paris (ESCP) Europe, whose first campus was established in Paris (Blanchard, 2009). The first curriculum was based on a combined theoretical and practical approach to business education, including pedagogical simulation games. Influenced by Vital Roux's insistence that a business school should be international in scope, ESCP Europe adopted a global perspective; about one-third of its students were from outside France, with 10 different languages being taught soon after the school's opening (Renouard, 1999). The school's approach to management was social and demand-oriented, owing to the influence of Jean-Baptiste Say, who was a neo-classical economist (Forget, 1999).

ESCP Europe was initially privately financed by a group of businessmen, until it was acquired by the Paris Chamber of Commerce in 1869. In fact, the Chamber of Commerce had refused a request to fund the school at its inception, rejecting any type of institutionalization of theoretical business education (Lemercier, 2003). Thus, French business schools evolved outside the public university system, with the chambers of commerce playing a predominant role in French management education (Blanchard, 2009).

A second pioneering institution was the Belgium Higher Institute of Commerce in Antwerp, founded in 1852. The program offered there was similar in content to ESCP Europe's interdisciplinary curriculum, including such courses as geography, history and foreign languages (Grunzweig, 1977; Renouard, 1999). However, in contrast to the privately financed ESCP Europe, the Antwerp Institute was state funded and university-like in nature.

Several schools based on the French/Belgian model were subsequently established in Europe's Mediterranean area, most notably in Italy. The curriculum of the first Italian school, the Ca' Foscari, established in Venice in 1868, was highly similar to that of ESCP Europe, with foreign languages being an important part (Kipping, Üsdiken, & Puig, 2004). While most Italian schools were state funded and of a university nature, and as such imitated the Belgian model (Longobardi, 1927), a notable exception was the privately financed Bocconi school, founded in 1902. Italian business schools, initially independent, became increasingly academicized and by the mid-1930s were integrated into the university system (Fauri, 1998).

The Northern (German) Model

The first German schools—founded several decades after the first business school in France—also served as role models for European business schools, particularly for schools in Northern European countries. The first German business school, Handelshochschule Leipzig, was founded in 1898, upon an initiative of the Leipzig Chamber of Commerce. The school, which was created outside the public university system, adopted a curriculum integrating theoretical and practical components as well as foreign language instruction. Additional areas of study, interdisciplinary in nature, included economics, law, geography, commodities, science and technology, commercial technique and humanities (Meyer, 1998). German business schools had to overcome opponents who were convinced that management could only be learned in practice, a problem that the founders of theoretical business education in France had also encountered (Kieser, 2004).

Whereas French business schools resisted an overly theoretical approach to business education, Germany moved rapidly towards academicization of the field, moving away from professionalization and interdisciplinarity. This led to the emergence of a completely new academic field, the so-called Betriebswirtschaftslehre (science of business administration). Humboldt's tradition of education through science, deeply rooted in Germany, rejected the distinction between educational and scientific activities, on the basis of the premise that only through scientific research can students acquire deep and specialized knowledge of a discipline.

Prominent academic and economist Eugen Schmalenbach, active during the early 1900s, insisted that a school's objective is to maximize common welfare rather than to increase individual profit. In making this claim, Schmalenbach encouraged the recognition of management as an academic discipline, an idea that public universities had previously rejected (Kieser, 2004). By the mid-1910s, most German business schools had been integrated into public universities and adopted a highly academic approach to teaching management; the initial, more practically oriented approach was abandoned (Üsdiken, 2004).

Other countries, particularly Scandinavian countries, adopted the German business school model. The first to do so was Sweden, whose Handelshögskolan i Stockholm, founded in 1909, was financed by the business community as an independent private institution (Engwall, 2004).

US Business Schools

The first business school in the US, the Wharton School of Finance and Commerce, was founded in 1881 by industrialist Joseph Wharton through a $100,000 donation. Influenced by Taylorism and inspired by the work of Adam Smith, the school's guiding principle was the improvement of economic efficiency, especially through labor productivity (Wren & Van Fleet, 1983). The Harvard Business School was established more than 25 years later, in 1908, and pioneered both the case-study approach and the MBA degree. Quite early on, in 1916, a group of prominent US business schools initiated the establishment of the AACSB (Association to Advance Collegiate Schools of Business), an accreditation institution that enabled US business schools to be standardized.

Whereas business schools in Europe were internationally oriented from the beginning, US business schools did not actively encourage a global perspective. For example, foreign languages were absent from Wharton's first curricula, and Joseph Wharton's stated objective was "to create a liberally educated class of leaders for American society" (Sass, 1982, p. 20).

Like their European counterparts, US business schools were not well received by the academic community, but for slightly different reasons. European schools, initially founded outside the established universities, were doubted in their capacity to teach business, a practical discipline, through a theoretical approach. US business schools, which were collegiate in nature, were accused of lowering the universities' academic standards and were criticized by professors of established university disciplines (Engwall & Zamagni, 1998). This critique led to the rapid establishment of a discipline, a process that was in line with Wharton's original objective: transforming the study of business from a trade into a rigorous profession. The school's first curricula were less interdisciplinary in nature than their European counterparts', comprising several business and finance courses. The influence of Frederick Taylor (1911), advocate for the development of a true science of management "resting upon clearly defined laws, rules, and principles, as a foundation" (p. 7), was clearly present.

Assimilation Period of Business Schools: 1945–Present Day

Americanization

After World War II, with Europe's economy in ruins, the US approach to training managers began to be perceived as a "weapon of social change" (Leavitt, 1957, p. 155). Several programs, such as the Ford Foundation, promoted US-style management across Western Europe (McGlade, 1998). France and Germany, role models during the Founding Period, were somewhat resistant to Americanization, whereas in other countries, such as Great Britain and Spain, the Americanization process took root more deeply (Engwall & Zamagni, 1998).

Although resistant to Americanization, French schools adopted parts of the US model by introducing permanent faculty who had been trained primarily in the US. The Institut Européen d'Administration des Affaires (INSEAD), founded in 1958 as a private institution and financed partly by the Ford Foundation, offered the first MBA degree in Europe. Germany's rapid post-war economic recovery, the Wirtschaftswunder ("economic miracle"), was attributed mainly to American management techniques (Kieser, 2004). However, the deep integration of German management education into universities prevented the rise of the more practically oriented US business school model (Locke, 1989). Only recently has the German model begun to return to its roots, adopting a more practical approach to management education. This approach is reflected in the establishment of such schools as the Wissenschaftliche Hochschule für Unternehmensführung (WHU), founded in 1984, as well as the reopened Handelshochschule Leipzig, both at the initiative of local chambers of commerce.

Motivated by the Frank report arguing that the UK needs US-type business schools (Williams, 2010), most universities in the UK began to offer MBAs and to apply the case-study approach. The London Business School was established in 1964 through Ford Foundation grants, and the Association of MBAs (AMBA) was created in 1967 to promote the MBA degree in the UK. Spain was also heavily influenced by the Americanization process and established US-style business schools. The first was the Escuela de Organización Industrial (EOI), founded in 1955, followed by the Escola Superior d'Administració i Direcció d'Empreses (ESADE) and the Instituto de Estudios Superiores de la Empresa (IESE), both established in 1958. IESE was even described by the Ford Foundation as Barcelona's Harvard (Mosson, 1965).

European (Re)Emancipation

In 1997 the EQUIS (European Quality Improvement System) accreditation system was founded, marking a turning point in the European business school landscape and the beginning of Europe's (re)emancipation from the domination of US-style business schools.

There are several important differences between EQUIS and the previously established US accreditation system AACSB; these differences reflect clear distinctions between European and US business school models. For example, EQUIS has strict requirements on internationalization, whereas AACSB only evaluates this area if it is part of the school's own mission. While EQUIS analyzes a school's general strategy and how it differentiates itself from other schools, AACSB looks more at curriculum design. The two accreditation systems also reflect differences in the structures of stand-alone European and collegiate-in-nature US institutions for management education, such that EQUIS only accredits business schools, whereas AACSB can accredit any management or accounting program in a university (e.g. a management program in a school of engineering) and grants university-wide accreditation.

Before the establishment of EQUIS, the UK Association of MBAs created the AMBA label in an attempt to curb the MBA "invasion" of the UK landscape. The situation had gotten out of hand; an article in *Management Today*, for example, discussed the overabundance of MBAs in the UK, stating that the "MBA glamour [of the '80s had] quickly faded in the harsh climate of the '90s" (Oliver, 1993, p. 26). Like EQUIS for Europe in general, AMBA tried to emancipate itself from US domination. This may explain why AMBA accreditation and, correspondingly, triple-crown accreditation (AACSB, AMBA, EQUIS) are pursued primarily by European institutions, whereas only one US school is AMBA accredited, and none has triple-crown accreditation.

The homogenization of European business schools has been fostered not only by the rise of European accreditation institutions but also by the EU. Specifically, in 1999 EU members initiated the Bologna process, through which European countries agreed to ensure comparability in the standards and quality of higher education and to facilitate mobility of students within Europe. This initiative transformed the European higher education landscape in general and that of business schools in particular.

Worldwide Trends in Business Education

In addition to the Americanization trend observed in the mid-twentieth century, followed by the emancipation of European schools, it is important to note two global trends promoting the standardization of business schools worldwide.

The first trend is the emergence of research-based business schools (e.g., Ghosal, 2005). This trend was triggered by a US Ford Foundation survey (Gordon & Howell, 1959) that pointed out the lack of research-based business education. Extensive financial resources have been invested towards reforming US business schools and promoting the 'scientization' of management education. This trend has taken root on a global scale, yet the US continues to dominate scientific management research. This development corresponds to the emergence of journals such as *Management Science*, whose first issues clearly reflect the objective of creating a science of business administration that adheres to the natural sciences model. In fact, some US business schools have shown a preference for hiring narrowly trained specialists able to publish in so-called A-journals (Bennis & O'Toole, 2005), a trend adopted by many business schools worldwide.

A second trend leading to more standardization worldwide is the heightened significance of international rankings for business schools (in addition to the aforementioned accreditations) as an effective magnet for recruiting students. Schools aiming to achieve a high ranking must comply with the various ranking criteria and therefore evolve in a specific, uniform direction. For business schools in Europe, the most important ranking is that of the British Financial Times (FT); this ranking was responsible for the creation of an entire organizational field of management schools (Wedlin, 2007). The FT first introduced an MBA ranking in 1999, and in 2005 it incorporated a ranking for the more traditionally European Master's Degree in Management. Business schools all over the world, including in China and India, have recently begun to apply for this ranking (as well as to pursue triple-crown accreditation), suggesting that the globalization of business schools is no longer unidirectional from the US to the rest of the world but has also started to be influenced by the European landscape.

European Management and European Business Schools

This section develops a definition of European management. Briefly, it suggests that European management entails cross-cultural, societal management based on an interdisciplinary approach. This definition is based on the values fostered by European business schools starting from their initiation: As discussed above, these schools were international in scope, created to deliver value for society at large; they were interdisciplinary in nature and practically oriented. After identifying the characteristics of European management, the question of how a European business school might prepare future managers to succeed in the unique European context will be addressed.

European Management and Its Defining Characteristics

Cross-Cultural Management

The cross-cultural management approach aims to understand how culture affects management practice, to identify means of increasing global management effectiveness and to identify cross-cultural similarities and differences in management practices (e.g. Calori & Dufour, 1995). As discussed above, the first business schools in Europe were more cross-cultural in their approach than their US counterparts; this difference can still be observed, for example, when comparing EQUIS, which emphasizes a school's international strategy, with AACSB, which does not. Current studies show that the cross-cultural approach is still a crucial component of European management. The European manager must develop strong cultural skills to be able to quickly adapt to different contexts. Calori and de Woot (1994, p. 237), for example, state that the European manager needs "international experience, competence in at least three languages, geographical mobility and global thinking".

The question is whether cross-culturalism is a distinctly European characteristic, that is, whether a European manager has a greater need for cross-cultural skills than do managers in other regions in the world. Trompenaars (1993, p. 8) answers by stating: "Nowhere do cultures differ so much as inside Europe". Indeed, several studies (e.g. Hofstede, 1980) have pointed to clear cultural differences among different European countries, grouping them into clusters with similar management styles. Europe can be described as embracing maximum cultural diversity at minimal geographical distances. As expressed through the EU slogan "United in Diversity", cultural diversity is considered to be a reflection of richness, leading to creativity and innovation. Thus, a key role of European management is to integrate different styles while acknowledging and respecting the differences amongst them.

Societal Management

In line with Takas (1974), societal management can be defined as management that takes into account society's overall welfare in addition to mere profitability considerations. European business schools are not necessarily the only business schools that are societal in their approach; however, it seems that the fundamental principles of European schools have historically been much more society-oriented compared with those of US schools. For example, as discussed above, Schmalenbach viewed societal welfare, rather than individual profit, as the main purpose of business schools (Kieser, 2004), whereas US schools were founded on principles of Taylorism. The US approach was criticized, in fact, by Wallace Donham (1933), dean of the Harvard Business School, whose article "The Failure of Business Leadership and the Responsibility of the Universities" questioned the lack of interest in considering business problems within their broader, societal context.

More recent research indicates that the societal notion of the welfare state continues to be more pronounced in most European states than in the US, although both regions have a common history of humanism (Calori, Steele, & Yoneyama, 1995). Pudelko and Harzing (2007), for example, argue that, compared with US management, European management has a more balanced approach of economic efficiency and social matters. Furthermore, the fact that public administration, whose raison d'être is a society's well-being (Kaplan & Haenlein, 2009), is of higher relevance in Europe than in the US is an indication of Europe's inherently more societal approach to management, as compared with that of the US.

Interdisciplinarity

Interdisciplinarity involves the combination of two or more academic disciplines into one activity. It is about creating something new by crossing boundaries and combining the knowledge encompassed in different domains (Klein, 1990). While studies within a single discipline tend to emphasize scientific rigor, the interdisciplinary approach aims to achieve greater practical relevance by applying a broader view to problems. Correspondingly, in teaching, an emphasis on scientific rigor is often considered to reflect a more theoretical approach, whereas interdisciplinarity reflects a more practically oriented teaching style.

Initially, both European and US management education approaches incorporated interdisciplinarity, since there was "no matter of scientific nature to teach in a commercial school [since] it still had to be created" (Locke, 1989, p. 71). However, as previously indicated, the collegiate structure of US schools rapidly led to the creation of a discipline of management. The fact that German-type business schools, which were quickly integrated into universities, partly overtook their US counterparts in their evolution toward academicization does not cancel out the fact that initially they were more interdisciplinary in nature.

More current studies indicate that European schools continue to be more interdisciplinary than their US counterparts. Calori and de Woot (1994, p. 237), for example, state that the European manager needs "a broad vision with an aptitude for interdisciplinary views and deep social, philosophical and ethical understanding". With respect to the research-based business school, Welter and Lasch (2008) suggest that, compared with US research, European research is more open to qualitative and exploratory approaches and is more contextual in nature.

How Can European Business Schools Train Future European Managers?

Cross-Cultural Management

In order to train a European manager, a business school first needs to develop the student's cultural intelligence. This is defined as an individual's capabilities to function and manage effectively in culturally diverse settings (Earley & Ang, 2003).

One means of enhancing students' cultural intelligence is to provide students with the opportunity to experience different cultural contexts. Several studies (e.g. Earley & Peterson, 2004) have shown that living in foreign countries increases a student's cultural intelligence. An effective duration of a stay in a foreign country should be longer than six months (Ang, Van Dyne, & Tan, 2011; Eisenberg et al., 2013). To provide students with such opportunities, business schools might set up exchange programs, offer double degrees with partner universities or develop cross-border multi-campus concepts. INSEAD, for example, has set up a campus in Singapore, and ESCP Europe has campuses in five European countries.

De Vita and Case (2003), however, argue that the development of a cross-cultural approach takes more than just "infusing" a few international elements into a program's contents. Doh (2010) supports this claim, stating that merely exporting students to foreign countries is not enough. Thus, another potentially effective means of fostering cross-culturalism is to offer specific courses on cross-cultural management. Such training might even serve as a substitute for some actual experiences abroad (Eisenberg et al., 2013).

Finally, Kedia and Harveston (1998) show that students become more culturally intelligent when they are taught by faculty with previous international experience. Cultural diversity within the student body further enhances this effect. This, together with the fact that international ranking systems such as the FT favour international diversity, might explain why business schools foster diversity in the national backgrounds of faculty and students. However, the extent of cultural diversity may have an upper limit; in some UK schools, for example, more than 80 percent of students come from China. This suggests that a highly international student body might not necessarily be culturally diverse.

Societal Management

A European manager's decisions must take into account the well-being of society at large. One means of developing this skill might be to offer classes in business ethics. Notably, the instruction of business ethics as a subject is mainly a US invention; business ethics courses have been offered in Europe only since the early 1980s (van Luijk, 2001). This might seem counterintuitive. Recall, however, that European business schools started out with clear societal objectives, suggesting that ethics should be inherently part of any course, be it accounting, finance or strategy. The fact that ethics were less pronounced in the first US schools might explain the development of designated business ethics courses. It might further explain why EQUIS attributes lower importance to business ethics than AACSB does (Moore, 2004).

Moreover, business ethics courses in the US and Europe do not focus on the same contents. Enderle (1996) claims that European courses discuss ethical choices made within tight constraints, whereas the US approach considers loose constraints. This difference might be a result of the fact that governmental influence is stronger in most European countries than in the US, which leads to tighter European regulation on employment rights, healthcare, etc. Managers in Europe thus need to devote less thought to morals in business; the State does this for them. In contrast, the more flexible US frameworks require firms to come up with their own moral guidelines for doing business.

Thus, instead of focusing on the instruction of business ethics, European schools might offer more value to their students by showing them the influence of the State and public administration on the private sector. As implied above, the prominence of the public sector in Europe as a funding resource for schools might play a role in European business schools' propensity to adopt a societal approach. Thus, several European business schools, such as ESADE, offer a so-called Master of Public Administration (MPA) in addition to an MBA in their portfolios.

Interdisciplinarity

The aim of interdisciplinary teaching is to offer a more cross- functional/integrative approach to management (Smart, Tomkovick, Jones, & Menon, 1999). McKeage, Skinner, Seymour, Donahue and Christensen (1999) stress that the success of an integrated interdisciplinary course is dependent on the level of communication and coordination between and within faculty and student populations. According to Wentworth (1995), faculty need to think "program, as opposed to courses". There are numerous different means of incorporating interdisciplinarity into a business school (a comprehensive review is beyond the scope of this article; the interested reader is referred, for example, to Klein, 1990). Briefly, there are two main approaches to encouraging interdisciplinarity: a broader approach that entails integrating non-business disciplines, and a more narrow approach that combines disciplines that are usually taught in business schools, e.g., marketing and accounting.

In the latter approach, simulation games are commonly used as a means of teaching students to take multiple management-related areas into account when making decisions. However, this teaching approach, and the ability to foster interdisciplinarity in general, may be hindered by the fact that many business schools are divided into departments with narrowly defined subjects. To overcome this limitation, Kates (1989, p. B3) advises "providing for the long-term security and sustenance of individual scholars working beyond disciplines" as well as "alternatives to tenure based solely on discipline or department".

The broader approach to interdisciplinarity—i.e., integrating non-business disciplines—is typically implemented to some extent within certain specializations, such as entrepreneurship, which might bring together different disciplines such as industrial design, marketing and creative industries. In many cases, however, this is done from a multidisciplinary approach and not a truly integrative interdisciplinary one. Another possibility is to offer entire programs combining two disciplines. Schools in Germany, for example, offer certification in engineering management, a specialized form of management that is concerned with the application of engineering principles to business practice.

The prevalence of interdisciplinary teaching has decreased since the recent emergence of research-based business schools, which emphasize the use of rigorous scientific methods (instead of practical relevance).

European Management on the Rise?

Identifying the distinctions between European and US business schools is relatively straightforward. As discussed above, there are clear differences between the two regions in terms of the content of the education they offer. Moreover, Europe and the US differ in their teaching methods. ESCP Europe initiated the use of pedagogical simulation games, whereas the Harvard Business School invented the case study approach. McNulty (1992) states that European business schools value professional projects, internships and action learning more than US schools do. Kipping and colleagues (2004) describe the rejection of the case-study approach by European business schools (with the exception of the UK) during the Americanization process.

Yet although this paper has attempted to derive general contours for the concepts of European management and the European business school, it is difficult to generalize these broad constructs across Europe, owing to the vast diversity of cultural contexts the continent encompasses. Indeed, Locke (1989) states that teaching methods vary substantially across European countries. However, management styles change over time, and it is possible that, at some point, there will be a homogeneous management style across Europe. New EU initiatives resembling the Bologna process or Erasmus might promote such a development. In fact, it is possible that culture at large will become global, with everybody watching the same TV shows, communicating globally on the same social media applications (Kaplan & Haenlein, 2010) and listening to the same massively open online courses (MOOCs; Kaplan & Haenlein, 2016; Pucciarelli & Kaplan, 2016).

However, at least two arguments speak against a homogeneous European management style. First, as indicated, Europeans see diversity as an advantage and thus are likely to try to maintain cultural differences. Second, Europeans speak different languages, which reflect their different cultures and impact their behavior. As long as there are different languages, it is likely that there will be different styles of management. This reaffirms the importance of language courses in business schools, since only through the comprehension of a language can one truly begin to understand a culture.

These ideas are reinforced by the principle that in times of globalization, cross-cultural competencies actually become increasingly important. This suggests that European management education—and particularly the international attractiveness of Europe's MBA programs and its uniquely European Master's in Management programs—should be on the rise. Pudelko and Harzing (2007, p. 206) "predict a more multi-polar world in which the virtual monopoly of the United States in setting the standards for 'best practices' in management will weaken". Indeed, in a recent statement, the AACSB (2009) indicated that its main challenges are "differences in organizational and cultural values" and "cultural diversity among employees and customers". European business schools have been dealing with these challenges for centuries.

References

AACSB (2009). *Eligibility procedures and accreditation standards*. Tampa, FL: AACSB.

Ang, Soon, van Dyne, Linn & Tan, Mei Ling (2011). Cultural intelligence. In R. J. Sternberg & S. B. Kaufman (Eds.), *Cambridge handbook on intelligence* (pp. 582–602). New York: Cambridge University Press.

Bennis, Warren G. & O'Toole, James (2005). How business schools lost their way. *Harvard Business Review*, 83(5), 96–104.

Blanchard, Marianne (2009). From "Ecoles Supérieures de Commerce" to "Management Schools": Transformations and continuity in French business schools. *European Journal of Education*, 44(4), 586–604.

Calori, Roland & de Woot, Philippe (1994). *A European management model: Beyond diversity*. New York: Prentice Hall.

Calori, Roland & Dufour, Bruno (1995). Management European style. *The Academy of Management Executive*, 9, 61–73.

Calori, Roland, Steele, Murray & Yoneyama, Etsuo (1995). Management in Europe: Learning from different perspectives. *European Management Journal*, 13(1), 58–66.

De Vita, Glauco & Case, Peter (2003). Rethinking the internationalization agenda in UK higher education. *Journal of Further and Higher Education*, 27, 383–398.

Doh, Jonathan P. (2010). From the editors: Why aren't business schools more global and what can management educators do about it? *Academy of Management Learning and Education*, 9, 165–168.

Donham, Wallace (1933). The failure of business leadership and the responsibility of the universities. *Harvard Business Review*, 11, 418–435.

Earley, P. Christopher & Ang, Soon (2003). *Cultural intelligence: Individual interactions across cultures*. Palo Alto, CA: Stanford University Press.

Earley, P. Christopher & Peterson, Randall S. (2004). The elusive cultural chameleon: Cultural intelligence as a new approach to intercultural training for the global manager. *Academy of Management Learning and Education*, 3, 100–115.

Eisenberg, Jacob, Lee, Hyun-Jung, Brück, Frank, Brenner, Barbara, Claes, Marie-Therese, Mironski, Jacek & Bell, Roger (2013). Can business schools make students culturally competent? Effects of cross-cultural management courses on cultural intelligence. *Academy of Management Learning and Education*, 12(4), 603–621.

Enderle, Georges (1996). A comparison of business ethics in North America and Continental Europe. *Business Ethics: A European Review*, 5(1), 33–46.

Engwall, Lars (2004). The Americanization of Nordic management education. *Journal of Management Inquiry*, 13(2), 109–117.

Engwall, Lars & Zamagni, Vera (1998). *Management education in historical perspective*. Manchester: Manchester University Press.

Fauri, Francesca (1998). British and Italian management education before the Second World War: A comparative analysis. In L. Engwall & V. Zamagni (Eds.), *Management education in historical perspective*. Manchester: Manchester University Press, 34–49.

Forget, Evelyn L. (1999). *The social economics of Jean-Baptiste Say*. London: Routledge.

Ghosal, Sumantra (2005). Bad management theories are destroying good management practices. *Academy of Management Learning & Education*, 4(1), 75–91.

Gordon, Robert A. & Howell, James E. (1959). *Higher education for business*. New York: Columbia University Press.

Grunzweig, Armand (1977). *Histoire de l'Institut Supérieur de Commerce de l'Etat à Anvers*. Brussels, Belgium: Cercle des anciens étudiants de l'ISCEA.

Hofstede, Geert (1980). *Culture's consequences: Comparing values, behaviors, institutions and organizations across nations*. London, UK: Sage.

Kaplan, Andreas M. (2014). European management and European business schools: Insights from the history of business schools. *European Management Journal*, 32, 529–534.

Kaplan, Andreas M. (2015). *European business and management*. London: Sage Publications Ltd.

Kaplan, Andreas M. (2018). Toward a Theory of European Business Culture. In G. Suder, M. Riviere & J. Lindeque (Eds.), *The Routledge Companion to European Business*. London, UK: Routledge.

Kaplan, Andreas M. & Haenlein, Michael (2009). The increasing importance of public marketing: Explanations, applications and limits of marketing within public administration. *European Management Journal*, 27(1), 197–212.

Kaplan, Andreas M. & Haenlein, Michael (2010). Users of the world, unite! The challenges and opportunities of social media. *Business Horizons*, 53, 59–68.

Kaplan, Andreas M. & Haenlein, Michael (2016). Higher education and the digital revolution: About MOOCs, SPOCs, social media and the Cookie Monster. *Business Horizons*, 59, 441–450.

Kates, Robert W. (1989). The great questions of science and society do not fit neatly into single disciplines. *The Chronicle of Higher Education*, 35, B2–B3.

Kedia, Banwari L. & Harveston, Paula D. (1998). Transformation of MBA programs: Meeting the challenge of international competition. *Journal of World Business*, 33(2), 203–217.

Kieser, Alfred (2004). The Americanization of academic management education in Germany. *Journal of Management Inquiry*, 13(2), 90–97.

Kipping, Matthias, Üsdiken, Behlül & Puig, Núria (2004). Imitation, tension, and hybridization: Multiple "Americanizations" of management education in Mediterranean Europe. *Journal of Management Inquiry*, 13(2), 98–108.

Klein, Julie T. (1990). *Interdisciplinarity: History, theory, and practice*. Detroit, MI: Wayne State University.

Leavitt, Harold J. (1957). On the export of American management education. *Journal of Business*, 30, 153–161.

Lemercier, Claire (2003). La chambre de commerce de Paris, acteur indispensable de la construction des normes économiques (première moitié du xixe siècle). *Genèses*, 1, 50–70.

Locke, Robert R. (1989). *Management and higher education since 1940: The influence of America and Japan on West Germany, Great Britain, and France*. Cambridge: Cambridge University Press.

Longobardi, Ernesto C. (1927). Higher commercial education in Italy. *Journal of Political Economy*, 35, 39–90.

McGlade, Jacqueline (1998). The big push: The export of American business education to Western Europe after the Second World War. In L. Engwall & V. Zamagni (Eds.), *Management education in historical perspective*. Manchester: Manchester University Press, 50–65.

McKeage, Kim, Skinner, Deborah, Seymour, Rose Mary, Donahue, Darrell W. & Christensen, Tom (1999). Implementing an interdisciplinary marketing/engineering course project: Project format, preliminary evaluation, and critical factor review. *Journal of Marketing Education*, 21(3), 217–231.

McNulty, Nancy G. (1992). Management education in Eastern Europe: "Fore and after". *Management Executive*, 6(4), 78–87.

Meyer, Heinz-Dieter (1998). The German Handelshochschulen, 1898–1933: A new departure in management education and why it failed. In L. Engwall & V. Zamagni (Eds.), *Management education in historical perspective*. Manchester: Manchester University Press, 19–33

Moore, Geoff (2004). Regulatory perspectives on business ethics in the curriculum. *Journal of Business Ethics*, 54(4), 349–356.

Mosson, Thomas Michael (1965). *Management education in five European countries*. London: Business Publications.

Oliver, Judith (1993). UK: A degree of uncertainty—MBA. *Management Today*, 7(6), 26–30.

Pucciarelli, Francesca & Kaplan, Andreas (2016). Competition and strategy in higher education: Managing complexity and uncertainty. *Business Horizons*, 59, 311–320.

Pudelko, Markus & Harzing, Anne-Wil (2007). How European is management in Europe? An analysis of past, present and future management practices in Europe. *European Journal of International Management*, 1(3), 206–224.

Renouard, Alfred (1999). *Histoire de l'École supérieure de commerce de Paris*. Paris: Raymond Castell éditions.

Sass, Steven A. (1982). *The pragmatic imagination: A history of the Wharton School 1881–1981*. Philadelphia: University of Pennsylvania Press.

Smart, Denise T., Tomkovick, Chuck, Jones, Eli & Menon, Anil (1999). Undergraduate marketing education in the 21st century: View from three institutions. *Marketing Education Review*, 9, 1–9.

Takas, Andrew (1974). Societal marketing: A businessman's perspective. *Journal of Marketing*, 38(4), 2–7.

Taylor, Frederick W. (1911). *The principles of scientific management*. New York: Harper Bros.

Trompenaars, Fons (1993). *Riding the waves of culture: Understanding cultural diversity in business*. London: Nicholas Brealey Publishing.

Üsdiken, Behlül (2004). Americanization of European management in historical and comparative perspective. *Journal of Management Inquiry*, 13(2), 87–89.

van Luijk, Henk J. L. (2001). Business ethics in Europe: A tale of two efforts. In R. Frederick (Ed.), *A companion to business ethics* (pp. 643–658). Cambridge: Blackwell.

Wedlin, Linda (2007). The role of rankings in codifying a business school template: Classifications, diffusion and mediated isomorphism in organizational fields. *European Management Review*, 4, 24–39.

Welter, Friederieke & Lasch, Frank (2008). Entrepreneurship research in Europe: Taking stock and looking forward. *Entrepreneurship Theory and Practice*, 32(2), 241–248.

Wentworth Jack R. (1995). Recent interdisciplinary evolution in Indiana University's MBA program. *Advances in Strategic Management*, 11, 129–132.

Williams, Allan P. O. (2010). *The history of UK business and management education*. London: Emerald.

Wren, Daniel A. & van Fleet, David D. (1983). History in schools of business. *Business and Economic History*, 12(1), 29–35.

14 Turning a Disadvantage into a Resource

Working at the Periphery

Tammar B. Zilber

'Center', 'Periphery', and a European Management Approach

A European, or American or Eastern, or any other approach to management scholarship—like any social identity—does not stand in itself, isolated from other approaches. Academic approaches like other social identities are formed within dialogues and relationships—real or imagined—with and against some Other. If a European approach is the in-group, there must be an out-group against which such a European approach, or an identity of the European scholar, is defined and formed (Lingard, Reznick, & DeVito, 2002; Somers, 1994). A European approach to management scholarship may well exist as scholars from Europe often describe themselves as having to adapt to, struggle with, negate or be measured against some "Other" approach, highlighting both sameness within their imagined community and differences from another community (Benhabib, 1996; De Cillia, Reisigl, & Wodak, 1999). Both approaches—European and non-European—are constituted through such interrelations.

For me, as a management scholar situated in Israel, issues of in-group and out-group, 'us' and 'them', are even more complex. Geographically, Israel is in the Middle East. While this location is crucial—religiously, historically, culturally and ideologically—to Israeli identity (Kimmerling, 2005), Israel has not been accepted as a legitimate member of this region. There is an ongoing conflict between Israel and Palestine and most other Arab countries, near and far from its borders. As a result, Israel occupies a somewhat ambiguous position in the world, as it has been constantly striving to transcend its geographical location. In some formal respects, Israel is considered to some extent part of Europe, for instance in sports (e.g. participating in soccer and basketball tournaments as a European country), commerce (association agreements with the European Union) and international relations (Israel is a major non-NATO ally of the North Atlantic Treaty Organization). Still, Israel is not 'in Europe', so I was actually somewhat surprised when Sabina Siebert approached me, and kindly asked me to write a piece for the "Reflections on Europe" series. The invitation inspired me to reflect again on my subject position, real and imagined. I am not a European, I thought, and I am neither 'Middle Eastern' nor American, that was clear to me. So, who am I?

In the following, I offer then a personal reflection of my experience of the perils and joys of doing research and publishing from the verge of Europe and facing the US. Granted, my experience is shaped by many factors—my gender, age, disciplinary background and many more; my location in the geopolitical periphery of the academic world being only one of them (Johansson & Sliwa, 2014). Still, while acknowledging this intersectionality, I will focus here on issues relating to the center–periphery complex and their relations to an elusive 'European approach to management'.

To begin with, as a management scholar situated in Israel, the Other against which I define myself professionally is US academia. That is true, especially after World War II, for most disciplines within the social and natural sciences in Israel (some disciplines within the humanities may be oriented towards Europe as well). Yet the US is not only the Other, but the better one. It defines quite thoroughly the discipline of organization studies. It is the center of the global scientific system, and we, in Israel, are at its periphery. There is nothing unique about this position within the center–periphery dynamics characterizing the scientific world (e.g. Cavazos, 2015; Heilbron, 2014; Lillis & Curry, 2010). It was found in various disciplines (Mosbah-Natanson & Gingras, 2014), management among them (Danell, 2000; Grey, 2010; March, 2005; Meriläinen, Tienari, Thomas, & Davies, 2008; Usdiken, 2014), and it has various implications within the diverse geographies of the periphery, even when one takes into account the espoused multilingualism of the European Union.[1]

The simplistic dichotomy between center and periphery has been much criticized in recent years—in geography (Potter, 2001) and sociology (Keim, 2011) and in relation to the academic world more specifically (e.g. Medina, 2013; Scott, 2015). Yet, its hold on our "geopolitical imagination" (Slater, 1993) is still strong and thus serves as my starting point, as I try to articulate how this position is formed, what it means to work academically in a periphery and what implications and possibilities are opened up from this vantage point. I will focus on three dimensions. Working at the periphery has linguistic implications, as I conduct most of my professional life in English, which is not my mother tongue. Being a means of communication and a cultural resource, language use has many effects. Moreover, working at the periphery has social consequences. Fresh out of graduate school I found myself with no relevant lineages in the (academic) community I wanted to be part of and had to find ways to make connections. Finally, there are also cognitive aspects involved. Working at the periphery means that one's taken-for-granted understanding of the rules of the academic game (defined by the center) is limited. Decoding the norms requires reflection, and that reflection and the insights it provides may turn out to be a real asset.

Know Thy Place: Early Socialization into a Peripheral Position

The US orientation of Israeli academia became evident—if sometimes implicitly—in the very first course of my BA studies, majoring in psychology and an interdisciplinary program in humanities. The reading materials were all in English, from Hilgard's Introduction to Psychology, and other books published by US publishers, through to numerous articles, most of them published in prestigious US journals. We read in English, while class discussions and written assignments were in Hebrew. Those who encountered difficulties—many of whom were trilingual, native speakers of Arabic, Russian and Amharic—had to take a reading comprehensive course in English (Bensoussan, 2015). As we progressed to the MA and PhD, it became apparent that English is not simply a barrier one needs to pass in order to finish one's studies, but rather the lingua franca of academia. English became the language one needs to master in order to be able to bridge one's peripheral location—linguistically, at least.

While English no longer is depicted as a monolithic language, but rather is composed of many "world Englishes—varieties of English used in diverse sociolinguistic contexts" (Bhatt, 2001, p. 527), I here refer to a specific linguistic voice—that of American English used by US academia. By linguistic voice I do not just mean the use of the right grammar or even the right American idioms. It is to become knowledgeable about the broader contexts of American English as used in academia; that is, its embeddedness within a wider ideological and cultural world. Indeed, the hegemony of English as the preferred language of Israeli academia stretches beyond presenting in English in international conferences and publications. It is part of the internationalization of academia worldwide, Israeli academia included (Cohen, Yemini, & Sadeh, 2014; Tietze, 2008; Yemini, Holzmann, de Wit, Sadeh, Stavans, & Fadila, 2015). In this context, it may not seem surprising that much of e-mail communication within Israeli academia, even if all participants are native Hebrew speakers, is carried out in English. Early on there may have been technical reasons for this, given that computer systems were mostly built for left-to-right languages (like English). Hebrew is written right-to-left, and the right indent used to be a major problem with computers back in the days. And still, even today, many Israeli academics correspond in English. Faculty hiring, promotion and remuneration practices all involve the counting of publications and lectures in English. One is measured by his or her standing in the global (that is, English speaking) network of scholars. Publications in Hebrew are hardly ever counted and scholars are often quite discouraged from publishing in Hebrew. This is the case in all the natural sciences and in most social science disciplines. Lately, there is also a pressure to teach in English—as part of an effort to boost international standing and meet international accreditation requirements. Israeli business schools work hard to create exchange programs with foreign universities, and Israeli students are encouraged to do their graduate studies abroad, which will help them later on to return and find tenure track positions in Israeli universities. Thus, an academic career for Israeli scholars, like other non-native English scholars, does not rest exclusively on their "individual academic knowledge and expertise" but will be equally "determined by their English language competence and their ability to link into knowledge networks and communities" (Tietze, 2008, p. 385).

Various policies and practices, from national to institutional levels, support the US orientation in Israeli academia. Access to resources, such as research databases, e-journals and other means of conducting and distributing research, match those of the best American universities. Moreover, Israeli scholars get special financing for 'outward relations'—funds to finance trips for conferences, seminars and sabbaticals abroad. Israeli academia, in this regard, is an outlier in comparison to other Middle Eastern and African countries (Lages, Pfajfar, & Shoham, 2015).

Notwithstanding those much needed resources, conducting professional life in one's non-native language carries some difficulties (Hanauer & Englander, 2011). One is always navigating between the languages, always translating, literally and metaphorically. Further, English being the professional language in one's writing and presentations, but also a second language in one's surroundings, creates divides between three language zones: discourse community, community of practice and speech community (Curry & Lillis, 2004). Maneuvering through these is an ongoing burden. It involves a 'loss of expressiveness' and 'semantic quality', because "language is much more than a code. It is at once a reference system and a cultural vehicle that represents reality and what we have to say in a singular and symbolic way. While translation makes it possible to disseminate ideas to a certain extent, there are nevertheless few concepts or models of interpretation that can be shared among different cultures in a completely analogous fashion" (Descarries, 2014, p. 566). Translation is a constant work on similarities and especially on differences. It is never transparent and simple and it always includes those gaps and the missing meanings you just could not capture in the Other, dominant language. As a result, oftentimes, you do not get to express what you know or think, but rather only what you can articulate (Pérez-Llantada, Plo, & Ferguson, 2011).

With much practice, it is sometimes possible to become, as it were, immersed enough in the other language—as if jumping over the need to translate. Indeed, as I write this text—twenty-something years into my life within academia—I no longer need to consult the dictionary or synonym finder as often as I used to. I no longer constantly simplify my arguments to match my ability to express them in English. I was lucky that the first academic text I wrote, while still a graduate student, was a book on narrative methodologies, co-authored with my doctoral supervisor and a colleague, a graduate student as well (Lieblich, Tuval-Mashiach, & Zilber, 1998). Part of the book we wrote together, and other parts were written by each of us individually. I was contemplating writing my parts in Hebrew and having them translated, as I believed it would be much easier and quicker. "No way", reacted my supervisor. "Write in English! If you write in Hebrew and have it translated, you will be forever crippled, forever dependent on crutches". She was right, and I pass the very same advice to my graduate students.

Yet it took much time and effort, and I often suspected that I was leaving a lot unsaid or not fully articulated. This was especially concerning because in my line of research, based on qualitative methods, writing is "a method of inquiry" (Richardson, 1998). Writing is not merely typing away my already clear and well-crafted findings. Writing in itself is a process of discovery in which I move back and forth between the empirical materials I have collected, my interpretations thereof and the theoretical questions in the relevant academic literature. Hence, while writing an article, I come to slowly understand what I am up to. Writing is complex because it is a transformative, constitutive process.

Writing in a second language makes the delicate and daunting creative process of moving along the 'hermeneutical circle'—connecting new findings, interpretations and theorizing—even more laborious. I have, of course, to translate my empirical materials and jump between Hebrew (the language of the world I study, and of my initial thinking of it) and English (the language in which I write and construct my analytical arguments). It does get easier with the years, but for me, writing in English is never as swift as writing in Hebrew. In Hebrew, my linguistic skills help me come up with more complex and nuanced ideas. Hebrew, as my native language, lifts my ideas higher. English, as my non-native language, sometimes feels like a weight that slows me down. At times, it feels as if I am talking with an echo, even if a faint one—constantly trying to figure out whether I have succeeded in crystalizing my argument properly, or whether the bouncing residues of my ideas, coming back from the linguistic walls surrounding me, are slightly twisted.

A Foot in the Door

I was trained in social and organizational psychology and did my BA, MA and PhD in the Department of Psychology at the Hebrew University. It took me that long to realize I was not in the right place. In social and organizational psychology, the individual is at the center. There is much attention to the social world around him or her, but this world is understood as some 'independent variables' that influence the individual. The focus (the 'dependent variables' in particular) always lies then in the various cognitive and emotional processes at the individual level. I, on the other hand, was interested in the social order itself. Not in cause-and-effect models but in the complexities of social textures. I was—and still am—fascinated by the process through which collectivities of people create a shared reality. Social psychology, I came to slowly understand, failed to offer deep insights about this collective process of social construction, partially due to its overdependence on positivistic research methods and given its paradigmatic assumptions about the presumably universal processes and mechanisms operating within individuals. So I started peeking into sociology and anthropology. This interest was evolving during my doctoral studies and research. Working as a research assistant and later as collaborator with Amia Lieblich, who was one of the very few faculty members in the psychology department that was doing qualitative research, I was slowly moving away from the dominant research paradigms of current psychology. To my great luck, Amia—a clinical psychologist by training and a student of life stories—agreed to supervise my PhD studies, and sensing my drifting away from psychology gave me a free pass to study whatever I found interesting.

In my PhD research, I studied a rape crisis center in Tel Aviv, Israel. Through this feminist organization I explored how organizations live and practice their ideologies. My understanding of the organization, after a long period of field work and analysis, focused on a constant tension between a psychotherapeutic discourse and feminist discourses prevalent in it. The thesis became an inquiry into organizational ambiguity—how an organization with a dual professional/ideological identity (psychotherapy and feminism) creates and maintains ambiguity in order to avoid annihilating some of its members and breaking down its social order.

Once I finished my graduate studies, I moved to the University of California in Berkeley for a year of postdoc, which was obviously the right thing to do for an aspiring academic. I was associated with the psychology department, thanks to my PhD supervisor's network, although by then it was clear to me that I had no future in psychology. With my interest in organizations and organizational life, a business school seemed like a much better fit. So, I crossed the beautiful green campus almost every day, heading from the old building of the psychology department to the magnificent modern new building of the business school. I spent hours in the library, reading management journals and books. There I came across a call for papers for a special issue of the *Academy of Management Journal*, on the subject of institutional change (Dacin, Goodstein & Scott, 2002). The guest editors gave a few examples of theoretical questions associated with the special issue, and one of the examples seemed to hit right at my own initial understanding of the complex rape crisis center I had studied. The only problem was that, at that time, I had only a scant knowledge of institutional theory (although I did have some vague sense of its insights with regard to the interface between organizations and their social environments). I was well read in social psychology, organizational psychology and life stories—not in organization theory. I had heard of institutional theory in an Introduction to Organization Theory course, but I was not versed in the ideas that would soon change the theoretical landscape in our field (Vogel, 2012). So there I was sitting at the UC Berkeley management school, dedicating my postdoc year to reading institutional theory from its early beginning and throughout its various developments—starting from

Berger and Luckmann (1967), through Meyer and Rowan (1977), Zucker (1977), DiMaggio and Powell (1983) and the so-called Orange Book, cover to cover (Powell & DiMaggio, 1991). I was moving slowly and quite thoroughly from the reference lists back, onward and sideways. It was time-consuming, and more than once I felt envious of my imaginary counterparts who were trained in American universities and learned from the very people whose writings I was reading—Powell, Scott, Meyer and others at Stanford; DiMaggio at Yale and later at Princeton; Zucker at UCLA; Hirsch at the University of Chicago and later at Northwestern; Greenwodd and Hinings at the University of Alberta and so on. Studying with them, I thought, would have saved me this year of catching up.

Only later did I realize that engaging those ideas through my own reading, and outside the face-to-face learning encounters, had its own advantages and fruitful outcomes. I was free to engage with the original formulations instead of their framing within certain specific understandings. The literacy gap between the written word and the spoken word was crucial then for opening up fresh understanding of institutional theory. Had I been exposed to these arguments through second-hand versions (in classes, seminars, or conferences), I would have been most likely socialized into their accepted social construction. "Centrality within a discipline, with its concurrent exposure to the dominant intellectual discourse, renders a scholar more likely to work with a socially constructed rather than a literal reading of a major work" (Mizruchi & Fein, 1999, p. 677). My peripheral position therefore created a space for learning and engagement that is different from the one opened up (and at times bounded) for scholars at the center.

My engagement with the original formulations of institutional theory, and my following of its genealogies and developments throughout the years, allowed me to detect how meanings were central to the original conceptualization of the institutionalization process (together with structures and practices) but abandoned from empirical studies of institutional theory. Assuming that meanings, structures and practices always go together, it may be reasonable to use easier-to-measure structures and practices as proxies of meanings. However—and here came in my close reading of the various formulations of institutional theory—what if meanings can change and be negotiated within an organization, even when practices and structures stay intact? This is what I believed was going on in the rape crisis center that I had studied. The original feminist meanings were swept aside by psychotherapeutic meanings, while the practices and structures were kept, to a large extent, in place. In retrospect, I think that my own training in narrative psychology, along with a fascination for the power of interpretation in social life, also contributed to my interest in the shifting grounds of meanings and in the ways actors may use various practices and structures to advance and negotiate different meanings. The interface between actors, meanings and practices in processes of institutionalization became the center of the theoretical formulation of my manuscript.

The manuscript went through a daunting review process, in three stages. This is typical to manuscripts in top-tier journals in our field, yet my manuscript was "peripheral" in many respects. It was an ethnography based on fieldwork, while the North American community is very much in favour of positivistic research (Amis & Silk, 2008; Bluhm, Harman, Lee, & Mitchell, 2011; Bort and Kieser, 2011; on the European qualitative research tradition, see Cassell, this volume). To add to that, the organization I studied—a non-profit, feminist collective—was not commonly explored within our discipline. Further, management scholars in the US are the community of scholars who, in effect, define standards of legitimate and good scholarship, research traditions and praxis. Those norms and standards are coded in language—textual conventions of scientific writing that may differ across cultures and "render non-native-English speakers' manuscripts to be considered 'poor' or 'awkward'" (Hanauer & Englander, 2011, p. 405). Even in a blind review, language may reveal locations (through the proxy of native or non-native English), and those revelations carry consequences. In cultural fields, for example, peers tend to favour others who are highly embedded within the field (Cattani, Ferriani, & Allison, 2014). Such center–periphery dynamics are so strong that they are apparent even across different Englishes (see re Australia, UK and US, Collyer, 2014).

Most importantly to my experience of the review process within the center–periphery interface was the issue of theory versus the empirical case. As often happens with empirical cases from the periphery, the editorial team found the case 'exotic', and challenged its theoretical relevance. Issues of generalizability seem to arise more critically in relation to studies based on non–North American data, as if such contexts are somehow more unique than any North American case study. Given center–periphery dynamics, centrally located or trained reviewers tend to treat North American empirical contexts as the norm (as interesting in itself), and everything else as a unique and peculiar setting that requires a serious theorizing in order to make it 'relevant'. This means that a special effort is required in order to transcend the bias to look at peripherally based cases as "other, specific, or culturally distinct" (Descarries, 2014, p. 564).

Indeed, I felt I was pushed to think more analytically with my case study in order to highlight analytical features that were relevant even to those readers not interested in rape crisis centers, feminist organizations or Israel. The effort was rewarding, and the paper developed through the review process. It came with a price—my nuanced, grounded and somewhat messy ethnographic study turned into a neat, conventional American research paper. Still, that first article, published in a special issue (Zilber, 2002), served as my ticket into the research community.

A Node in the Network

The linguistic dimension of working at the periphery connects to a social one, further touching upon issues of power structure and the asymmetrical relations between center and periphery. American English, like any language, carries with it ideology, thought patterns and a world-view that are all "coded into its syntactical structure and its semantic fields" (Tietze & Dick, 2009, p. 120). American English is an instrumental and symbolic capital that enables—or disables—the performance of academic habitus (Sliwa & Johansson, 2015). Language draws specific maps of the field's social network and power structure so that English-speaking scholars, located in well-regarded US institutions, are set at its center. Scholars from the periphery of the US and even more from the periphery of the world are located at the periphery of this academic network.

No surprise then that, even with the internationalization of science, networks of production and dissemination are still embedded within center–periphery geopolitical relations. Certainly within our discipline of organization studies, scholars "are gathered into guilds and live in groups of small cottages" (Battilana, Anteby, & Sengul, 2010, p. 695). Academic fields cohere around "invisible colleges"—comprising members who "had similar training, meet regularly at conferences and workshops, circulate manuscripts among colleagues to gather friendly reviews, publish in much the same journals, participate in the activities of the same research associations, and visit one another at their universities and business schools" (Vogel, 2012, pp. 1015–1016). Invisible colleges are crucial for the flow of resources (like information and legitimacy), and they seem to reflect center–periphery dynamics as well (Usdiken, 2014). In actuality, "internationalization" is not a reciprocal dynamic, in which the relative weight of peripheral contribution rises. Rather, it means "Westernization". The direction of influence runs from center to periphery, and not vice versa (Battilana et al., 2010; Mosbah-Natanson & Gingras, 2014).

As a graduate of the Hebrew University in Jerusalem, who did all my studies in Israel, my invisible college was quite local and not much use for supporting me in a global career. I returned from my postdoc year at UCB with a top-tier publication, which got me into a tenure track position with the Jerusalem Business School at the Hebrew University. Now that I had an institutional and disciplinary affiliation, it was time to take networking more seriously. Off I went to three international conferences—the Standing Conference on Organizational Symbolism (SCOS) 2002 annual meeting in Budapest, Hungary; the 2002 annual meeting of the European Group of Organizational Studies (EGOS) in Barcelona, Spain; and the 2002 annual meeting of the Academy of Management (AoM) in Denver, Colorado. At these conferences I learned more about the differences in academic cultures between the US and Europe. Whereas EGOS is structured around small working groups that enable meeting like-minded people and making connections over two and a half days of intensive discussions, AoM is a much more individualized endeavour. Attendees run around to catch relevant sessions and present their work. I realized that there is more to this chaos—in particular that symposia were gravitating points and that they were the crucial events. They were, I came to understand, the most fruitful format in which to present a paper. Whereas paper sessions were collections of papers submitted separately and put together by the organizers, symposia sessions were very different, as their organizers assembled a group of scholars around a coherent theme, usually with a discussant that gives it all an added value. Consequently, and following my basic new understanding of how things worked and how networks are formed, a year later, in 2003, I wanted my work to be presented in a symposium. But no one bothered to invite me to take part in any. Well then, I should invest my own time and energy and arrange a session myself. However, I knew no one I could invite based on my personal relations. People I studied with were mainly psychologists, not organizational theorists. And, like me, they were all Israelis. Again, I was reminded that my PhD supervisor was centrally located in narrative psychology, but her network was not useful in my new business school environment. In addition, I still had not met new colleagues through seminars and workshops, and felt quite lonely.

Luckily, I had my AMJ paper, which had just been published. So, I approached other authors in the special issue whose work seemed relevant to mine. I did not know any of them, but I played heavily on us sharing the pages of AMJ. All responded positively to my e-mails. Some of them even accepted my invitation to present their work, while others declined but were kind enough to connect me with their students or colleagues. I also contacted the guest editor who handled my manuscript, and asked him to serve as a discussant. He kindly agreed and so I managed to put together a proposal for a session, and finally got to meet, in person, those authors whose work I had read and admired. We had some good conversations, and I felt this was working well. I thought I should develop the conversation into the realm of the broad questions in institutional theory, those that bothered many of us yet were not always discussed explicitly enough. Thus, for the next six years I co-organized Professional Development Workshops (PDWs) at the Academy. Each year we invited people whose work I appreciated and whom I wanted to get to know, to discuss issues that I found important and underdeveloped.[2] Organizing these PDWs was time-consuming, but they were a lot of fun and a great way to get to know new people and exchange ideas. In that way, I was slowly creating my own invisible college.

I was happy and content. I felt that I understood "the system" and made it work for me . . . only to find out that apart from the AoM and EGOS annual meetings, a host of small-scale gatherings were going on all around North America and Europe. As a keen reader of acknowledgements in publications, I knew such meetings were being held and were the birthplace of many books and articles. But how do I get in? It took time before I was even in the know—that is, found myself on some mailing lists for the call for papers. Thus came a series of intimate conferences and workshops that allow one to expand and deepen one's intellectual horizons as well as network.

Let me highlight again the center–periphery interface and this time in its quite material aspects. Living in Israel, attending such conferences and workshops takes a lot of effort—schlepping from afar, changing time zones and paying for expensive travel and accommodation. But for me, as a Jerusalem-based scholar, the efforts are well deserved and the opportunities they open are priceless. These include invitations to write chapters for edited books (Zilber, 2008, 2009), conversations that have turned into journal special issues (Lawrence, Leca, & Zilber, 2013; Suddaby et al., 2010) and organizing or co-convening conferences.

These endeavours involved getting to know many new people and developing a good feel for research and writing still in progress. Indeed, given the long process of bringing research into print, even the keenest reader of management outlets lags far behind what is going on right now. Seminars, conferences and workshops (serving as a reviewer as well) are a wonderful way to follow the developments in our theoretical field in real time. As no one just happens to 'drop by' in Jerusalem and give a talk (as people who happen to be in Boston are happy to present their work at Harvard or MIT), seminars are not an option for me at the periphery. I therefore worked hard on the conference circuit.

Balancing In-Group and Out-Group Positions

Back in Jerusalem, another aspect of working at the periphery is trying hard to find new resources and new networks within our own community of scholars. Thus, at the Hebrew University we try to create and maintain intellectual and social networks by strengthening our ties with organizational scholars across disciplinary divides. We also put much effort into hosting small, yet intensive, international workshops and conferences at the Hebrew University. Bringing leading scholars from North America and Europe to Israel gives ourselves and our students the opportunity to meet and converse with them on a personal level. I encourage my graduate students to attend conferences as early as possible and to present their work in symposia they organize with me, in order to create the best context for their voice to be heard. Hopefully, all this will make their integration into our scholarly conversation a little easier.

Situated in the periphery, one becomes (painfully) aware of the "cultural peculiarities" of the center's "style of inquiry" (Bendix, Mills, & Noyes, 1998). While members of an intellectual community often have little awareness of their style of inquiry, "foreigners" are constantly engaged in comparisons and tackle surprises, and may thus be in a better position to be reflective about the production of knowledge in our discipline. Without too much psychodynamic reductionism, I believe that my peripheral position also directs my meta-theoretical and meta-methodological writings, in which I read and analyze the development of theory and methods in the study of institutions.[3] My interest in the production of knowledge in our field also extends to my empirical projects. I am interested in the translation both of images in the business world (Zilber, 2006) as well as of research methods in academic circles (Zilber & Zanoni, 2015).[4]

These meta-theoretical and meta-methodological writings stem from my own experience as a non-native English speaker and non–North American trained scholar. I believe that my efforts, as a young scholar, to decode how the system works resulted in applying a reflective and critical gaze at the very production of scientific knowledge.

All this would not have happened had I not managed to position myself on the 'radar' of North American scholars through a series of publications in prestigious North American and European outlets (Zilber, 2002, 2006, 2007, 2011). It would not have happened had I not maintained my network through extensive travels to participate at conferences and workshops, giving seminars and serving as external examiner (North American system) or opponent (European system). At the same time, it probably would have not happened had I been totally immersed within the North American conversation. Being—unwillingly at first, and later on purpose—somewhat off the main current, kind of 'a stranger', was a subject position that was helpful in having some fresh analytical distance that could serve as an added value to contribute. I still see it as a challenge to balance my in-group and out-group positions in the service of my research.

My approach to management studies developed out of my peripheral location in Israel and bilingual experience (widely defined in both the literal and symbolic realms). In my experience, this peripheral position has linguistic, social and cognitive implications. It comes with both disadvantages and advantages. Overall, though, and at least for now, mine is a happy story. English, as "the language of knowledge generation and dissemination", is "both a medium to articulate and express knowledge as well as a constitutive force which shapes the content of knowledge" (Tietze, 2008, p. 371). In this context, being bilingual (literally) and holding a bridging position between academic worlds may help one carve a space for exploration and freedom unattainable to those who were trained and pursue their careers within North American academia and the English language. To the degree that a European management approach stems from an experience of periphery within a center–periphery interface, it holds much promise for scholars to make use of certain degrees of freedom that are dear in our gradually globalized, quantified and capitalized process of knowledge production (Curry & Lillis, 2013; Slaughter & Leslie, 2001). Let us rejoice in that.

Acknowledgements

This work was supported by the Leon Recanati Center of the Jerusalem School of Business Administration, The Hebrew University. Special thanks to Yehuda Goodman for the ongoing discussion of the ideas presented in the article.

Notes

1. See for example the positions of the non-English speaking European countries (Anderson, 2013; Curry & Lillis, 2004; Descarries, 2014; Mur Dueñas, 2012; López-Navarro, Moreno, Ángel-Quintanilla, & Rey-Rocha, 2015; Olsson & Sheridan, 2012). See also the experience of academics at the Arabian Gulf (Buckingham, 2014), Argentina (Beigel, 2014), Australia (Collyer, 2014), China (Flowerdew & Li, 2009), Jordan (Pedersen, 2010), Mexico: (Englander, 2009), South Korea (Lee & Lee, 2013), Taiwan (Chiu, 2011) and Turkey (Usdiken & Wasti, 2009).
2. Early on, I organized these PDWs with Kate Thomson, and the very last one with Julie Batilana.
3. I devoted a review chapter (Zilber, 2008), to trace the development of the various schools that deal with meanings and ideas within institutional theory. In a chapter published in a special double volume on "Institutional Logics in Action" in the series *Research in the Sociology of Organizations* (Zilber, 2013), I explore the intellectual genealogy of two current streams within Institutional Theory—Institutional Logics and Institutional Work, evaluate their relative contributions as well as their shortcoming and offer a division of labor and possible collaborations between them. In another *RSO* special issue, I review recent studies of Institutional Logics and argue for a fuller constructivist approach, necessary for us to be able to study their work on the ground (Zilber, 2017). In an article published in the *Journal of Management Inquiry*, I compare institutional theory with its former counterpart 'organizational culture' theory and point to ways by which the former can contribute to the latter (Zilber, 2012). In a co-authored article (Hatch and Zilber, 2012), we offer more ways to foster a constructive dialogue between the two theories (both of these papers resulted from a 2009 Academy symposium organized by Kathryn Aten and Jennifer Howard-Grenville). I am also directing a reflective gaze at the qualitative research methods I use, which are closely related to the very theoretical contributions I am making. Based on my experience with ethnographic studies, I wrote about the innovative use of ethnography in exploring organizational fields—rather than examining organizations alone (Zilber, 2014, a paper that resulted from an Academy PDW organized by Hila Lifshitz-Assaf and Michell Anteby; Zilber, 2015).
4. In an ongoing research project with Patricia Zanoni we examine the institutionalization of ethnography as a legitimate research method in Organization Studies. By analyzing published scientific articles, we examine the construction of organizational ethnography in different journals, representing various sub-academic communities within the field. The first co-authored paper out of this project (Zilber & Zanoni, 2015) focuses on the discipline's top-tier journal, *Administrative Science Quarterly*, showing how ethnography, brought into our discipline from anthropology, has been adapted to fit the discipline's institutional order as to what constitute 'science', 'research' and 'knowledge'.

References

Amis, John M. & Silk, Michael L. (2008). The philosophy and politics of quality in qualitative organizational research. *Organizational Research Methods*, 11(3), 456–480.

Anderson, Laurie (2013). Publishing strategies of young, highly mobile academics: The question of language in the European context. *Language Policy*, 12(3), 273–288.

Battilana, Julie, Anteby, Michel & Sengul, Metin (2010). The circulation of ideas across academic communities: When locals reimport exported ideas. *Organization Studies*, 31(6), 695–713.

Beigel, Fernanda (2014). Publishing from the periphery: Structural heterogeneity and segmented circuits: The evaluation of scientific publications for tenure in Argentina's CONICET. *Current Sociology*, 62(5), 743–765.

Bendix, Regina, Mills, Margaret & Noyes, Dorothy (1998). International rites: Introduction. *Journal of Folklore Research*, 35(1), 1–4.

Benhabib, Seyla (1996). The Democratic movement and the problem of difference. In S. Benhabib (Ed.), *Democracy and difference: Contesting the boundaries of the political* (pp. 3–18). Princeton, NJ: Princeton University Press.

Bensoussan, Marsha (2015). Motivation and English language learning in a multicultural university context. *Journal of Multilingual and Multicultural Development*, 36(4), 423–440.

Berger, Peter L. & Luckmann, Thomas (1967). *The social construction of reality: A Treatise in the sociology of knowledge*. New York: Anchor Books.

Bhatt, Rakesh M. (2001). World Englishes. *Annual Review of Anthropology*, 30, 527–550.

Bluhm, Dustin J., Harman, Wendy, Lee, Thomas W. & Mitchell, Terrence R. (2011). Qualitative research in management: A decade of progress. *Journal of Management Studies*, 48(8), 1866–1891.

Bort, Suleika & Kieser, Alfred (2011). Fashion in organization theory: An empirical analysis of the diffusion of theoretical concepts. *Organization Studies*, 32(5), 655–681.

Buckingham, Louisa (2014). Building a career in English: Users of English as an additional language in academia in the Arabian Gulf. *TESOL Quarterly*, 48(1), 6–33.

Cattani, Gino, Ferriani, Simone & Allison, Paul D. (2014). Insiders, outsiders, and the struggle for consecration in cultural fields: A core-periphery perspective. *American Sociological Review*, 79(2), 258–281.

Cavazos, Alyssa G. (2015). Multilingual faculty across academic disciplines: Language difference in scholarship. *Language and Education*, 29(4), 317–331.

Chiu, Yi-hui (2011). Exploring non-native science scholars' perspectives of writing for publication in English. *Asia-Pacific Education Researcher*, 20(3), 469–476.

Cohen, Anat, Yemini, Miri & Sadeh, Efrat (2014). Web-based analysis of internationalization in Israeli teaching colleges. *Journal of Studies in International Education*, 18(1), 23–44.

Collyer, Fran (2014). Sociology, sociologists and core-periphery reflections. *Journal of Sociology*, 50(3), 252–268.

Curry, Mary Jane & Lillis, Theresa (2004). Multilingual scholars and the imperative to publish in English: Negotiating interests, demands, and rewards. *TESOL Quarterly*, 38(4), 663–688.

Curry, Mary Jane & Lillis, Theresa (2013). Introduction to the thematic issue: Participating in academic publishing-consequences of linguistic policies and practices. *Language Policy*, 12(3), 209–213.

Dacin, M. Tina, Goodstein, Jerry & Scott, W. Richard (2002). Institutional theory and institutional change: Introduction to the special research forum. *Academy of Management Journal*, 45(1), 45–56.

Danell, Richard (2000). Stratification among journals in management research: A bibliometric study of interaction between European and American journals. *Scientometrics*, 49(1), 23–38.

De Cillia, Rudolph, Reisigl, Martin & Wodak, Ruth (1999). The discursive construction of national identities. *Discourse & Society*, 10(2), 149–173.

Descarries, Francine (2014). Language is not neutral: The construction of knowledge in the social sciences and humanities. *Signs*, 39(3), 564–569.

DiMaggio, Paul J. & Powell, Walter W. (1983). The iron cage revisited: Institutional isomorphism and collective rationality in organizational fields. *American Sociological Review*, 48, 147–160.

Englander, Karen (2009). Transformation of the identities of nonnative English-speaking scientists as a consequence of the social construction of revision. *Journal of Language Identity and Education*, 8(1), 35–53.

Flowerdew, John & Li, Yongyan (2009). English or Chinese? The trade-off between local and international publication among Chinese academics in the humanities and social sciences. *Journal of Second Language Writing*, 18(1), 1–16.

Grey, Christopher (2010). Organizing studies: Publications, politics and polemic. *Organization Studies*, 31(6), 677–694.

Hanauer, David I. & Englander, Karen (2011). Quantifying the burden of writing research articles in a second language: Data from Mexican scientist. *Written Communication*, 28(4), 403–416.

Hatch, Mary Jo & Zilber, Tammar B. (2012). Conversation at the border between organizational culture theory and institutional theory. *Journal of Management Inquiry*, 21(1), 94–97.

Heilbron, Johan (2014). The social sciences as an emerging global field. *Current Sociology*, 62(5), 685–703.

Johansson, Marjana & Sliwa, Martyna (2014). Gender, foreignness and academia: An intersectional analysis of the experiences of foreign women academics in UK business schools. *Gender Work and Organization*, 21(1), 18–36.

Keim, Wiebke (2011). Counterhegemonic currents and internationalization of sociology theoretical reflections and an empirical example. *International Sociology*, 26(1), 123–145.

Kimmerling, Baruch (2005). *The invention and decline of Israeliness*. Berkeley: University of California Press.

Lages, Christina R., Pfajfar, Gregor & Shoham, Aviv (2015). Challenges in conducting and publishing research on the Middle East and Africa in leading journals. *International Marketing Review*, 32(1), 52–77.

Lawrence, Thomas B., Leca, Bernard & Zilber, Tammar B. (2013). Institutional work: Current research, new directions and overlooked issues. *Organization Studies*, 34(8), 1023–1033.

Lee, Hikyoung & Lee, Kathy (2013). Publish (in international indexed journals) or perish: Neoliberal ideology in a Korean University. *Language Policy*, 12(3), 215–230.

Lieblich, Amia, Tuval-Mashiach, Rivka & Zilber, Tammar B. (1998). *Narrative research: Reading, analysis and interpretation*. Newbury Park, CA: Sage.

Lillis, Theresa M. & Curry, Mary Jane (2010). *Academic writing in a global context: The politics and practices of publishing in English*. New York: Routledge.

Lingard, Lorelei, Reznick, Richard, DeVito, Isabella & Espin, Sherry (2002). Forming professional identities on the health care team: Discursive constructions of the 'other' in the operating room. *Medical Education*, 36(8), 728–734.

López-Navarro, Irene, Moreno, Ana I., Ángel Quintanilla, Miguel & Rey-Rocha, Jesús (2015). Why do I publish research articles in English instead of my own language? Differences in Spanish researchers' motivations across scientific domains. *Sciento-Metrics*, 103(3), 939–976.

March, James G. (2005). Parochialism in the evolution of a research community: The case of organization studies. *Management and Organization Review*, 1, 5–22.

Medina, Leandro R. (2013). *Centers and peripheries in knowledge production*. New York, NY: Routledge.

Meriläinen, Susan, Tienari, Janne, Thomas, Robyn & Davies, Annette (2008). Hegemonic academic practices: Experiences of publishing from the periphery. *Organization*, 15(4), 584–597.

Meyer, John W. & Rowan, Brian (1977). Institutionalized organizations: Formal structure as myth and ceremony. *American Journal of Sociology*, 83, 340–363.

Mizruchi, Mark S. & Fein, Lisa C. (1999). The social construction of organizational knowledge: A study of the uses of coercive, mimetic, and normative isomorphism. *Administrative Science Quarterly*, 44(4), 653–683.

Mosbah-Natanson, Sébastian & Gingras, Yves (2014). The globalization of social sciences? Evidence from a quantitative analysis of 30 years of production, collaboration and citations in the social sciences (1980–2009). *Current Sociology*, 62(5), 626–646.

Mur Dueñas, Pilar (2012). Getting research published internationally in English: An ethnographic account of a team of finance Spanish scholars' struggles. *Iberica*, (24), 139–155.

Olsson, Anna & Sheridan, Vera (2012). A case study of Swedish scholars' experiences with and perceptions of the use of English in academic publishing. *Written Communication*, 29(1), 33–54.

Pedersen, Anne-Marie (2010). Negotiating cultural identities through language: Academic English in Jordan. *College Composition and Communication*, 62(2), 283–310.

Pérez-Llantada, Carmen, Plo, Ramón & Ferguson, Gibson R. (2011). "You don't say what you know, only what you can": The perceptions and practices of senior Spanish academics regarding research dissemination in English. *English for Specific Purposes*, 30(1), 18–30.

Potter, Rob (2001). Geography and development: "core and periphery"? *Area*, 33(4), 422–427.

Powell, Walter W. & DiMaggio, Paul J. (1991). *The new institutionalism in organizational analysis*. Chicago: The University of Chicago Press.

Richardson, Laurel (1998). Writing: A method of inquiry. In N. K. Denzin & Y. S. Lincoln (Eds.), *Collecting and interpreting qualitative data* (pp. 345–371). Thousand Oaks, CA: Sage.

Scott, Peter (2015). Dynamics of academic mobility: Hegemonic internationalisation or fluid globalisation. *European Review*, 23, S55–S69.

Slater, David (1993). The geopolitical imagination and the enframing of development theory. *Transactions of the Institute of British Geographers*, 18(4), 419–437.

Slaughter, Sheila & Leslie, Larry L. (2001). Expending and elaborating the concept of academic capitalism. *Organization*, 8(2), 154–162.

Sliwa, Martyna & Johansson, Marjana (2015). Playing in the academic field: Non-native English- speaking academics in UK business schools. *Culture and Organization*, 21(1), 78–95.

Somers, Margaret R. (1994). The narrative constitution of identity: A relational and network approach. *Theory and Society*, 23(5), 605–649.

Suddaby, Roy, Elsbach, Kimberly D., Greenwood, Royston, Meyer, John W. & Zilber, Tammar B. (2010). Organizations and their institutional environments: Bringing meaning, values, and culture back in: Introduction to the special research forum. *Academy of Management Journal*, 53(6), 1234–1240.

Tietze, Susanne (2008). The work of management academics: An English language perspective. *English for Specific Purposes*, 27(4), 371–386.

Tietze, Susanne & Dick, Penny (2009). Hegemonic practices and knowledge production in the management academy: An English language perspective. *Scandinavian Journal of Management*, 25(1), 119–123.

Usdiken, Behlül (2014). Centres and peripheries: Research styles and publication patterns in "top" US journals and their European alternatives, 1960–2010. *Journal of Management Studies*, 51(5), 764–789.

Usdiken, Behlül & Wasti, S. Arzu (2009). Preaching, teaching and researching at the periphery: Academic management literature in Turkey, 1970e1999. *Organization Studies*, 30(10), 1063–1082.

Vogel, Rick (2012). The visible colleges of management and organization studies: A bibliometric analysis of academic journals. *Organization Studies*, 33(8), 1015–1043.

Yemini, Miri, Holzmann, Vered, de Wit, Hans, Sadeh, Efrat, Stavans, Anat & Fadila, Dalia (2015). The drive to internationalize: Perceptions and motivations of Israeli college directors. *Higher Education Policy*, 28(3), 259–276.

Zilber, Tammar B. (2002). Institutionalization as an interplay between actions, meanings, and actors: The case of a rape crisis center in Israel. *Academy of Management Journal*, 45(1), 234–254.

Zilber, Tammar B. (2006). The work of the symbolic in institutional processes: Translations of rational myths in Israeli High Tech. *Academy of Management Journal*, 49(2), 281–303.

Zilber, Tammar B. (2007). Stories and the discursive dynamics of institutional entrepreneurship: The case of Israeli high-tech after the bubble. *Organization Studies*, 28(7), 1035–1054.

Zilber, Tammar B. (2008). The work of meanings in institutional processes and thinking. In R. Greenwood, C. Oliver, K. Sahlin & R. Suddaby (Eds.), *Handbook of organizational Institutionalism* (pp. 151–169). London: Sage.

Zilber, Tammar B. (2009). Institutional maintenance as narrative acts. In T. Lawrence, R. Suddaby & B. Leca (Eds.), *Institutional work* (pp. 205–235). Cambridge: Cambridge University Press.

Zilber, Tammar B. (2011). Institutional multiplicity in practice: A tale of two high-tech conferences in Israel. *Organization Science*, 22(6), 1539–1559.

Zilber, Tammar B. (2012). The relevance of institutional theory for the study of organizational culture. *Journal of Management Inquiry*, 21(2), 88–93.

Zilber, Tammar B. (2013). Institutional logics and institutional work: Should they be agreed? In M. Lounsbury & E. Boxenbaum (Eds.), *Research in the sociology of organizations* (Vol. 39A, pp. 77–96). Emerald

Zilber, Tammar B. (2014). Beyond a single organization: Challenges and opportunities in doing field level ethnography. *Journal of Organizational Ethnography*, 3(1), 96–113.

Zilber, Tammar B. (2016). Studying organizational fields through ethnography. In K. Elsbach & R. Kramer (Eds.), *The Handbook of qualitative organizational research* (pp. 86–95). New York: Taylor & Francis/Routledge.

Zilber, Tammar B. (2017). How institutions matter: A bottom-up exploration. In J. German, M. Lounsbury & R. Greenwood (Eds.), *Research in the sociology of organizations* (Vol. 48A, pp. 137–155). Emerald.

Zilber, Tammar B. & Zanoni, Patrizia (2015). Translation as a continuous process: The case of "ethnography" in organization studies (Unpublished manuscript).

Zucker, Lynne G. (1977). The role of institutionalization in cultural persistence. *American Sociological Review*, 42, 726–743.

Index

Note: Page numbers in **bold** indicate tables, and page numbers in *italics* indicate figures.

www.ingramcontent.com/pod-product-compliance
Ingram Content Group UK Ltd.
Pitfield, Milton Keynes, MK11 3LW, UK
UKHW020938180425
457613UK00019B/457

* 9 7 8 0 3 6 7 8 8 7 5 8 2 *